Y0-BQV-941

WITHDRAWN
L. R. COLLEGE LIBRARY

# Piracy in the Graeco-Roman World

This book is an innovative historical study of piracy in the Graeco-Roman world from the Archaic period to Late Antiquity. It explores the conditions which allowed piracy to flourish in the ancient Mediterranean, especially the close relationship between warfare and piracy, and examines the impact which pirates had upon ancient society. Particular attention is paid to the numerous states and rulers who claimed to be actively suppressing piracy for the good of all. In many cases these claims turn out to be highly exaggerated ones, intended to enhance the prestige of those on whose behalf they were made. Surprisingly, in view of the prominence of pirates in many works of Classical literature, this book is the first to offer detailed analysis of the portrayal of piracy by ancient writers, including Homer, Cicero and the ancient novels, taking account of the political, social and literary contexts which shaped their accounts.

PHILIP DE SOUZA is Senior Lecturer in Classical Studies, St Mary's University College, Strawberry Hill.

# Piracy in the
# Graeco-Roman World

Philip de Souza

CAMBRIDGE
UNIVERSITY PRESS

CARL A. RUDISILL LIBRARY
LENOIR-RHYNE COLLEGE

PUBLISHED BY THE PRESS SYNDICATE OF THE UNIVERSITY OF CAMBRIDGE
The Pitt Building, Trumpington Street, Cambridge, United Kingdom

CAMBRIDGE UNIVERSITY PRESS
The Edinburgh Building, Cambridge CB2 2RU, UK   http://www.cup.cam.ac.uk
40 West 20th Street, New York NY 1011-4211, USA   http://www.cup.org
10 Stamford Road, Oakleigh, Melbourne 3166, Australia

© Cambridge University Press 1999

This book is in copyright. Subject to statutory exception and to the provisions of
relevant collective licensing agreements, no reproduction of any part may take
place without the written permission of Cambridge University Press.

First published 1999

Printed in the United Kingdom at the University Press, Cambridge

Typeset in Times New Roman   [AO]

A *catalogue record for this book is available from the British Library*

ISBN 0 521 48137 6 hardback

DE
88
.D4
1999
am.2001
ABM 1048

LEMOIR-RHYNE COLLEGE

*This book is dedicated to the memory of John M. Carter*

# Contents

# Plates

# Acknowledgements

A book such as this cannot be written without the support of academic libraries and their staff. I should like to thank the librarians and staff at the University of Leicester, the British Schools at Athens and Rome; and in London, where most of the work was done, Royal Holloway College, University College, St Mary's University College, the University of London Library, the Warburg Institute, the Institute of Historical Research, and, above all, the excellent Joint Library of the Hellenic and Roman Societies and the Institute of Classical Studies.

Throughout this book I have deliberately quoted or referred to a wide range of textual evidence. Most of these quotations are in English translations which are my own unless stated otherwise. The abbreviations used follow the scheme of *The Oxford Classical Dictionary*[3]. It is important to acknowledge that I have been able to draw upon such a wide range of sources thanks to the exceptional work of numerous scholars of the nineteenth and twentieth centuries, whose unselfish efforts in editing, publishing, surveying and discussing Greek and Latin texts has given those of us who work on ancient history at the end of the second millennium AD an invaluable resource. This book would not have been possible without the work of many better scholars than myself.

The book is based upon my PhD thesis: 'Piracy in the ancient world: from Minos to Mohammed' (University of London, 1992). The thesis was researched and written under the excellent supervision of Tim Cornell and examined by Alastar Jackson and Boris Rankov. I take this opportunity to thank all three for their comments on the thesis and their help and support with the long process of turning it into a book. I held a British Academy scholarship for the first two years of my research, which was invaluable in getting me started; thereafter the generosity of Royal Holloway and Bedford New College, the Institute of Historical Research and the University of Leicester enabled me to support my studies through part-time work.

The book is considerably different in structure from the thesis on which it is based. There have also been some changes in the content, where I have tried, albeit rather unevenly, to take account of new source material and scholarly publications which appeared after the summer of 1992. The text of the book was completed in the summer of 1998.

I have been fortunate to have the opportunity of presenting my research findings at a variety of conferences and seminars in British universities and colleges. Thanks to all those who invited me, organized and chaired the sessions and offered a myriad constructive criticisms. Most of the arguments put forward in this book have been improved with the help of colleagues and friends who have patiently listened to or read my work. I thank them all for their perceptive comments and suggestions. Special mention must be made of several individuals who have, I believe, contributed significantly to the final work, although they are not to be held in any way responsible for its shortcomings. A big thank you to Richard Alston, Tim Cornell, Michael Crawford, John Davies, Keith Hopwood, Boris Rankov, Nick Rauh, Graham Shipley and Hans van Wees. Thanks are also due to Pauline Hire, Susan Moore and the staff and anonymous reader of Cambridge University Press for their expertise, efficiency and patience.

I should like to thank all the colleagues, students, friends and members of my family, especially my parents Collin and Maureen, who have encouraged and supported me in my efforts to finish this book. The final mention, with the greatest affection, belongs to my wife Debra, without whom I could never even have started.

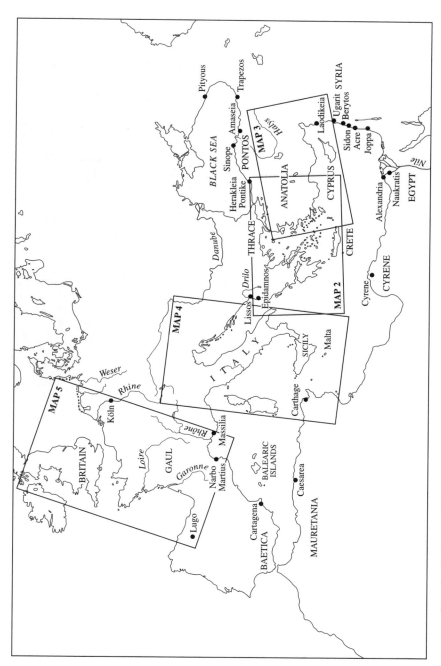

Map 1. The Roman Empire.

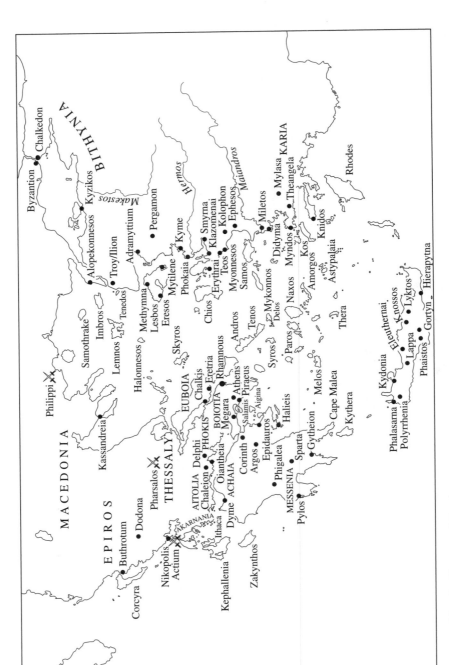

Map 2. Greece and the Aegean.

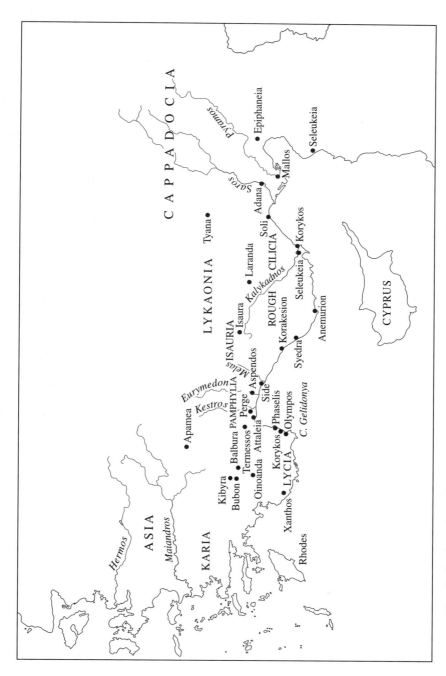

Map 3. Southern Anatolia.

LIGURIA

Ravenna

ISTRIA

ILLYRIA

*Adriatic Sea*

ETRURIA

CORSICA

Cosa

*Tiber*

Rome

Ostia

Antium

Tarracina

Sinuessa

Caieta

Cumae

Puteoli

Misenum

Neapolis

CAMPANIA

APULIA

Brundisium

Tarentum

SARDINIA

*Tyrrhenian*

*Sea*

Pharos

Issa

Lipari Is.

Naulochus

Zankle/Messana

Mylasa

Marsala

SICILY

Syracuse

Elorus

*C. Pachynus*

Map 4. Italy.

Map 5. Britain and France.

# 1    Introduction

Sometime in the second century BC the citizens of the Athenian colony on Imbros in the Northern Aegean had the following decree inscribed in stone:

Decided by the people. Teleas, son of Aristokratos, of Cholargos proposed: since Lysanias is benevolent towards the people, and, there being a hostile attempt by some people against the island, he did not make light of it, nor shrink back from the danger to himself, but stood firm and brought news of the descent of the pirates. Therefore, so that the people may show their gratitude, it is proposed: With good fortune, it has been decided by the people that Lysanias, son of Aristokratos, of Deradiotai, is to be praised, and he is to be crowned with a crown of gold . . .[1]

It would seem that as soon as he was aware of the hostile strangers' approach, Lysanias knew exactly what word to use to rouse his compatriots: pirates! Their enthusiastic praise of his actions reflects a mortal fear of the sudden descent of pirates and the panic and suffering which might result. Murder, pillage and kidnap by seaborne raiders were familiar terrors for many of the inhabitants of the Mediterranean in Classical times. The surviving historical records contain many instances of piratical attacks on both land and sea. From the poems of Homer to the works of St Augustine pirates and piracy are a recurring theme in Classical literature. Why was piracy such a problem in the Graeco-Roman world? What efforts were made to suppress it, and how successful were they? These are some of the questions which this book will address through a detailed examination of the ancient sources.

Piracy is a term normally applied in a pejorative manner. Pirates can be defined as *armed robbers whose activities normally involve the use of ships.* They are men who have been designated as such by other people, regardless of whether or not they consider themselves to be pirates. In the

---

[1] *IG* XII.8.53, lines 1–13. The inscription continues with further honours for Lysanias. The date of some time before 166 BC, proposed by the editors (*IG* XII.8.4), is to be preferred to Ormerod's suggestion of the first century BC; Ormerod (1924): 139.

Graeco-Roman world the use of pirate as a term for undesirable 'others' is the usual way in which piracy is presented to the scholar. The pirates of Classical Antiquity are identified by their victims and their enemies, they do not claim the label of pirate for themselves.

It is important to establish at an early stage that *all* evidence of piracy in the Graeco-Roman world is textual. Piracy is not a phenomenon which can be documented from the material remains of Classical civilizations. Ancient pirates did not leave any distinct trace in the archaeological record, unlike soldiers, whose graves, equipment and habitations are fairly easy to identify.[2] A history of piracy can, therefore, be written only on the basis of texts which mention pirates or piracy in explicit terms, or which can be shown to refer implicitly to pirates or piracy, according to the normal usage of these terms in the culture which produced the texts.

There have been several histories of ancient piracy by modern scholars, notably Sestier, Ormerod and Ziebarth.[3] All of these have tended to treat piracy as a relatively straightforward and unchanging phenomenon, assuming, implicitly or explicitly, that the terms pirate and piracy meant much the same in the Graeco-Roman world as they did up to the end of the nineteenth century.[4] This book presents a new and radically different historical interpretation of the ancient Graeco-Roman texts relating to piracy, in which the emphasis is on understanding the use of the labels pirate and piracy in their historical and cultural contexts. I have deliberately taken a sceptical approach to mentions of pirates in ancient texts. In each case I have tried to determine why the individuals or groups described as pirates have been labelled in this way. My aim has been to produce not merely a narrative of piratical events, but an historical analysis of the development of the terms piracy and pirate in the Graeco-Roman world from *c.* 800 BC to AD 700.

## Language

Since the basis of this study is an examination of Classical texts relating to piracy, it is necessary to explore briefly the Greek and Latin vocabulary

---

[2] For an optimistic attempt to assemble archaeological evidence which *may* relate to piracy see Gianfrotta (1981). There was no distinctive visual image of piracy in the Graeco-Roman world, but see Pls. 1–4 for a range of images.

[3] Sestier (1880); Ormerod (1924); Ziebarth (1929).

[4] Recent studies of particular importance include the excellent essay by Jackson (1973); the detailed analysis of Cretan piracy by Brulé (1978); the attempt at categorization of piracy by Garlan (1978), which reappeared in a revised form as Garlan (1989). Since the thesis on which this book is based was completed there have also been studies of the Romans' attitude to piracy by Pohl (1993); Braund (1993); and a very good article on the Cilician pirates by Avidov (1997).

for piracy. Piracy and banditry were much more closely linked in the ancient world, in terms of both language and perception, than they are today. It is, therefore, also important to consider how far the ancient language of piracy and banditry overlap and to what extent it is possible to distinguish between the two in ancient writings.

Ancient Greek has two common words which can be translated as pirate, ληστής (*leistes*) and πειρατής (*peirates*)[5]. The former is attested in Homer in various forms[6] and it continues to be used by Greek writers throughout the period covered by this book. It derives from the same root as ληίς (*leis*), meaning booty or plunder, i.e. the Indo-European root *laϝ* or *lau*, and its essential meaning is armed robber or plunderer, for which the common English terms are bandit or pirate.

The second word, πειρατής (*peirates*), is a later arrival in the vocabulary of the ancient Greek sources, not being found in Homer or any of the writers of the Classical period (*c*. 500–330 BC). *Peirates* and words derived from it continue to be used in the sources right up to the end of our period, and have meanings synonymous with *leistes* and its derivatives[7]. The derivation of *peirates* is probably from the word *peira*, meaning a trial or attempt, and it may be connected with *peirao*, meaning to make an attempt at something. An alternative derivation from the word *prasso*, meaning to pass through, achieve, is also possible, but unlikely.[8]

The earliest datable occurrence of the word *peirates* is in an Attic inscription of the mid third century BC from Rhamnous. It is a deme decree in honour of Epichares, who was elected as *strategos* with special responsibility for coastal defence during the archonship of Peithidemos,[9] and undertook vigorous defensive measures during the Chremonidean war. The decree mentions a ransoming or exchange of prisoners arranged by Epichares and also indicates that the prisoners were taken by *peiratai*, who had been brought into the area by people described as 'from the city', i.e. Athens. Epichares held an enquiry and punished the guilty:

... ἐκόλασε δὲ καὶ τού-
[ς κ]αθηγουμένους εἰς τ[ὴ]ν χώραν τοῖς **πειραταῖς**, λαβὼν καὶ ἐξετάσας αὐτούς, ὄν-
[τα]ς ἐκ τῆς πόλεως, [ἀξίω]ς ὧν ἔπραττον.

---

[5] There is also another word for pirate, the much rarer καταποντιστής (*katapontistes*), which is found only occasionally in Greek literature; see below pp. 9–11.
[6] Ebeling (1885): 985–7.
[7] See LSJ s.v. πειρατής.
[8] See LSJ s.vv.
[9] The date of Peithidemos' archonship is disputed, but must fall in or near to 267 BC, that is to say during the Chremonidean war, with the dating of which it is closely connected; see Will (1979): I 223–4 and Meritt (1977): 174, who suggests 265/4 for Peithidemos' archonship.

... he also punished those who had introduced the pirates/bandits into the land, men from the city, arresting and interrogating them in a way that was fitting for what they did.[10]

The episode took place in a time of war, when Athens was supported by the Ptolemaic forces against those of the Macedonian king Antigonos Gonatas (c. 277–239 BC), but it was not itself a significant act of war. It may be that the *peiratai* were allied in some way to Antigonos, but their identity is not known, possibly because it was not clear to their victims. Speculation about them is pointless since the inscription is too badly damaged to yield any further information, and it is our only source for this event. The simplest and most logical interpretation of the use of *peirates* is that it is a pejorative term for a raider or plunderer, as it is found in later texts.[11]

The word *peirates* also occurs in an inscription from Aigiale on the northern coast of the island of Amorgos, describing a raid on the town which took place at night:[12]

... ἐπειδὴ **πειρατῶν** εἰς
[τ]ὴν χώραν ἐμβαλόντων νυκτὸς ...

... since, when pirates made an incursion into the countryside at night ...

During the raid a variety of people from the city were captured and two of the citizens managed to negotiate their release:[13]

... συνέπεισαν τὸν ἐπὶ τῶν **πει**-
[ρ]**ατῶν** ἐπιπλέοντα Σωκλείδαν ἀπο-
λῦσαι τά τ' ἐλευθέρα ...

... he persuaded Sokleidas, the captain of the pirates, to release the free persons ...[14]

The editor of *Inscriptiones Graecae* vol. XII.7 dates the inscription to the third century BC, from the lettering. There is no reason to question the translation of *peiraton* as 'pirates', although any attempt to identify the perpetrators can only be speculation. Attempts to date the inscription more exactly on the basis of such speculation are futile. The fact that

---

[10] *SEG* 24 (1968), no. 154, lines 21–3.
[11] Whether pirates or bandits should be used to translate the word *peiratais* here is not entirely clear. Rhamnous is a coastal town, but it is close to Boiotia and it could be penetrated quite easily by land. Later references to men called *peiratai* show that they can be bandits or pirates (see below) and insufficient context is provided by the inscription itself. Austin (1981): no. 50 translates 'pirates'.
[12] *IG* XII.7.386, lines 4–5.
[13] Ibid., lines 15–17.
[14] Translation from Austin (1981): no. 87.

there may have been similar raids by Aitolian pirates in this area in the middle of the third century BC does not mean that this incident can be attributed to them and dated to a particular period of Aitolian piratical activity.[15] The inscription can, therefore, be dated to before 200 BC only on the basis of the lettering.

A word derived from *peirates* does occur in an Attic inscription which can, perhaps, be assigned to an earlier date, permitting the conclusion that this word was in use at the same time as it occurs in the noun form in the Epichares inscription discussed above. The relevant decree is in honour of Herakleitos of Athmonon, who protected Salamis from piratical attacks from the direction of Epilimnion:[16]

... καὶ πολέμου γενομένου τοῦ περὶ Ἀ-
λεξάνδρον καὶ **πειρατικῶν** ἐκπλεόντων ἐκ τοῦ Ἐπιλιμνίου ...

... and when the war of Alexander broke out, and pirates were sailing out from Epilimnion ...

Herakleitos was the Macedonian *strategos* of the Piraeus. The attacks occurred during the revolt of Alexander of Corinth, son of Krateros, which means that the honorific decree should be later than *c.* 250 BC, but not necessarily much more than a few years later, which would also be consistent with the lettering of the inscription.[17]

The Greek word *peirates* is, therefore, first attested in inscriptions from the middle of the third century BC, the earliest of which can be dated to 267 BC. There is nothing in these inscriptions which indicates a different meaning from that found in later literary and epigraphic sources. It is necessary, however, before continuing to discuss the early use and meaning of *peirates*, to consider two alternative explanations which have been advanced in recent scholarly works.[18]

In an appendix to an article on Athenian involvement in the war of Agis III,[19] D. S. Potter put forward the view that it is possible to discover the earliest use of the word *peirates* in Book 20 of Diodorus' *Universal History*.[20] He is of the opinion that the text of Diodorus Books 18–20 is

[15] Ziebarth (1929): ch. 4, does just this, associating the Aigiale raid with a decree of nearby Naxos relating to 'Aitolian piracy' (*IG* XII.5.36). See also Tarn (1913): 208–15, and Benecke (1934): 11–16.
[16] *SIG* no. 454 = *IG* II².1225, line 13.
[17] On the date of Alexander of Corinth's revolt see Walbank (1957–79): I 235–6 and Will (1979–82): I 316–18.
[18] For similar conclusions to mine, and further, detailed discussion of literary and epigraphic sources see Pritchett (1991): 315–18.
[19] The attempt of the Spartan king Agis III to throw off Macedonian control of the Peloponnese while Alexander was in Asia in 331 BC.
[20] Potter (1984).

based mainly on Hieronymos of Kardia, who was contemporary with the events described in Book 20. He argues that since *peirates* first appears in Diodorus' text in Book 20, with the alternative *leistes* being used earlier, Diodorus is following the linguistic usage of Hieronymos. Since all the references to *peiratai* occur in connection with an Antigonid king's army, Potter takes them to refer to some kind of special mercenaries, engaged in a 'respectable entrepreneurial activity'.[21] He also believes that the inscriptions from the third century discussed above refer to people who are '"naval mercenaries" operating under some legitimate authority ... synonymous with *polemios*'.[22] Potter does not believe that the word has a pejorative sense at this time, but that it acquired one later. Thus for him it is a late fourth-century term for a naval mercenary, possibly coined and almost certainly first used by the historian Hieronymos.

The view has several weaknesses. In the first place, Hieronymos' influence on the text of Diodorus is not clear-cut. Potter's authority for Diodorus' preservation of Hieronymos' language, Jane Hornblower, suspects that Diodorus did not use Hieronymos' original work, but a later recension, probably by a Rhodian scholar of the second century BC, who reworked the text of Hieronymos, adding some material and changing some of the original. She concludes that: 'Direct comparison between Diodorus and his source for xviii–xx as yet eludes us ...'[23] Secondly, Potter's interpretation rests on the assumption that *peirates* first appears in Diodorus at 20.82.4, in a list of the forces of Demetrios Poliorketes at the siege of Rhodes in 305 BC. Yet Diodorus has just used the same word in the previous chapter, during his description of the high esteem of Rhodes in the eyes of the Greeks (Diod. 20.81.3):

ἐπὶ τοσοῦτον γὰρ προεληλύθει δυνάμεως ὥσθ' ὑπὲρ μὲν τῶν Ἑλλήνων ἰδίᾳ τὸν πρὸς τοὺς **πειρατὰς** πόλεμον ἐπαναιρεῖσθαι καὶ καθαρὰν παρέχεσθαι τῶν κακούργων τὴν θάλατταν.

Indeed, she attained such a position of power that she took up the war against the pirates by herself, and cleared the sea of their evil manifestation.

This passage may well reflect the language of a Rhodian version of Hieronymos' history, but could not possibly have been written by Hieronymos himself, because it refers to the exploits of the Rhodians in the third and early second centuries BC.[24] For Diodorus there was no doubt that *pei*-

---

[21] Potter (1984): 235.
[22] Potter (1984): 231.
[23] Hornblower (1981): 276–7. See also Sacks (1990) who argues strongly against the view that Diodorus was a slavish copier of his sources.
[24] See below pp. 49–53, 80–92.

*rates* was a pejorative term, as it was for his contemporary Strabo.[25] The passage cited above makes no sense if it is simply a term for some kind of 'naval mercenary' who is completely 'respectable' and whose activity is 'legitimate'. As a general point about Diodorus' vocabulary, it should be noted that Diodorus usually tries to bring his sources closer to his own clear, simple style. Hornblower cites the case of his use of Agatharchides in Book 3: 'He prefers the more modern Hellenistic usage, ... and in general replaces unusual with usual words.'[26] The fact that Diodorus is using the word in a military context repeatedly in Book 20 is indicative of the nature of Hellenistic warfare at this time, rather than the nature of the word itself.

It has also been suggested that *peirates* was a fourth-century creation to provide a distinctive word for seaborne plunderers (pirates) as a supplement to *leistes*.[27] The idea comes from entries in the tenth-century AD Byzantine lexicon *The Suda* (1454 and 474):

πειρατῶν: καταποντιστῶν, κατὰ θάλασσαν ληστῶν ... ὅθεν καὶ πειραταὶ οἱ κατὰ θάλατταν κακοῦργοι.
λῃσταί: καὶ λῃστὴς μὲν ὁ ἐν ἠπείρῳ πειρατὴς δὲ ὁ ἐν θαλάσσῃ.

*peiraton*: *katapontistai*, plunderers on the seas ... whence also *peiratai*, those who are evildoers by sea. *leistai*: *leistes* is on the land as *peirates* is on the sea.

While these entries make it clear what the Byzantine lexicographers thought were the appropriate meanings of *peirates* and *leistes*, they should not be taken as indicators of the fourth-century BC usage. In any case *peirates* is not attested in the surviving fourth-century sources. Nor can they be used to represent later Classical usage, since they are not borne out by examination of any other writers. Later authors continue to use both of the words *leistes* and *peirates* as synonyms. For example, Achilles Tatius, writing in the third century AD, uses both words together in the following passage, describing a malicious servant (Ach. Tat. 2.17.3): ... ἦν γὰρ καὶ ἄλλως εὔρωστος τὸ σῶμα καὶ φύσει **πειρατικός** ... ('... he was exceptionally strong of body and by nature piratical'). The sentence continues: ... ταχὺ μὲν ἐξεῦρε **λῃστὰς** ἁλιεῖς ἀπὸ τῆς κώμης ἐκείνης ('... he quickly sought out some pirate sailors from that village'). The obvious translation of both words here is pirate, rather than bandit.[28]

The earliest surviving author to make considerable use of the word *peirates* is Polybius, writing in the mid second century BC. He uses it to

---

[25] See below p. 8.
[26] Hornblower (1981): 274.
[27] McKechnie (1989): 117 & 131.
[28] Achilles Tatius also treats *leistes* and *peirates* as synonyms meaning pirate in other places, e.g. Ach. Tat. 5.7.6 and 7.

describe a variety of individuals and groups ranging from the bandit Dorimachos and his gang to a flotilla of pirate ships chased by the Romans in 190 BC during the war with Antiochos. A brief look at some examples of his usage and that of Strabo, writing in the first century AD, will suffice, along with the passages of Achilles Tatius cited above, to illustrate the usual practice among Greek authors. In his account of the Aitolian Dorimachos' raiding in the Peloponnese in 222 BC Polybius writes as follows (Polyb. 4.3.8):

συνδραμόντων δὲ **πειρατῶν** καὶ παραγενομένων πρὸς αὐτὸν εἰς τὴν Φιγάλειαν, οὐκ ἔχων τούτοις ἀπὸ τοῦ δικαίου συμπαρασκευάζειν ὠφελείας . . .

When a newly formed gang of bandits came to him [Dorimachos] at Phigaleia, not having a justifiable project to provide them with plunder . . .

Polybius cannot possibly be referring to pirates in this context, so the translation of *peiratai* must be bandits.[29] In a later book, however, when he is describing the naval battle of Myonnesos, he uses *peirates* with the meaning of pirate (Polyb. 21.12): . . . οἱ δὲ **πειραταὶ** θεασάμενοι τὸν ἐπί-πλουν τῶν Ῥωμαϊκῶν πλοίων . . . ('. . . the pirates, seeing the Roman fleet bearing down upon them . . .'). Again the obvious translation of *peiratai* is pirates, and this can be confirmed by referring to the text of Livy 37.27.4, which goes into greater detail than the fragment of Polybius.[30] In Book 4 Polybius uses *leisteia* to describe the plundering activities of the Cretans (4.8.11) and the Aitolians (4.9.10). He refers in these instances to plundering both by land and by sea. Strabo is even freer in his use of *leistes*, *peirates* and their cognates. He also treats them as synonyms and even employs them both in the same sentence, when contrasting the Lycians with their neighbours the Pamphylians and the Cilicians (Str. 14.3.2):

ἀλλ᾽ ἐκεῖνοι μὲν ὁρμητηρίοις ἐχρήσαντο τοῖς τόποις πρὸς τὰ **ληστήρια** αὐτοὶ **πειρ-ατεύοντες** ἢ τοῖς **πειραταῖς** λαφυροπώλια καὶ ναύσταθμα παρέχοντες.

But the former used their places as bases for piracy, when they practised it themselves, or made them available to other pirates as markets for their plunder.[31]

From the texts cited above it can be seen that *peirates* is a synonym for *leistes*. They both mean pirate or bandit, and can both be translated by either English word, or by the neutral term plunderer.

---

[29] It is significant that Polybius' language throughout this section on the Aitolians in the late 220s BC (Polyb. 4.3–6) is generally polemical and pejorative. Hence his choice of *peiratai* to describe Dorimachos' band, because it is not a technical, military term, but a pejorative, damnatory one. See further below pp. 73–6 on Polybius and the Aitolians.

[30] See Walbank (1957–79): III 105. Livy's text reads *apparuit deinde piraticos veloces et lembos esse* ('Then it became clear that they were fast pirate *lembi*'). On the *lembos* see Casson (1971): 125–7.

[31] *Leisteria* is a noun derived from *leistes* meaning the practice of piracy or banditry.

The word *peirates* is, therefore, first attested in the third century BC and is apparently a common word in the Greek world by the end of the century. In literary sources either or both may be used. Suggested specific meanings for *peirates* are not borne out by its usage, and the precise circumstances of its appearance in the ancient Greek language are not ascertainable. It is possible that, since Greek was a spoken language with a strong oral tradition, the 'newer' word may have been in use for some considerable time before its earliest occurrence in any written context. The habits of Greek epigraphy were generally conservative, with innovations being incorporated only very slowly.

### Differentiation between pirates and bandits in Greek sources

As has been stated above, the modern English words pirate and bandit are both possible translations of the Greek words *leistes* and *peirates*. The clear semantic difference which is found in modern English, that pirates operate mainly at sea and use ships, and that bandits always operate on land, is not inhererent in the ancient Greek words as they are used in the surviving sources. This does not mean, however, that ancient writers could not distinguish between the two. On the contrary they often did so, when they had reason to, by using either a qualifying description, or by use of another (less common) word which means pirate. An example of the former method of differentiation is found in Strabo's description of the Bosporan peoples near Colchis (11.2.12): ζῶσι δὲ ὑπὸ τῶν κατὰ θά-λατταν **λῃστηρίων** ('They live by plundering at sea' – i.e. piracy). There is only one word in Greek which means a pirate, not a bandit: *kata-pontistes*,[32] which translates literally as 'one who throws into the sea'. It is used almost exclusively to mean pirate.[33] It is not a commonly used word in Greek literature, possibly because, although useful for specifying pirates as opposed to bandits or plunderers in general, it is a long and rather inelegant one. There can be no doubt that even those authors who did employ it were reluctant to make continuous use of it, for whatever reason. Isokrates uses it only once in the *Panegyrikos* and twice elsewhere (Isoc. *Paneg.* 115; *Panath.* 12 and 226). He also uses *leistes* (e.g. *Panath.* 226). Demosthenes uses both *katapontistes* and *leistes*. At one point he

---

[32] It is translated by LSJ under the verb from which it derives, καταποντίζω, which means 'throw into the sea, plunge or drown therein': LSJ s.v.

[33] Pausanias (8.52.3) uses this word metaphorically, saying of all who fought against Athens in the Peloponnesian war: ... φαίη τις ἂν αὐτόχειρας καὶ ὅτι ἐγγύτατα καταποντιστάς εἶναι τῆς Ἑλλάδος ('... they may fitly be described as the assassins and almost the "wreckers" of Greece'. Trans. Frazer). Pausanias prefers to use *leistes* for pirate, e.g. 1.7.3.

employs both as a pair of pejorative terms to describe conditions on the island of Alopekonnesos (Demos. 23.166).

The only author who makes regular use of *katapontistes* is the historian Cassius Dio, writing in the third century AD. He prefers *leistes* to *peirates*, which he never uses. He employs *katapontistes* as a specific term for a pirate when he wishes to make an explicit distinction between maritime and land-based activities. His use of it is concentrated round his discussion of Pompey's early career and the *lex Gabinia* of 67 BC (Dio 36.20–37). The distinction between pirates and bandits is clearly made in the opening part of this section (Dio 36.20.1): οἱ **καταποντισταὶ** ἐλῄπουν πλέοντας, ὥσπερ καὶ τοὺς ἐν τῇ γῇ οἰκοῦντας οἱ τὰς **λῃστείας** ποιούμενοι ('The pirates had always attacked shipping, just as the bandits did those who live on the land'). Having differentiated between the two types of plunderers, Dio explains why, with the continual wars providing cause and opportunity for many to turn to armed robbery or plundering (*leisteia*), it was piracy which had caused the greatest concern at Rome at this time (Dio 36.20.3–4):

While the bandits' (*leistika*) plunderings on the land, being under the very eyes of the locals, who could discover the injury nearby and apprehend them without much difficulty, were easily stopped, the plundering by sea [i.e. piracy] had increased dramatically. For while the Romans were occupied against their enemies, they [the pirates] were flourishing, sailing all over the place and all joining together as groups, so that some of them came to each other's aid like regular allies.

The point which Dio stresses here is the pirates' ability to operate everywhere (36.22.4). It is the range and comparative strength of piracy which makes it so different from banditry and allows it to become a serious menace. Dio, however, does not use only the specific term *katapontistes* to refer to pirates in this section. He initially employs it to make a clear distinction between pirates and bandits. Then, when he has established that it is the pirates who will be the subject of his narrative, he alternates it with *leistes* (Dio 36.24.1; 36.36.4). Thus it can be seen that Dio could use a specific term for pirate rather than bandit, but did not always feel it necessary to do so, allowing the context to make it clear which was meant (as at 36.20.1). At other times he might leave it up to the reader to decide the significance of *leistes*. In a later book Dio explains that Aulus Gabinius (*cos.* 58 BC) had been a rather disastrous proconsul for the people of his province of Syria. In 55 BC, when he toyed with intervention in Parthia and then turned instead to an invasion of Egypt, he left behind him a province bereft of soldiers. Dio says of him: 'Gabinius did much to ruin Syria, so much that he caused more harm to the people than did the pirates (*leistikon*), who were flourishing still ...' He repeats the point at

39.56.5. The irony of the situation is apparent only if the translation is 'pirates', for it was Gabinius who, as tribune in 67 BC, proposed the law which gave Pompey the Great his famous command against the pirates. Dio's subtle humour is well served by his choice of words.[34]

It was possible, therefore, to differentiate between pirates and bandits in ancient Greek. From at least the beginning of the fourth century BC there was a word available which meant only pirate (i.e. *katapontistes*), but it was rarely used. It was always possible for ancient authors to add a qualifying adjective or participle or phrase to the words *leistes* and *peirates* and their cognates in order to make the meaning clear. Alternatively it could be obvious from the context of a particular passage which of the two was meant. There remained, however, an inherent ambiguity of meaning in the two main Greek words for armed robbers or plunderers which reflected a close association of the two in the minds of the Greek-speaking peoples of the ancient world. This close association derived particularly from the disapproval which both types of armed robbery often merited in the eyes of many in the Graeco-Roman world.

If bandits and land-based plunderers in the Graeco-Roman world can be described in the same language as pirates, what is there about the pirates that is significantly different? The answer, which has already been provided, but is worth emphasizing, is that piracy involves the use of *ships*, which require a greater initial commitment of resources and offer a greater range and freedom of opportunity to the would-be plunderers than can be obtained from wholly land-based activities.[35] Ships also need harbours or anchorages, so that the pirates' *bases* become an important factor in their success, and the suppression of piracy requires the control of such bases.

It is appropriate at this stage to consider what might mark piracy out as different from any other forms of violence among the Greeks, especially warfare. Linguistically this is done by referring to acts of war and warriors with distinct words. A good example, from the fifth century BC, is the inscription recording a treaty between Athens and Halieis in 424/3 BC:[36]

... πα]ρέχεν ἁλι-
ὰς Ἀθεναί[οις ναύσταθμον καὶ προθύμος ὀφελὲ]ν Ἀθεν-
αίοις καὶ **λ[ειστὰς** μὲ ὑποδέχεσθαι μεδ' α]ὑτὸς **[λε]ίζε[σ]**-
θαι μεδὲ χσ[υστρατεύεσθαι μετὰ τὸν **πο]λεμίον** ἐπ'
['Ἀθε]ναίος ...

---

[34] See below Chapter 5 for Pompey's campaign against the pirates.
[35] See, for example, the passage quoted above from Dio's *Roman History* 36.20.
[36] *IG* I (3rd edn) 75, lines 6–10. See Meritt (1935).

The people of Halieis are to make available to the Athenians their harbour and to help them readily. They are not to admit pirates, nor to practise piracy, nor are they to join in a campaign with the enemy against the Athenians ...

The inscription clearly differentiates between pirates and enemies. This does not mean, of course that enemies do not plunder, but the Athenians' opponents in warfare (who, in the context of this treaty, would be the Spartans and their allies) are described by a different word (*polemioi*) to the one used for pirates (*leistai*), who might also plunder the Athenians, as, indeed, might the people of Halieis themselves.[37] A distinction between war and piracy was regularly made in the Graeco-Roman world, but the ancient sources do not always make one, nor do they all make it in the same way and for the same reasons. Most of the ancient Greek historians and other authors whose works are used in this book were highly sophisticated writers, capable of exploiting the associations of commonly used terms to present their own interpretations of people and events. For example, two words which are derived from *leistes* – *leisteia* and *leizomai* – are regularly used by the Greek historians Thucydides and Polybius to refer to acts of banditry or piracy (e.g. Thuc. 1.5; 3.85; 4.41; 5.115; Polyb. 3.24.4; 4.8.11; 5.101.1; 13.8.1). The language of these two authors can be taken as reasonably representative of the vocabulary and ideology of the Classical and Hellenistic periods. They use these words typically to refer to acts of maritime armed robbery which meet with their disapproval, for one reason or another, but the variety of contexts in which they employ them, ranging from the aristocratic raiding of Homeric times to seaborne plundering on behalf of Hellenistic kings, are a strong warning against simply placing all such references under the heading of 'piracy', and assuming that they had an unchanging, negative image in the eyes of contemporaries.[38] Hence it is important to approach piracy through a detailed analysis of the sources, establishing, as far as is possible, what they are saying and why they are saying it. The gradual development of a negative image of piracy in the Graeco-Roman world is one of the main themes of this book.

### Latin language

The Latin vocabulary for piracy is similar in some respects to the Greek. There are two main words for pirate: *praedo*, derived from *praeda* (booty/plunder), which is the one most commonly found in Latin literature, and

---

[37] On the historical context of this inscription see below pp. 31–3.

[38] For more detailed analysis of these and other passages in Thucydides and Polybius see de Souza (1992): 41–50.

*pirata*, which clearly derives from the Greek word *peirates*. *Praedo* is similar to *leistes* and *peirates* in that it can mean 'bandit' or 'pirate'. In addition, the Latin word *latro* is sometimes used to mean pirate. In its earliest usage, in Plautus, it seems to have meant 'mercenary', but it quickly became a synonym for *praedo*.[39]

Pirates could be differentiated from bandits with the use of an adjective or qualifying phrase, as in this extract from Nepos' *Life of Themistokles* 2.3: *qua celeriter effecta primum Corcyraeos fregit, deinde* **maritimos praedones** *consectando mare tutum reddidit* ('This being quickly achieved, he first humbled the Corcyraeans, then, by pursuing the pirates, he made the sea safe'). Piracy, or banditry, is usually signified in Latin by the word *latrocinium*.[40] There are no significant controversies or academic debates over the meaning of these Latin words. As with the Greek authors, however, the Latin writers whose works are analysed in this book were fully capable of exploiting the wide range of meanings and associations inherent in these words to achieve a suitable literary or rhetorical effect.

### Structure of the book

The arrangement of the main chapters of this book is broadly chronological. I trace the origins and early use of the terms pirate and piracy in the Archaic period of Greek history (*c.* 800–500 BC) in Chapter 2, focussing on the world of the Homeric poems and the rise of the Greek *poleis* in the Eastern and Western Mediterranean. Much of the source material which is discussed in the rest of the second chapter is provided by the famous Athenian historians and orators of the fifth and fourth centuries BC, especially Herodotus, Thucydides, Xenophon and Demosthenes. Their evidence is supplemented by other literary sources, not all of them contemporary with the Classical period (*c.* 500–323 BC), and by inscriptions, which furnish important documentary evidence of piracy from the middle of the fifth century BC onwards.

Chapter 3 begins the analysis of ancient piracy in what has often been considered its heyday, the Hellenistic period (*c.* 323–31 BC). I have not attempted to adhere so closely to a chronological structure in this chapter, mainly because of the lack of reliable narrative sources for much of the third century BC, until the 220s, when the *Histories* of Polybius throw a fascinating, but complex, light upon the period of rise of Rome and the

---

[39] On *latro* meaning mercenary see *OLD* s.v. *latro* (1). Both *latro* and *pirata* are used to mean pirate in August. *De civ. De.* 4.4.

[40] E.g. Livy 37.13.11–12; Cic. *II Verr.* 1.89. See below pp. 149–50 for further examples and discussion of the vocabulary of piracy in Cicero's works.

decline of the Hellenistic kingdoms in the Eastern Mediterranean. The activities of the Aitolians, Illyrians and Cretans, who acquired considerable notoriety as pirates in the third century BC, are discussed in this chapter. Numerous inscriptions are considered in both this and the following chapter, 4, which examines piracy in the second and first centuries BC, paying particular attention to the Cilicians and the history of Roman suppression of piracy in the Late Republican period (133–31 BC). This topic reaches a climax in Chapter 5, which presents a new interpretation of the famous campaign against the pirates of Pompey the Great in 67 BC. Analysis of Cicero's treatment of the theme of piracy in several of his works is fundamental to this chapter.

Chapter 6 assesses the extent of Pompey's success and explores the nature of piracy in the Roman Principate (31 BC – AD 284). The geographical scope of the book widens somewhat in this chapter, going beyond the Mediterranean region to the edges of the Roman Empire. I consider that the era of the Roman Imperial Peace (*pax Romana*) had a profound effect on perceptions of piracy in many of the ancient sources written during or after this period, especially the *Geography* of Strabo, which is discussed in some detail in this chapter, along with several other literary sources. The main section of the book ends with Chapter 7, in which I examine piracy in the Graeco-Roman world in Late Antiquity (AD 284 – c. 700), ending with the arrival of the Muslims in the Mediterranean in the seventh century BC. Chapter 8 briefly draws some general conclusions from the analyses and interpretations of the preceding chapters.

# 2 The origins of piracy from the Bronze Age to Alexander

It would be tempting to trace the history of ancient piracy well back into the second millennium BC, to the era when the peoples of the Eastern Mediterranean began to travel regularly by sea and to trade across long distances. Nautical and terrestrial archaeology, and the records of Egypt and the Near Eastern civilizations, show that ships carrying valuable cargoes were sailing between Egypt, Cyprus, the Levantine coast and the Aegean by *c.* 1200 BC. There were also busy sea lanes in the Red Sea and the Persian Gulf. Ships capable of carrying large cargoes and numerous warriors are depicted on various artefacts and in carvings and wall paintings from Egypt, Crete and the Cyclades.[1] There are even some scenes which illustrate fighting at sea, most notably the Medinet Habu reliefs from Thebes, which depict the triumph of the Egyptians under Rameses III against the 'Sea Peoples' *c.* 1190 BC.[2] When the available historical records for the Mediterranean in the Bronze Age are analysed, however, reliable evidence of piracy is found to be lacking.

It might be argued that the earliest records of piracy are the legends preserved by the Greeks about Minos, the powerful ruler of Crete. Both Herodotus and Thucydides claim that Minos ruled the seas, and the latter says of him: 'It is likely that he cleared the sea of piracy as far as he was able, to improve his revenues' (Thuc. 1.4). Herodotus also associates the Karians with Minos, saying that they were his subjects and that they manned his ships, thus acquiring a reputation for prowess in war (Hdt. 1.171). The Athenians preserved a tradition that they had once paid tribute to Knossos, a tribute which they associated directly with Minos and the story of Theseus.[3] Some scholars have argued that the so-called Minoan Thalassocracy can be associated with the period of Minoan cultural pre-eminence in the Aegean in the second millennium BC, perhaps around the periods Middle Minoan II, IIIA and IIIB (*c.* 1700–1400 BC).[4]

---

[1] See Casson (1971): chs. 2–3; Bass (1972): ch. 1.
[2] Illustrated in Casson (1971): fig. 61 and Bass (1972): 21, fig. 18.
[3] Philochoros, *FGrHist* no. 328, fr. 17; Plut. *Thes.* 16–19.
[4] Buck (1962); Hägg and Marinatos (1984).

If so, then the fact that Minos and his successors 'ruled the sea' could be held to show that they had the power to suppress piracy. I do not subscribe to this view of an historical Minoan Thalassocracy. The explanation of Thucydides' account which was advanced by George Grote still holds good today: 'Here we have conjectures, derived from the analogy of the Athenian Maritime Empire, in the historical times, substituted in the place of fabulous incidents, and attached to the name of Minos.'[5] In short the Minoan Thalassocracy is a myth, and it has no sound historical basis.[6] Legendary exploits of the ancestors of the Greeks reported in the authors of the Classical period cannot be taken as evidence for the history of piracy in the Bronze Age.

In any case, what does it mean to talk of piracy in this period? The scanty written sources for the history of the Mediterranean in the second millennium BC contain no mention of piracy, because there was no such concept. Warfare and piracy had not come to be differentiated in this early period. Ormerod and others have taken Egyptian and Near Eastern records which speak of groups like the Lukka and the Sea Peoples as evidence of piracy in the fourteenth, thirteenth and twelfth centuries BC.[7] Yet it seems to me that there is no distinction between piracy and warfare in these records. For example, letters from the late thirteenth-century BC king of Ugarit, 'Ammurapi, to the king of Alashiya (probably Cyprus) speak of ships and attacks by sea. In one letter the Ugaritic king says that he has no ships available to defend his city against the ships that have been sighted off the coast: 'My father, did you not know that all my troops were stationed in the Hittite country, and that all my ships are still stationed in Lukka and have not yet returned? So that the country is abandoned to itself...' This letter has been associated with a tablet of the Hittite king Supiluliuma II (c. 1210 BC), recording a victory at sea, and the two assumed to refer to piracy against Ugarit: 'The ships of Alashiya met me in the sea three times for battle, and I smote them; and seized them; and I seized the ships and set fire to them in the sea.'[8] While it is tempting to associate these references to fighting at sea with an attempt to suppress piracy in the Eastern Mediterranean, it seems to me that the most appropriate term for this activity is warfare. It might help if some motivation could be established for these conflicts, whether they were attempts to obtain territory, or just to plunder, but in general the sources are not full enough to analyse them in such a fashion. Similarly, attempts

---

[5] Grote (1888): 220–1. See below pp. 26–30 on the Athenian Empire and piracy.

[6] See the excellent discussion by Starr (1955).

[7] Ormerod (1924): ch. 3; Sandars (1985).

[8] Nougayrol (1968): 87–9; see also Sandars (1985): 142. On the often uncertain chronology of the Ugaritic and Hittite rulers in this period see Kuhrt (1995): 229–32, 264–66, 305–14.

to find in references to the land of Ahhiyawa and its people an early record of Mycenaean piracy and raiding, of the kind sometimes thought to be reflected in the Homeric poems, also fall foul of the lack of any criteria for differentiating piracy from warfare.[9] It cannot be said that there is evidence of piracy in the historical records without some distinctive terminology. People using ships to plunder coastal settlements are not called pirates, so they cannot really be said to be practising piracy.

## Piracy in the Archaic Greek world

It is only in the Archaic period of Greek history, roughly 800–500 BC, that the concept of piracy starts to emerge. As was noted above, the Homeric poems are the earliest written sources which refer to individuals and groups who are labelled *pirates*. The Homeric poems were probably composed in Ionia around 750–700 BC. They portray a society and a culture that is largely based upon the poet's contemporary world, but which has fantastical elements in it, particularly the attributes of the gods and heroes.[10] I am in agreement with the widely held view that the values and ideals of the Homeric poems also reflect contemporary society, so that, in general terms, the poems can be used as a reasonable source of evidence for the social history of the Greeks of the late eighth century BC. An obvious difficulty is that separating 'fact' from 'fantasy' is not an easy thing to do, since even what seems plausible may not necessarily be true to life. Comparison is possible with a few references in later literature to the activities of the early Greeks, and the comparison seems to indicate that the picture of plundering and raiding which emerges from Homer was at least partly based on contemporary conditions.

It would be possible to write an entire book on the subject of Homeric piracy alone, but that is not my purpose here. Instead I shall present a brief study of piracy in the Homeric poems to illustrate certain fundamental points. The first is that although pirates are, from their earliest appearance in ancient literature, regarded with some disapproval, it is also possible for a pirate to achieve high status as a result of his plundering, so that in the Homeric world piracy was not necessarily a shameful or

---

[9] See Sandars (1985); Bryce (1986) and (1989); Kuhrt (1995). Note also Catling (1975) and Barnett (1975) on Sea Peoples, Alashiya, and Ahhiyawa. See below pp. 17–22 on the Homeric poems and history.

[10] On the fantasy world of Homer see van Wees (1992): ch. 1. The bibliography on 'Homeric society' is vast and ever-increasing; for recent discussions with further references see Osborne (1996): ch. 5; Raaflaub (1998). The *Iliad* was apparently composed earlier than the *Odyssey*, but the two poems share a similar set of values and may well be the work of the same poet.

deplorable activity, as Thucydides noted in the introductory section of his history of the Peloponnesian War, known as the *Archaeologia* (Thuc. 1.5). A further important point is that piracy is so closely related to warfare in both aims and methods that they are virtually indistinguishable in the Homeric world.[11]

The passage which best illustrates the ambiguous nature of pirates in Homer is a formulaic greeting used twice in the *Odyssey*, and also once in the *Homeric Hymn to Apollo*.[12] The first time the greeting is encountered is at Pylos, the second in the cave of the Cyclops: 'O strangers, who are you? From where have you come along the sea lanes? Are you travelling for trade,[13] or are you just roaming about like pirates,[14] who risk body and soul, bringing harm to other people?' (*Od.* 3.71–4; 9.252–5). The first time the greeting is employed, after Nestor has welcomed Odysseus' young son Telemachos and his companions to a feast, dispels any sense of realism in its use. If they were pirates the king and his followers would all know the answer by now, and would probably have died as a result. The second instance, when the Cyclops discovers Odysseus and his companions hiding in his cave, confirms this conclusion. The essence of the question seems to be something between, 'Are you friend or foe?' and, 'Are you good or bad?' There can be no doubt that this elaborate formula implies some disapproval for the activities of pirates. They are 'bringers of harm' whose presence may be less beneficial than that of traders, but there is also a suggestion that pirates are more 'glamorous', since they risk so much in their pursuit of gain. It is important to note that in neither case does the party questioned answer affirmatively, either by claiming to be traders or more like pirates. The audience, of course, knows in each case that they belong to the group called *basilees*, or aristocrats, as all Homeric heroes do.[15] Some specific persons are called pirates in the *Odyssey*. Odysseus himself, when he is pretending to be the son of the Cretan Kastor, describes his companions on plundering raids as pirates (*Od.* 17.425). The swineherd Eumaios says that his nurse was captured in Phoenicia by 'Taphian pirates' (*Od.* 15.427). It is significant, however, that no individual Achaian hero is directly called a pirate, and especially not Odysseus. There seems to be a definite separation between heroes and

---

[11] The arguments put forward here differ somewhat from those advanced in de Souza (1995a). I have benefited enormously from discussions of Homeric society with Hans van Wees.

[12] *Hom. Hymn Apoll.* 452–55. These hymns were composed at intervals after the two main epics.

[13] κατὰ πρῆξιν.

[14] οἷά τε ληϊστῆρες ὑπεὶρ ἅλα.

[15] On the nature of the Homeric *basilees* see van Wees (1992): 31–6 and 78–83.

pirates in the poet's mind, although there is very little difference between them in terms of their actions in the poems.

What do heroes and pirates regularly do in the Homeric poems? The best illustration of this is provided by Odysseus' Cretan guise:

Farming I never cared for, nor life at home, nor fathering fair children. I revelled in long ships with oars; I loved polished lances, arrows in the skirmish, the shapes of doom that others shake to see. Carnage suited me; heaven put those things in me somehow. Each to his own pleasure! Before we young Achaians shipped for Troy I led men on nine cruises in ships to raid strange coasts, and had great luck, taking rich spoils on the spot, and even more in the division. So my house grew prosperous, my standing therefore high among the Cretans. (*Od.* 14.222–34)

But Zeus the son of Kronos brought me down. No telling why he would have it, but he made me go to Egypt with a company of pirates – a long sail to the South – for my undoing. Up the broad Nile and in to the river bank I brought my dipping squadron. There, indeed, I told the men to stand guard at the ships; I sent patrols out – out to rising ground; but reckless greed carried my crews away to plunder the Egyptian farms; they bore off wives and children, killed what men they found.[16] (*Od.* 17.424–33)

In short, both pirates and heroes set off in their long ships to distant shores to plunder and kill. The difference between those who are heroes and those who are pirates seems only to be their god-given fate. It cannot be coincidental that the luck of the son of Kastor changes when he joins a group identified as pirates. Their greed and lack of discipline cause them to be slaughtered and their new recruit to be sold as a slave. Yet the raids which they undertake are indistinguishable. The Homeric poems, especially the *Odyssey*, contain a large amount of this kind of robbery with violence, often, but not always, in the context of a larger-scale conflict which merits the description of warfare. It is significant that Odysseus makes his Cretan claim that he earned high status among his countrymen because of the booty he obtained from his raids. This same idea can be seen in the way that Zeus ensures Odysseus himself will have a suitable amount of 'booty' with him when he finally returns to Ithaca, twenty years after setting off for the Trojan War, although in this case it is not the result of warfare, but of the generosity of the Phaiakians: 'They will send him in a ship back to his own country with gifts of bronze, gold and many garments, even more than he would bear if he had returned unharmed from Troy, laden with his share of the booty' (*Od.* 5.37–40).

The hero's booty can consist of metals and objects of value, as in the last quotation, but it can also consist of cattle or slaves.[17] It is an essential

---

[16] Both passages are quoted from the translation of Fitzgerald (1961), with minor alterations.

[17] See *Il.* 18.28; *Od.* 1.397–8 for slaves; *Od.* 23.356–8 for cattle.

aspect of Homeric warfare that the heroes should amass plenty of booty. As well as the wealth which this brings, there is also a direct equation of booty with status, hence the deeply damaging quarrel between Achilleus and Agamemnon is over a woman who is part of the spoil. Without his booty an Homeric hero is incomplete. Homer does not, however, neglect the other side of the story, the victims of plundering are taken notice of by the poet as well. It should not be overlooked that Odysseus, in his attack on the Kikones (*Od.* 9.39–52), or the raids of his fictional Cretan, brings misery to the victims. It is noticeable that most of these raids seem to go wrong because of the greed of the perpetrators, which gets them into trouble with their victims' neighbours. It seems to me that this represents a feeling of moral indignation and disapproval for such actions. The poet is indicating that they deserve to suffer for what they have done.

Nevertheless, it cannot be denied that the acquisition of booty through violence brings prestige and status to most of those who engage in it. It is contrasted implicitly with trading, an activity which also involves the accumulation of wealth through maritime expeditions, but which is unsuitable as an occupation for a hero.[18] The story of the kidnapping of Eumaios, who became Odysseus' swineherd after he was taken from the island of Syrie (*Od.* 15.403–84), shows the Phoenician traders who abducted him in the worst possible light, as liars and cheats, rather than warriors. That which is honourable and will confer prestige and status in Homer can be defined as that which is done by the heroes. If it comes to a choice between trader or pirate, as in the greeting quoted above, the more honourable and prestigious title is the latter. But the ambiguous and potentially disapproving label pirate is never applied to Odysseus. Ideally a hero like Odysseus will engage in warfare, which is essentially a communal or public activity, but he will be competing with his peers for individual honour, prestige and status. The Trojan War itself represents the highest level to which this violent competition can rise, but the piratical raids of Odysseus and others carried out in reprisal for previous attacks, for example Nestor's youthful exploits, as described to Patroklos (*Il.* 11.685–762), reveal a wide range of activities which might be described as warfare, raiding or piracy. A private raid, whether it is carried out in reprisal for previous injuries or simply to obtain booty, may escalate into a public confrontation involving whole communities.

It would seem, therefore, to be very difficult for the modern student of Homeric society to determine exactly, or even approximately, where any boundaries between warfare and piracy might be drawn, although it has

---

[18] See *Od.* 8.159–64 for Odysseus being insulted with the label 'trader'; *Od.* 14 and 15 for the low status of Phoenician traders.

been argued by some scholars that there is a clear distinction between war and piracy in the Homeric poems.[19] Piracy or raiding for plunder is considered by Nowag to be less important than warfare, which conveys a higher status on the (successful) combatants. He contrasts small raids with the sacking of major cities, such as Troy. But the *Iliad*, because it focuses on the siege of Troy in such a spectacular fashion, is bound to make all other raids appear petty in comparison, although, as Nowag acknowledges, they are conducted in a very similar fashion. Most of the warfare in the *Odyssey* is on a smaller scale, and it is this poem which seems to me to present a wider and more comprehensive picture of Homeric values. In his important study of Homeric warfare and society van Wees has argued that there is an important distinction between what he calls predatory warfare (carried out by 'freebooters') and status warfare (carried out by heroes). I do not think that this distinction is easily maintained either. A significant case for the demonstration of van Wees' argument is the Cretan guise of Odysseus, the son of Kastor. Van Wees argues that the reluctance of this Cretan to participate in the Trojan War (*Od.* 14.235–9) is due to his preference for predatory rather than status warfare. Yet the passage quoted above shows that his plundering raids, which in van Wees' scheme must be predatory warfare, have nevertheless earned him high status. He goes to Troy because, if he does not, he will lose that status, which also seems to indicate that he is just as involved in status warfare as he is predatory warfare; the two cannot be easily separated.[20]

It may have been Helen's face that launched a thousand ships, but it was Homer's poems that provoked a thousand academic debates. Alternative interpretations of piracy and warfare in Homer can be argued just as persuasively as my own. I am confident, however, that the main points are valid. Pirates and their activities can be, and are, looked upon with disapproval in the Homeric poems. Piracy is an evil business from the victims' point of view, yet for the heroic practitioner it brings high status and prestige, largely because of the fighting involved and the booty that is obtained. Warfare and piracy are virtually indistinguishable in Homer. The ingredients of violence and booty are equally important in both, and the methods of war and piracy are essentially the same.[21] Warfare can also be motivated by other factors, such as honour, vengeance and pride, all of which are to be found in the poems. In the historical world of the early Archaic Greeks the difference between the two was probably a

---

[19] E.g. Bravo (1980): 975–7; Nowag (1983): chs. 2 and 3, especially 94–106; Jackson (1985) and (1993).

[20] See van Wees (1992): ch. 4, especially 207–17.

[21] Note that no Homeric pirate (or hero) attacks ships at sea. See below pp. 22–36 on the development of trade and the threat of piracy to it in the Archaic and Classical periods.

matter of perceptions and labels. Many of the activities which a status-conscious aristocrat would have felt made him worthy of the title *basileus* would seem to his victims to have justified their labelling him a pirate.

References in later literary sources to the activities of the Archaic Greeks in both the Eastern and the Western Mediterranean do lend some support to the view that the image of war and piracy in the Homeric poems reflects a contemporary reality quite closely. According to a brief remark in Thucydides' Sicilian *Archaeologia*, the city of Zankle (later called Messana), the establishment of which can be dated to about 730–720 BC on archaeological grounds,[22] was founded by pirates from the existing settlement of Kyme (Thuc. 6.4.5). They were later joined by people from Chalkis and other parts of Euboia. What can a reference like this mean? Were the founders of Zankle looking for a base from which to practise piracy, and chose this one because it was situated on the straits between Italy and Sicily? Or did they found a city first, and then carry out raids which their victims labelled piracy? Such references, fascinating though they are, cannot easily be interpreted. Thucydides seems to imply that piracy was common among the colonising Greeks of the eighth century, as does Strabo when he reports the claim of Eratosthenes that the Early Greeks sailed abroad for both trade and piracy (Str. 1.3.2). Herodotus also mentions Greeks from Ionia voyaging to Egypt for plunder in the time of the first Saite pharaoh, Psammetichos (664–610 BC). These particular men, equipped with bronze armour, stayed and were recruited as mercenaries (Hdt. 2.152).[23] In slightly different circumstances, the Phokaians who settled in Corsica in the mid sixth century BC began to plunder their neighbours, until they provoked war as a reaction from the Carthaginians and Etruscans which culminated in an inconclusive battle at sea (Hdt. 1.166). There is abundant archaeological evidence for Greek trade and settlement across the Mediterranean in the Archaic period,[24] but the lack of reliable and clear literary evidence makes it very difficult to assess to what extent piracy was also practised by the people who were involved in this trade. Nevertheless it seems clear, on the basis of the Homeric poems and the later literary references, that not all interaction between those who roamed the Mediterranean in the Archaic period was of a peaceful or 'commercial' nature.

Trade and piracy are both forms of economic activity. They can have a similar motive (the accumulation of wealth) and achieve similar results (the movement of goods and/or persons across long distances). The dif-

---

[22] See *CAH* III.3.162.
[23] See Lloyd (1975–88): ad. loc.
[24] See *CAH* III.3; Boardman (1980); Wells (1980).

ference between them is that piracy involves violence and the forceful obtaining or transfer of property. Maritime trade has a longer history than piracy. The oldest known shipwrecks in the Mediterranean, found off the coast of Turkey at Ulu Burun and Cape Gelidonya, were almost certainly trading vessels, operating between the coasts and islands of the Eastern Mediterranean in the fourteenth and thirteenth centuries BC.[25] They carried mixed cargoes of basic necessities and luxuries, as well as all the paraphernalia required to trade in several different lands and with several different peoples. There is, however, little that can be said about the relationship between trade and piracy until the end of the Archaic period. By the sixth century BC it seems that there was a clear distinction in the Mediterranean between cargo ships, short and rounded in most cases, powered only by sails, and warships, longer and slimmer, powered by oars and sails and with a ram on the prow.[26] The Greeks began to use specific words for merchants, and to create institutions for the facilitation and practice of trade.[27] An Athenian law attributed to the time of Solon (c. 594 BC) and preserved through a quotation in the *Digest of Roman Law* (*Dig.* 47.22.4), recognizes the swearing of oaths for associations of citizens for the conduct of religious rites, burials, revelling, trade and plundering. Jackson has suggested that a fragmentary sixth-century inscription from the oracle of Apollo at Didyma relates to raiders wanting to establish the 'legitimacy' of their proposed targets.[28]

Thucydides says that the Corinthians were among the first to put down piracy in order to help traders (Thuc. 1.13), but there is no secure date for this remark, which may be an invention on the basis of contemporary attitudes to piracy and trade.[29] Mention has already been made of the distinction between pirates and traders in Homer, the latter apparently not receiving the same high status as the former, although this may not reflect the prevalent attitude among the poet's contemporaries and his upper-class audience. It would seem reasonable to suppose that as trade became more significant for the élite in Greek society their attitude to indiscriminate piracy would have started to change. As the Greeks expanded their trading connections and colonized many places in the Mediterranean, it is likely that the status of traders could have become higher and relatively better in moral terms than that of pirates, although this would have been a very gradual process. There is plenty of evidence from

---

[25] See Bass (1967) and (1987); Parker (1992). The cargoes included pottery, semi-precious stones, metal ingots and some foodstuffs.

[26] See, for example, Pls. 1 and 2.

[27] Reed (1984).

[28] Jackson (1995).

[29] See below pp. 26–9 on this and other passages from Thucydides' *Archaeologia*.

Pl. 1. Athenian Black Figure drinking cup of the mid sixth century BC, showing a merchant ship, propelled by sail, and a warship, propelled by sail and by oars rowed at two levels. A smaller ship is being towed behind the warship. The merchant ship is broad-beamed and has a deep draught, while the warship is long and narrow, with a ram on its prow.

Pl. 2. Opposite side of the cup in Pl. 1. The crew of the warship appear to be furling the sail. This scene may be an attempt to depict pirates preparing to attack the merchant ship.

the Classical and Hellenistic periods that piracy could be perceived as a considerable threat to merchants and long-distance trade.[30] The origins of this view may lie in the Archaic period.

It begins to be possible to differentiate between warfare and piracy in the Greek world towards the end of the Archaic period. The general trend from the Archaic into the Classical period (*c.* 500–330 BC) is towards the development of organized states with citizen and/or mercenary armies which engage in more sophisticated and large-scale forms of warfare.[31] The activities of Polykrates, tyrant of Samos (*c.* 546–522 BC), characterized in Herodotus as plundering, seem to amount to a kind of early imperialism:[32]

All his campaigns were victorious, his every venture a success. He had a fleet of a hundred fifty-oared galleys and a force of a thousand bowmen. His plundering raids were widespread and indiscriminate – he used to say that a friend would be more grateful if he gave him back what he had taken than if he had never taken it. He captured many of the islands and a number of towns on the mainland as well. Amongst other successes, he defeated at sea the Lesbians, who had sent their whole fleet to the help of Miletos; the prisoners he took were forced to dig, in chains, the whole moat which surrounds the walls of Samos.[33] (Hdt. 3.39)

Polykrates' capture of many cities and his large fleet and army seem to be characteristic of warfare, a public activity involving a political entity – the *polis* of Samos – rather than piracy. It is also around this time that naval warfare begins to be reported in the sources, here among Greek states, and earlier in Herodotus' reference to the adventures of the Phokaians among Greeks and non-Greeks (Hdt. 1.166).

The limitations of piracy as a method of waging warfare are illustrated by the Ionian revolt (499–494 BC). A plundering raid against Sardis in 498 BC, conducted by an allied force of Ionians, Eretrians and Athenians, served only to aggravate relations with the Persian king (Hdt. 5.97–101), and the various piratical enterprises of Histiaios of Miletos achieved nothing of value either (Hdt. 6.5 and 26–30). It seems to me that a greater variation in Greek warfare develops clearly in the fifth century BC. Some campaigns and expeditions are more politically motivated than others. Clashes of city-states with each other, and with the Persians, produce organized violence on a very large scale. Plunder can still be an important motivation, however, and there is still a close correspondence between

---

[30] See below Chs. 3 and 4.
[31] Garlan (1972): ch. 1A distinguishes a political form of warfare from 'la forme "sauvage"'. This is probably too crude a characterization, but the aims and intensity of Greek warfare do seem to change with the rise of the *polis*; see also de Souza (1998b).
[32] On the nature of the Polykratean regime see Shipley (1987): chs. 4 and 5.
[33] Translation by de Sélincourt (1972).

piracy and some types of warfare. In 490 BC the unsuccessful expedition of Miltiades of Athens to Paros seems to have combined a political motive (or excuse), to punish the Parians for their alleged medizing, with a less noble motive, namely to obtain money for the Athenians (Hdt. 6.132–5). The point at which the distinction between warfare and piracy can be most clearly marked is, perhaps, the creation of the Delian League in 478 BC. Some scholars have tried to characterize this as just an association of Greek states to practise piracy against the Persian Empire by plundering the king's lands.[34] The early campaigns of the League produced far more than mere plunder, however, as they involved conquest of territory. The members of the League soon become involved in inter-state warfare, and the imperialist ambitions of the Athenians took precedence over the idea of exacting reparations from the Persians. Warfare and piracy are no longer the same thing in the fifth century BC, although, as will be seen, there is still a certain amount of overlap between the two.

### Athens and piracy

It has often been suggested that the Athenian maritime empire of the fifth century BC took an active role in controlling piracy, and that the suppression of piracy was an important, if undeclared, justification for the establishment of its precursor, the Delian League, in 478 BC.[35] There is evidence that the idea of suppressing piracy was current in Athens in this period, principally in the history of the Peloponnesian War by the Athenian Thucydides. He suggests that the legendary king Minos, who he claims was the first Greek ruler to establish a navy, would probably have put down piracy in the Aegean in order to increase his revenues, and he later attributes a similar policy to the Corinthians (Thuc. 1.4; 1.13). It is obvious that Thucydides is here making a connection between the exploits of Minos and the Corinthians in the earlier history of the Greeks and the recent achievements of the Athenians. The extent of that connection is a matter for careful interpretation, however, since nowhere in his work does Thucydides *explicitly* credit the Athenians with any action to suppress piracy outside the operations of the Peloponnesian War.[36] What Thucydides seems to be doing in his introductory section is emphasizing the importance of sea power in the turbulent history of the Greeks, and the

---

[34] E.g. Sealey (1966), who argues that the original purpose of the League was piratical. See the convincing response of Jackson (1969) on the language used in Thuc. 1.96.

[35] E.g. Hornblower (1983): 30–1; Hornblower (1991): 21–2 and 150; Ormerod (1924): 110. Ormerod notes, however, that '...this very real benefit is passed over almost in silence by our authorities'.

[36] See below pp. 31–2 for action taken against pirates during the Peloponnesian War.

way that sea power could only be exercised by states which had substantial revenues at their disposal. By giving a brief account of the powerful states and rulers of earlier Greek history, stressing the themes of revenues and sea power, he encourages his readers to see the maritime empire created by the Athenians in the period leading up to the start of the Peloponnesian War as the greatest manifestation of military power the Greek world had ever seen. This in turn serves to substantiate his claim that the Peloponnesian War, which resulted in the downfall of that empire, was the greatest conflict in the history of the Greeks, surpassing the Trojan War and even the Persian Wars (Thuc. 1.1–19).[37]

It is clear that Thucydides perceived a marked difference between the nature of warfare in his own time and in the Heroic era of Minos and the Homeric epics. He seems to envisage the heroes as pirate leaders, and he links the growth of seaborne trade and the appearance of walled coastal cities to a reduction in the prevalence of piracy (Thuc. 1.5–8).[38] He is dismissive of the length and scale of the Trojan War, saying that it lasted so long because the forces involved were relatively small and the Greeks spent much of their time cultivating the land in the Chersonese and carrying out plundering raids (Thuc. 1.10–11). The main 'evidence' for these conjectures must have been the *Odyssey* and the *Iliad*, in which there is a heavy emphasis on the predatory nature of warfare and the individualistic values of the heroes.[39] Thucydides must have been struck by the 'progress' in military organization and political aims which the hoplite and trireme warfare of his own day represented in comparison with the crude, predatory style of the warfare in the Homeric epics.

It is, however, often overlooked that Thucydides implies at several points in his *Archaeologia* that such piracy is no longer as widespread a phenomenon among the Greeks as it was in earlier times. He presents the archaic world of the Homeric heroes as one in which, among other things, piracy was so common that a formal greeting to a stranger would include the question, 'Are you pirates?' Furthermore, he connects Corinthian prosperity with the suppression of piracy, in both cases implying that conditions are very different in his own time (Thuc. 1.5; 1.13).

For Thucydides, then, the suppression of piracy played a very important role in the establishment of earlier sea powers, like Minos and the Corinthians, but in the recent rise of the Athenian Empire it was not an essential matter and therefore he does not mention it in his summary ac-

---

[37] See especially 1.1, 1.10 and 1.18–19. On the structure and themes of the *Archaeologia* see Hornblower (1991): 3–56.

[38] His argument is essentially that trade generates revenue which provides the resources to build the walled cities.

[39] See above pp. 17–22 on Homeric piracy and plundering.

count of the development of this empire, usually called the *Pentecontaëtia* (Thuc. 1.89–118). How did he reach these conclusions? One explanation could be that Thucydides believed that there was much less piracy around in the Greek world to threaten the revenues and security of the Athenian Empire. Whereas the earlier Greeks had frequently made piratical attacks on each other and on the barbarians, necessitating the carrying of arms at all times and the building of cities away from the coast, in his own time it was only the rather backward regions of Greece north of the Gulf of Corinth where such behaviour was still the norm (Thuc. 1.5–6). That is not to say that piracy was completely eradicated, but it had been reduced to a level which presented far less of a threat, partly as a result of the actions of Minos and the Corinthians, and also partly as a consequence of the development of that great social and political phenomenon, the Greek city-state – the *polis*. A further explanation could be that the Athenians, in spite of their thriving overseas trade, did not depend upon maritime commerce for their revenues in the same way that the Corinthians did. Their principal sources of income were the tribute of their allies and the products of their own land. They could be vulnerable to pirates, as the occasional mentions of piracy in the course of the Peloponnesian War indicate, but they were not, in Thucydides' view, dependent upon the suppression of piracy to maintain their revenues and their power in the period 478–431 BC.

Given that Thucydides is explicit in his description of the ways in which the Athenians, like Minos and the Corinthians, and others whom he mentions in the *Archaeologia*, increased their revenues and established their rule over other Greeks, if he took the view that suppression of piracy was in any sense a significant feature of their rise to power, then he would surely have mentioned it at some point in his work, most logically in Book 1. Since he does not do so, it is a reasonable conclusion that, in Thucydides' eyes, controlling piracy was not a function of either the Athenian Empire or the Delian League out of which it developed.

A possible objection to this analysis is the argument that the model for the relationship between increasing revenues and suppressing piracy on the part of Minos and the Corinthians was furnished for Thucydides by the Delian League and the Athenian Empire. Since, by his own admission, Thucydides was basing his account of the early history of the Greeks on probable deductions from uncertain sources (Thuc. 1.20–1), then he would have taken the fifth-century Athenians as an analogy for the behaviour of earlier sea powers, and his emphasis on controlling piracy could, therefore, reflect contemporary Athenian practice.[40] The answer

---

[40] This interpretation goes back at least as far as Grote (1888): 220–1. See above pp. 15–16.

to this objection is that, as has already been noted, Thucydides saw *leisteia* (encompassing both piracy and banditry, but particularly the former) as a major feature of the early Greek world, preventing safe communications and so hampering the growth of long-distance trade. This view was based largely on his reading of the Homeric poems, in which predatory warfare and piracy are very prominent. His conclusion that the suppression of piracy must have been necessary in order to permit commercial development was a logical one which did not require a fifth-century model.

Evidence that piracy was still a common problem for the Greek *poleis* in the mid fifth century BC comes from epigraphic sources. An inscription from Teos on the western coastline of Asia Minor, dated to *c.* 470 BC, details curses to be pronounced against the betrayal of the community by the *aisymnetes*, an important local magistrate. The death penalty (for families as well as magistrates) is prescribed for several offences including committing banditry or piracy, and sheltering men known to be bandits or pirates who have plundered the territory of Teos or have committed piracy out at sea.[41] From this text it would appear that the Teians were likely to be troubled quite often by pirates raiding their territory. Another, slightly different practice, the taking of plunder by way of reprisals, is mentioned in an inscription of *c.* 450 BC, recording an agreement between Oiantheia and Chaleion, which restricts the custom to the seas outside the harbours of the two cities, where seizures are deemed to be lawful.[42] This form of piracy was apparently very common in the fifth century BC, as the instances from the Peloponnesian War discussed below indicate. It is also noteworthy that these two *poleis* are located in the region of central Greece where Thucydides claims that 'old-fashioned' attitudes to warfare and piracy persist (Thuc. 1.5–6).

The only evidence for the Athenians and their allies taking direct action against pirates before the Peloponnesian War occurs in literary sources which are much later than the fifth century and cannot be given as much weight as Thucydides. One instance is Plutarch's account of the Delian League expedition to the island of Skyros which occurred in 476 BC, led by the Athenian general Kimon. The conquest of the island is mentioned by Thucydides, but Plutarch's version in his *Life of Kimon* is much more detailed (Thuc. 1.98; Plut. *Kim.* 8). According to Plutarch the island was inhabited by Dolopians whose constant plundering of ships, including those which were trading with them, eventually resulted in a request for Athenian intervention, addressed directly to Kimon, whose expedition

---

[41] *SIG* 37, 38 = Fornara (1983): no. 63. This text is very specific about the distinction between piracy and banditry, using the rare word κιξάλλης for 'bandit'.
[42] Tod (1946): no. 34.

'cleared the sea of pirates'. Plutarch says that it was the Dolopian pirates themselves who invited Kimon to invade and seize control, because they were anxious to avoid paying compensation to some Thessalian merchants who had complained to the Delphic Amphictyony. Kimon also 'discovered' the bones of the Athenian hero Theseus on the island and returned them to Athens. Thucydides' version is much less elaborate than Plutarch's. He simply says that the Athenians enslaved the local population and established a colony of Athenian citizens there. The description of Dolopian piracy in Plutarch is not very credible, and the whole account has many features which look like attempts to justify Athenian 'imperialism'. It would seem that the capture of Skyros was intended to benefit the Athenians collectively, by providing them with an island to colonize, and Kimon in particular through the prestige of the conquest and the return of Theseus' bones to Athens. The suppression of piracy would appear to be a later addition to the story, included by Plutarch because it places Kimon in a better light as a benefactor of the Greeks in general.[43]

In his *Life of Perikles* Plutarch gives an account of what is known as the 'Congress Decree' (Plut. *Per.* 17). This was a proposal apparently put to the Athenian assembly by Perikles for a congress of Greek states to be held at Athens. Plutarch does not clearly date this measure, but modern scholars have assigned it to 448/7 BC, after the 'Peace of Kallias'. Among the items on the agenda for this congress was ensuring the safety of the seas, which has led some scholars to conclude that Perikles was looking to obtain general Hellenic approval for existing or proposed Athenian naval operations against pirates, although there is no other evidence for Athenian naval actions against pirates around this time.[44] Many scholars believe, however, that this decree was a forgery, composed in the fourth century BC, and that no such congress was ever proposed.[45] The fifth-century Athenians had no policy of suppressing piracy in general, nor do their imperial activities and alliances seem to have had much indirect effect on the prevalence of piracy, at least as far as the Teian inscription indicates. Indeed, as the power of the Athenians caused alarm among the Peloponnesians, the incidence of piracy in the Aegean sharply increased.

[43] See Podlecki (1971) on the significance of Theseus' bones. A similarly untrustworthy claim that an Athenian leader of the period suppressed piracy occurs in Nepos' short life of Themistokles: Nepos, *Them.* 2.3.

[44] E.g. Ormerod (1924): 108–9. Plutarch, *Per.* 11 refers to regular expeditions of Athenian triremes, but does not indicate that these had anything to do with piracy. At *Per.* 19 he mentions an expedition to the Thracian Chersonese c. 447 BC which dealt with 'groups of bandits' (*leisterion*), but there is no suggestion that piracy was a particular problem in this region.

[45] E.g. Seager (1969) and Macdonald (1982).

## War and piracy

The Peloponnesian War (431–404 BC) was, according to its historian Thucydides, greater than any previous conflict in Greek history, involving thousands of soldiers and sailors, and hundreds of ships. Thucydides also notes the diverse forms which the war took in its many theatres of conflict, ranging from full-scale hoplite and trireme battles of the traditional kind, to 'guerrilla' actions and plundering raids by forces which Thucydides often describes as pirates.[46] He makes a distinction between formal warfare and what he calls *leisteia* (plundering), a form of warfare which the Spartans in particular were unused to before this time (Thuc. 4.41). It seems that the Peloponnesian War also saw widespread use of the principle of taking reprisals against an enemy for injuries perceived to have been done, by carrying out (or promoting) plundering raids on their territory and their shipping, or that of their allies. Thus, in 416 BC, in response to the provocation of Athens' subjugation of Melos and the Argive invasion of Phliasia, the Spartans announced their support for plundering against the Athenians, their intention being to encourage their citizens and their allies to raid Attica without actually abandoning the treaty concluded in 421 BC (Thuc. 5.115).

The nature of the raids clearly varied according to circumstances. In such cases as the Corcyran oligarchs who raided their former homeland from bases on the mainland in 427 BC, the main intention was to harass the inhabitants and undermine the authority of their political opponents (Thuc. 3.85). A similar aim lay behind the attacks carried out by the raiders who were established by the Athenians on Lakonian territory, or the Peloponnesian flotilla which attacked merchant shipping from its base at Knidos in 411 BC (Thuc. 4.41; 7.26; 8.34). Whether these raiders used ships, or only operated on land like bandits, their objectives were essentially political ones, although their methods, in the eyes of Thucydides at least, lay beyond the bounds of formal warfare. Wherever raiding was carried out those who claimed to be the legitimate political leaders would naturally be expected to justify their authority by protecting the local population from the attackers. Failure to do so could result in their downfall. In a like manner any occupying force or garrison which could not deal with plundering raids would be shown to be weaker than its opponents and, therefore, find it harder to control the subject population. As a result various measures were undertaken to control or prevent such raids, such as the fortification of Atalante to guard Euboia and the dispatch of a small Athenian flotilla in the region of Karia and Lycia to

---

[46] E.g. 2.32; 2.69; 3.51; 3.85; 7.26; 8.35.

prevent 'Peloponnesian' pirates from attacking the merchant shipping coming from Phaselis and Phoinike into the Aegean (Thuc. 2.32 and 69).[47] Another method which the Athenians seem to have adopted during the War was to demand that their allies should not to allow pirates to use their harbours as bases. A clause specifying this is found in two treaties of c. 427–424 BC, between Athens and Mytilene, on the island of Lesbos, and between Athens and Halieis in the eastern Peloponnese.[48] The latter treaty states: 'The people of Halieis are to make available to the Athenians their harbour and to help them readily. They are not to admit pirates, nor to practise piracy, nor are they to join in a campaign against the Athenians. . .'[49] The requirement to make the harbour available to the Athenians would seem to allow the possibility of its use as a base for Athenian vessels to plunder the Peloponnesian coastline. The distinction between enemies and pirates does not mean that enemies might not set sail in search of plunder, but allows some differentiation between the Spartans and their allies, who are the Athenians' enemies in the current war, and anyone else, including the people of Halieis, who might seek to raid Attica from a base at Halieis.

The identity of the pirates involved in episodes related by Thucydides is often difficult to establish. Sometimes he is specific about the origin of ships and/or their crews,[50] but often he gives no indication or only a vague generalization. Those whom the Athenians were trying to prevent establishing themselves in Karia and Lycia in 430/29 BC are described by Thucydides as 'Peloponnesian', but this term is not specific enough to be of much help. They might have come from anywhere in the Peloponnese, or indeed from areas closer to hand. All that can be deduced from the label is that they were operating on behalf of the Spartans and their allies against the interests of the Athenians and their allies (Thuc. 2.69).[51] When the Spartans proclaimed reprisals against Athens in 416 BC they invited 'anyone of their own people' to raid the Athenians, but this would not have been intended to include only Spartans, especially as it was their allies and friends who were most likely to have the ships to carry out seaborne raids (Thuc. 5.115). By the end of the war the Peloponnesian fleet seems to have attracted some 'hangers-on' who were looking for

---

[47] The Karian/Lycian expedition was not very successful. Its commander Melesandros marched inland (presumably to collect tribute) and was defeated by Lycian forces. On the nature of his operations see Hornblower (1991): 354–5.
[48] IG I³ nos. 67 and 75.
[49] IG I³ no. 75, lines 6–10 (424/3 BC).
[50] E.g. Thuc. 3.85; 4.41; 8.35.
[51] Similarly in 3.51 Thucydides refers to pirates 'sent out' by the Peloponnesians, but their identity is unclear.

opportunities to carry out piratical raids against their opponents. When Lysandros wanted to send news of the Spartan victory at Aigospotamoi in 405 BC back to Sparta he chose a Milesian pirate called Theopompos as his messenger (Xen. *Hell.* 2.1.30).

In the latter stages of the Peloponnesian War another objective seems to become prominent – obtaining funds and/or supplies to prosecute the war. The Athenians, as they became more and more desperate for funds, resorted to the methods of piracy in order to obtain them. Their unfortunate victims tended to be the Greeks of Asia and the Hellespontine cities. The renowned politician Alkibiades is a prime example of the general turned plunderer. In 410/9 BC he plundered the territory of the Persian satrap Pharnabazos. Plutarch says that he generously allowed priests and priestesses to go free without demanding a ransom, but he attacked the city of Chalkedon with the intention of obtaining as much money as he could. Unfortunately he found that the wealth of the city had been sent to Bithynia for safekeeping, presumably because the Chalkedonians had anticipated his actions. Alkibiades then approached the borders of Bithynia with his army and forced its people to hand over the booty to him and conclude a treaty of friendship (Plut. *Alc.* 29.3). After defeating both Pharnabazos and the Spartans outside Chalkedon he sailed to the Hellespont and then into the Aegean to collect money, his purpose being to impress upon the allies of Athens the importance of staying loyal to her, and to obtain from them the funds he needed to pay and provision his forces. Diodorus describes the process even more bluntly than Plutarch, recounting Alkibiades' actions in 408 BC, after the capture of a stronghold on Andros: 'He then sailed off with his forces to ravage Kos and Rhodes, and he also collected huge amounts of booty for the maintenance of his soldiers' (Diod. 13.69.5). Another raid on the city of Kyme in 407 BC yielded much booty and many captives, and caused the Kymeans to protest strongly to the Athenian assembly (Diod. 13.73). It is clear that Alkibiades exploited the mobility his ships enabled and the capacity for intimidation which his army provided. He cannot be called a pirate, but his methods could easily be termed piratical.

Such methods continued to be used by the armies and fleets of the Greek city-states in the fourth century BC. The famous Athenian general Iphikrates, for example, used *leistai* in the Hellespontine region during the Corinthian War (395–387 BC), as did his opponents, and there were several other generals who were accused of operating like pirates in the fourth century (Xen. *Hell.* 4.8.35).[52] The Thessalian tyrant Alexander of Pherai, one of the leaders prominent in the power politics of the mid

---

[52] See the evidence collected in Pritchett (1974): 82–5 on Chares and 85–9 on Charidemos.

fourth century, is called a pirate in the main historical acounts. He seems to have earned this label more as a result of his attacks on the Cycladic islands than for his operations on the Greek mainland, but his methods were no different from those of his contemporaries (Diod. 15.95.1; Xen. *Hell.* 6.4.35).[53]

The practice of raiding in reprisal became a considerable problem for the Athenians (and others) in the first half of the fourth century BC. A lawcourt speech of 399 by Lysias notes that the Athenian *polis* is desperately short of money and that while the Spartans are making threats because of the non-payment of the amount owing to them, the Boiotians (whose territory borders Attica) are already taking reprisals for unpaid debts (Lys. 30.22). In 389 BC, during the Corinthian War, the Spartan *harmost* Eteonikos, who was based on Aigina, with the full backing of the Spartan *ephors*, invited volunteers from among the island's inhabitants to plunder Attica. In response the Athenians sent a force of hoplites under the general Pamphilos to Aigina. They built siege walls to blockade the main city by land and sent ten triremes to cut it off by sea. A Spartan admiral, Teleutias, was able to drive off the Athenian ships, but the fortifications were held for several months, until another Athenian squadron removed the occupying force (Xen. *Hell.* 5.1.1–5).[54] After a subsequent Athenian attack on Aigina had inflicted a defeat on the Spartan forces and embarrassed Eteonikos they refused to sail out again because they had not been paid. Teleutias, returning to take command of them, resorted to attacking the merchant ships in the harbour at Piraeus and seizing ships and boats along the coastline of Attica. He sold his booty and captives in Aigina, where there must have been quite a market for Athenian plunder by now, and used the proceeds to pay his sailors and keep his operations going (Xen. *Hell.* 5.1.14–24).

This series of raids and counter-attacks illustrates how unclear the distinction between warfare and piracy could be in the fourth cenury BC. Xenophon is careful to note that the Aiginetans had been peacefully trading with the Athenians prior to Eteonikos' declaration of reprisals, so that they effectively swapped one method of obtaining profit from the Athenians (trade) for another (piracy). They presumably did not have any specific dispute with the Athenians, but were simply taking advantage of the justification offered by the Spartan declaration of reprisals, which was itself intended to increase the pressure on the Athenians' own territory and resources without any increase in the size of the Spartan forces.[55]

---

[53] Compare Evagoras of Cyprus in Diodorus 15.3.

[54] Quoted in de Souza (1995a): 184.

[55] Aigina is ideally situated for attacks on Attica and its coastal shipping, and Xenophon reports the Athenians suffering from Aiginetan-based piracy again in 374 BC (Xen. *Hell.* 6.2.1).

The fact that reprisals might not even have been declared against a particular state would not necessarily prevent the seizure of property, since opportunists would strike (in the best tradition of pirates) wherever the chance arose. This would tend to make almost anyone at sea, on coastlines, or in a harbour fair game. One of the private lawcourt speeches in the Demosthenic corpus tells how, in about 369 BC, Lykon of Herakleia, having deposited some money in the bank of Pasion at Athens for payment to his partner Kephisiades, set out on a voyage to Libya: 'But misfortune befell this Lykon, so that as soon as he had set out on the voyage across the Gulf of Argos he was attacked by pirate ships, his goods were taken to Argos, and he was shot with an arrow and later died' (Demos. 52.5). The speaker says no more about the pirates, so their identity and their possible allegiance is unknown. Indeed, a record of the whole episode survives only because a court case developed out of a dispute over the money which had been deposited with Pasion. Thus, when in his *Panegyric*, written about 380 BC, Isokrates complains that 'the pirates rule the seas', he is surely referring to the activities of a whole range of evildoers who might be individual opportunists, with or without the 'legitimation' of a declaration of reprisals, or they might belong, however loosely, to one or other of the many naval detachments operating in the Aegean at this time (Isoc. 4.115).

In his speech *Against Timokrates* Demosthenes describes an incident which occurred in 355 BC and shows how the informal 'rules' concerning reprisals might be ignored or manipulated in particular circumstances. Some Athenian ambassadors, who were on their way to Mausolos of Karia in a trireme, captured a ship from Naukratis in Egypt and seized 9½ talents' worth of property. It was decided by the people that, although the Athenians and Egyptians were not at war and had no current disputes, Athens' friendly relations with the king of Persia, from whom the Egyptians were in revolt, justified the seizure of Egyptian plunder. The goods became the property of the state, since they had been taken by men on an official mission, and a tithe of the proceeds was paid to Athena. With such a large sum involved it was not difficult to find an excuse for this opportunist act (Demos. 24.11–12 and 120). The frequency with which Athenian ships and their commanders made seizures is often commented on in the speeches of the Demosthenic corpus. In his criticism of a decree proposed in 352 BC by Aristokrates in favour of Charidemos, which sought to make it a crime to harm him, Demosthenes argues that it prevents someone from resisting the Euboian mercenary turned Athenian general should he make an unjust attempt at seizure. This, says Demosthenes, is a very likely scenario, because generals are constantly taking people and property by force. Thus, someone may legitimately be resisting Charidemos and kill him, only to be arrested for contravening Aristokrates' proposed decree (Demos. 23.60–1). Another speech, of *c.* 359 BC, delivered before the Athenian *boule*, claims that the many instances of Athenian trierarchs carrying off people and property have provoked reprisals against Athenian citizens, making it very dangerous for them to travel abroad. This problem is illustrated by the case of the Athenian Nikostratos who was pursuing some runaway slaves when he was captured by a warship and sold into slavery on Aigina. His new owner eventually ransomed him for twenty-six minai, doubtless a huge profit ([Demos.] 53.6–7; *c.* 366 BC).

## The rise of Macedon

In the 350s BC, after more than a century of warfare among the *poleis* of central and southern Greece, often involving the Greek communities of the Aegean and western Anatolia, and sometimes drawing the Greeks of Sicily and South Italy into the fray, the political balance of the Greek world was changed by the rise of a new power – the kingdom of Macedon. In fourth-century Athens complaints about piracy seem to have been made fairly often, to judge from the works of Demosthenes and his fellow orators. Philip of Macedon and his allies were a favourite target for accusations of promoting piracy. In his speech *On the Crown*, delivered in 330 BC, Demosthenes claimed that, but for his strong policies towards Philip, the Athenians would have suffered attacks from pirates based on the island of Euboia. His rival Aischines had earlier accused Philip of being responsible for an attack by pirates on Phrynon of Rhamnous which violated the sacred truce during the period of the Olympic games, a charge which Philip appears to have accepted (Aeschin. 2.12). The Macedonian monarch is also directly accused of acting like a pirate, preying on commercial ships to provide himself with resources, a practice which led Demosthenes to call him, 'the pirate of the Greeks' (Demos. 10.34).[56]

Although he frequently condemned such actions on Philip's part, Demosthenes was fully aware of the usefulness of piratical methods and even went so far as to advocate using such tactics in the war against Macedon (Demos. 4.23). The difference between legitimate warfare and piracy was often only a matter of opinion and interpretation,[57] leaving Athenian generals open to criticism over their indiscriminate plundering for the

---

[56] See also Demos. 4.32–4. The great orator himself is called a *leistes* by Aischines 3.253.

[57] Philip himself attempted to allay Athenian fears by releasing their citizens without demanding any ransom in 348 BC, after the fall of Olynthos (Aeschin. 2.12). He also tried to counter what he saw as biased presentation of his actions by politicians like Demosthenes by writing his side of the story in a letter to the Athenians in 342 BC (Demos. 7.33–5).

purpose of obtaining supplies. Thus, in 342 BC, Demosthenes was called upon to defend the actions of Diopeithes, an Athenian general who had been in command of some mercenaries escorting Athenian kleruchs to a settlement in Thrace. In the course of defending the Athenian settlers against the neighbouring Kardians he carried the conflict deeper into Thrace and ravaged some of Philip II's territory. Philip, who had a peace treaty with Athens at this time, wrote a letter to the Athenians complaining about Diopeithes' activities ([Demos.] 12.2–4), which added to the criticisms of other allies whose ships had been seized in the Hellespontine area and forced to make 'contributions' to the Athenian funds. In response Demosthenes argued that Diopeithes was only doing what was necessary in order to maintain an effective army. The Athenians had not granted him any resources for his pay, so he had to manage as best he could (Demos. 8.9 and 24–34).[58] Nor is he doing anything unusual, claims Demosthenes, since virtually all Athens' generals have taken money from the islanders and mainland inhabitants of the Aegean and Hellespontine area, operating a kind of 'protection racket' by promising to leave ships and harbours alone, or offering 'escorts' in return for 'gifts' which will be used to finance the Athenian navy (Demos. 8.24–5).[59]

Philip II also accused the Athenians of turning a blind eye to acts of piracy carried out by others, especially in the important Hellespontine region, which the Athenians claimed as their special area of responsibility, largely because it commanded the vital trade route from the Black Sea ([Demos.] 12.2). A further case of piracy which the Macedonian king held the Athenians responsible for was the actions of Kallias of Euboia, who captured numerous cities allied to Philip, in spite of the peace treaty between them which specifically covered these cities. Nor, claims Philip in his letter to the Athenians in 340 BC, did he stop there:

He captured and sold as slaves all those sailing to Macedonia, treating them as enemies. And you decreed him a vote of thanks! So I find it hard to imagine how things could be worse, if you were actually to declare war on me. For when we clearly had our differences you also used to send out pirates and make slaves of those sailing to us, you helped my enemies and harmed my territory. ([Demos.] 12.5)

The Athenian attitude towards Kallias is similar to their tolerance of the mercenary leader Charidemos, mentioned above, who was also accused of piracy and supporting pirates. Demosthenes' description of Charidemos' career in his speech against Aristokrates shows clearly how the actions of

[58] See Pritchett (1974): 92–3 for a full set of references and discussion of this episode.
[59] Quoted in de Souza (1995a): 182.

such a man could be considered acceptable while they were in the interests of Athens, but could be condemned as wanton plundering and piracy when they were directed against those interests (Demos. 23.148–9 and 166–7).

### The suppression of piracy

Given the apparent ubiquity of pirates in the Eastern Mediterranean in this period it is hardly surprising that the idea of concerted action to suppress piracy became an important political issue. Both Philip of Macedon and the Athenians claimed the right to carry out the job of locating pirates and destroying their bases in the interests of all the Greeks. Although both sides argued that they were acting out of a wish to make the seas safe for all, it is clear from the way that they practised and promoted acts which, from their victims' point of view, were indistinguishable from piracy, that they were not seriously concerned with the matter beyond their own short-term political advantage. They saw an opportunity to justify their aggressive and acquisitive military and naval policies in terms of the suppression of piracy. The political significance of the debate is brought out in the speech *On the Halonnesos*, probably written by the Athenian politician Hegesippos *c.* 343 BC ([Demos.] 7). The island of Halonnesos had been captured by Sostratos, who is called a pirate in the speech, but he was expelled by Philip's forces. The king offered to give the island to the Athenians, but they claimed it as their own and sent an embassy to Philip to demand, among other things, its immediate return. Early in his speech Hegesippos warns the Athenians that Philip wishes to demonstrate to all the Greeks that his superior military power has won Halonnesos, and that the Athenians can get it back only as a gift from him. Accepting this would amount to an admission that Athens is not strong enough to protect even her own possessions from pirates, let alone those of her allies ([Demos.] 7.6–8). In general Hegesippos shows more concern for the preservation of Athenian prestige than for the actual suppression of piracy:

Regarding pirates, Philip says that you and he are duty-bound to co-operate in guarding against evildoers at sea, but what he is really after is to be established at sea, by your agreeing that without Philip you do not have the strength to mount guard at sea, and, furthermore, by giving him free rein to go sailing from island to island, stopping off on the pretext of guarding against pirates, corrupting the exiled islanders and taking them away from you. ([Demos.] 7.14–15)

This speech clearly shows the level of concern which existed among many Athenian politicians that their naval standing in the Aegean, already badly compromised by the Social War (357–355 BC), was in danger of being completely lost unless they could reassert their power in the face of the growing might of Philip of Macedon. It is in this context that an Athenian decree mentioned in another speech of the 340s BC should be considered. In the speech *Against Theokrines* the speaker refers to the decree of Moirokles which enjoined the Athenians and their allies to guard against those who injured shipowners or merchants travelling by sea. Moirokles is known to have been a contemporary of Demosthenes and Hypereides, and it appears that he also advocated anti-Macedonian policies ([Demos.] 58.53).[60] The speaker mentions a fine of ten talents to be imposed upon the Melians, in accordance with the provisions of Moirokles' decree, for harbouring pirates ([Demos.] 58.56).[61] On the face of it this seems to be an example of the Athenians making a firm stand against pirates, and that is doubtless the way that their actions were meant to appear. With so many accusations of piracy being flung around it would have been very important for the Athenians, who depended heavily on seaborne commerce, to be able to reassure merchants that they could expect some protection from them against pirates. Yet fining the Melians (a relatively small and weak community) would also have been a way for the Athenians to flex their political muscles and demonstrate their readiness to punish those whom they considered to have committed some misdemeanour. In both respects rivalry with the growing power and authority of Macedon may have been the primary motive behind the measures taken.[62]

A further reason for doubting Athenian claims to be actively suppressing piracy in this period is the obvious impracticality of such an enterprise. On the one hand piracy was still an accepted method of conducting maritime warfare in the fourth century BC, as can be seen from the references in the Attic orators discussed above. Suppressing such activities would have seriously hampered Athenian efforts to maintain their military power in the Greek world. Even a campaign to identify and punish selected pirates would require an enormous military effort to tackle them in the most effective way, that is by denying them the bases from which to operate. It was not without reason that the possession or control of

---

[60] On Moirokles' opposition to Philip II see Arr. *Anab.* 1.10.

[61] The provision of Moirokles' decree under which the Melians were liable to a fine may have been similar to the clauses in the treaties between Athens and Mytilene (427–424 BC) and Athens and Halieis (424/3 BC) *IG* I³.67.7–8; 75.6–10; see above p. 32. The difference in the case of Moirokles' decree was that it applied to all allies of the Athenians. There is no indication that the decree of Moirokles, which perhaps dates to the 350s BC, committed the Athenians to undertaking any military actions.

[62] This atmosphere of political rivalry provides a plausible context for the forgery of the so-called Congress Decree of Plut. *Per.* 17, discussed above on p. 30. See Seager (1969) and Macdonald (1982).

islands and coastal sites was so prominent in both Athenian and Macedonian strategy. In friendly hands they could be used as bases from which to harry the opposing sides' territory and disrupt commercial and military traffic, as had been done during the Peloponnesian War.[63] In the hands of enemies they could represent a serious threat to one's own security. In a region littered with such potential pirates' nests it was difficult for one state to control even a few of them, and the capability to ensure the safety of the seas in general was probably beyond even the combined resources of Athens and Philip of Macedon, whatever the wily Macedonian king may have claimed.

According to the Attic oration *On the Peace with Alexander*, when Alexander renewed the peace treaty between the Greek states known as the Common Peace in 336 BC a clause was included to the effect that all the participants in the Peace should be allowed to sail the seas safely and without hindrance. The speaker of this oration, which is not the work of Demosthenes himself, claims that the treaty has already been broken by the seizure of some Athenian ships by Macedonian forces at Tenedos ([Demos.] 17.19).[64] This special provision, which bears some similarity to the Athenian decree of Moirokles mentioned above, suggesting a possible Athenian origin, was presumably intended to deter the kind of piracy and seizure in reprisal which had been such a danger to maritime traffic in the previous hundred years. That it did not ensure safety at sea is hardly surprising. 'Enemy' ships and seafarers remained a tempting and vulnerable target. In practice it seems to have been left to individual states to protect their own maritime interests as far as they could. Accounts of the naval operations undertaken along the coast of Anatolia in 332 BC indicate that pirates continued to seek opportunities to profit from warfare even against the forces of Alexander the Great (Arr. *Anab.* 3.3.4; Curt. 4.5.18 and 21).[65] Alexander is credited by the Roman historian Quintus Curtius with sending one of his admirals, Amphoteros, on a mission to deal with piracy in 331 BC, which some historians have seen as an attempt to realize the ideal of clearing the seas of pirates put forward by Philip II in the 340s BC (Curt. 4.8.15).[66] It is difficult to tell what Amphoteros was supposed to do in this respect, and no mention is made of pirates in the generally more reliable narrative of Arrian.[67]

---

[63] See above pp. 31–4.

[64] The Athenians despatched a 'rescue' force of 100 triremes.

[65] *IG* XII.2.256 mentions *leistai* among the forces of the tyrants who controlled the Lesbian city of Eresos in 324 BC, but these need not have been pirates.

[66] See Ormerod (1924): 121–2. The mission is connected with King Agis III of Sparta's revolt against Macedonian rule in 331 BC by Bosworth (1975).

[67] See Bosworth (1975).

There is also some evidence of Athenian military efforts to deal with the problem of piracy at this time, although they seem to have been intended only to protect Athenian interests. An entry in the records of the naval magistrates for 335/4 BC mentions the despatch of some triremes under the command of Diotimos, 'to take guard against pirates', but there is no further information about the nature of this expedition. To see it as some kind of regular patrol or police action to suppress piracy would be a mistake, as such arrangements were not practical. The triremes must have had some specific destination and a particular mission: they could not have simply sailed around looking for pirates. Nor is there any substance to the suggestion that Diotimos was honoured for his successful completion of this particular mission.[68] In 325/4 BC the Athenians founded a colony on the Adriatic, partly to provide a safe haven against attacks by Tyrrhenians.[69] Acccording to Diodoros pirate ships had made the whole of the Adriatic coastline unsafe for merchants in the mid fourth century BC (Diod. 16.5.3).[70] He also credits the Corinthian Timoleon with capturing and executing in 339/8 BC a pirate leader called Postomion, whose twelve galleys had been plundering the coast of Sicily (Diod. 16.81.3).[71]

## Pirates in the Classical Greek world

It can be seen that in the Classical period the term pirate was widely used in the Greek world to refer to almost anyone who attacked people by sea. Although the attackers might have considered themselves to be engaged in legitimate raiding or warfare, their victims (and their allies) were likely to label them pirates as a way of illegitimizing their actions. Piracy had become a potentially deplorable activity among the Classical Greeks, but it was still a common feature of warfare and, in the form of reprisals, an alternative or supplement to larger-scale conflict. The ways in which the sources refer to the activities of Athenian generals and other 'condottieri', especially in the mid fourth century BC, indicate that there was a growing conflict between, on the one hand, recognizing a general need to reduce the danger of piracy and to accept collective responsibility for actions taken on behalf of a particular state, and, on the other hand, the desire of

[68] *IG* II[2].1623, lines 276–85. Contra Pritchett (1991): 337–8. It may be significant that Diotimos was one of those named by Alexander for extradition after the sack of Thebes: Arr. *Anab.* 1.10. His 'mission' could have been a convenient form of exile, to protect him from the Macedonians.

[69] *IG* II[2].1629, lines 217–33.

[70] Recorded under the events of the year 359/8 BC, but the situation is likely to have prevailed for a considerable period of time.

[71] No other sources mention this Postomion. See below pp. 51–3 on the general problem of identifying 'Tyrrhenian' pirates in this period.

some Greeks to take advantage of any opportunity for booty on their own initiative, without regard for the niceties of 'international relations'. The various individuals and groups who are called pirates in this period are often far more than mere 'outlaws'. In many cases, however, it seems to have been their misfortune to fall victim to accounts generated by enemies who have sought to justify opposing them by describing them as pirates.

# 3    Hellenistic piracy

After the death of Alexander the Great in 323 BC the vast empire which he had conquered stretched from the Adriatic in the West to the Hindu Kush in the East, but it quickly fragmented as his generals fought each other to gain control of as much of it as they could. The conflicts of these 'Successors' and the almost continuous wars waged by their descendants, who became rulers of kingdoms of varying size and stability in the Mediterranean and Near East, provided many opportunities for piracy of the kind that had become so common in the mid fourth century BC. The Hellenistic monarchs were warrior-kings whose armies of Greek and Macedonian mercenaries, native troops and various irregulars campaigned across the Greek-speaking world, capturing, plundering and destroying for the political and economic benefit of their commanders and themselves. It is no surprise, therefore, to find that the piratical activities familiar from the history of the Classical Greeks continue to be described and (occasionally) condemned in the sources for the wars of the Hellenistic period. Modern scholars have characterized this period as the heyday of Greek mercenary warfare, and when pirates are referred to in the literary and epigraphic texts they are usually assumed to be employed as mercenaries by one or other of the leading Hellenistic monarchs, or they are considered to be 'unemployed' mercenaries, making a (dishonest) living in between campaigns.[1] As the following pages will show, however, there was a great deal more variety among the various pirates who appear in the sources for this period.

### Demetrios and the siege of Rhodes

The unsuccessful attempt by Demetrios I Poliorketes (the Besieger) to lay siege to and capture Rhodes in 305/4 BC provides an excellent opportunity to examine the contribution of those described as mercenaries and

---

[1] E.g. Rostovtzeff (1941): index s.v. mercenaries and piracy; Griffith (1968); Miller (1984); McKechnie (1989).

pirates to the warfare of this period.[2] Diodorus Siculus, whose *Library of History* is the main source for the events of the siege, opens his account with an (exaggerated) appraisal of the Rhodians' naval strength and prestige among the Greeks, which made their island a major target for the Successors (Diod. 20.81).[3] The large island and its mainland territories (the *Peraia*) could only be conquered and controlled through a major amphibious campaign. The origins of the conflict seem to lie in an attempt by the Rhodians to resist the pressure from Demetrios and his father, Antigonos Monophthalmos (the One-eyed), to side with them in their war against Ptolemy I, son of Lagos, the ruler of Egypt, a monarch with whom the Rhodians had begun to establish strong links. The Rhodians had supplied Antigonos with warships, which he used against both of his main rivals, Ptolemy and Kassandros, in 314–311 BC,[4] but they refused a further demand to assist in the confrontation with their new ally Ptolemy in 306 BC (Diod. 20.82).[5] The aged Antigonos then provoked war with a piratical act reminiscent of the conflict between Philip II and Athens in the 340s BC:

When they did not agree, he sent one of his generals with some ships. The plan was to bring to land ships sailing out of Egypt for Rhodes and to seize the cargoes. This general having been driven off by the Rhodians, he [Antigonos] threatened to besiege the city with great forces, saying that they had started the war unjustly.[6] (Diod. 20.82.2)

The Rhodians at first tried to conciliate Antigonos through negotiations with his son Demetrios, but, after Demetrios demanded 100 noble hostages and use of the island's harbours against Ptolemy, they decided that war was inevitable (Diod. 20.82.3).

Demetrios arrived at the city of Rhodes with an army of 40,000 soldiers, plus cavalry, and a mixed assortment of 200 warships and about 170 lesser vessels (Diod. 20.82.4). In addition to this 'official' force, Diodorus says he was accompanied by about a thousand cargo ships belonging to pirates and traders, and a host of 'those who are accustomed to regard the misfortune of war as an opportunity for their own profits' (Diod. 20.82.5–83.1). Once he had established his camp Demetrios sent out these

---

[2] See Griffith (1968): 52.
[3] His account seems to be based upon a lost work called *The History of the Successors*, by Hieronymos of Kardia, a follower of Demetrios, although the version which Diodorus used for the siege was probably a later (Rhodian) recension, which describes Rhodes in terms of her later (third- and second-century) power; see Hornblower (1981).
[4] Diod. 19.57–58; 61–2; 64.5–7; 77.3. See Billows (1990): 359.
[5] See Billows (1990): 116–17 and 162–9; Hauben (1977).
[6] Note that Antigonos is apparently claiming the right to act in reprisal for the injury inflicted by the Rhodians when they 'attacked' his ships.

'pirates and others' to plunder the island by land and sea. These large numbers of 'irregulars' who were attached to Demetrios' army need not have been recruited directly by him, nor need they have been in his pay. Their presence was surely voluntary and inspired by the prospect of rich pickings at the expense of the defeated Rhodians. It is significant that Diodorus refers to them as traders and merchants, distinguishing them from the more professional military personnel, mercenaries and other troops levied from the Antigonid domains, who would be expected to play a major role in the fighting and would be well rewarded for their work.[7] The irregulars are what modern historians would call 'camp followers'. They provided a market (and other services) for the besieging army and would have expected the opportunity to participate in looting captured cities and territories. Diodorus describes a similar group who attached themselves to Demetrios' forces when he invaded Thessaly to challenge Kassandros in 302 BC (Diod. 20.110.4). Rhodes is a large island, and the resources of the mainland were within easy reach. In order to maintain an effective siege, Demetrios had to try to blockade the Rhodians by sea as well as by land. They probably did not have a large fleet of their own – most of the ships they had built in recent years were for Antigonos – but they were experienced sailors and had help from Ptolemy in Egypt and Kassandros in Greece. No doubt the size of the undertaking he had embarked upon encouraged Demetrios to make use of as many of these irregulars as he could. Thus, the pirates and some of the merchants were soon in action. although their efforts were unimpressive, in spite of their large numbers.

Demetrios tried sending out ships to intercept supply vessels coming to Rhodes from Egypt, but this enterprise was defeated by the weather (Diod. 20.96.1). Then a Rhodian admiral called Amyntas, sailing towards the *Peraia*, encountered some of the pirates operating for Demetrios:

These pirates had three undecked ships, they were apparently the strongest of those who fought alongside the king's forces. But the Rhodians overpowered them in a brief sea fight capturing the ships and their crews, among whom was a certain Timokles, the 'archpirate'.[8] (Diod. 20.97.5)

Several important points emerge from this brief description. A distinction is clearly implied between Demetrios' own ships ('the king's forces') and those of the pirates, who cannot be considered a regular part of his army or navy. The captured vessels are said to have belonged to the strongest of Demetrios' allies, yet the ships used by the pirates are 'undecked', in-

---

[7] On the composition of Demetrios' and Antigonos' forces see Billows (1990): app. 2.

[8] The term 'archpirate' (ἀρχιπειράτης) probably means simply the leading pirate, and does not have any special connotations of expertise or influence.

dicating that they were not proper warships, and thus no match for the naval forces commanded by Amyntas.[9] The same admiral later captured some merchants who were bringing grain to Demetrios' camp and diverted their ships and cargoes to the besieged city. No more is said about pirates in Diodorus' account of the siege after the capture of Timokles, which may indicate that any other pirates who accompanied Demetrios' army decided to stay clear of the action until a more favourable opportunity presented itself, such as the fall of the city. In spite of his large fleet Demetrios did not have the forces to mount a complete blockade at sea. It was obviously cheaper and easier to use the merchants and pirates who were following his army in the expectation of profiting from his success. He clearly hoped that weight of numbers would compensate for their naval inadequacies, although their contribution to his operations seems to been a very minor one. There have been few occasions before the advent of modern navies when this kind of privateering has proved truly successful, although blockades and raiding were sometimes an effective adjunct to more conventional forms of conflict.[10]

### More Hellenistic 'pirates'

The connection of pirates with forces of Demetrios I is repeated in accounts of the siege of Ephesos in 287 BC, but this time it is Demetrios' general Ainetos who is besieged, and the army trying to take the city belongs to the rival Hellenistic monarch Lysimachos.

When Ainetos, the general of Demetrios, was defending Ephesos and ravaging the environs with many pirates,[11] Lykon, the general of Lysimachos, bribed the archpirate Andron with money and took possession of Ephesos. The archpirate led into the city some of Lykon's soldiers, unarmed, in cloaks and rough garments and with their hands bound, as though they were prisoners, and getting near to the citadel he issued them with daggers, which they kept hidden under their arms. Having killed the gate keepers and the guards on the acropolis, he raised the signal to those with Lykon. These men marched in, laid hold of Ainetos and occupied Ephesos. And, having given the pirates their reward, straightaway escorted them

---

[9] The essential difference between decked and undecked ships in the Graeco-Roman world is that the former are vessels designed for warfare, while the latter are merchant crafts and smaller oared ships which might be used by pirates; see Casson (1971): 88 and 116.

[10] See Jackson (1973) for a survey of ancient examples. See above pp. 31–4 on the Peloponnesian War and below pp. 46–8, 75–6 for discussion of further instances in the Hellenistic period. Andrews (1964) and (1985) and Bromley (1987), demonstrate how the impact of the privateers and pirates on events in the early modern period was often insignificant when compared to the regular armies and navies.

[11] πολλοῖς πειραταῖς.

out of the city, believing that their faithlessness towards their former friends made it unsafe to have them around.[12] (Polyaen. 5.19)

It seems clear that Andron and his men were operating around Ephesos in much the same way as the pirates at the siege of Rhodes. Ainetos was prepared to allow them to come and go because they were causing harm to his opponents and hence their leader, the so-called archpirate Andron, was admitted to the city with what seemed like another bunch of captives for sale. Andron and his men were camp followers exploiting the conflicts of the warring successors of Alexander for their own profit. They owed no particular allegiance to either side, and so they were happy to betray their erstwhile allies and customers to their opponents. It may be that they had decided that Lykon's forces were more likely to emerge victorious, so they changed sides at an opportune moment. When Lykon, an experienced general, had got the upper hand he immediately dispensed with their services, however, as he knew that they could not be trusted to the same extent as the regular mercenaries who fought in the armies of the Hellenistic monarchs.[13]

Another individual who is labelled an 'archpirate' is Ameinias, who was with the army of Demetrios' son Antigonos Gonatas at the siege of Kassandreia in 277/6 BC. Like Andron he betrayed the city, after winning the trust of the tyrant Apollodoros and using his position to allow 2,000 soldiers over the walls (Polyaen. 4.18). He apparently reappears in Antigonos' army as a general a few years later (Plut. *Pyrr.* 29.6). Gabbert concludes that Ameinias, like Andron, had 'pursued a career as a pirate or brigand', before joining Antigonos and rising to a position of great trust and authority.[14] She characterizes Timokles, Andron and Ameinias as 'political and military entrepreneurs', taking advantage of a climate of opportunity for rapid advancement.[15] What evidence is there to back up this conclusion? The authority for describing Ameinias as a pirate is presumably Polyaenus' unnamed source, perhaps a Hellenistic historian. Gabbert, working on the principle that there is no smoke without fire, says of Ameinias: 'our sources, though late and lacking in detail must have had some basis for labelling him an archpirate'.[16] Unless we can be clear about what that basis was, however, it is not possible to construct

[12] Another version of this incident is recorded in Frontinus' *Stratagems* 3.3.7, specifying the use of ships by Andron. This justifies the translation of πολλοῖς πειραταῖς as 'many pirates'.

[13] Contra Gabbert (1986): 157.

[14] Gabbert (1986): 158–60.

[15] Gabbert (1986): 162.

[16] Gabbert (1986): 159.

elaborate hypotheses about such individuals. The literary sources for the Hellenistic period are generally less detailed and circumstantial than those for the mid fourth century, principally because of the declining significance of Athens. The narratives and collections which are available to us are more concerned with the main topics of warfare and politics than with the relatively trivial matter of piracy. It merits occasional mention, but often without important details regarding the background, the precise allegiance and the motives of the people involved. Only when some rhetorical or moral point is being made does the organization of piracy in the Hellenistic period become a suitable subject for ancient historians. Timokles' naval failures hardly seem to make him a military specialist, Andron's treatment at the hands of Lykon makes the label pirate look appropriate; but Ameinias seems more like a mercenary general, whose principal fault may have been to incur the displeasure of a contemporary or later historian with a flair for literary embellishment.[17]

## Rhodes

The Rhodians were merchants, obtaining a great deal of their revenues from the practice and promotion of long-distance trade. It is clear from Diodorus that in the early Hellenistic period one of their most important trading partners was the Ptolemaic kingdom of Egypt: 'They were especially inclined to honour Ptolemy. For it was the case that the majority of their revenues came from merchants sailing to Egypt and the city was largely fed from that kingdom' (Diod. 20.81.4). Egypt was, however, far from being the only source of income, and the revenues of the Rhodians grew as they established connections with many other regions. The island's several harbours for merchant ships enabled it to function as a major entrepôt in the Hellenistic period, particularly for trade from Egypt and the Levant, and there was a substantial slave market there. The Rhodians themselves were famous sailors whose extensive trading activities are attested to by the wide dispersal of their pottery in the Hellenistic period, especially in the Eastern Mediterranean and the Black Sea area.[18]

It is hardly surprising, therefore, that the Rhodians were renowned in antiquity for their suppression of piracy. Early evidence of their concern and determination to protect merchant shipping comes from one of the Attic orators, Lykourgos, in his speech against Leokrates. The Athenian

---

[17] Gabbert (1986): 159 also says that Ameinias commanded an Antigonid garrison at Korinth, which would be further indication of his 'legitimate' mercenary status, but there seems to be no clear evidence for this claim.

[18] See Rostovtzeff (1941): 676–92, 1484–90; *CAH* VII.1.270–5; Berthold (1984): 49–54, 100–1; Casson (1954); Gabrielsen (1997): ch. III.

statesman says that after the Battle of Chaironeia (338 BC) his opponent falsely reported to the Rhodians that Athens had been captured by the Macedonians and the Piraeus blockaded. The Rhodians' reaction was to despatch warships to escort their merchant vessels to port (Lyk. *Leokr.* 18). Diodorus also mentions the Rhodians driving off the ships sent to attack their cargo vessels on the way to Egypt by Demetrios Poliorketes, just before the siege of Rhodes, which suggests that they either used escort ships, or had armed merchantmen (Diod. 20.82.2) He prefaces his introduction to the siege of Rhodes in 305 BC as follows: 'Indeed, she had attained such a position of power that she took up the war against the pirates by herself, on behalf of the Greeks, and cleared the sea of their evil infestation' (Diod. 20.81.3). Diodorus is, of course, exaggerating here, possibly because he is using a pro-Rhodian source, but there is plenty of evidence to back up the claim that the Rhodians went to war with pirates in the Hellenistic period.[19] It was during the third and second centuries that they established their reputation as the friends of merchants and the suppressors of piracy.

Another celebrated case of Rhodian intervention to ensure the freedom of merchants is the war against Byzantion in 220 BC, which came about because the Byzantines tried to impose tolls on ships passing in and out of the Black Sea. Polybius says that the imposition of these tolls produced widespread discontent, largely because it was causing a sharp drop in profits for the merchants operating along the route. The Rhodians were invited to take action 'because of their pre-eminence in maritime affairs' (Polyb. 4.47.1). This incident shows not only how far the Rhodians were prepared to go in order to protect their trading activities, but also the extent to which their reputation among the Hellenistic naval powers made it natural for others to look to them for leadership in such circumstances. The Rhodians do not seem to have been unique among the states of the Hellenistic world in claiming to operate a policy of deliberately opposing those whom they considered to be pirates. Although they came under pressure from the Rhodians and others in the third century BC for imposing tolls, the Byzantines were also anxious to protect the shipping which was the source of much of their revenue. Polybius praises their efforts to prevent attacks on traders, slavers and even fishing vessels by local tribes from the Black Sea littoral (Polyb. 4.50.3). In this respect the Byzantines were in a similar position to the Rhodians, since they both had an interest in suppressing piracy in order to allow maritime traffic to flourish. Indeed, the Byzantines' demand that ships passing in and out of

---

[19] See above pp. 5–7 on Diodorus' source for this section. See also Trog. *Prol.* 35 on Rhodes and piracy.

the Black Sea should pay tolls to them was probably linked to an assurance of safe passage through the waters which they considered to be under their supervision.[20]

There was, however, a difference in scale between Byzantine activities to ensure the safety of seafarers and the anti-piratical operations of the Rhodians, whose naval forces were substantial and very well organized. It has even been claimed that the Rhodian navy was 'designed as an anti-pirate force'.[21] This is, perhaps, a rather over-enthusiastic statement, especially in view of the fact that most of our information about the Rhodian navy comes from accounts of its activities in warfare, often alongside Pergamon and Rome.[22] The Rhodians used a variety of ships, including triremes, quadriremes and quinqueremes, but their most distinctive vessel was probably the *trihemiolia*. This was a fast, decked ship which (unlike the trireme) did not have several levels of oarsmen, but was still capable of dealing with the larger warships of the Hellenistic monarchs.[23] Speed would be useful when chasing enemy ships, whether pirates or not, and decks allowed plenty of marines to be carried, including archers and heavily armed infantry for amphibious operations. It should not be forgotten that one of the principal uses of any ancient warship was to transport soldiers to fight on land, as well as at sea. There is, however, some direct evidence which shows elements of the Rhodian navy in action against pirates.

An inscription found on the island of Rhodes and dated to the early third century B.C. records the names of three Rhodian brothers who died fighting with the Rhodian navy:

The earth shrouds these brave [men] in death: ———— son of Timakrates, acting as a bow officer [on a trihemio]lia he died fighting against [the Tyrrhenians]. ———— es son of Timakrates, sailing on the [guardship] among the rowers(?), he died fighting against the Tyrrhenians. [Polemarcho]s son of Timakrates, [having been sent out] as a detachment leader he died fighting against the pirates(?). The *damos* of Kasareis [erected this].[24]

The Rhodian custom of erecting public monuments to their war dead is attested as early as 305 BC by Diodoros (20.84.3). It has been suggested

---

[20] See also Walbank (1957–79): I 504–7; Gabrielsen (1997): 44–5.
[21] Berthold (1984): 98.
[22] See Schmitt (1957); Thiel (1946): esp. ch. III. On the inscriptions discussed below and the Rhodian navy in general see Rice (1991) and Gabrielsen (1997).
[23] See Morrison (1980).
[24] *SIG* (3rd edn) 1225. See also *GVI* no. 41. Discussion in Hiller (1895); Blinkenberg (1938): 14, 45; Torelli (1975); Rice (1991). There are several lacunae and restorations are indicated by [–]. Precise line lengths are difficult to determine. The date is uncertain and could be much later. The term translated as 'detachment leader' is συνταγματάρχας, the precise meaning of which is unclear.

that this monument records casualties suffered in attempts to combat Tyrrhenian (i.e. Etruscan) pirates.[25] The third of the brothers, Polemarchos, is the only one who is specifically said to have been killed by pirates. His brothers' opponents may also have been pirates, but with the difference that their identity was more clearly established than was the case with Polemarchos.[26] The identity of the brother Polemarchos is suggested by another inscription in which a Rhodian officer called Polemarchos, son of Timakrates, of the deme of Kasareis, is honoured along with other naval personnel for his participation in an attack on the island of Aigila, modern Antikythera.[27] This might also have been an expedition which the Rhodians construed as anti-piratical, but a precise indication of its purpose is lacking.

Why were the Rhodians fighting people they described as Tyrrhenian pirates in the early third century BC? If the name Tyrrhenians is interpreted broadly, as referring to any pirates from the Italian peninsula, rather than specifically from Etruria, then it is possible to place this episode in the context of several references in historical sources to the Tyrrhenians as pirates in the late fourth and early third centuries BC. According to Diodoros, it was because merchants crossing the Adriatic between Greece and Italy were suffering at the hands of Apulian pirates that Dionysios II, tyrant of Syracuse (367–344 BC), established two cities in the barbarian territory of Apulia to act as safe havens for merchant ships (Diod. 16.5.3). An Athenian colony was founded on the Adriatic coast in 325/4 BC partly in order to provide a safe harbour from Tyrrhenian attacks.[28] Two speeches composed by Attic orators towards the end of the fourth century BC have titles which suggest a general problem of Tyrrhenian attacks on Athenians or their allies,[29] and Tyrrhenian pirates are mentioned by Diodoros, who says that the Greek mercenary leader Timoleon captured some in the harbour of Syracuse c. 339 BC, along with their leader Postomion, whose Latin name suggests that 'Tyrrhenians' had a wider application than just Etruscans (Diod. 16.81.3).

Livy refers to attacks of 'Greek' pirates on the coast of Latium around

---

[25] See Ormerod (1924): 130; Ziebarth (1929): ch. 4. Hiller's supplement in line 5, [ναυάρ-χιδ]ι, might indicate an escort vessel of some kind, possibly intended to guard merchant ships against pirates.

[26] A possible alternative translation to 'pirates' is 'bandits', but Tyrrhenians would presumably have to have been pirates (i.e. operating in ships) in order to have reached a place where they could come into conflict with the Rhodians. It seems to me unlikely that all three brothers died on the same expedition.

[27] *Clara Rhodos* 2.169, no. 1; see Rice (1991) on the prosopography.

[28] *IG* II².1629, lines 217–33; see above p. 41.

[29] The Τυρρανικός of Deinarchos and the Περὶ τῆς φυλακῆς τῶν Τυρρηνῶν of Hypereides; see Ormerod (1924): 128–9.

350 BC and as early as 338 BC the Romans seem to have tried to reduce the plundering raids of the people of Antium by barring them from navigation and establishing one of several citizen colonies there, apparently in an effort to improve the general defences of the Latin coast.[30] Rome herself had to deal with complaints about pirate raids in the fourth century BC from several quarters, including Alexander the Great and Demetrios I Poliorketes (Str. 5.3.5). According to Strabo Demetrios apprehended some Tyrrhenian pirates and sent them to Rome with the message that the leaders of Italy should not send out pirates, especially to attack the land of the *Dioskouroi*, whose temple the Romans had erected in their Forum.[31] In 298 BC it was necessary for the Delians to borrow money from the temple of Apollo 'for protection against the Tyrrhenians', which could imply the financing of expeditions against them, but it is more likely that it was used to pay for improvements to the island's defences, perhaps including the hiring of mercenary guards.[32] Finally, the involvement of the Rhodians in a long-running conflict, or series of conflicts, with Tyrrhenians, which they justified as suppression of piracy, can be inferred from a passage in a speech included among the works of the second-century AD orator Aelius Aristeides which comments on the magnificent collection of booty taken from Tyrrhenian pirates to be seen in Rhodes.[33]

All these pieces of evidence can be considered as indicators that Tyrrhenian pirates were considered to be a major problem in Magna Graecia and parts of the Aegean during the late fourth and early third centuries BC. Ormerod interpreted the sources as indicating a dramatic rise in Etruscan and central Italian piracy after the demise of the Syracusan tyranny in the mid fourth century.[34] Yet the references are so diverse in terms of the location and possible identity of the pirates that it seems implausible to ascribe a common origin to the various groups mentioned. It is better to see these passages as evidence of the activities of a variety of Italian-based seafarers whose precise origins may in many cases have been unknown to their victims or captors, who simply applied the label 'Tyrrhenian pirates' to maritime armed robbers, whom they knew or sus-

---

[30] Livy 8.14 Antium; 8.21 Tarracina (329 BC); 9.28 Sinuessa (313 BC); see Salmon (1969): ch. 4. The creation of a small Roman naval force under the *duumviri navales* in 311 BC, which Ormerod is inclined to link with piratical raids, is probably best understood as part of the general enhancement of the Romans' military capacity in this period, rather than an anti-piratical provision; Ormerod (1924): 161. On Rome in the fourth century see Cornell (1995): chs. 14, 15.

[31] The mention of Alexander by Strabo may be a literary embellishment to a story about Demetrios. The historicity of the whole episode, which is undated, is doubted by Tarn (1913): 48.

[32] *IG* XI.2.148, line 73 (εἰς φυλακὴν τῶν τυρρηνῶν). Gabrielsen (1997): 43 and 59–60 suggests the hiring of naval forces, possibly from Rhodes.

[33] Pseudo-Aristeides 25.4.

[34] Ormerod (1924): 158–61.

pected to be from Italy, whenever they encountered them. It may be that the apparent increase of Tyrrhenian piracy is merely a manifestation of the greater intensity of seafaring activity in the fourth and third centuries BC. Maritime trade and military expeditions produced a substantial amount of traffic between Italy and the Eastern Mediteranean and there was considerable instability in the political alignments of Greeks or Italians in this period. In the third century Agathokles, the tyrant of Syracuse, is said to have supplied the Apulians with ships for their piratical attacks, presumably in order that his enemies would suffer at their hands (Diod. 21.4) These are similar conditions to those which prevailed in the Aegean in the mid fourth century BC and which help to explain the frequent mentions of piracy in the literary sources.[35]

### The Ptolemaic kingdom

It is appropriate at this point to consider briefly a few scraps of evidence for activity by the forces of Rhodes' ally, the Ptolemaic kings of Egypt, against pirates. An Athenian inscription from c. 286 BC honours a Ptolemaic naval commander who escorted grain ships coming to Athens '... in order that the supply of grain might be brought with utmost security to the people'.[36] It is tempting to suppose that this was a regular occurrence, but I think not, since the Ptolemaic navy had many other duties to perform, besides helping the Athenians with their grain ships. There is no explicit literary evidence to indicate that this episode was not exceptional. Another Ptolemaic officer is honoured in an inscription from Thera dated to about the middle of the third century BC:

... decided by the council and the people; decree of the council: since Hermaphilos son of Philostratos of Rhaukos who was sent by king Ptolemy as *phrourarch* (garrison commander)[37] and general of the city has been responsible for a great many very good things for the citizens, and when there was an attack of pirates in long ships against the North harbour at Oia and the temple, while a crowd of women and children and other persons were staying there, not less than 400 of them, and having launched an attack against the pirates he drove them off in the night ...[38] who, coming down into the harbour by night with the citizens beat off the pirates and pursued them closely to their ships, and running considerable risks ...[39]

---

[35] See above pp. 33–41.
[36] *IG* II$^2$.650 lines 15–16.
[37] I read [φρούρ]αρχος where the editors restore [ναύ]αρχος; see Bagnall (1976): 132–3.
[38] The text is too fragmentary too be understood for about $2\frac{1}{2}$ lines. It resumes with the actions of Hephaistios of Myndos, a subordinate officer, and his soldiers.
[39] *IG* XII.3.1291. The inscription continues by detailing the honours to be paid to Hermaphilos and Hephaistios.

The intention of these pirates seems to have been to capture people and sell them as slaves, possibly on the island of Crete, which is not far away to the south. The Ptolemaic forces on Thera are clearly decisive in driving off the pirates, but it is noticeable that the local population are also involved, and that the island seems to have been prepared for some kind of attack. It is possible that the incident occurred during one of the many wars of the third century BC. A large number of islands in the Aegean and some mainland sites were used as bases by the Ptolemaic navy and army, especially in the third century BC, but this was because of their strategic importance in the wars with the Antigonids and other monarchs.[40] As a result there were opportunities for Ptolemaic forces to deal with attacks like this one, or to carry out convoy duties. Ormerod thought that there was a Ptolemaic 'policing' of the Aegean, arguing that because the Rhodians were active against pirates and headed a League of islanders, then the Ptolemies must have done the same, although the evidence for such a policy does not survive.[41] With no explicit literary testimony, and only a couple of apparently fortuitous epigraphic instances of Ptolemaic officers tackling pirates,[42] I do not think that it is reasonable to conclude that the Egyptian kings pursued a major anti-piracy policy in the Aegean in the manner of the Rhodians.

### Kings and pirates in the Black Sea

Piracy was not, of course, confined to the Aegean and the Eastern Mediterranean. Wherever there were ships and places or people to plunder there were likely to be pirates in the Hellenistic period. The majority of the literary sources for the period, and almost all of the surviving inscriptions, deal with a relatively small region. Beyond this area there were some attempts to suppress or reduce piracy, in the interests of trade or the security of coastal settlements. In the Black Sea region local Hellenizing monarchs and some of the Greek cities are credited with trying to suppress the piracy of tribes and peoples, who apparently preferred raiding cities and plundering merchants to the less exciting business of trade. The efforts of the Byzantines have already been noted, as have their demands

---

[40] See Bagnall (1976). For an example of a Ptolemaic base see Shipley (1987) on the strategic importance of Samos in the third century.

[41] Ormerod (1924): 130–5.

[42] See also *SIG* 502; *IG* XII.8.156, which honours a Ptolemaic governor of the Hellespont who provided soldiers to protect the island of Samothrace (*c.* 228 BC?). Pirates are not mentioned in this inscription, although Tarn (1913): 87 thought they were the reason for the garrison. Ormerod (1924): 129–30 connects this incident with *SIG* 372; *IG* XII.8.150 (late fourth century BC). See also Bagnall (1976): 159–68.

for tolls, which provoked a war with Rhodes.[43] The benefactions of
Eumelos of the Kimmerian Bosporos are lauded by Diodoros in extravagant fashion, rivalling the praise he accords to the Rhodians:

On behalf of those who sailed to the Pontos he waged war on the barbarian tribes
who were accustomed to plunder them, the Heniochoi and the Tauroi as well as
the Achaians. Thus he cleared the sea of pirates, so that not only within his own
kingdom, but throughout nearly the whole world, his magnanimity was proclaimed by the merchants, enabling him to receive the very finest of rewards for
his good deeds. (Diod. 20.25)

Doubtless Diodoros is exaggerating, but the benefit for a Hellenizing
monarch of a policy of supporting merchants and opposing pirates, or at
least claiming to do so, would not just be increased opportunities for
trade, but also prestige and recognition within the Hellenic world. Polybius calls Kavaros, the king of the Thracian Gauls, 'kingly and magnan-
imous in his actions', because he 'did much to ensure the safety of merchants sailing into the Pontos' (Polyb. 8.22). It is conceivable that the
deeds of such monarchs, especially wars against neighbouring 'barbarian'
tribes, were motivated primarily by the political and material benefits they
could bring to the kings, and would have been undertaken regardless of
the concerns of visiting traders, but they could be presented to visiting
Greek embassies as acts of suppression of piracy for the common good.

The diplomatic and political implications of this concern to safeguard
commercial traffic are evident from a letter of Ziaelas, the king of Bithynia, to the people of Kos, inscribed at Kos c. 240 BC, in which the king
recognizes the inviolability of the temple of Asklepios on the island of
Kos and promises to be as friendly and well disposed towards the Koans
as his father Nikomedes had been, and to ensure the safety of Koan sailors
who visit his shores. He explains that he is anxious to be friendly to all the
Greeks who come to his kingdom, 'as we are convinced that this contrib-
utes in no small way to one's reputation', and he cites the friendship of
Ptolemy III, king of Egypt, 'our friend and ally', towards the Koans as a
further reason for his decision to continue the policy of his father.[44] It
should be noted that the Koans are the ones who have sent an embassy to
Ziaelas, a move which was presumably prompted by the change of monarch, and the Koans' desire to ensure that there was no change of attitude
towards their traders. Such concerns seem to have been of greater importance to the Koans than the Bithynian monarch, and the king's assurances, while no doubt welcome, did not necessarily amount to much more
than a promise that their ships would not be plundered while they were

---

[43] See above pp. 49–50.     [44] Welles (1934): no. 25.

in Bithynian harbours, or if they happened to be wrecked upon the Bithynian coast. Our literary sources make no mention of any military operations undertaken by Ziaelas, or his father or brothers, to deal with pirates. Nevertheless, it is clear that the Koans, whose merchants travelled regularly to this region, sought any kind of protection they could find.[45] It is likely that other cities would have sent ambassadors to the court of the new king to renew whatever agreements they had made with his father, a situation which was complicated by the fact that after the death of Nikomedes the kingdom had been divided among his sons.[46] The mention of Ptolemy III shows how the influence of a powerful monarch could be beneficial to a small state like Kos. The Seleukid monarch Seleukos II played a similar role in obtaining *asylia* (immunity from reprisals) for Smyrna from the Aitolians.[47] The complex nature of Hellenistic politics meant that the Koans had more than one powerful king to reckon with, however, and it appears from another inscription that one of the ambassadors who was sent to Ziaelas, Diogitos, also visited Seleukos II in order to obtain his favour for the temple and the Koans, possibly as part of the same diplomatic mission, although both Ziaelas and Ptolemy were enemies of Seleukos at the time.[48] The problems facing merchants in this area, particularly the conflict between urbanizing, Hellenizing monarchs and the warlike, predatory neighbouring tribes, continued well into the period of the Roman Empire.[49]

### The profits of piracy

There is another way of looking at the relationship between trade and piracy in the Hellenistic period. Piracy itself could be considered as a form of trade. Pirates, like merchants, are often engaged in a commercial activity, trying to make some kind of profit from their plunder. In simple terms the ships and manpower which the practice of piracy required could be seen as investments, and the plunder which piratical activities yielded could be seen as a return on that investment. When Agathokles supplied some of the Apulians with ships for piratical purposes in the early third century BC, he did not merely expect friendship or alliance from the Apulians in return. He wanted, and he obtained, a share of their booty (Diod. 21.4). A similar relationship existed between Philip V of Macedon and Dikaiarchos the Aitolian. Ships were supplied by the king in return

---

[45] On Koan trade with the Black Sea area see Sherwin-White (1978): 243–4.
[46] See Will (1979–82): I 246–7.
[47] *OGIS* nos. 228, 229. See below p. 69.
[48] Welles (1934): no. 26.
[49] See below pp. 206–09.

for a substantial share of the plunder they were used to obtain (Diod. 28.1.1).[50] When Skerdilaidas the Illyrian was cheated of his profits by Philip V, he endeavoured to make up for this by his raids on merchant ships. He seems to have met the initial expense of the plundering he undertook on Philip's behalf from his own resources, so he had even more incentive to obtain a quick profit (Polyb. 5.95; 101).

A further example of a quarrel over booty is found in a third-century BC inscription from Thera which deals with captives taken by pirates from Allaria in Crete. It seems that some of the pirates' associates were themselves originally from Thera and they objected to the sale of the captives, who were presumably also Therans, and had tried to secure the intervention of a Ptolemaic officer serving in a garrison on Thera to help them in their negotiations. The inscription is apparently a letter from this officer, in which he gives a brief history of the Therans:

> ... on their side the Allariotes say that they [the Therans] were originally captives and that they spent three years with the Allariotes who gave them a share in their home and freed them as not merely assistants, but partners in their struggles. But no promise was made that they should receive any booty ...[51]

These Therans seem to have been slightly more than slaves but slightly less than free partners. They did not become Allariote citizens, and their labours on behalf of their former masters were not rewarded with any booty. It is impossible to say whether these were the normal practices of Cretans, but the reluctance of the Allariotes to share their booty is striking. It indicates that there was a well developed hierarchy among the Cretans, with only an élite being granted the chance to benefit directly from the profits of piracy.[52] The essential point here is that the Therans saw themselves as 'partners' with their Allariote superiors. The matter was eventually settled by an exchange of prisoners, the Allariotes not being prepared to lose out in their dealings with the Therans. The Ptolemaic officer's letter concludes: '... the persons who were with us we yielded up. Of these there were ----- Greeks and the rest, being 45 in number, were foreigners.'[53] These unfortunates were presumably kept or sold as slaves by the Allariotes.

An important element in the success of piracy was often the availability of a suitable market for the pirates' plunder. Aigina has already been seen to figure in several accounts of plundering in reprisal and piracy in the fourth century BC. Its proximity to both Attica and the Peloponnese would have made it an ideal place for the disposal of booty obtained from

---

[50] See below pp. 75, 81–2 on Philip V and Dikaiarchos.
[51] *IG* XII.3.328, lines 2–7; *SEG* 29, no. 744.
[52] See Brulé (1978): 12–16 for further discussion and bibliography.
[53] *IG* XII.3.328, lines 18–20. The number of the Greeks is not preserved.

such actions.[54] It is no coincidence that the Cretans were infamous as pirates and that many of the Cretan cities had thriving slave markets, especially Polyrrhenia, although there were also major markets on Rhodes and Delos. Some places seem to have deliberately chosen to provide facilities for certain groups of pirates to dispose of their plunder. With regard to the results of raids carried out in reprisal, or as part of a recognized war there was apparently no legal or moral objection to selling the proceeds and profiting thereby. Indeed, the considerable body of evidence which indicates that both people and property were regularly recovered after such attacks, through the intervention in the place of sale of *proxenoi* or even citizens of the victims' own state,[55] suggests that in these circumstances pirates would openly dispose of booty in their home port. Even where there was no legal or moral justification for piracy, or in cases where the booty was clearly illicit, the possibility of profiting through trade in 'stolen goods' was enough to persuade some communities to cooperate closely with those recognized to be pirates. Strabo accuses several of the coastal cities of Pamphylia, Cilicia and eastern Lycia of being 'partners in crime' with the region's notorious pirates in the last two centuries BC:

But they [the Pamphylians and Cilicians] made use of such places as bases for the practice of piracy, either being pirates themselves, or else furnishing the pirates with markets for their plunder and docking facilities. In Side, at any rate, a city of Pamphylia, the docks were set up for the benefit of the Cilicians, who used to sell their captives there by auction, admitting that they were free men.[56] (Str. 14.3.2)

The fates of Delos and Aigina, both of which were sacked by pirates in the first century BC are, however, an indication that there was no sense in which such markets were exempt from attack by pirates. Offering assistance to one group did not necessarily mean neutrality in the eyes of others.[57]

It would seem logical that if a place could flourish as the result of 'legitimate' trade, as in the case of Hellenistic Rhodes, then it might also be possible for piracy to be the making of a city's fortune. Unfortunately there is little evidence, beyond the rather vague comments of the literary sources, to indicate that any particular place might have owed its prosperity to the ill-gotten gains of pirates. For example, the relative wealth of the Cilician and Pamphylian cities, which are closely associated with

---

[54] See above p. 34.
[55] See below pp. 65–9.
[56] Cicero makes similar accusations about Phaselis and its co-operation with pirates; Cic. *Verr.* 4.21; see further below pp. 129–30.
[57] See further below pp. 162–3.

piracy in the late second and early first centuries BC by our literary
sources, cannot be properly assessed because of the relative lack of archaeological evidence, although some efforts are being made to improve
this situation.[58] It would, however, seem reasonable to suppose that few,
if any, places are likely to have specialized in the handling of piratical loot
to the exclusion of other forms of trade. It is in any case highly unlikely
that the piratical revenues of any city would be easily distinguishable from
more legitimate ones. Even for historical periods where the documenta-
tion is of a far higher quality only rough estimates are possible, based
upon impressionistic accounts, rather than precise data.[59] A good example of the difficulties inherent in trying to assess the profitablilty of ancient
piracy is provided by the city of Phalasarna on the western coast of Crete.
Phalasarna's harbour and town have been exposed for excavation by the
uplifting of the western end of Crete since Antiquity. The excavations
there have revealed a greater degree of prosperity than might have been
expected for a small Cretan city in the Hellenistic period, particularly evident in the fine quality of the harbour facilities and fortifications.[60] Phalasarna seems, therefore, to have been a wealthy place in the Hellenistic
period, although it is likely that the campaign of Metellus Creticus
brought its prosperity to an abrupt end around 67 BC.[61] The excavators
of Phalasarna seem confident that they have uncovered a prosperous
'pirates' port'. There is however, no specific literary or epigraphic testimony to connect Phalasarna with any acts of piracy in the Hellenistic
period, although it is reasonable to suppose that some Cretan pirates did
use Phalasarna as a port, whether because it was their home city or because
it was conveniently situated on he extreme western end of the island.
There is, however, no clear evidence to suggest that its wealth depended in
any significant way upon piracy. Other sources of revenue, such as agri-
culture, trade in stone, commercial links with nearby Polyrrhenia and
later with Egypt, and the service of local mercenaries overseas, are all attested in some form, and seem to provide adequate explanations for the
city's relative prosperity.[62] My own general impression for the Hellenistic

---

[58] The Rough Cilicia Regional Survey Project, under the direction of Professor Nick Rauh
from Purdue University, Indiana, is the most promising initiative in this regard. Preliminary reports indicate evidence of substantial economic activity in the area of Side and its
hinterland.

[59] See, for example, Ritchie (1986) on New York in the late seventeenth century, or Rediker
(1987) on the home ports of the Anglo-American pirates in the 'Golden Age' of the early
eighteenth century.

[60] See Frost & Hadjidaki (1990); Hadjidaki (1988a), (1988b).

[61] See below pp. 157–61.

[62] On all of these see Hadjidaki (1988a). Polyrrhenia, but not Phalasarna, is one of the cities
which granted asylia to Teos in 204/3 BC (ICret II Polyrrhenia 3); see below pp. 67–9.

Mediterranean is that the profits of piracy are unlikely to have accounted for any dramatic changes in local prosperity over an extended period of time, such as might make some impression on the archaeological record of a particular city. Whatever our literary sources might claim, the contribution of piracy to the economy of any place in Antiquity is unknowable, because it cannot be detected.

### Piracy and the Hellenistic slave trade

Several instances have already been mentioned of pirates capturing people and then selling them into slavery, from the Archaic, Classical and Hellenistic periods.[63] It is in the Hellenistic period, however, that the connection between piracy and the slave trade seems especially prominent. There is plenty of evidence to indicate that piracy was an important source of slaves in this period. The literary evidence includes New Comedy, for the plays of Menander (343–291 BC), Plautus (*fl.* 204–184 BC) and Terence (185–159 BC) often feature individuals who are captured by pirates and sold as slaves. The following example comes from Menander's play *The Sikyonian*:

A god:    ... his daughter, I say. And when they [the pirates] had all three persons in their power, they decided it wasn't worth their while to take the old lady, but they carried off the young girl and the servant to Mylasa, a town in Karia, and there they put them up for sale in the market.[64]

That the girl and her servant had been captured by pirates and sold as slaves is shown by another fragment of the same play:

Theron:    They say that you lost your daughter from Halai when she was four years old, along with Dromon, a servant.

Kichesias:    Yes, I did.

Theron:    Good!

Kichesias:    She was kidnapped by pirates. You have reminded me of sorrow and suffering, and of my poor child.[65]

The capture and sale of individuals as slaves by pirates is also a common theme in inscriptions of this period, further demonstrating a close associ-

---

[63] See above pp. 20, 35–6, 57–8.

[64] Men. *Sik.* lines 3–7.

[65] Men. *Sik.* lines 355–9; the word translated as pirates is ληστῶν. Both quotations are from the translation by Miller (1987). For further examples see Plaut. *Poen.* lines 896–7; *Mil. Glor.* line 118; Ter. *Eun.* lines 114–15.

ation between piracy and the slave trade.[66] An inscription recording an
honorific decree of the people of the Aegean island of Amorgos in the mid
third century BC gives details of an incident which seems to have been
typical of piratical attacks:

Resolved by the council and the people; Soterides, son of Phidias, of Kosyllos was
president, Philoxenos, son of Philothemis of Alsos moved: since, when pirates
made an incursion into the countryside at night and captured a total of more than
thirty girls, women and other persons, free and slave, and scuttled the ships in the
harbour and captured the ship of Doreios, in which they sailed off with their
captives and the rest of their booty; when all this had happened Hegesippos and
Antipappos, the sons of Hegesistratos, who were themselves prisoners, persuaded
Sokleides, the captain of the pirates, to release the free persons and some of the
slaves, and volunteered to act as hostages on their behalf, and showed great concern that none of the citizen women should be carried off as booty and be sold, or
suffer hardship, and that no free person should perish; thanks to these men the
prisoners were saved and returned home without suffering harm . . .[67]

The gallantry of the two young men is clear, albeit with the assumption
that the lives and virtues of the free citizens matter far more than those of
the slaves. Yet the inscription fails to indicate how they were able to persuade the pirates' leader to release so many of his prisoners. It seems
highly likely that some kind of deal was done, involving a ransom for the
free persons and selected slaves, perhaps domestic servants, nurses and the
like. The sons of Hegesistratos presumably relied upon the fact that getting their hands upon the wealth of their fellow citizens would seem more
profitable to the pirates than selling their captives as slaves at one of the
Aegean's main slave markets – Rhodes, or Delos, or Crete. The fate of
the individual captives was determined according to their social status and
the likelihood that others would be prepared to purchase their freedom. A
comparison might be made with the third-century BC inscription from
Thera mentioned above, reporting a dispute between some pirates from
Allaria in Crete and their Theran partners. In this case it would appear
that some of the captives were freed because they also were Therans, but
that other captives, including both Greeks and foreigners, were required
in exchange.[68]

Individuals seem to have relied heavily upon the diplomatic and com-

---

[66] There is an excellent catalogue of instances, relating to war and/or piracy, in Pritchett
(1991): 272–83.
[67] *SIG* 521 = *IG* XII.7.386. I quote from the translation of Austin (1981): no. 87. Sokleides
is referred to in lines 15–16 as: τὸν ἐπὶ τῶν πειρατῶν ἐπιπλέοντα. Gofas (1989): 429–30
suggests that this designation should be understood in terms of an overseer of cargo,
rather than a commanding officer, but the military analogy seems to be more appropriate
than the commercial one; see LSJ Suppl. s.v.
[68] *IG* XII.3.328; see above p. 57.

mercial ties of their cities and states to protect them from capture and sale as slaves. Captives might be transported long distances and sold far away from their homes, reducing the likelihood of intervention by relatives or fellow-countrymen. Decrees of *proxenia* (appointment as the official local representative of a foreign state), *asylia* (immunity from reprisals) and *isopoliteia* (equal citizenship rights) are very well attested for the Hellenistic period, indicating a network of agreements and alliances which could offer some chance of rescue for the victims of pirates. For example, Eumaridas of Kydonia in Crete was honoured as *proxenos* by the Athenians in 228 BC, partly because of his assistance in ransoming Athenians who had been captured in earlier raids on Attica and sold in Crete, possibly by Aitolians.[69] The larger slave markets of the Aegean seem to have afforded opportunities for wealthy individuals to obtain honours and status in distant communities through charitable acts of this kind. An inscription from Delos, dating to some time in the late third century BC, records how the people of Theangela in Karia honoured Semos, son of Kosimados, of Delos for freeing some Theangelan women who had been captured by pirates and sold in the slave market.[70]

A particularly good example of a community's efforts to safeguard its citizens is a treaty between Miletos and various Cretan cities, found in Miletos and dated to some time between 260 and 230 BC. It records a decree of the Knossians, in response to an embassy of the Milesians. Initially a formal agreement was concluded between Knossos and Miletos, which remained in force even though it was lost in a fire. Thereafter, as a result of an embassy from the Milesians inquiring about this agreement, a new copy of the treaty was drawn up for display in Miletos:

And so that the other Cretans should themselves make a treaty with you with greater willingness, we think it necessary to make a treaty as you have requested. A Knossian shall not knowingly purchase a Milesian who is a free man nor a Milesian a Knossian. Anyone who purchases knowingly shall forfeit the price paid and the person [bought] shall be free. If he purchases unknowingly, he shall return the person and get back the price he paid. If anyone buys a slave, he shall get back the price he paid and return the person. If he does not return it, he shall be brought at Knossos before the *kosmoi* and at Miletos before the *prytaneis*. The magistrates in each state shall compel him to return the person to whoever [rightfully] claims him, in accordance with the agreement.[71]

The inscription continues to outline procedures for disputes and convictions. Finally the names of nineteen other Cretan communities are ap-

[69] *SIG* 535; see below pp. 66–7 for further discussion of this inscription.
[70] *IG* XI.4.1054A.
[71] *SdA* III.482 = *ICret* I Knossos, no. 6. I quote here from the translation in Austin (1981): no. 89. See further Ducrey (1968): 243–6; Brulé (1978): 6–12.

pended as parties to the same agreement. Two further treaties of a very similar nature with Gortyn and Phaistos, both of which were at the head of their own groups of Cretan cities, were added below this one. The effect of these treaties would have been to provide some security for Milesians who were captured as a result of piracy (or war) and taken to Crete for sale. Citizens would be freed and slaves returned to their masters. This would only happen, however, if the people involved in the transactions were from cities party to the agreements, and there is nothing in the treaty to prevent goods being seized. Nor would such an agreement prevent the sale of Milesians away from Crete. The Milesians could not prevent the seizure of people by pirates in this way, only moderate some of its effects.

There can be no doubt that large numbers of men, women and children were moved around the Mediterranean as a result of the slave trade in the Hellenistic period. Many of them were foreigners, from the Black Sea area and from the 'barbarian' margins of the Greek world.[72] It is clear from the sources, however, that many were Greeks, and that they were commonly bought and sold by other Greeks. There was a certain amount of philosophical and moral opposition to the practice, but little was actually done to prevent it. The need for slaves was just too great.[73] There has long been an assumption about the role of pirates in the slave trade, especially in the Hellenistic period, as the following quotation from a classic historical work shows: 'The pirate had a most useful place in the economy of the old world; he was the general slave merchant.'[74] Statements such as this imply two things. Firstly, that piracy was a major source for the slave supply in the ancient world, and, secondly, that most pirates were after captives whom they intended to sell as slaves. As Garlan has observed, however, the ancient Greeks were rather reticent about the slave trade, especially after the development of the ideas of citizenship and equality in the Classical period.[75] Slave merchants are rarely heard of in the sources, and the nature of the slave supply system is often misunderstood. Pirates may appear to be major suppliers of slaves, but that is largely because the literary sources are more than willing to mention the slave trade in connection with piracy. Pirates, after all, are already disapproved of for their piracy, the fact that they deal in slaves just confirms their low status and enhances condemnation of them.

It is, however, unlikely that pirates provided a high proportion of the slaves to be found in the Hellenistic world. Many were of 'barbarian'

[72] See Finley (1962); Braund & Tsetskhladze (1989).
[73] On the attitudes of the Greeks to Greek slaves and their preference for non-Greeks see Garlan (1987): 13–18.
[74] Tarn (1913): 88. For a more recent example see Pohl (1993): 33–6.
[75] Garlan (1987).

origin, not Greeks, and the main sources of supply were probably outside the Mediterranean. Warfare and piracy may have been significant contributors, but they were not the main ones. It is also probable that the numerous agreements about immunity, guarantees of safety and treaties providing for the return of citizens sold as slaves, would have tended to reduce the effectiveness of piracy as a means of supplying slaves. It seems to me very likely that many of the slaves who were sold by pirates were already slaves when they were captured, so that the pirates were not supplying new slaves but simply 'redistributing' old ones. Citizens and other free persons could be ransomed or reclaimed more easily and with greater urgency than slaves. Hence the important distinction made between purchasing free persons and purchasing slaves in the agreement between Miletos and the Cretan cities quoted above.

Things may have changed to some extent with the arrival of large Roman armies making huge numbers of Greeks, and others, slaves from the early second century BC onwards.[76] The market at Delos seems to have boomed after the arrival of the Romans, and the trade in slaves was an important contributor to its success.[77] Barbarians would still have accounted for many of the slaves being sold to the Italians and Greeks, as is suggested by the complaint of Nikomedes III, king of Bithynia (c. 127–94 BC), recorded by Diodorus, that the *publicani* had seized most of his people as slaves (Diod. 36.3). Strabo seems to imply that the growth of Cilician piracy in the second century BC and the large market for slaves were coincidences:

> The export of slaves greatly encouraged them in their wickedness, since it became profitable for all concerned. The slaves could be obtained easily, and not far away there was a big and prosperous market, Delos, capable of taking in and sending out tens of thousands of slaves every day, hence the saying which arose: 'Merchant, sail in, unload, everything has been sold.'[78] (Str. 14.5.2)

The ancient sources also give the impression that slaves were a major source of income for the Cilicians, although here too I suspect that it was 'used' slaves that were the usual objects of pirate attacks. In the Late Republic, as in the Hellenistic period, 'fresh' slaves came from outside the Mediterranean area, or from its barbarian margins.[79] What may, however, have been different in the case of the Cilicians was the extra demand

---

[76] See Harris (1979): 74–93.

[77] See Rauh (1993): 41–68. Coarelli (1982) even argues that the 'Agora of the Italians' on Delos was basically a slave market.

[78] The word μυριάδας (tens of thousands) is not to be taken literally. It simply means, 'a huge number'.

[79] See Crawford (1977) on the shift away from Anatolia as a source of slaves after 63 BC.

for slaves which was produced by the Romans, which the Cilicians undoubtedly helped to satisfy.[80]

## Ransom

The third-century BC inscription from Amorgos quoted above seems to refer to a typical outcome of piratical raids in the Hellenistic period – the release of prisoners after payment of a ransom. This method of extorting wealth from their victims had obvious advantages to Hellenistic pirates. On the one hand it could be a more direct way of obtaining money than selling the captives as slaves, since it was not necessary to find a market. On the other hand it also had the potential to produce greater profits, since the 'price' of the individuals was determined by their value to their fellow citizens and families, rather than merely the going rate for slaves obtained in dubious circumstances. The ransom for a few captives of high status could easily outweigh the sale price of a large number of slaves. Epigraphic evidence suggests that ransoming prisoners from pirates was common in the Hellenistic period,[81] and may even have been the principal aim of much piracy in the Eastern Mediterranean. It is also worth noting that ransoming prisoners of war was a very well established practice in the Greek world, as the opening and closing events of the *Iliad* attest, which meant that pirates could take advantage of established customs and procedures in the pursuit of ransoms.[82]

An inscription from Rhamnous on the north-east coast of Attica honours a certain Epichares, *strategos* in charge of coastal defence, for his help in rescuing people who were seized by pirates around the time of the Chremonidean War (*c.* 267–262 BC):[83]

... and he also made a deal about the prisoners who had been captured, that they should be freed through the mediation of a herald on payment of a ransom of 120 *drachmai* [each], that none of the citizens should be carried off and that the slaves should not be made away with,[84] he also punished those who had introduced the pirates into the land, men from the city, arresting and interrogating them [in a way that was fitting] for what they did ...

[80] See Hopkins (1978): ch. 2.

[81] E.g. the inscription from the end of the third century BC which honours five ambassadors from Aulon on the island of Naxos who obtained the ransom of 280 captives from the Aitolians (*SIG* 520).

[82] For a general survey of ransom in the Greek world see Pritchett (1991): 245–97.

[83] *SEG* XXIV.154, lines 19–23; dated to 264/3, *vel paulo post*. I quote from the translation in Austin (1981): no. 50, to which I have made a few changes. See also *BE* (1968), no. 247. See above pp. 3–4 for more detailed discussion of the date and language of this inscription.

[84] Austin tranlates ἀφανίζεται here as 'killed', but I think it is unlikely that the pirates would have decided to carry off the citizens but kill the slaves.

The details provided in this honorific decree are both fascinating and alarming. It would appear that some people from the city of Athens had tried to take advantage of the confusion brought about by the Chremonidean War to engage in some kidnapping and extortion at the expense of their fellow citizens.[85] The actual perpetrators of the attack, the unidentified pirates, were not caught, but the Athenians who encouraged them, and presumably showed them where to find their victims in expectation of a share in the profits, were. The episode neatly illustrates the close connection between ransoming and the slave trade. The pirates were clearly prepared to negotiate with Epichares for a suitable ransom, but if the negotiations had not been successful, then the prisoners would have been taken away, presumably by sea, and sold as slaves. Epichares' investigation must have turned up information about the link between the pirates and the men from the city, perhaps revealed to the prisoners while they were being held, but the decree does not elaborate on this, concentrating instead on Epichares' services as local commander.[86]

Another Athenian inscription reveals what might happen to captives who were taken away from their homeland by pirates who were not prepared to wait around and negotiate for an immediate ransom. The stone preserves the text of an honorific decree passed in 217/16 BC for Eumaridas of Kydonia, a Cretan.[87]

Gods. In the archonship of Heliodoros, in the eleventh prytany, of the tribe of Kekropis, in the month Thargelion; Lysistratos, son of Phylarchides, of Oinoe proposed: since Eumaridas both previously, and at the time when Boukris overran the countryside and carried off to Crete a large number of the citizens and of the others from the city, performed many great services for the people and contributed money from his own pocket for the twenty talents that had been agreed [as ransom] for the prisoners; and [since] he lent money to the captives for their travel expenses; and [since] now, when the people [of Athens] has sent ambassadors so that good relations may be preserved with all the Cretans and so that this might be achieved, if anywhere the right to plunder has been given to those who sail against the shore [of Attica],[88] this right is ended,[89] he pleaded his case so that everything should be done in the best interest of the people; and [since] he also took part in an embassy to Knossos and her allies, and also gave letters to the ambassadors for his

---

[85] On the date, course and consequences of this complicated war see Will (1979–82): I 219–33.

[86] Hammond and Walbank (1988): 283 suggest that the pirates were employed by Antigonos Gonatas, but this cannot be conclusively demonstrated.

[87] *SIG* 535, lines 1–20; the translation is basically that of Austin (1981), no. 88, with alterations and additions where necessary. See also Brulé (1978): 17–20(ii); Pritchett (1991): 143–7.

[88] εἴ που ἀποδέδοται τοῖς καταπλέουσιν.

[89] Austin omits the phrase ἀρθεῖ τοῦτο, in lines 13–14, from his translation. See further Brulé (1978): 19–20(ii).

friends in Polyrrhenia, so that they would co-operate with him over the interests [of the people]; and [since] he undertakes to show every care to ensure the preservation of good relations between the people [of Athens] and all the inhabitants of Crete . . .[90]

The Boukris mentioned in this inscription might have been an Aitolian, perhaps the son of another Boukris who was honoured at Delos in the middle of the third century BC.[91] The connections between Aitolians and Cretans are well attested for this period, so it is no surprise to find the Athenian captives being disposed of in Crete, even if they were taken by Aitolians rather than Cretans.[92] Their fate was not, however, sealed from the moment they were captured. As has already been noticed above, the obvious choice which lay before pirates with prisoners was either to sell them as slaves or to attempt to obtain a ransom. For Boukris and his party, who had sailed away from the region in which their raid had taken place, the latter option required a suitable go-between and the availability of funds for the ransom. This was obviously where Eumaridas came in. He was a Cretan and apparently had considerable wealth at his disposal. He used it to help the Athenians and was accorded honours and influence as a result. Good relations between Athens and Kydonia seem to go back at least to the late fourth century BC.[93] Eumaridas then went on to play a crucial role in negotiations between Athens and various Cretan cities. These negotiations seem to have been aimed at reducing attacks on the Attic coast by pirates emanating from Crete. It would appear that certain cities had been allowing their citizens to take booty from Attica, and the people of Athens were making a concerted effort to prevent further occurrences. It is impossible to tell how successful they were, although there is plenty of epigraphic evidence for the capture of Athenian citizens by Aitolians and others, over whom the Cretan cities would have no control.[94]

A recently discovered inscription from the Ionian city of Teos has provided further, dramatic evidence of both the vulnerability of coastal

---

[90] The rest of the inscription is concerned with the honours to be given to Eumaridas. *SIG* nos. 536–7 are two more inscriptions put up with this one in honour of Eumaridas and his son Charmion.

[91] Durrbach (1921): no. 42. The identification is far from certain.

[92] See Brulé (1978): 21.

[93] See Brulé (1978): 16–17 on *IG* II$^2$.399, honouring Eurylochos of Kydonia for ransoming and returning Athenian prisoners *c.* 320 BC. See Potter (1984) for discussion of the possible context of this incident.

[94] *IG* II$^2$.1130, which records Athenian ambassadors complaining of the same problem to another Cretan community, of unknown identity, in the second century BC. *SIG* 520 = *IG* XII.5.36 honours the successful public envoys in another case of capture by pirates (Aitolians) and ransom, earlier in the third century on Naxos. *IG* II$^2$.746, a fragmentary Athenian decree of the mid third century BC apparently records the ransom of persons captured and then sold by Aitolians; see Brulé (1978): 22–4.

communities in the Mediterranean to piratical attacks in the second half of the third century BC and the profitability of taking prisoners to hold for ransom, rather than to sell as slaves.[95] The inscription records public decrees concerning the raising of a large sum of money, which the Teians are using to pay as ransom to some pirates who are holding a number of Teians, including women and children, as hostages. The sum is calculated as a tenth of the wealth of the Teians and must be collected by the city's magistrates and officials to pay the pirates, some of whom have remained in the city, whilst the rest have apparently taken the hostages to a convenient hiding-place. The inscription describes the process by which the Teians must declare their personal wealth in order to obtain the relevant sum in coinage, precious metals, fine fabrics and other easily transportable forms. Much of the surviving *stele* is taken up with a list of those whose contribution is above a certain level, probably one *mna* or about 100 *drachmai*. These individuals are to be specially honoured and treated as public creditors.

It is clear from the nature of the decrees' provisions that the Teians are completely at the mercy of the pirates, who, after striking a deal with the magistrates, have allowed 23 days for the collection of the ransom money, during which time the pirates still in the city must be presuming that they are completely safe, and those holding the hostages are not expecting any rescue to be effected. From this comfortable position the pirates have arranged for the Teians to supervise their own ransacking, saving themselves much time, effort and danger by having the plunder collected and delivered to them. A further peculiarity of this episode is that the ransom may have been envisaged by the pirates as a kind of tithe, similar to that which might have been offered to the gods after a battle. Such offerings were often made as 'tenths' of the booty accumulated from raids or campaigns. This practice is attested by inscriptions for the proceeds of piratical raids by the Cretan cities in the Hellenistic period.[96] The editor of the Teian inscription, Sencer Şahin, argues that the pirates who attacked Teos may well be Cretans, since the events took place around the time of the Cretan War.[97] In addition, when the Teians sought *asylia* for their city at the end of the third century BC, with the aid of Antiochos III and Philip

---

[95] Text, German translation and commentary in Şahin (1994). The editor only dates the inscription to 'etwa in die zweite Hälfte des 3. Jahrhunderts v. Chr.' The attackers are described as πειραταί in line 65 of the inscription. The translation as 'pirates' seems appropriate since Teos is a coastal city which it would have been relatively straightforward to attack from the sea, with the element of surprise, but not from the land.

[96] See Brulé (1978); Pritchett (1991): 366–8.

[97] See below pp. 80–4.

V, a major objective was to gain immunity from piratical raids by the Cretans.[98]

### *Asylia*

Grants of *asylia* and, to a lesser extent, *isopoliteia* were clearly one way in which the communities of the Eastern Mediterranean attempted to cope with the problem of piracy. It was possible to persuade one or more of the Hellenistic monarchs to declare a city and its territory *asylos* and to encourage others to follow suit. Cities sent out their own ambassadors, or sought the assistance of other people's envoys to obtain such grants from the major states and Leagues, especially the Aitolian federation and the Cretan *koinon*. The efforts of the Teians towards the end of the third century BC are among the best documented, probably because of their success. Antiochos III, the Aitolians, the Delphic Amphiktyony, many of the Cretan cities and, even, with the persuasion of Antiochos' representative, the Romans, all recognized the claims of Teos (and the resident Dionysiac Artists) with grants of *asylia*.[99] The aim in such cases was partly to discourage piratical raids by getting the agreement of those who were likely to attack, or were in a position to influence the actions of other potential attackers, but it is important not to see these conventions as something specifically related to piracy. The main focus of *asylia* seems to have been the guarantee of inviolability to sanctuaries, such as that of Aphrodite Stratonike at Smyrna, which was granted *asylia*, along with the city, by the Delphic Amphiktyony and Seleukos II (246–225 BC).[100] Individuals or groups with sacred duties could also obtain this privilege, as in the case of the Dionysiac Artists at Teos. The grant of *asylia* might discourage attacks, whether piratical or not, and it might provide help and redress for the victims of such attacks, but all recorded cases indicate that it was the weaker parties to the agreement who were seeking protection and/or assurances from the stronger ones. If the stronger party wished to ignore or violate the agreement there was little that the weaker one could do about it. A declaration of *asylia* did not guarantee protection or immunity from piracy for anyone.

---

[98] Şahin (1994): 19–20, 25–36; see also Herrman (1965). See Brulé (1978): 72–4 on the agreements between Teos and nearly 20 Cretan cities, dated to 204/3 BC; some of the agreements were extended and/or renewed *c.* 160 BC.

[99] See Brulé (1978) 72–4 (Cretans); *SIG* 563–5 (Aitolians and Delphi); *SIG* 601 (Romans). For general discussion see Herrmann (1965). The Roman grant is recorded in a letter from the praetor Marcus Valerius Messala in 193 BC.

[100] *OGIS* 228 and 229; translation of the latter in Austin (1981): no. 182.

### The Aitolians

The Aitolians expanded their territory in Central Greece at the expense of the neighbouring Phokians, Amphilokians and Akarnanians during the fourth and early third centuries BC. They played a prominent role in the victory over the invading Gauls in 279 BC and took control of the Delphic Amphiktyony in 277 BC. By the middle of the third century BC the Aitolian confederation included not only cities from Aitolia proper, but also many other *poleis*, whose inhabitants were not Aitolians, but who were persuaded, one way or another, to join the alliance. For a long time they dominated the Delphic Amphiktyony, which gave them a degree of political influence outside their immediate region. When, in the late 270s BC, the Aitolians gained direct access to the Aegean via central Greece, they also achieved the capacity to involve themselves in the politics of the Greek world beyond the mainland.[101] Their naval power grew at the same time as that of the Ptolemies waned, until, by the end of the 250s BC, they were a force to be reckoned with in the Aegean and around the coastline of Greece.[102] The festival of the Nikoleia on Delos, founded in 252 BC by an Aitolian called Nikolaos, is often taken as an indication of the high status of the Aitolians in general at this time.[103] Their tendency to be hostile towards Macedon, a rival for influence over central and southern Greece, made them appropriate allies for Rome in the struggle against Philip V in 212 BC. They eventually fell out with Rome after the defeat of Philip V at Kynoskephalai in 197 and, after a brief but disastrous alliance with Antiochos III, they were deprived of their conquests and forced to accept an inferior status as subject allies of Rome in 189 BC, effectively bringing their period of influence to an end.

The nature of Aitolian sea power has been discussed at length by Benecke, who argued that the Aitolians exploited their lax customs and laws regarding plunder and reprisals to terrorize many of the smaller states of the Hellenistic world into establishing favourable diplomatic and economic relations with them. In effect, according to Benecke, they employed piracy as a means of increasing their political power. The extent of their influence is ascertained principally from a series of inscriptions of the mid third century BC which record the conclusion of treaties and agreements between the Aitolians and various other states. Many of these texts record the granting of freedom from reprisals and general guarantees of safety to

---

[101] See Will (1979–82): I 217.
[102] See Benecke (1934); Flacelière (1937); Will (1979–82): I 325–8.
[103] *IG* XI.2.287B; see Benecke (1934): 20.

sanctuaries and communities.[104] One example, the granting of *asylia* to the sanctuary at Smyrna *c.* 246 BC, shows the involvement of Seleukos II Kallinikos in the process. He proclaimed the immunity of Smyrna, and then the Delphic Amphiktyony, which effectively meant the Aitolians, confirmed this position by a decree of its own.[105] Other examples seem to indicate that it was the individual cities or communities which approached the Aitolians and asked for a recognition of their immunity, or a guarantee of safety, as the Teians did *c.* 260 BC.[106] Some places seem to have gone even further, as is shown by an inscription from Delphi recording a grant of *isopoliteia* and *asylia* to Chios, along with admission to the Delphic Amphiktyony, in return for a grant of Chian citizenship with full rights to the Aitolians:[107]

... since the [Aitolian] League, because of the ancestral kinship and [friendship] which exists between [our] people and the Aitolians, voted previously to grant us citizenship [and] forbade all to plunder the property of [the Chians] from whatever starting base [on] pain of being liable to prosecution before the [councillors] on a charge of harming the common interests of the Aitolians; for this the people voted that the [Aitolians] should be citizens and share in all the rights the Chians share in ... and now the sacred envoys and the ambassadors have returned and [reported] to the people the goodwill felt [towards our] city by the Aitolian League, who display their anxiety to grant [all] the requests of the ambassadors, and especially have granted to our people one vote as *hieromnemon* in the Amphiktyonic Council, in conformity with the feelings of kinship and friendliness [they have] had before towards our city.

It is difficult to assess the relative importance of these rights. Whether the Aitolians were always the main beneficiaries of such grants is not clear. Was it, as Benecke has argued, the deliberate policy of the Aitolians to use the fear of piracy to extort concessions from the people of Chios and other communities? While it is obvious that Chian citizenship would help Aitolian traders and provide the Aitolian League with a potential friendly base in the Aegean, the Chians obtained through this agreement a certain amount of security for their citizens and a vote on the Delphic Amphiktyony, a notable political and diplomatic advantage.[108]

---

[104] For a full list see Benecke (1934): 17–29. These treaties usually grant *asylia* or *asphaleia*. It may be that similar treaties were also concluded with communities closer to Aitolia in the fourth century BC.

[105] *OGIS* nos. 228–9; Benecke (1934): 23.

[106] *IG* IX.15.191; Benecke (1934): 21.

[107] *SIG* 443 = *IG* IX.1².195A. Note the revisions in *BE* (1977): 231. Quotations from Austin (1981): no. 52. See Benecke (1934): 17–19.

[108] The Aitolians did not grant a seat on their own federal council to the Chians, or to anyone else outside the Aitolian confederacy. See Larsen (1968).

Both sides would seem to have made substantial gains as a result of this agreement.

An important objection to Benecke's hypothesis of the Aitolians plundering, or threatening to plunder, for political purposes is the relatively small amount of evidence which can be used to show them practising piracy in the Aegean *before* the 220s BC. Of the evidence collected by Ormerod and Benecke,[109] only an inscription from Naxos, recording an attack by Aitolians on the town of Aulon *c.* 280 BC, belongs to the period before the middle of the third century BC.[110] At all stages in the expansion of the Aitolian League there may well have been a considerable amount of what could be termed predatory warfare. The importance of obtaining booty in war was deeply ingrained in Greek culture, and it may have been particularly prominent among the peoples of central Greece. Thucydides says that it was in this region that the Homeric style of warfare, which primarily aimed at acquiring status and honour through raiding and plundering, was still prevalent in the fifth century BC (Thuc. 1.5–6). Alastar Jackson has pointed to the personal name Laistas, derived from *leistes*, which occurs in an inscription of the late third century BC, as an indicator of the extent to which piracy or raiding could be a prestigious and respectable activity.[111] These factors may have had some influence on the decisions of individual communities to conclude agreements with the Aitolians to limit the damage that might be done to them, but I am not convinced that this was a key element of Aitolian political influence. Even such all-embracing agreements as the Chian treaty quoted above were not necessarily much protection outside of the fairly limited jurisdiction of the Aitolian League, whose political ambitions are less significant here than the need of many small states in the Aegean region to preserve their safety by maintaining good relations with the wide variety of 'powers' in the political world of the third century BC. An alliance with Aitolia was only one method by which this might be done. At best it was a potentially useful supplement to the benefactions of the Antigonid, Ptolemaic and Seleukid monarchies, the goodwill and practical assistance of the Rhodians, or the regional influence of the various petty monarchs of the Hellespont and Black Sea.[112] The main source of information

---

[109] Ormerod (1924): 139–42; Benecke (1934): 11–29.

[110] *SIG* 520.

[111] *SIG* 539A, line 6; Jackson (1973): 251.

[112] See above pp. 48–56. Unfortunately we lack a complete list of such alliance for any individual state, although the example of Smyrna cited above shows that a city would energetically seek the protection of more than one power at a time. The apparent prominence of Aitolian *asylia* agreements is partly to be accounted for by the fact that so many of them were inscribed at Delphi, being officially actions of the Amphiktyonic council.

about Aitolian piracy is Polybius, whose account relates almost entirely to incidents from the time of the Social War (220–217 BC) or later, suggesting that the Aitolians' reputation for widespread piracy and plundering was gained as a result of their activities in the last quarter of the third century BC. Treaties and agreements between the Aitolians and others from this period represent only a very small proportion of the documents cited by Benecke.[113] At this point it is worthwhile to examine Polybius' views in more detail.

## Polybius and the Aitolians

Polybius was born about 200 BC, the son of Lykortas, a prominent political figure in the Achaian Confederation. His own political career was cut short after the defeat of Perseus of Macedon in 168 BC. Polybius was one of 1,000 Achaians deported to Rome and Italy. He became friendly with many of the leading Roman politicians of the mid second century BC, especially Publius Cornelius Scipio Aemilianus. He was freed in 150 BC but continued his close association with Scipio Aemilianus and played a significant role in the reorganization of southern Greece after 146 BC. He was a fiercely patriotic Achaian and an ardent admirer of the Romans, writing his *Histories* principally to describe and explain their rise to power and their defeat of Carthage, Macedon and the Seleukids. Polybius is rightly regarded as one of the finest historians of the ancient world. He was a remarkably industrious researcher by ancient standards, studying many original documents as well as the work of earlier writers. His *Histories* were published around the middle of the second century BC and provide one of the most important sources for the history of the Hellenistic period and the rise of Roman domination in the Mediterranean.[114] Polybius has a lot to say about pirates in the course of his work, much of it highly informative and important for our understanding of ancient piracy. In order to appreciate the value of Polybius, however, it is necessary to consider how his attitude towards different groups in the Hellenistic Mediterranean was shaped and expressed. His highly polemical treatment of the Aitolians and their associates requires special attention.

An important aspect of Polybius' portrayal of the Aitolians is the contrast between them and their rivals and sometime allies, the Achaians. In

---

[113] *SIG* 522 (*c*. 220 BC) and *SIG* 554 (*c*. 207 BC).
[114] Only Books 1–5 out of the original 40 survive intact. Much of what can be reconstructed of the remaining books comes from quotations and excerpts in collections of other ancient writers. For the sources of the various fragments referred to see Walbank (1957–79).

Book 2 Polybius eulogizes the Achaian League, its history and its institutions in his account of the background to the Social War (220–
217 BC). He reserves special praise for the Achaian *strategos* Aratos of
Sikyon, whose deeds, partly recorded in his historical memoirs, were an
inspiration to Polybius (Polyb. 2.37–44). He then depicts the Aitolians as
jealous of the achievements of the Achaian League under Aratos, and
desirous of destroying it for their own gain. By painting a picture of the
cunning, agresssive, greedy and perfidious nature of the Aitolians, Polybius makes Aratos, the man who was responsible for thwarting their ambitions, all the more heroic and virtuous (Polyb. 2.45).

In Book 4 of Polybius' *Histories* all the Aitolians are portrayed as
sharing an unhealthy predilection for plunder, so that, for example, Polybius' account of the outbreak of the Social War focusses on the exploits
of the Aitolian Dorimachos, who is described as 'a young man full of the
Aitolians' violent and grasping impulses' (Polyb. 4.3.5). Although he has
been sent to the Peloponnese in 222 BC as a representative of the Aitolians, supposedly to help protect the territory of Phigalea, Dorimachos
takes up with a group of bandits whom he leads in illegitimate raids
against the Messenians (Polyb. 4.3.6–10).[115] After this brief foray has
been brought to an end by the complaints of the Messenians, Dorimachos
is able to persuade Skopas in 221 BC to back his idea of a war against
the Messenians by appealing to the latter's baser instincts: 'But, this being
the most effective argument to use with the Aitolian, he held up before his
eyes the prospect of the huge amount of booty to be gained from the territory of the Messenians, as they would have no warning ...' (Polyb.
4.5.5). The result is that the Aitolian leaders declare war against the
Messenians, Epirotes, Acharnians and Macedonians without even con-
sulting their own people (Polyb. 4.5.10). One of their first operations in
this war, as it is described in Polybius' narrative, is a piratical act – the
seizure of a Macedonian naval vessel, whose crew are sold as slaves in
Aitolia (Polyb. 4.6.1).[116] In the subsequent chapters Polybius continuously presents the Aitolians as aggressive and untrustworthy. He offers
love of plunder as their main motive in the Social War. This is, however,
a highly selective and obviously biased presentation. The Aitolians were
under considerable political pressure from the Achaian League, and their
intervention in Messenia, which was about to ally with their rivals, has to

---

[115] See above pp. 7–8 on the language of this passage.
[116] Polybius labels the Aitolians involved as pirates (πειραταί), just as he has earlier called
Dorimachos and his associates bandits, using the same word. Clearly it is a matter of
perspective; since the Aitolian leaders considered themselves to be at war, they would
not have thought of such an act as piracy.

be seen in the wider context of relations among the mainland Greeks after the death of Antigonos Doson in 221 BC.[117]

Another highly revealing book of Polybius' *Histories*, as far as his attitude to the Aitolians is concerned, is the fragmentary Book 13.[118] In the course of describing the events which led to Roman intervention in the affairs of the Greeks at the end of the third century BC, he deals with the activities of the leaders of the Aitolian League around 205 BC. He criticizes the new legislation introduced by Skopas and Dorimachos, saying they were motivated by typical Aitolian greed and corruption to change their older (i.e. better) laws (Polyb. 13.1–2). He then contrasts the treacherous behaviour of Philip V of Macedon, who enlisted the Aitolian 'pirate' Dikaiarchos to help the Cretans against Rhodes, with earlier rulers and with the Romans, who do not stoop to tricks or deception in warfare or public affairs (Polyb. 13.3). Then he describes a degenerate renegade called Herakleides, whom Philip used to stir up the Cretans against the Rhodians (Polyb. 13.4–5). Next he describes the evil nature and deeds of Nabis, the Spartan tyrant and an ally of the Aitolians (Polyb. 13.6–8). The last few surviving paragraphs of Book 13 go on to narrate affairs in Asia. In this book there is no mention of piracy, or pirates, but what makes it significant is the invective and criticism which Polybius heaps upon the Aitolians and upon their associates.[119] There can be no doubt that he hated and despised the Aitolians, blaming them, in particular, for the troubles of the Greeks from the Social War onwards. It is important to bear in mind this attitude of Polybius when using him as a source for the study of piracy in the Hellenistic period.[120]

There can be no doubt, however, that the Aitolians deserved, at least in part, the poor reputation they attained as a result of their piratical activities in the third century BC. Several chapters of Polybius' Book 4 contain a catalogue of Aitolian piracy and banditry, featuring incidents which were shocking even by ancient Greek standards of violence and plundering, like the pillaging in 219 BC of the sanctuary of Zeus at Dodona (Polyb. 4.67). It seems to have been their liking for sudden, unexpected

[117] See Walbank in *CAH* VII$^2$.1.5473–81; Walbank (1957–79) ad loc.; Will (1979–92): II 71–2; Fine (1940).

[118] See Walbank (1957–79): ad loc. for suggestions as to missing contents and the relationship of fragments.

[119] The level of abuse is maintained throughout most of Polybius' *Histories*. See, for example, his description of the deaths of Skopas and Dikaiarchos (Polyb. 18.54). Associates of the Aitolians also come in for criticism like the piratically inclined Cretans (Polyb. 4.8.11). Polybius can be more sympathetic to the Aitolians; see Sacks (1975).

[120] See below pp. 76–80, 84–6 on Polybius' use of accusations of piracy in his presentation of the Illyrians and of Nabis, the Spartan 'tyrant'.

attacks on potentially rewarding targets which made the Aitolians particularly to be feared. Although most Greek states seem to have accepted that a declaration of reprisals was a necessary preliminary to any retaliatory plundering action, this does not seem to have been the case among the Aitolians in the Hellenistic period. Polybius has Philip V of Macedon complain that they have a custom which permits them to take reprisals without any public announcement (Polyb. 18.4.8–5.2). Yet the Aitolians were not alone in this attitude to reprisals. It was also apparently a local custom of permitting plundering without 'official' sanction that was partly responsible for the excesses of the Illyrians in the latter part of the third century BC.[121]

## Rome and the Illyrians

It is with the above observations about Polybius' treatment of the Aitolians in mind that the Illyrians, whose activities prompted the appearance of the first Roman forces in the Eastern Mediterranean in the third century, should be considered. The Illyrians were a group of warlike Hellenizing tribes, occupying a large part of the eastern coastline of the Adriatic and its hinterland, neighbouring Macedonia and Epiros, whose power increased with the decline of the Epirote and Macedonian kingdoms in the third century BC. Relatively little is heard about the Illyrians before the second half of the third century BC, when the Ardiaean kings expanded their territory southwards along the Dalmatian coast. The First Illyrian War (229 BC) was the occasion of Rome's first military intervention on the Greek mainland. It is often asserted that the primary motive for Roman intervention was the protection of Italian traders against Illyrian pirates.[122] Not surprisingly, this war is the subject of a detailed discussion by Polybius in which the protection of traders against pirates figures prominently. He describes the Illyrians under their ambitious king Agron, and their surprise defeat of the Aitolians at Medion in Akarnania (232 BC), which vividly demonstrated their military potential to the rest of the Greeks.[123] According to Polybius the king died soon after and was succeeded by his queen, Teuta. Polybius castigates Teuta for her feminine weakness, and her inability to take a long-term approach to political authority. According to him, emboldened by the recent success against the

---

[121] See below pp. 76–80 on the Illyrians; see also Dell (1967). The Aitolians seem to be deliberately exploiting the uncertainties inherent in Greek customs which allowed delayed or unequal reciprocity.

[122] E.g. Harris (1979): 195–7; Pohl (1993): 58–89.

[123] Polybius uses this episode to make more criticisms of the Aitolians and their love of plunder (Polyb. 2.2).

Aitolians, she allowed her subjects free rein to plunder the shipping of the Adriatic, and formed a piratical fleet which attacked neighbouring states indiscriminately (Polyb. 2.4.8–9). The Illyrians made their way to the territory of Epirotes, where, with the help of some treacherous Gaulish mercenaries, they captured the city of Phoinike. The arival of a combined Aitolian and Achaian force persuaded the Illyrians to withdraw, but not before they had engaged in further piracy, using Phoinike as a base:

For some time previously it had been the custom of this people to prey upon vessels sailing from Italy, and at this moment, while they were occupying Phoinike, a number of them, operating independently of the Illyrian fleet, attacked Italian traders; some of these they had robbed, some they had murdered, and a large number were carried off into captivity. In the past the Roman government had always ignored complaints made to them about the Illyrians. But now, as more and more people approached the senate on this subject, they appointed two commissioners, Gaius and Lucius Coruncanius, to travel to Illyria and inquire into what was happening. (Polyb. 2.8.1–3)

The ambassadors found Queen Teuta and her forces besieging Issa, an island off the coast of Dalmatia which was resisting her domination of Illyria, and were assured that the Illyrian monarchy meant no harm to Rome, but that it was not their custom to restrain their subjects from practising piracy. The younger of the Coruncanii told her that Rome would take steps to make the Illyrians reform their customs. Polybius then says that the queen 'gave way to a fit of womanish petulance' (Polyb. 2.8.12), and sent people to assassinate the Roman ambassadors. The result was a war with Rome and defeat for the Illyrians at the hands of a large force of 20,000 infantry, 2,000 cavalry and 200 ships, led by both the consuls of 229 BC.[124]

Polybius' rather sexist account places the blame for the war on Illyrian piracy, which he describes as a long-standing problem for the vulnerable Greeks of the Adriatic coastline (Polyb. 2.5.2), and a lack of civilized restraint by the emotional queen. He says of Queen Teuta that, after seeing the booty obtained from Phoinike, she became more determined than before to injure the Greeks (Polyb. 2.8.4). Such an attitude is also found in Polybius' treatment of the Carthaginians, Aitolians, Nabis and the Cretans. This pejorative tone, accusing his subjects of an unreasonable desire for plunder which leads to piracy, comes easily to Polybius when he is describing enemies of the Achaians and Romans.[125] The Romans act

[124] For an imaginative reconstruction of the chain of events, involving 'blockade-running' by Italians, which puts Rome in the wrong when war is declared, see Badian (1952).

[125] In this instance the Aitolians are on the same side as the Achaians, although Polybius is clearly more interested in and better informed about the part played by the latter (Polyb. 2.6; 2.9.8–10.5; 2.12.4).

initially to protect Italian traders, but also to protect 'the Greeks' from the evil of Illyrian piracy. In this regard it is important to note that, for Polybius, the First Illyrian War takes place in the context of failure by the combined Achaian and Aitolian Leagues to help the Greek cities which were the Illyrians' principal targets, firstly Phoinike, and then Corcyra, which was occupied by an Illyrian garrison. Polybius emphasizes the Corcyreans' eagerness to place themselves under Roman protection, describing them as 'accepting this as the only effective safeguard for themselves against the future lawlessness of the Illyrians' (Polyb. 2.11.6). When the Romans step in to punish the Illyrians for their unrestrained piracy, therefore, they are delivering the Greeks from fear of their 'common enemy' (Polyb. 2.12.6).[126]

Polybius' version of the events of 229/8 differs markedly from that given by Appian (App. *Ill.* 7). In his *Illyrike* the later author includes several details which are not mentioned by Polybius and which indicate that there were other pressures coming to bear. According to Appian, Agron was still alive and had already captured a large amount of territory from neighbouring Illyrians and Greeks including Corcyra, Epidamnos, Pharos and parts of Epiros, when he began the siege of Issa. In Appian's version it is the people of Issa who appeal to Rome, and the Roman embassy never reaches its destination, but is attacked by *Illyrikoi lemboi* and forced to retreat.[127] The casualties include an Issaian called Kleemporos, as well as one Coruncanius. In addition Appian says that Agron, who died after the attack on the Roman ambassadors, left behind an infant son, Pinnes, whose stepmother and regent was Teuta.

These differences cannot be fully reconciled, and a choice has to be made as to which of the accounts is more reliable. Although Polybius is traditionally given more credit than Appian in such matters, arguments in favour of the latter are far stronger in this instance.[128] Appian wrote his *Roman History* in the mid second century AD, arranging his account of the rise of Rome in terms of the Romans' conflicts with various ethnic groups. His most detailed narrative, an account of the *Civil Wars* at the end of the Republic, is a carefully constructed interpretation of the internal conflicts which followed Rome's conquest of the Mediterranean, and which led to the establishment of the Principate. It is replete with specially

---

[126] Polybius uses the phrase κοινοὺς ἐχθρούς to describe the Illyrians.

[127] *Lemboi* and *liburnai* are ancient ship types commonly associated with pirates, although the use of such vessels does not automatically indicate that their crews are pirates; see Casson (1986): 141–2.

[128] The case is most convincingly put by Derow (1973). For an important reappraisal of Appian's historical technique and reliability see Goldmann (1988).

composed speeches and moralizing observations on the descent into anarchy in the late Republic, and the redundancy of the republican political system. By contrast his brief account of Rome's Illyrian Wars, which has relatively little significance in his wider historiographical scheme, is far less moralistic and rhetorical than Polybius' version. Although Polybius probably did not have very good sources of information for these events, he was sharply aware of their symbolic importance for the wider theme of his *Histories*, that is, the rise of Roman power in the Mediterranean. As a consequence Polybius was keen to make the First Illyrian War into a major 'set-piece' early in his work, with Rome's earliest intervention in Greek affairs foreshadowing later events.[129]

The course of the war which followed the Roman embassy to Agron seems to indicate that the Romans' main concern was to protect the straits of Otranto and the coastline of Italy, rather than to help Issa, which had to wait almost a year until the siege was lifted. The subsequent settlement with Teuta, which bound the Illyrians not to sail beyond Lissos, on the river Drilo, thus keeping them away from the Epirotes and Rome's other allies in this area, also barred them from the narrowest part of the straits. The military strength of the Illyrians certainly commanded respect, especially as they could easily be persuaded to fight for others. If nothing else, the experience of fighting Pyrrhos of Epiros in the 270s BC must have made the Romans wary of having strong and belligerent neighbours across the Adriatic.

It is difficult to determine how far the Romans were acting to protect trade when they complained to the Illyrians in 229 BC. According to Polybius the senate was eventually responding to the protests of Italian traders, who had suffered for a considerable time at the hands of the Illyrian pirates. In spite of his comments, and the statement in Strabo's *Geography* that Illyrian piracy had a long history, Dell has argued that significant problems of this kind were a relatively recent phenomenon, the result of population growth and the disappearance of the restraining influence of the Epirote monarchy.[130] The main threat in his view was not really to the Italian traders, but to the Greek cities and the local tribes of the area to the south of Illyria. What is called piracy by Polybius is characterized by Dell as 'large-scale raids for booty and incipient imperialism'.[131] The condemnatory tone used to describe the Illyrians' methods and aims in warfare by Polybius may well reflect contemporary Greek

---

[129] See Walbank (1957–79): ad loc. On the other sources for this war, which do not offer anything more than does Appian or Polybius, see Derow (1973): 123–4.
[130] Dell (1967).
[131] Dell (1967): 358.

complaints of a kind which were also levelled against the Aitolians and Cretans.[132]

Nevertheless, it seems unlikely that Polybius, in spite of the limits of his account, would have included the mention of attacks on Italian traders if these did not take place, or had no significance. What indications are there that trade across the Adriatic was important enough to warrant Roman military intervention to protect it? Early Roman coinage has been found in the general area of Illyria, but Crawford has argued that coin hoards found on the eastern side of the Adriatic contain too little Roman coinage to suggest that it was circulating as a medium of exchange in Illyria or neighbouring regions, although the third-century BC bronze coins found in hoards from the Mazin area might have been exported as metal, rather than coinage.[133] Crawford suggests that Phoinike shows most numismatic evidence for contacts with the West in general, and Derow argues for the importance of Issa and the Dalmatian islands in cross-Adriatic exchange. Since these two places figure prominently in accounts of the First Illyrian War, it seems likely that Italian traders' interests did have some influence on events, but that Polybius has magnified the extent to which they were a reason for Rome to go to war with the Illyrians. The war was less about protecting merchants against pirates, and more about curbing the Illyrians' aggression towards their neighbours in an area strategically important to Rome. Polybius, however, is deliberately reticent about the strategic implications, preferring to present the Romans as acting in the interests of Italian traders and the Greek cities, protecting them against the 'common enemy', as he calls the Illyrian pirates, in a fashion which seems more altruistic and, in his view, more suitable, for the future masters of the Mediterranean world.[134] The idea of a powerful state being on a kind of mission to suppress piracy was hardly a new one, but Polybius seems to have been the first to portray Rome in this guise.

### Rhodes and the Cretan cities

The First Cretan War (c. 206–203 BC) provides the most dramatic manifestation of the complex nature of piracy in the Eastern Mediterranean

---

[132] See above pp. 70–6 on the Aitolians and below pp. 80–4 on the Cretans. Polybius' main source of information for the Illyrian War may be the accounts (written or oral) of those Achaians who witnessed either the unsuccessful joint expedition with the Aitolians, or the embassy from the Roman consul Postumius, which he says gave the Romans' explanation for their involvement (Polyb. 2.12.4).

[133] Crawford (1978). See also the discussion in Derow (1973): 125–6.

[134] See Derow (1973) for further discussion of Polybius' reticence regarding the strategic aspects of the First Illyrian War. It is also noteworthy that the Romans imposed tribute on the Illyrians after the conclusion of the war (Polyb. 2.12.3).

and the Rhodians' anti-piracy activities. The origins of the war are not fully presented in any of the surviving historical narratives, but they seem to go back to earlier rivalries among the Cretan cities and a series of inter-city disputes which led to the involvement of their allies.[135] The relation-ship between Rhodes and some of the Cretan cities went back well into the third century. In 305 BC the Knossians had given help to Rhodes when the island was besieged by Demetrios Poliorketes (Diod. 20.88.9), and in 220 BC the Knossians successfully appealed to the Rhodians for assistance in their war with Lyttos, gaining the help of a Rhodian naval force under the admiral Polemokles. This intervention resulted in the Eleuthernaians, who claimed that one of their citizens, Timarchos, had been killed by Polemokles in order to please the Knossians, declaring re-prisals against the Rhodians and beginning a war with them (Polyb. 4.53.1–2). The almost continuous warfare among the Cretan cities en-abled the Rhodians to play off one group of them against the other,[136] in an effort to control Cretan attacks against Rhodes' allies in the Cycladic islands, who suffered particularly from Cretan 'piracy', doubtless justified by the Cretans as acts of war or reprisal (Diod. 27.3). Although Rhodes did not, at this time, control the Nesiotic League, it seems that the lesser islands looked to her for leadership and protection. A decree of the second half of the third century BC from the island of Delos honours three Rhodian trierarchs and a navarch who were 'appointed by the people of the Rhodians for the protection of the islands and the safety of the Greeks'.[137] The nature of the mission that these men were carrying out is unclear. It could have been explicitly designed to control piracy, but the inscription does not say so. On the other hand, the language of the inscription illustrates nicely the Rhodians' own rather grandiose attitude to their position as the leading Aegean naval power, which the Cretans were challenging by their attacks on the islands.[138]

An important role in the First Cretan War is assigned to Philip V, king of Macedon, who had been president of the Cretan *koinon* since 217 BC,[139] and who took an active part through the agency of the Aito-

---

[135] On the origins and course of the war see Brulé (1978): 29–56; van Effenterre (1948): 213–24. Polybius makes Philip V responsible for the war, claiming that he sent Her-akleides to incite a war between Rhodes and the Cretans (Polyb. 13.5). I cannot see any reason to give credence to the unlikely story of Herakleides' ruse in Polyaen. 5.17.2.

[136] See Willetts (1955): 234–41 for a brief account of these 'Social Wars'.

[137] *IG* XI.4.596; Durrbach (1921), no. 39. See also no. 40, a dedication of booty to Apollo by a Rhodian navarch and his men. On the date of no. 39 (*c.* 250–220 BC?) see Fraser and Bean (1954): 158.

[138] On the relative prominence of Egypt and Rhodes in the Cyclades see Will (1979–82): I 1231–3, 239–41; Fraser and Bean (1954): 94–108.

[139] Polyb. 4.53–5. The Antigonids, like other Hellenistic monarchs, saw Crete as a valuable recruiting ground for mercenaries and were keen to maintain good relations with as many of the Cretan cities as possible.

lian Dikaiarchos. According to Diodoros, Philip provided Dikaiarchos with 20 ships for the practice of piracy and instructed him to assist the Cretans against Rhodes: 'In accordance with these instructions he plundered merchant shipping and extorted money from the islands by raiding' (Diod. 28.1.1). In this version of events it appears that Dikaiarchos' main purpose was to raise money for Philip V, perhaps in order that the king could provide himself with a suitable navy for his ambitious foreign policies.[140] Were Dikaiarchos' activities simply plundering raids, worthy only of the designation piracy, or was he engaged in warfare and merely the victim of pejorative labelling? The answer to this question would seem to depend on one's point of view. Polybius says that his targets included the Hellespontine cities, which could mean that he concentrated his attacks on vessels trading between the Black Sea and Rhodes, though he may not have been too precise about selecting his prey (Polyb. 18.54.8–10). To the victims of his raids and his attacks on merchant shipping the answer would probably have been yes, he was a pirate, as were the Cretans whom he was supposedly assisting. Yet if it is assumed that he was paid for his efforts, then he could be called a mercenary, and from his employer's point of view he was collecting revenues, and helping Philip V's Cretan allies in their war with the Rhodians.[141] He was provided with ships by the Macedonian monarch. Were these ships, therefore, in some sense a part of the Macedonian royal navy? Unfortunately it is not possible to provide clear answers to these sorts of question. It may be that Philip operated through an agent in order not to be held *directly* responsible by the Greeks in general for the piratical activites of Dikaiarchos and the Cretans, since it is clear that what they were doing could be widely perceived as piracy, although systematic extortion of plunder had long been and was still an integral part of Greek warfare.[142] The scale of Dikaiarchos' operations and their political purpose make warfare seem a more appropriate modern label than piracy, but the distinction is a fine one. The First Cretan War shows how closely piracy and warfare were related in this period.

The First Cretan War seems to have been conducted in a series of raids and counter-raids, with the Rhodians' main opponents, besides Dikaiarchos, being Gortyn, Hierapytna and Eleuthernai. That the Rhodians eventually gained the upper hand is indicated by a treaty they made with Hierapytna in about 200 BC.[143] This treaty states that the Rhodians may

---

[140] Will (1979–82): II 104. The date of Dikaiarchos' expedition is uncertain, although the suggestion of 205 BC seems reasonable, Brulé (1978): 44–6.

[141] On the later mercenary activity of Dikaiarchos (and other Aitolians) in Ptolemaic service see Walbank (1957–79): II 625–6.

[142] See Jackson (1973) and above pp. 31–8.

[143] *SIG* 581 = *SdA* III no. 551. A date of 205/4 BC is suggested by Brulé (1978): 51–6.

recruit mercenaries in Crete, that they may use Hierapytna as a military and naval base and that they may require the Hierapytnians to assist them with auxiliary troops for warfare in defence of Rhodes. The Rhodians are clearly making demands from a position of strength, which the Hierapytnians have acceded to in return for the promise of Rhodian help if they fall foul of their Cretan neighbours, or their allies. The treaty also specifies ways in which the Hierapytnians must assist the Rhodians in the suppression of piracy:

(X) And if pirates establish bases in Crete and the Rhodians wage war at sea against the pirates or those who provide shelter or assistance to them, the Hierapytnians shall take part in the operations by land and sea with all possible strength and at their own expense. The pirates who are captured shall be handed over to the Rhodians together with their ships, while each of the allies shall take half of the rest [of the booty].

(XVII) And if during a campaign which the Hierapytnians are waging with the Rhodians to destroy a pirate base, any of those who provided shelter or assistance to the pirates wage war on the Hierapytnians because of this campaign, the Rhodians shall come to the help of the Hierapytnians with all possible strength, and anyone who acts in this way shall be an enemy of the Rhodians.[144]

The treaty seems to envisage a continued Rhodian interest in the suppression of piracy which will involve them in campaigns against Cretan-based pirates and their supporters. An immediate Rhodian desire to prevent further initiatives like that of Dikaiarchos would seem to be the most obvious reason for these anti-piracy clauses, although a longer-term policy of suppressing piracy would be most effective if the Rhodians could deny bases and ships to those they considered to be pirates. It is worth noting, however, that the treaty also included a clause excusing the Hierapytnians from participating in a war between the Rhodians and any other state with which they had an alliance. If the Rhodians could claim that this third party was engaged in piracy, or was sheltering or supporting pirates, then the Hierapytnians would not have an excuse for maintaining their neutrality. Fragments have been discovered of a similar treaty which was drawn up between Rhodes and the Cretan city of Olontos, at about the same time as the Hierapytnian one. There are corresponding passages on assistance in warfare, but nothing survives about the suppression of piracy. It is possible, however, that clauses of a similar nature to the ones in the Hierapytnian treaty were included in the full version.[145] It is easy to read too much into such documents, since they are literally preserved in

[144] I quote here from the translation in Austin (1981): no. 95.
[145] *SdA* III no. 552. For details of the corresponding clauses, partly restored with help from the Hierapytna treaty see Garlan (1969).

stone and suggest a permanence in political alignments which may be
illusory. Although the Rhodians had been the victors in the First Cretan
War and they were able to detach several cities away from the large *koi-*
*non* headed by Philip V, they had neither the opportunity nor the resources to bring all of the island's many communities under their control
by force. Treaties with former enemies could not be expected to last very
long, and even Knossos could not be guaranteed to remain on the Rhodian side.[146] In the short term, however, the prestige of the Rhodians was
greatly enhanced in the Aegean as a result of their chastisement of the
Cretans. Their position among the islanders was that of a strong protector, as a series of honorific inscriptions for Rhodians from this period indicates.[147] It is most likely that the reputation of the Rhodians as the
suppressors of piracy for the common good which Diodorus mentions
dates to this period (Diod. 20.81.3). Furthermore, in the early years of the
second century BC they were involved in a series of campaigns as allies of
the Romans, culminating in the defeat of Antiochos III in 189 BC, following which the Rhodians were rewarded with increased possessions on
the mainland and substantial trading privileges.[148]

### Nabis

The ruler of Sparta from *c.* 207 to 192 BC, Nabis, son of Demaratos, is
another good example of a victim of Polybius' character assassination. He
may, or may not, have been a legitimate king. The sources are unclear on
this point, as they are on many others concerning his fifteen-year period
of domination.[149] Polybius calls him a tyrant, and it is clear that he has
no sympathy for Nabis or his rule. He introduces him in the following
way:

Nabis, the tyrant of the Lakedaimonians, having already been ruling for two
years, had so far tried nothing of any consequence, the defeat of Machanidas by
the Aitolians being a recent occurrence, but he was busily laying the foundations
of a long-lived and oppressive tyranny. (Polyb. 13.6.1–2)

This part of Polybius' *Histories* continues with a catalogue of Nabis'
crimes and outrages. He murdered or drove into exile leading Spartans,
encouraged mercenaries, thieves and assassins and generally behaved in

---

[146] See van Effenterre (1948): 213–21.
[147] See van Gelder (1900): 450–64. On the revival of the Nesiotic League *c.* 200 BC, under
    Rhodian direction, see Fraser and Bean (1954): ch. V; Will (1979–82): II 80; Berthold
    (1984): 142–4; Gabrielsen (1997): 56–63.
[148] See Schmitt (1957); Will (1979–82): II chs. II, III.
[149] See Forrest (1980): 148–9; Cartledge and Spawforth (1989): 67–9.

the manner appropriate to an oppressive tyrant. Polybius next provides a particularly salacious description of an 'iron maiden' device which Nabis used to torture rich citizens in order to obtain their money.[150] Having finished with this he continues by saying: 'The rest of what he did during his rule was much the same as this. For he took part in piracy with the Cretans; he filled the Peloponnese with temple-looters, robbers, murderers ...' (Polyb. 13.8.1–2). The catalogue of wickedness continues in the same vein, with more spicy details. Polybius' bias in the case of Nabis is obvious and undisputed, but historians have, on the whole been prepared to believe the accusations of piracy. Livy makes the Roman proconsul Titus Quinctius Flamininus accuse him of the same:

You arranged not only an alliance with Philip our enemy, but, if the gods may allow, you even fixed a close union through Philocles, his prefect, and waging war against us, you made the sea around Malea unsafe with pirate ships, and you captured and killed almost more Roman citizens than Philip, and the coast of Macedonia was safer than the promontory of Malea for the ships carrying provisions to our armies. Refrain, therefore, if you please, from boasting about trust and the rights of alliance, and, putting popular oratory aside, speak as befits a tyrant and an enemy. (Livy 34.32.17–20)

Livy has already made Flamininus repeat some of the accusations brought against Nabis in Polybius' description, and there is no doubting that Polybius is the ultimate source of this speech.[151] Livy has taken the opportunity provided by the appearance of Nabis in his narrative to work in a fine display of historical rhetoric, but the accusation of practising piracy carries even less weight here than it does in Polybius. The function of the charge of piracy is to discredit Nabis, and to highlight the moral rectitude and military power of Romans who intend to suppress the evil of piracy. Yet Brulé argues that during the First Cretan War Nabis sided with the Rhodians and their allies, against Philip V and the Cretan cities grouped around Gortyn.[152] This might appear to place him on the side of the anti-piratical forces in the Aegean, although consideration of the nature of Rhodes' Cretan allies suggests that there were no such clear divisions.[153] Later on in the second century BC Nabis is clearly siding with the Aitolians, and Polybius' attitude to him is likely to be coloured by this, as well as his pro-Achaian bias. Nabis also had connections with Delos, where he was acknowledged as a benefactor of the sanctuary,

---

[150] On the nature of this description, slightly garbled by the Epitomator, see Walbank (1957–79): ad loc.
[151] See Briscoe (1973–81): ad loc.
[152] Brulé (1978): 49–50.
[153] See above pp. 80–4; see also the discussion of Nabis' relations with Crete in Karafotias (1997): ch. 6.

which was also a major trading centre.[154] There is, however, a danger of reading too much into this kind of thing. While a large number of the dedications and inscriptions of Delos in the third and second centuries BC relate to the Rhodians and speak of order and peace, there are also plenty that are dedicated by or to Aitolians.[155] Polybius' picture of Nabis as wholly bad is not necessarily borne out by other sources. His associations with others who are regularly called pirates has resulted in a similar label being applied to him. He was a leading figure in the violent and often unprincipled world of Hellenistic politics, so he cannot be viewed as any kind of saint; but then neither can most of his contemporaries.[156]

## Rhodes and Rome

The fleet which Philip V of Macedon put into action in the Aegean during the last few years of the third century BC was not particularly successful.[157] His activities seem to some extent to have stimulated piracy in this region, however, and the Roman commanders who started to make regular appearances in the Aegean at this time were called upon to counter it.

In 200 BC the consul Publius Sulpicius Galba, who was wintering at Apollonia, despatched one of his legates, Gaius Claudius Centho,[158] to Athens with some Roman triremes to deal with raids by land and piratical attacks on the coastline from Chalkis.

Their arrival at Piraeus brought much needed relief for the allies, who were in a desperate state. They had been subjected to regular attacks on their territory out of Corinth and Megara, which now ceased; and the pirate ships from Chalcis, which had not only infested the sea, but also all the coastal lands of the Athenians, would neither sail past Sunium nor dare to venture beyond the Straits of Euripus into the open sea. There also came an additional three Rhodian quadriremes, and there were three undecked Athenian ships, all gathered to defend the coastal lands.[159] (Livy 31.22)

Who was operating these pirate ships? It may have been allies of Philip V, or it could have merely been that independent pirates were exploiting the state of war to raid one territory from the relative safety of another, which was held by enemy forces.[160] In the peace settlement between Flamininus

---

[154] *SIG* 584; Durrbach (1921): no. 58. On Delos as a trading centre see Rauh (1993) and Rostovtzeff (1941).
[155] See Durrbach (1921): 273–6 for a list of dedicators arranged geographically.
[156] The revisionist view of Cartledge in Cartledge & Spawforth (1989): ch. 5 is most important for all of the above.
[157] See Will (1979–81): II 121–30.
[158] *MRR* I 323 and 325.
[159] See Briscoe (1973–81): ad loc.
[160] Chalkis was Philip V's last major stronghold on Euboia; see Will (1979–82): II 167.

and Nabis in 195 BC, a major concern of the Romans seems to have been to limit the potential of the Spartans to interfere in naval activity by freeing the coastal settlements of Lakonia from their control, severing Nabis' ties with Crete and limiting him to only two small galleys (Livy 34.35–6). Thus he was left with neither the ships nor the bases to engage in 'piracy'.[161]

Philip V was not the only Hellenistic monarch who is said to have benefited from the participation of pirates in warfare. In 190 BC the Seleukid king Antiochos III was engaged in a naval struggle in the Aegean against the forces of Eumenes II of Pergamon, the Rhodians and a Roman navy. His admiral Polyxenidas defeated the Rhodians, under the command of Pausistratos, at Panhormos, in which engagement a certain Nikandros was prominent on the Seleukid side: 'Then he ordered Nicander, a certain pirate chief, to make for Palinurus with five decked ships, and then to lead the soldiers by the shortest route across the fields to the rear of the enemy, while he himself made for Panhormus, dividing the fleet in order to hold the harbour entrance on both sides' (Livy 37.11.6).[162] Nikandros' arrival forced Pausistratos to abandon his plan to attack on land and attempt a breakout by sea, which was defeated by Polyxenidas. Nikandros captured some of the Rhodian ships on a beach, while they were still trying to embark (Livy 37.11.7–13). Nothing more is said about this pirate chief in Livy's narrative. He seems to have been a competent commander, and one trusted by Polyxenidas, but the significance of the term *archipirata* which Livy applies to him is difficult to determine. Does it mean that Nikandros was in command of a large force of pirates? Does it mean that he had once been a pirate leader? Or is it merely a pejorative label which has been applied to him by his (Rhodian?) opponents?[163] It is very difficult to reach clear conclusions about such individual cases which are reported in non-comtemporary sources.

Evidence of continued Rhodian interest in the control of piracy comes from another Delian honorific inscription, dated to the early second century BC:

Decided by the council and the people. Telemnestos, son of Aristeides, proposed: since Epikrates, son of Polystratos, of Rhodes, sent to war by the people in decked

---

[161] Cartledge and Spawforth (1989): 75–7.

[162] The same events are reported by Appian, who calls Nikandros a *peirates* (App. *Syr.* 24–5).

[163] See above for other 'archpirates'. Note the reference in the third-century BC inscription *SIG* 521 to a pirate leader as: 'the one in charge of the pirates on ship' (τὸν ἐπὶ τῶν πειρατῶν ἐπιπλέοντα). Why not use the term ἀρχιπειράτης? Perhaps, given the date of all the sources which use it, ἀρχιπειράτης was a late Republican invention? It is conceivable that it comes from a phrase which had the meaning 'formerly a pirate' (ἐν ἀρχῇ πειρατής), but there are no obvious linguistic parallels.

ships, accompanied on campaign by the triremes of the islanders and the undecked ships of the Athenians, took care of the safety of shipping and the islands, with due reverence for the sanctuary, passing an edict that the ones practising piracy against the enemies should base themselves in their own ports, and that no-one should use Delos as a base, in accordance with the manifest wishes of the people ...[164]

The date of this inscription has been the subject of some debate. It is impossible to assign an exact context to it from the internal evidence, and the external evidence is inconclusive. Some scholars believe that it refers to events at the time of the Second Macedonian War (200–196 BC), while others prefer to assign it to the period of the Syrian War between Rome and Antiochos III (192–189 BC).[165] Evidence to support the latter view includes the mention of undecked Athenian ships among the vessels accompanying Epikrates, described by Livy in his account of Roman and Rhodian naval activities in 190 BC (Livy 37.13.11–14.1):

The praetor [Gaius Livius] sent two allied triremes from Italy and two Rhodian ones under the command of the Rhodian Epicrates to guard the straits of Cephallenia. The Spartan Hybristas was practising piracy there with the Cephallenian young men, and the sea was now closed to supplies from Italy. At Piraeus Epicrates met Lucius Aemilius Regillus, who had succeeded to the naval command. When he heard about the Rhodian débâcle he led Epicrates and his four ships back with him to Asia, since he only had two ships of his own; they were also accompanied by some undecked Athenian ships.[166]

Nothing more is said by Livy about Hybristas and the Kephallenians, so it must be assumed that the problem was only a temporary one. Possibly another force was sent to deal with the pirates, or they ceased their operations before the Romans had time to organize anything more. Polybius, commenting on Philip V's attack on Kephallenia in 218 BC, claims that the Kephallenians regularly joined the Aitolians in plundering the mainland (Polyb. 5.3.7). This observation might indicate that the Kephallenians were simply taking advantage of the piratical opportunities offered by the frequent sea traffic between Italy and Greece during the war with Antiochos III. On the other hand the presence of a Spartan commander, albeit one whose name means 'arrogant', is suggestive of a co-ordinated

---

[164] *SIG* 582 = Durrbach (1921): no. 67, lines 1–17. The last few lines speak of the importance of good order and justice. The phrase translated as 'the ones practising piracy' is οἱ πειρατεύοντες.

[165] Second Macedonian War: Ormerod (1924): 133; Briscoe (1973–81): notes to Livy 31.22. Syrian War: Durrbach (1921): 89–91; Jackson (1973): 252–3; Berthold (1984): 155.

[166] The Rhodian fleet had recently suffered a heavy defeat at Samos. Their admiral Pausistratos had been killed (Livy 37.11; App. *Syr.* 24–5). Livy calls Nikandros, one of the Seleukid fleet commanders, an archpirate, although Appian simply calls him a pirate.

approach by Rome's enemies. It is, however, unclear whether Hybristas was operating on behalf of anyone else.[167]

Epikrates may have stopped off at Delos on his way to or from Piraeus. The measures for which he is honoured in the Delian inscription seem not to be aimed at suppressing piracy, but merely at forbidding those who are practising it from operating out of Delos. The victims of the pirates in this instance are apparently also enemies of the Rhodians. The pirates may, therefore, be allies of Rhodes, perhaps even from Crete.[168] The implication of this honorific inscription is that piracy practised against Rhodes' allies should be suppressed, but piracy practised aginst Rhodes' enemies can be tolerated.[169] Epikrates' status as a naval ally of Rome would have lent an extra bit authority to his edict, perhaps even the hint of Roman force to back it up. The attraction of Delos to the pirates was that it offered ample opportunities for the disposal of booty, being already a thriving market for all kinds of trade. The danger for the Delians was that they might become the object of counter-raids, and so be swept up in the current war, much as the Aiginetans were caught up in the Corinthian War in 389 BC.[170] In order to preserve their security and a certain degree of neutrality they persuaded the representative of a powerful naval alliance to warn any pirates off.

Later on in the same year, just before the naval battle of Myonnessos, some Roman ships encountered pirates who had been plundering the island of Chios, where the Romans had recently established their main supply-base. The pirate vessels fled at the approach of Lucius Aemilius and his ships (Livy 37.27–8; Polyb. 21.12). Once again it is possible that these ships may have been attached to the forces of Antiochos III,[171] but equally they could have been opportunists who seized the chance offered by the war between Antiochos and Rome to raid the island while the Romans and their allies were busy elsewhere. There seems at first glance to have been quite a lot of piracy going on in conjunction with the wars in the Eastern Mediterranean at this time, although the extent to which the pirates were *directly* involved in the warfare is often unclear and seems

---

[167] Polybius associates the Spartan tyrant Nabis with piracy (13.8.1–2) and Livy (34.32.17–20) has Flamininus accuse him of making the seas around Cape Malea unsafe for shipping with his pirate vessels, but there are no indications of direct Spartan involvement in the war with Antiochos. On Sparta and Rome at this time see Cartledge and Spawforth (1989): 75–9.

[168] As suggested by Brulé (1978): 48–9.

[169] It should be noted that there is nothing in the terms of the treaty between Rhodes and Hierapytna, discussed above, which prevents the Hierapytnians from practising piracy against those designated as enemies of Rhodes.

[170] See above p. 34.

[171] As suggested by Briscoe (1973–81): ad loc.

in general to have been very limited. Certain named individuals (e.g. Nikandros, Hybristas) may have been labelled 'pirates' in the sources in order to present them in an unfavourable light, as is perhaps the case with some of the 'archpirates' discussed earlier in this chapter. The main historical narratives for this period are very biased in their presentation of the enemies of Rome, Rhodes and other states. The mention of pirates fighting for the 'other' side could well be the result of such a bias. The Epikrates inscription from Delos suggests that both sides in the conflicts of the early second century might tolerate or even promote piracy in their own interests. The literary image of the Rhodians and their Roman allies was one which required them to be kept out of the story.

It is also important to realize that while the ancient sources make a great deal out of the strategic implications of piratical activities, which threatened military supply routes and the movement of troops, the main object of the perpetrators of such raids would have been the acquisition of booty, which was so much a commonplace of ancient warfare that it could usually be taken for granted by ancient historians and their readers. When Hybristas led the young Kephallenians out to attack ships coming from Italy, it is more likely to have been the prospect of obtaining goods and slaves than the possibility of disrupting the Roman war effort which prompted them to act. It is no surprise that the pirates encountered by Aemilius in 190 BC chose to flee rather than engage with the Roman naval forces and risk losing the plunder with which they had filled their ships at Chios.

The difficulty of coping with piracy remained a serious concern for the Rhodians in the second century BC, particularly when it was compounded by the external political policies and the internal social tensions of the Cretan cities.[172] The Rhodians' own problems with reluctant subjects on the mainland also involved them in long bouts of warfare, as did commitments to their Roman allies. After 164 BC, when the senate undermined their privileged position in the Aegean, making Delos a free port and liberating several cities of the *Peraia*, two of the mainstays of the Rhodian economy, maritime trade and exploitation of the resources of the mainland, were severely reduced, as was the Republic's ability to act against pirates (Polyb. 30.31.10). Rhodes went to war with her Cretan enemies again in 155–153 BC, having failed to get satisfaction by diplomatic means, which suggests that although the treaties of the third cen-

---

[172] On the troubled relationships between the aristocracy and the lower classes in Hellenistic Crete see Willetts (1955) and Brulé (1978). The latter's researches indicate a complex range of economic and social imperatives behind the rise of Cretan piracy in the third century, but see Walbank (1980) and Karafotias (1997).

tury may stil have been valid, their effectiveness was heavily dependent
upon the perceived status of Rhodes. Her forces were defeated, apparently on more than one occasion, but they did have some success in re-
pulsing the Cretans from the Cyclades (Polyb. 33.17; Diod. 31.43–5).[173]
This time, however, the conflict was brought to an end by Roman intervention, underlining the humiliating decline in the position of Rhodes.
She had gone from being an independent maritime power to a weak, dependent ally of the Romans.

Laudable though their efforts were, the Rhodians could not have been
expected to suppress piracy over a large area, or for a long time. No
amount of successful campaigning on Crete or elsewhere, with or without
Rome help, could remove the menace of piracy from the seas. In the first
place there were far too many locations for pirates to operate from, and,
secondly, the conflicts and rivalries of the Hellenistic period provided a
wealth of targets and opportunities to attack them. Even at the height of
their power it is likely that the Rhodians were barely scratching the sur-
face of a deep-rooted problem. The inscription from the Athenian colony
on the island of Imbros quoted at the opening of this book shows the kind
of unexpected piratical attack to which exposed coastal settlements were
vulnerable in this period.[174] Once again the identity of the attackers and
the particular reason for their raid are unknown. From the potential victims' point of view these things were of little consequence. It was the immediate threat to lives and possessions which dominated their perceptions
of such episodes. Lysanias' warning may not have prevented the attack,
but at least the people had a chance to defend themselves, or to flee with
their valuables to places of safety, which might have discouraged the
pirates. There is no sign in this inscription of any protection from one of
the naval powers of the Hellenistic Mediterranean.

In the long run it was only the Romans, as masters of the Mediterranean, who would be in a position to offer general protection against
piracy, but their assumption of the mantle of the Rhodians was a long
and slow process. It has been suggested that the Romans' solution to the
problem of piratical attacks on the western coasts of Italy in the fourth
and third centuries BC was to occupy the potential bases, as at Antium
in 338 BC (Livy 8.14).[175] It would, however, be rash to presume that
the prevention of piracy was the motive behind the foundation of all of
Rome's maritime colonies. The Roman colonies founded on the Italian
coast in the 190s BC may have had some impact in discouraging piracy,

---

[173] See Brulé (1978): 57–66; Schmitt (1957): 145–51.
[174] IG XII.8.53, lines 1–13; see above p. 1.
[175] Ormerod (1924): 161–6.

but other, more convincing explanations have been advanced for them (Livy 32.29.3; 34.45.2–4).[176]

The Romans seem to have become involved in the suppression of piracy during the third and second centuries BC. Polybius' claim that their intervention in Illyria in 229 BC was to protect traders against pirates may be doubted (Polyb. 2.8),[177] as may the explanation of the Istrian war of 221 BC (Eutr. 3.7; App. *Ill.* 8),[178] but one result of these campaigns could well have been to reduce the dangers to shipping and coastal settlements in this region.

The Ligurians also had a reputation for piracy which is advanced by the sources at several points to explain Roman campaigns in the second century BC. Roman armies were active against them from 197 BC onwards (Livy 37.57.1–2). In 182 BC complaints about both the Histrians and the Ligurians were received at Rome:

When the consuls had been inaugurated, the provinces were assigned as follows. Liguria went to the consuls ... the Histrians were added on because it was announced by the people of Tarentum and Brundisium that their coastal territories were under threat from pirate ships from across the sea. The people of Massilia made the same complaint about the ships of the Ligurians. (Livy 40.18.3–4)

After a defeat by Lucius Aemilius Paullus, Livy says that the Romans rounded up the captains and crews of the Ligurian pirate ships, and the *duumvir* Gaius Matienus captured 32 vessels (Livy 40.28.7; Plut. *Aem.* 6.2–3). There were many more campaigns against the Ligurians, who continued to resist Roman domination and, according to our sources, to practise piracy, well into the first century BC.[179] The sort of priorities which determined Rome's external policies in both the Eastern and Western Mediterranean towards the end of the second century BC can, however, be illustrated from a relatively minor episode in Roman history.

### Metellus Balearicus

The year 123 BC was a momentous one in the history of the Roman Republic. The first tribunate of Gaius Gracchus saw much political activity and the introduction of a series of measures which affected the lives of millions of people across the whole of the Roman world. At the same time one of the consuls, Quintus Caecilius Metellus, probably taking the *pro-*

[176] Salmon (1969): ch. 4: Briscoe (1973–81): ad loc.
[177] See above pp. 76–80.
[178] See Dell (1970): 34–6. He prefers Appian's explanation of the aggression of Demetrios of Pharos as a motive for Roman intervention.
[179] See below and also Harris (1989): 114–18.

*vincia* of Hispania Citerior (Nearer Spain),[180] campaigned successfully in the Balearic Islands and celebrated a triumph on his return in 121 BC. His conquest of the islands even earned him the title 'Balearicus'. The Epitomator of Livy, more concerned with the excitement surrounding Gracchus than 'foreign affairs', is very brief in his reporting of this event: 'Another thing contained in this book is the achievement of Quintus Metellus against the Baleares, whom the Greeks call "nudists", because they spend the summer lying around naked. They are called Baleares from the missiles they sling, or on account of Balius, a companion of Hercules whom he left behind when he sailed off after Geryon' (Livy, *Per.* 60). The crucial detail which the Epitomator omits is the reason for Metellus' conquest of the islands. Fortunately this is supplied by other sources. Orosius gives a brief notice: 'Metellus, having gone to the Balearic Islands to make war, conquered them and, in the course of quashing an outbreak of piracy which had arisen there, killed many of the inhabitants' (Oros. 5.13.1). This account is further supplemented by Florus who, after describing Quintus Caecilius Metellus Creticus' exploits, continues the story of Metellan triumphs: 'Since the house of Metellus Macedonicus was becoming accustomed to assuming surnames from wars, another of his sons was not slow in following the example of Creticus, this one being called Balearicus. At this time the Balearic islanders were plaguing the seas with their ferocious piracy' (Florus 1.43.1–2).[181] Florus explains that the islanders, who were primitive people, used roughly made rafts to attack passing ships. They employed their famous slings against Metellus' fleet and soldiers, but to little effect.

A slightly different version of the events is given by Strabo in the third book of his *Geography*. In the course of a discussion of the peaceable nature of these people, which is apparently due to the fertility of their soil, he says: 'On account of the dealings between a few of their worse elements and the pirates,[182] they were all falsely accused, and Metellus, who was surnamed Balearicus, came against them. He it was who founded the cities' (Str. 3.5.1). Strabo also mentions the fact that Metellus settled 3,000 'Romans' (probably veterans) from Spain in the islands. They formed two

---

[180] See Richardson (1986): 157 n. 5 and Appendix III.

[181] Florus' chronology is more than a little wayward. Creticus and Balearicus were certainly not brothers. His accounts of wars against pirates in Book 1 of his *Epitome of all the Wars over 1200 Years*, written in the second century AD, are arranged geographically – Cilicia, Crete, Balearics, Cyprus.

[182] Strabo's Greek here is: τοὺς ἐν τοῖς πελάγεσι λῃστάς, which the Loeb translation of H. L. Jones (1917–32): 125 renders as 'pirates of the high seas'. Morgan (1969) bases a lot of his argument about Metellus' campaign on this over-elaborate translation. It is simply a case of Strabo using a qualifying phrase to indicate that λῃστής in this instance means 'pirate', rather than 'bandit'.

settlements on Mallorca. He adds the comment that the islanders have always suffered from the desire of others to possess their fertile land.[183]

Most modern historians have made little of this episode in the Romans' suppression of piracy, being content simply to mention it or to pass over it entirely.[184] The only recent attempt to analyse Metellus' conquest, by M. G. Morgan, has sought to explain it in terms of a sudden outbreak of piracy, caused by 'the pirates of the high seas' being driven out of their bases in Sardinia and Transalpine Gaul by the Romans, and escaping to the Balearics. The decision of the Romans to send a consul to conquer the islands is explained by pressure from the people of Massilia.[185] Morgan wants to absolve the Baleares of blame for piracy, and sees the campaign of Metellus as a continuation of Roman efforts to drive out pirates along the route from Italy to Spain. This is possible, but there is no clear evidence of any pirates being driven out of these areas at this time. Morgan seizes upon Orosius' description of piracy having 'arisen' in the islands to claim that it was 'a sudden outbreak of piracy', which 'provided the Romans with an excellent reason for taking action when they did and as they did'.[186] A passage in Diodorus' description of the islands, however, indicates that pirates had been active there for some time.[187] Florus indicates that there was no sudden influx of pirates. Since both Florus and Orosius are likely to have derived their accounts from Livy, and Florus' account, in spite of his mistake about Metellus, is the longer one, it seems to me that he cannot be brushed aside in favour of a rather forced interpretation of Orosius. The sources do not agree, either, as to who the pirates were. Florus is quite clear that it was the Baleares themselves who were to blame, and his description of their methods is a perfectly credible one.[188] Strabo seems to be sure that only a few of the islanders were involved in piracy. This may be true, but it does not follow that any pirates

---

[183]  Strabo's comments on the peaceable life of the Baleares need not necessarily be believed. His brand of geographical determinism, derived in part from Poseidonios, requires that piratical peoples inhabit sterile and unproductive areas. See Str. 11.2.12 and 17.3.24 on the Heniochi and others; see below pp. 200–04 on Strabo and piracy.

[184]  E.g. Scullard (1982): 41; Harris (1979); Stockton (1981); Greenidge & Clay (1960). Ormerod (1924) is the obvious exception.

[185]  Morgan (1969).

[186]  Morgan (1969): 223. Orosius' word is *exoriebatur*.

[187]  Diod. 5.17.3, referring to the, apparently, common problem of pirates sailing in and stealing women.

[188]  'You might think that these savage woodsmen would not even dare to look out to sea from their rocks. Yet they also used to board simple rafts and terrorize passing ships with their sudden, unexpected attacks. Indeed, when they observed from on high the approach of the Roman fleet, thinking of plunder, they even dared to launch an attack ...' (Flor. 1.43.2–4). Compare the description of the Uskoks' methods in Tenenti (1967). They also employed small vessels to launch surprise attack on much larger ones.

based in the islands were recent arrivals from the southern coast of Gaul. In addition, I think that Strabo's main concern here is to make the situation conform to his theory that piracy is the product of poor lands.[189]

Why did the Romans choose this moment to conquer the Balearic Islands? In the first place, it would seem reasonable to associate the move with a real concern to remove the problem of pirates emanating from these islands. Their methods were strikingly effective. Florus describes the natives fleeing from the Romans, 'like bellowing cattle', and mentions a prolonged search-and-destroy operation among the hills (Flor. 1.43.6).[190] The effectiveness of this aggressive Roman action, and of the subsequent garrisoning of Mallorca, seems to be borne out by the fact that we hear nothing more about pirates from the Balearics in the Late Republic after Metellus' campaign.[191] Pompey stationed one of his legates there during the campaign of 67 BC, but there is no indication of any action (Flor. 1.41.9). Communities of Roman citizens were being established in Southern Gaul at this time, partly to consolidate the route from Italy to Spain.[192] Campaigns against the Ligurians had been a regular feature of Roman military activity since early in the second century BC, with piracy a complaint made against them by the Massilians.[193] It should also be noted that archaeological evidence indicates that the volume and intensity of trade between Italy and the southern coast of France was increasing in this period. Finds of amphorae and especially shipwrecks suggest that there was plenty of shipping for the Baleares to attack.[194] Metellus' campaign is best seen as part of this process of conquest of the Western Mediterranean. Piracy may have been particularly troublesome at this time, but the establishment of veteran settlements at Palma and Pollentia on Mallorca ensured that Roman control was secure.[195] It should also not be overlooked that Metellus gained a triumph and the resultant pres-

[189] Morgan (1969) argues that it is Poseidonios' theory on the peaceable nature of the inhabitants of fertile lands which is behind Strabo's account. According to Morgan, Poseidonios wrote an account of the Baleares which was 'apologetic' in tone and based on interviews with the islanders. The problem with this approach is that it is too conjectural. The version which we have is Strabo's, not Poseidonios'. Whatever the latter may have written or done, it is impossible to know without direct attestation.

[190] Compare Orosius' reference to many deaths among the inhabitants (Oros. 5.13.1).

[191] In 81 BC Sertorius and his Cilician 'allies' briefly captured Ibiza, but left after a battle with the forces of Gaius Annius (Plut. *Sert.* 7–9). See below pp. 132–4 on Sertorius.

[192] Aquae-Sextiae (124 BC); Narbo Martius (c. 118 BC). There was some political opposition to these colonies at Rome. See Scullard (1982): 39–41; Drinkwater (1983): 5–7; Salmon (1969): 121–36. See also Stockton (1979): App. 1 on the Gracchan colonies.

[193] See above pp. 91–2.

[194] See in general Cunliffe (1985). On shipwrecks note especially Almagro & Vilar (1973), Charlin et al. (1978), Long (1988) and Company (1971); more recent finds in Parker (1992).

[195] Morgan (1969): 226 tries to link the episode with Gaius Gracchus' tribunate.

tige from his victory. This aspect of Roman military action was just as important as any strategic considerations.[196]

[196] See Harris (1979). Note the phrasing of Orosius' account: 'Metellus, having gone to the Balearic islands to make war' (Oros. 5.13.1). See below pp. 141–5 for further Roman attempts to secure the navigation of the Western Mediterranean.

# 4    Cilician piracy

By the 70s BC the region of Southern Anatolia known as Rough Cilicia and the neighbouring district of Pamphylia were notorious as the homeland of pirates whose exploits terrorized the inhabitants of the Mediterranean. The origins of these 'Cilician' pirates are obscured by two main factors: firstly, the lack of contemporary sources for the second half of the second century BC, particularly for events in the Eastern Mediterranean; secondly, the tendency of later sources to portray the growth of piracy in this region in moralistic terms which oversimplify the phenomenon and distort its development. Since many of them are essentially discussing piracy as a problem which was 'solved' by Pompey in 67 BC, they also tend to present it as a continuously growing menace to the Mediterranean world which assumes such enormous proportions that only a heroic figure like Pompey can possibly defeat it.[1] The most important source is Strabo, who had scant regard for the Pamphylians and Cilicians. He believed that they had exploited the rugged coastline of Southern Anatolia, with its many harbours for piracy, in contrast to the Lycians, who refrained from piracy:[2]

For that matter the nature of their territory is more or less the same as that of the Pamphylians and Rough Cilicians. But they (the Pamphylians and Rough Cilicians) made use of such places as bases for the practice of piracy, either being pirates themselves, or else furnishing the pirates with markets for their plunder and docking facilities. At Side, at any rate, a city of Pamphylia, the docks were set up for the benefit of the Cilicians: they used to sell their captives there by auction, admitting that they were free men. (14.3.2)

Other writers of the Principate, including Appian (*Mith.* 92), Dio (36.20–23) and Plutarch (*Pomp.* 24) present a similar picture of the Cilicians and Pamphylians as dyed-in-the-wool pirates. While it is impossible to reconstruct a full, detailed narrative of events relating to the Cilician pirates, there is enough evidence to enable the modern historian to discern the broad outlines.

---

[1] See below pp. 172–8 on the 'legend' of Pompey and the pirates.
[2] See below pp. 200–04 on Strabo's general approach to piracy.

## Tryphon and the growth of Cilician piracy

The earliest example of a pirate leader in this region is Diodotus Tryphon, who led a revolt against the rule of the Seleukid monarchs in the late 140s BC. Strabo attributes the origin of Cilician piracy to the operations conducted by this rebel who seized control of much of Syria from his base at Korakesion.[3] Korakesion was a safe base for Diodotus because it lay well beyond the geographical limits of Seleukid power as defined by the treaty of Apamea in 188 BC.[4] On the other hand it was ideally situated for attacking the Syrian coastline and the cities of the Levant.[5] Tryphon's aim seems to have been to supplant the Seleukids in Syria and to this end he encouraged Cilicians to carry out piratical raids. Strabo says very little about the operations of Tryphon, nor do our other sources offer much help. It seems clear, however, that he used his small fleet and the resources of his Cilician 'allies' in an attempt to force the coastal cities of the Levant to submit to his rule.[6] He was ultimately unsuccessful, as Strabo relates:

> However, having been blockaded in a certain place by Antiochos, son of Deme-trios, he was compelled to take his own life. But for the Cilicians this was the be-ginning of organized piracy, Tryphon being responsible for establishing them, along with the incompetence of the succession of kings who ruled over both Syria and Cilicia at that time. (Str. 14.5.2)

What Strabo appears to be saying here is that Tryphon was initially responsible for the establishment of pirates operating out of Cilicia; perhaps he furnished them with ships, in the manner of Philip V and Dikaiarchos.[7] Thereafter the political chaos which followed his rebellion, as the rival Syrian kings fought amongst each other, made it easy for 'undesirable elements' to take control in Cilicia, and allowed piracy to continue from the same fortified bases.[8] The piratical activities of the Cilicians probably had little effect on the outcome of Tryphon's wars. They would have raided the rich cities of the Syrian and Phoenician coastline, and the

---

[3] Str. 14.5.2.

[4] See McDonald (1967) and McDonald & Walbank (1969).

[5] Str. 16.2.19 records that Berytos was destroyed by Tryphon.

[6] See Maróti (1962b) for speculations about Tryphon from the very meagre sources. His desire to rule a unified kingdom seems to have run up against opposition from the prosperous coastal cities, which preferred weak kings, or even no kings at all, to strong rulers who might expect far more from them. Arados, for example, refused to co-operate with the Cilician-based 'pirates' (Str. 16.2.14).

[7] See above pp. 81–3.

[8] Several other Seleukid pretenders based themselves in Cilicia at one time or another between c. 150 and 70 BC. On the political situation see Will (1979–82): II 373–79, 404–13, 434–57. For the latest research on the location and nature of the coastal bases used by pirates and others in this period see Rauh (1999b).

shipping which passed into the Aegean for profit. After his demise they continued to do so, with considerable success. Appian speaks of the leaders of these pirate groups as 'tyrants' or 'kings' (App. *Mith.* 92; 117), some of whom were notorious (and powerful) enough to enter the historical record.[9] According to Strabo the enemies of the Seleukids, principally the Ptolemaic kings of Egypt and Cyprus, did little to hinder this development as they saw it as a means of weakening their rival (Str. 14.5.2). The pattern which seems to emerge from these examples is of the creation of 'fiefdoms' of varying sizes along the southern coast of Anatolia, from Rough Cilicia to Pamphylia, in which individual leaders exercise autocratic power and from which (it is implied) they direct piratical forces against their neighbours and more distant targets. Rulers of small fiefdoms which lay further inland were less of a threat as they could not easily project their power across long distances. They remained small-scale 'bandit' leaders, acknowledging neither the authority of the Seleukids, nor that of Rome, nor (unless it suited them) that of any of Rome's enemies. Those whose domains were coastal in nature had the opportunity to extend their sway across the sea, raiding (or threatening to raid?) in a manner reminiscent of the Aitolians and Cretans.[10]

Strabo continues his explanation of the growth of Cilician piracy by linking it with the slave trade (Str. 14.5.2). He says that the ready availability of persons for capture and the proximity of a rich market at Delos, fuelled by the wealth of the Romans and their demand for slaves, meant that the pirates operating out of Cilicia seized people to sell as slaves, as well as other plunder.[11] Indeed, Strabo speaks of the Cilicians 'passing themselves off as slavers' (Str. 14.5.2).[12] Modern scholars have drawn attention to this comment and deduced that the lack of decisive Roman intervention against the Cilician pirates was a result of their selfish desire to preserve the Cilicians as an important source of slaves.[13] This interpretation seems to be unnecessary, as there is no firm evidence that the Cilicians were vital to Rome's slave-supply. Roman indifference to piracy is

---

[9] E.g. Zeniketos (Str. 14.5.7); Kleochares (Memnon, *FGrHist.* 434 fr. 1.53); Niko (Cic. *II Verr.* 5.77). See below pp. 134–6.

[10] See above Ch. 3. Rauh (1998) argues that Cilician pirate communities differed significantly from those of Aitolia and Crete because they involved *only* the inhabitants of coastal plains and *not* those who dwelt in the mountains. On the nature of mountain and coastal interaction in Cilicia see Hopwood (1990) and (1991).

[11] Compare the 'haul' of the pirates who attacked Ephesos in the inscription quoted below, p. 100.

[12] The Greek text reads: οἱ λῃσταὶ προσποιούμενοι σωματεμπορεῖν.

[13] Ormerod (1924): 206–7; Marasco (1987b); Pohl (1993): 186–90. An exception is the excellent article by Avidov (1997), which appeared too late for me to give it full consideration here.

more appropriately explained by the fact that it did not, for a long time, affect the Romans in any significant way. Strabo says that a senatorial fact-finding mission to the Eastern Mediterranean led by Scipio Aemilianus (*c.* 140 BC) blamed the weakness of the Seleukids for the problem of piracy. The Romans clearly did not consider themselves responsible for the general 'security' of this region until at least the end of the second century BC, although they were partly to blame for the relative ineffectiveness of the Seleukids, and the weakness of Rhodes.

It should not be thought that pirates roamed freely in the Mediterranean during the second century BC, except when they were checked by the Romans in the campaigns outlined below. The friends, allies and subjects of Rome were not wholly dependent on Roman initiatives when it came to dealing with piracy. Unfortunately, because of the highly selective nature of the historical records available to us for this period, it is difficult to document the kinds of action which might be taken. Only occasionally are we given glimpses of actions against pirates which do not involve Rome. One such glimpse comes from an inscription recovered from Astypalaia. It is an honorary decree of the Ephesians for the Astypalaians, dated to the end of the second century, when Ephesos was part of the Roman province of Asia:[14]

Decided by the Council and the People. Moschion son of Menetos proposed, following the motion put to the Council by the *strategoi*, concerning the honours for the people of Astypalaia; since the Astypalaian men have conducted themselves like good and faithful friends of our People, having fought bravely against[15] ... [1 line] ... the pirates ... and wickedly ... [3 lines] ... from the sea ... [½ line] ... and[16] after the pirates sailed here and made an attack on our territory at Phygela and carried off persons from the shrine of Artemis Mounichia,[17] both free people and slaves, and plundered their property and many places in the surrounding area, the Astypalaians, drawn up for battle in response to the earlier reports from the Ephesians, sailed out against the pirates and, risking their lives, sparing no effort of mind or body, but exposing themselves to great danger in the ensuing fight, put to flight all their opponents[18] ... [2½ lines] ... among the ships ... [½ line] ... having driven the pirates and wrongdoers into the city of the Astypalaians, and having punished them on the spot, in accordance with their hatred of evildoers,

---

[14] The inscription is *IG* XII.3.171; also published in *IGSK* Ephesos 1a no. 5, which is the text I have translated here. Numbers in brackets refer to the length of the lacunae. See also Ziebarth (1929): 40. It is dated fairly certainly on the basis of the letter forms.

[15] There is little of lines 6–14 which can be made out. I have translated only those words which seem clear: πει[ρ]ατ[ῶν on lines 5–6, καὶ ἀνοσίος on lines 10–11 and ἐκ τῆς [θα]-λάσ[σης on lines 13–14.

[16] The text is virtually complete for the next ten lines (15–25).

[17] These places are on the coast to the south of Ephesos.

[18] The text is fragmentary again for the next three lines (25–7).

and having rescued the ones who were snatched away from our territory, and having discovered them to be our citizens, they looked after all of them and received them into their homes, providing each and every one with all that they needed for their daily care and bodily sustenance, caring for them just as for their own children. Similarly, they cared also for the dearly beloved children of free persons, protecting and nursing them ...[19]

It is clear that pirates have raided Ephesian territory and then been intercepted and defeated by the Astypalaians. The inscription implies that a signal, or a message, or report reached Astypalaia ahead of the pirates, and enabled the islanders to make military preparations. The sequence of events is obscured by the lacunae in the inscription. I would hazard a guess that the pirates might have been making for Crete, perhaps to dispose of their captives and their booty. Astypalaia is the 'last stop' before Crete, so it *could* have been a logical step to assume that the pirates would head that way, but this is only speculation.[20] The Astypalaians appear to have had some ships at their disposal, but this need not have been more than a handful of oared vessels and not a substantial war-fleet.

I would lay particular emphasis on two points which arise from this episode. In the first place, there is nothing in the inscription to connect the events with Cilicia, even in the widest sense of that term. The identity of the pirates is a mystery, since it is no more than a guess that they were connected with Crete. So the point to be made is that, in this period, not all pirates were necessarily Cilicians (or even Cretans). Secondly, the actions are carried out independently of any Roman authorities. Ephesos was part of a Roman province, and it is possible that this inscription dates from after 105 BC, when Astypalaia had a treaty of alliance with Rome, which included provisions to resist the enemies of Roman allies and subjects, by land and sea.[21] This particular episode concerns only the Ephesians and the Astypalaians, however, who seem to be capable of dealing quite effectively with piracy on a small scale. The point to be made, then, is that the suppression of piracy was the concern of both the Romans and their allies. Indeed, allied involvement was vital at all stages and in all areas, as will be demonstrated below.

[19] The remaining five lines of the inscription are very fragmentary and cannot be deciphered.

[20] See below pp. 145–7 on Cretans and piracy in this period. The summary justice meted out by the Astypalaians is no great surprise, but it would have prevented the pirates from explaining how they came to be there if the circumstances were at all suspicious.

[21] *IG* XII.3.173; Sherk (1969): no. 16, lines 29–34. It is conceivable that the treaty was prompted by Roman recognition of the strategic importance of Astypalaia as revealed by the sort of incident recorded in this inscription.

CARL A. RUDISILL LIBRARY
LENOIR-RHYNE COLLEGE

## Marcus Antonius the orator

The earliest evidence we have for military action by Rome against Cilician pirates is the campaign of Marcus Antonius the orator (*cos.* 99) in 102 BC. An attempt has been made by J.-L. Ferrary to argue that there was a campaign against the pirates in 103 BC, which could have been led by Marcus Antonius.[22] He bases this idea on a pair of undated inscriptions from Messene.[23] The inscriptions were set up in honour of Aristokles, secretary (*grammateus*) of the Messenian *synedrion*. They praise his skill and honesty in rendering the financial accounts for a special tax, and record the figures for the seventh month.[24] The tax itself was a 2% levy on individual and institutional wealth. It would appear to have raised the sum of nearly 100,000 *denarii*, encouraging two Romans, Memmius and Vibius, to give Aristokles a gold ring. Although both soldiers and oarsmen are mentioned in the accounts, they only figure as people from whom payment is outstanding. Ferrary plausibly identifies the Memmius mentioned as Gaius Memmius (*tr. pl.* 112) who could have been governor of Macedonia somewhere between 106 and 102 BC.[25] He appears to have been prosecuted in 103 BC on a *repetundae* charge, perhaps even for irregularities connected with the levy recorded on the Messenian inscriptions.[26] There is, however, nothing in the inscription to connect the levy with an expedition against pirates, nor any mention of an expedition before that of Marcus Antonius in the literary sources. Ferrary's suggestion is, in any case, highly speculative.[27] The only candidate for the leader of such an expedition would be Marcus Antonius himself, but the evidence indicates that his campaign was in 102 BC and not 103 BC.[28] It is also possible that in 103 BC he was in Rome for the trial of the tribune Gaius Norbanus.[29] What remains certain is that the only date which we have for

---

[22]   Ferrary (1977): 657.

[23]   *IG* V.1.1432 and 1433.

[24]   See Wilhelm (1914) for discussion of the details of the inscriptions and the tax itself. Giovannini (1978): 115–20 has tried to establish an imperial date for these inscriptions but I do not find his arguments convincing. Hopkins (1980): 121 n. 59 cites these inscriptions as evidence of the normal method of tax collection in the Principate, although the inscriptions seem to indicate an exceptional situation. I have benefited from discussion of these inscriptions with Tony Spawforth.

[25]   *MRR* I 559, 562, 564, 566. Memmius was the consular candidate killed on the orders of Saturninus in 100 BC (App. *Bell. civ.* 1.32–3; Livy, *Ep.* 69). He would therefore have been a praetor around 104 BC.

[26]   Val. Max. 8.5.2; Cic. *Font.* 24.

[27]   Ferrary (1977): 657 n. 138.

[28]   Obseq. *Prodig.* 44. The date is given by Obsequens as 'In the consulship of Gaius Marius and Quintus Lutatius', or 102 BC.

[29]   Cic. *Orat.* 2.107. It is more likely, however, that Norbanus' trial was in 95 BC; see Badian (1964): 34–70.

his campaign against the pirates is 102 BC. It seems to me that Ferrary's suggestion is plausible as far as it explains the use to which the levy was put, but I do not agree with his date for Antonius' expedition. It is probable, given the enormous military pressure that the Romans were under at this time, that the expedition was financed almost entirely from provincial resources.

The precise nature of Antonius' command has been the subject of some dispute.[30] The Epitomator of Livy records his activity thus: 'Marcus Antonius, praetor, pursued the pirates into Cilicia' (Livy, *Ep.* 68).[31] Julius Obsequens offers a similar account, under the year 102 BC: 'The pirates of Cilicia were destroyed by the Romans' (Obseq. *Prodig.* 44). An inscription from Rhodes which honours a naval officer who served under Antonius calls him proconsul,[32] and he is referred to as proconsul in a Latin inscription from Corinth.[33] He must have been praetor in either 103 or 102 BC. I would opt for the former, which means that he went out to his province immediately after his praetorship. His triumph is mentioned by Plutarch, and was possibly the reason for his presence outside Rome with troops in 100 BC.[34]

The extent of Antonius' campaign is not easy to establish, nor is it possible to be certain of the circumstances which led to his appointment.[35] He may have been assigned the province of Asia, rather than Cilicia, although it is evident that he did campaign in Cilicia.[36] It seems to me that there is no need to depart as far as some have done from the apparent meaning of the few references to this campaign which we do have.[37] The date of 103 BC for the praetorship fits perfectly well with

---

[30] See *MRR* II 568–70 and III 19.

[31] The precise wording of the Latin is of some interest here: *Marcus Antonius praetor in Ciliciam maritimos praedones id est piratas persecutus est.* It seems that the Epitomator thought his readers might not understand the true significance of *maritimos praedones*, Livy's usual way of saying 'pirates', and so he added the word *piratas*, which was now in common use, in order to clarify his point. This would suggest that the text of Livy is being quoted directly.

[32] *IGRRP* 4.1116 στρατηγοῦ ἀνθυπάτου.

[33] *ILLRP* 1.342; Taylor & West (1928), *pro consule.* This was the usual terminology for provincial governors at that time.

[34] Plut. *Pomp.* 24, referring to the capture by pirates of his daughter, and describing him as 'a man who had celebrated a triumph'. The same incident is mentioned by Cicero, *Leg. Man.* 33. His presence outside Rome at the time of Saturninus' death is also mentioned by Cicero (*Rab. Post.* 26) who says he was there *cum praesidio.*

[35] For various suggestions see Ormerod (1924): 208; Sherwin-White (1984): 101; Benabou (1985); Pohl (1993): 210–11.

[36] See Sherwin-White (1976): 5. Coarelli (1982) provides a more extensive list of governors of Asia, drawing on some unpublished inscriptions, which suggests that Antonius could not have been assigned to Asia.

[37] E.g. Magie (1950): II 1161 and Ferrary (1977). The interpretation of Ormerod (1924): 208–10 is rendered only partially obsolete as the result of new evidence.

Antonius' career pattern. Two years between the end of a praetorship and the beginning of a consulship was common among Roman aristocrats at this time. It is quite understandable that he should have attempted to boost his chances of being consul by gaining a triumph from his provincial assignment, and this may even have been the main objective of his campaign.[38] This campaign was clearly aimed at reducing the menace of certain local fiefdoms, of the kind described above, in a region which was designated 'Cilicia'. That is not to say that the problem of piracy was not a reason for the assignment of Marcus Antonius' province. I do think, however, that he did not expect or even attempt to eradicate the problem. His objective was to mount an attack on some communities in 'Cilicia', with a combined naval and land operation, demonstrating the willingness of Rome to carry out decisive action in the region, and obtaining sufficient military credit to further his career back in Rome. This appraisal is based on the following interpretation of the evidence.

The sources refer to Marcus Antonius as both praetor and proconsul.[39] The obvious interpretation of this is that he was praetor (in 103 BC) and that he was sent to Cilicia in 102 BC, where he held proconsular *imperium*. There are two possibilities for the title of the province which was assigned to Antonius. Either it was Asia, or Cilicia.[40] If Asia was the province assigned to him, it would have been intended as a base for his operations outside the normal territorial area of that province. Sherwin-White argues that it would be virtually impossible for a Roman magistrate to carry out a military campaign in this area without using Asia and its resources.[41] This is probably true, but it does not mean that Asia had to be the *provincia* which was designated for him. The picture of his activities which is presented by the available evidence is very clearly centred on Cilicia and the immediately adjacent areas, with no suggestion that he was in any of the main areas of the province of Asia. Literary references can be combined with epigraphic evidence to show where Antonius campaigned against the pirates.[42]

There are two contemporary inscriptions which indicate the operational sphere of Antonius' forces. The Latin verse inscription from Corinth,

---

[38] See Harris (1979): 262–3 for the high success rate of praetorian *triumphatores* in the consular elections.

[39] Livy, *Ep.* 68; Cic. *Orat.* 1.82; *ILLRP* 1.342; *IGRRP* 4.1116.

[40] Sherwin-White (1976); (1984); Ferrary (1977); Benabou (1985). Sherwin-White is rightly critical of Magie (1950): 1161, who suggests a maritime command with no territorial basis. Such roving commissions were a later development, as is shown below pp. 141–67. Antonius was given a geographical area, with a specific mission to act against pirates in that area.

[41] Sherwin-White (1977b); (1984): 97–100.

[42] This is the explanation suggested by Michael Crawford, as part of his new interpretation of the *lex de provinciis praetoriis*; Crawford (1996): 261–2.

mentioned above, commemorates a crossing of the Isthmus of Corinth by a Roman fleet: 'Under the auspices of [[Marcus Antonius]] proconsul', the name having been erased and restored by the editors.[43] The text continues: '... the fleet was transported across the Isthmus and despatched over the sea. The proconsul himself set out for Side. Hirrus, his propraetor, because of the season of the year, stationed the fleet at Athens.' The verses were inscribed on a block which had previously been used for an inscription in Greek. The lettering and the language indicate that a date between 146 BC, the destruction of Corinth by Mummius, and 44 BC, the establishment of a new Caesarian colony, would be appropriate. Consequently, there are only two likely candidates for the identification of the erased name, Marcus Antonius the orator, and Marcus Antonius Creticus, repectively the grandfather and father of Marcus Antonius the triumvir, whose *damnatio memoriae* would account for the (accidental) erasure of the name.

Although it is known that Marcus Antonius Creticus was active in Greece and in the Eastern Mediterranean, there is nothing to suggest that he ever went as far as Side.[44] Marcus Antonius the orator, on the other hand, is known to have visited Athens on his way to Cilicia, thanks to a chance reference in one of Cicero's works, in which he features as a speaker: '... when, on my way to Cilicia as proconsul, I came to Athens, I was delayed there for several days on account of the difficulties in putting to sea ...' (Cic. *De orat.* 1.82). Furthermore, it is much easier to understand him setting out for Side, in Pamphylia, than his son. If Pamphylia was, as Sherwin-White has suggested,[45] part of the Roman province of Asia at this time, and Side was not a haven for pirates, as in later years, then it would have made a good base for a maritime expedition against Cilicia. The fact that the proconsul went ahead of his forces is odd, if these were the only naval contingents involved, but there is evidence to suggest that Antonius used forces from several different parts of the Roman world. Tacitus, in describing a speech attributed to some Byzantine ambassadors who tried to get on the right side of Claudius, says: 'They recalled the forces they had sent against Antiochos, Perseus, Aristonikos, and the help they gave to Antonius in the war against the pirates ...' (Tac. *Ann.* 12.62). Also to be considered is the unusual presence of a propraetor in the proconsul's retinue, which is unusual, but not impossible at this time. Thus, I would argue that the Corinth inscription says that Marcus Antonius the orator set out from Greece for Side, in Pamphylia,

[43] *ILLRP* 1.342; full text, translation and discussion in Taylor & West (1928).
[44] See Foucart (1906) and below pp. 141–8.
[45] Sherwin-White (1976): 1–3.

and Cicero adds the further detail that he called in at Athens on his
way.[46]

In addition, the inscription from Rhodes mentioned above honours a
naval officer who served under Antonius *in Cilicia*. Rhodians were probably involved in all the Roman campaigns against pirates at this time.[47]
While these two inscriptions do not 'formally' designate Marcus Antonius'
*provincia*, they do give a clear indication of the area in which he was
active. Taken in conjunction with the passages from Livy, Obsequens and
Cicero quoted above, they provide adequate evidence for the conclusion
that the *provincia* was Cilicia, with specific instructions to campaign
against the pirates operating from that region.[48] The scrappy nature of
our sources makes it impossible to reconstruct Marcus Antonius' campaign of 102 BC in great detail. The following points are, however, reasonably well founded upon the evidence.

We know that Antonius and his propraetor Hirrus transported a fleet
across the Isthmus at Corinth from the inscription which commemorated
this event. The inscription was probably set up by Hirrus himself, hur-
riedly, before he followed Antonius to Athens. He stationed the fleet here
'because of the season of the year'.[49] Hirrus' actions, taken in conjunction
with Cicero's mention, quoted above, of the difficulty in sailing which
Antonius encountered, are consistent with the interpretation that all this
took place in the early spring, before the best of the sailing weather. The
fleet may have come from Italy,[50] and the impression given by Hirrus'
boastful inscription, as well as the number of naval officers under Antonius' command, is that it was quite large.[51] The Byzantine contingent in

[46] Sherwin-White (1976): 1–3 prefers to assign the Corinth inscription to Marcus Antonius
Creticus. He thinks that the presence of a propraetor in the proconsul's retinue makes this
more likely to refer to Creticus, but his argument does not account for the journey to
Side. Sherwin-White argues that the details of this journey do not fit with what is known
about Marcus Antonius, i.e. that he visited Athens, but there is no reason why the com-
poser of the Corinth verses (Hirrus himself?) should have mentioned this. The inscription
seems to have been erected in great haste, probably near the *diolkos*, so Hirrus and the
fleet may not even have known that their commander was delayed at Athens when they
put it up; see Taylor & West (1928).

[47] *IGRRP* 4.1116: ... [Μ]άρκου Ἀντωνίου στραταγοῦ ἀνθυπά[του καὶ] Αὔλου Γαβεινίου
τ[α]μία ῥωμαίων ἰς [Κ]ιλικίαν ... Sherwin-White (1976): 4, rightly points out that in a
Rhodian inscription Cilicia would be a precise geographical term, i.e. 'Rough' Cilicia.

[48] As Sherwin-White points out (1976): 5, only a few years earlier, although the consuls who
fought Jugurtha were based in the existing province of Africa, their own *provincia* was
designated as 'Numidia' and their specific task was the war with Jugurtha.

[49] *ILLRP* 1.342, lines 5–6; see Taylor & West (1928).

[50] As suggested by Reddé (1986): 459.

[51] 'In a few days all this was accomplished with little confusion, and at the same time with
great skill and security' *ILLRP* 1.342, lines 7–8. Another inscription, *IG* XII.5.841 from
Tenos, honours a prefect called (?)Quintus Calpurnius who may well have been one of
Antonius' naval officers.

Antonius' forces, mentioned above, may have joined this fleet at Athens, but it is more likely that it, along with other allied forces from the Eastern Mediterranean, joined up closer to Cilicia. Side would be an obvious place to collect maritime contingents for a campaign aimed at Cilicia. The port is sheltered and the mountains separate it from Cilicia itself, but the sea distance to the Cilician coast is relatively short. The fleet could have 'shadowed' the land forces using the coast road to approach Cilicia, or even transported a large force for an amphibious operation. It is highly unlikely that Antonius brought a substantial army from Italy. The Cimbri and Teutones still menaced Italy at this time. He probably relied on levies from allies and the provinces.[52]

What did Antonius do with his forces? Most of our information about them is concerned with naval contingents, and the relatively high rank of Hirrus (propraetor) would make most sense if the fleet was an important element of Antonius' command. It is possible that some kind of naval battle was fought, since Cicero tells us that a prefect, Marcus Gratidius, who was serving under Antonius, was killed in action: 'My uncle Marcus Gratidius was a man who really knew his Greek! He was born to be an orator. He was a close friend of Marcus Antonius, whose prefect he was in Cilicia when he was killed ...' (Cic. *Brut.* 168).[53] The description of Antonius' campaign in the Epitome of Livy, saying he 'pursued the pirates into Cilicia' (Livy, *Per.* 68), suggests that little of his activity actually took place within the borders of Rough Cilicia. Antonius' campaign against the pirates was probably an attack on one or more coastal positions, with some fighting on land (and possibly at sea). The main thrust of his operations would appear to have been against actual, or possible, pirate *bases*, with the intention of denying the pirates the necessary safe havens from which they could operate. He was successful enough to gain a triumph (at the expense of at least one prefect), which he probably celebrated in 101 BC.[54] There were good reasons for him to return quickly to Rome in order to campaign for the consulship in person. The elections for 99 BC were hotly contested.

Antonius clearly did not 'destroy' the Cilician pirates, as Obsequens' exaggerated notice claims. The apparent prominence of allies in his forces, and in the *lex de provinciis praetoriis* discussed below, indicates that it was Rome's allies in the Eastern Mediterranean (above all the Rhodians) who were pressing for some positive action against the pirates

[52] See Brunt (1971): 431 and Sherwin-White (1984): 99–101.
[53] Cic. *Leg.* 3.36 adds the detail that Marcus Gratidius was Cicero's great-uncle, his grandmother's brother. If *praefectus* here means 'prefect of the fleet', then a naval battle would be a possible context for his death.
[54] See *MRR* III 19; Ferrary (1977): 624–7.

in Cilicia. Through Antonius, Rome had shown her willingness to act against the perceived problem of Cilician piracy, and that action could be effective, but there was to be no short, simple solution. Further efforts were required almost immediately, as the law discussed below shows.

## The *lex de provinciis praetoriis*

This Greek translation of a Roman law has been known about since the end of the nineteenth century, when fragments of it were found inscribed on the monument of Lucius Aemilius Paullus at Delphi. The discovery in 1970 of a further, slightly different, translation at Knidos has rendered all earlier discussions obsolete, as a far greater proportion of the text is now available for study.[55] The date of the law cannot be fixed precisely, but it must fall after the election of the consuls for 100 BC, that is Gaius Marius and Lucius Valerius Flaccus, who are named in the text, and before the allocation of the praetorian provinces for 100 BC, a measure which cannot have been long delayed. It should also be noted that, at the point at which the Knidos translation was made, the status of the kingdom of Cyprus was rather doubtful, hence the careful phraseology employed to describe its ruler.[56] The choice of date among recent commentators has varied from late 101 BC to 99 BC.[57] The most likely date seems to be early in 100 BC.[58]

To a certain extent, the date of the law has to be determined by considering its purpose and the intentions of those involved in its promulgation. Lintott argues that it 'seems to be filling a lacuna in senatorial business'.[59] On his interpretation it is essentially a collection of pieces of routine administration, which would normally have been dealt with by *senatus consulta*, and which have had to be carried through by legislation at the end of the year because 'the senate was likely to be less active and in that year lacked consular leadership'.[60] Ferrary attempts to place the law

---

[55] See Hassall, Crawford, Reynolds (1974) for first publication of the new text. I am especially grateful to Michael Crawford for providing me with a copy of his latest edition of the law before it was published; see now Crawford (1996): 231–70.

[56] See Hassall et al. (1974): 198. The law requires the governors of Asia and Macedonia to publish its provisions. As a result, the two surviving copies represent different translations of the Latin original, presumably made locally, soon after its passage; see Crawford (1996): 234 and 258–70.

[57] Giovannini & Grzybek (1978); Lintott (1978); Sumner (1978).

[58] Hassall et al. (1974) argued originally for late 101 BC; the suggestion of Ferrary (1977) that February 100 BC is the most appropriate date is favoured by Crawford (1996): 236–37.

[59] He is seeking to explain the nature of the law's contents, which he describes as 'humdrum'; Lintott (1976): 71–2.

[60] Lintott (1976): 72.

within the wider context of *popularis* legislation. He has shown that the law is formally a *lex de provinciis praetoriis* and not, as is assumed by most commentators, a collection of measures passed *per satura* in a fashion which was forbidden by the *lex Caecilia Didia* of 98 BC.[61] He draws particular attention to the provisions for Cilicia which are found in both versions:[62]

The senior consul is to send letters to the peoples and states to whom he may think fit, to say that the Roman people ⟨will have⟩ care, that the citizens of Rome and the allies and the Latins, and those of the foreign nations who are in a relationship of friendship with the Roman people may sail in safety, and that on account of this matter and according to this statute they have made Cilicia a praetorian province.[63]

If Cilicia had been made a praetorian province in 102 BC, and allotted to Marcus Antonius, it would seem strange that the Roman legislators found it necessary to explain their reasons for doing the same again.[64] If, on the other hand, Marcus Antonius' *provincia* in 102 was Asia, with special instructions to deal with Cilician pirates, as suggested by Sherwin-White,[65] then the purpose of this part of the law becomes much clearer. I find it unlikely, however, that Asia was the province which Marcus Antonius held. All the sources speak of his activity in and around 'Cilicia', with little mention of places in Asia. It is also possible that he spent only one year, or less, in his province, campaigning long enough and hard enough to gain a triumph and lose a prefect, but not doing enough to secure Roman control over Cilicia. This might only require him to be active in his command for a few months. He could, therefore, have left the province by the end of 102 BC and returned to Rome. This hypothesis would allow Cilicia to be 'vacant' in the year 101 BC, and hence provide a plausible reason for legislators in 100 BC to need to explain its designation as a province for that year. Cilicia is to be, for this year, a *provincia* for a

---

[61] Ferrary (1977). See Cicero, *Dom.* 53. for a definition of this practice.

[62] All quotations are from the translation in Crawford (1996): 253–7. Words wrongly omitted by the translators or the engravers have been included in angle brackets. The Knidos copy (column III, lines 28–37) is the main source for this passage, but the Delphi text clearly included the same clauses (block B, lines 5–7).

[63] Sherwin-White (1976) argues that the Greek term used here (στρατηγικός) means only 'military' and not 'praetorian', because the status of the magistrates governing the provinces of Macedonia and Asia is elsewhere left open (e.g. Knidos copy, column II, lines 12–13). This is refuted by Ferrary (1977): 637–45.

[64] The possibility suggested by Hassall et al. (1974), that the territory of Cilicia is being 'annexed', would partially explain the need for this pronouncement, but this explanation lacks any supporting evidence and does not accord with the course of events in the following 30 years. See Sherwin-White (1984): 99.

[65] Sherwin-White (1976): 5; (1984): 97–9.

Roman magistrate of praetorian rank, and the local rulers are being informed of this extension of the Romans' sphere of military action. Crawford and his collaborators also note that the law makes a great deal of the decision to make Cilicia a praetorian province, in spite of the fact that this had been done two years earlier.[66] This 'fuss' is best explained by the prominent anti-piracy sections of the law. Here the Romans appear to be picking up on Polybius' suggestion that they have a duty to protect the Greeks against piracy.[67] The Romans can therefore be seen as aligning themselves with the celebrated suppressors of piracy from Greek history, like Athens, Alexander and Rhodes.[68]

It is noticeable that no direct references are made in the law to Marcus Antonius or to his earlier campaign in Cilicia. This would not be very remarkable if they had ended a year before the law was promulgated, as I have argued above. The victories of Titus Didius in Macedonia were, on the other hand, much more recent,[69] and so they receive a special mention in the text of the law, which gives detailed instructions to the new praetor of Macedonia on how the conquered territory is to be administered.[70] There are also several references to the current and future governors of Asia and Macedonia, both of which have been held as *provinciae* for many years. They are required to swear an oath concerning the law's provisions,[71] but the same is not required of any magistrate holding Cilicia, for the simple reason that, at the time of the law's promulgation, there was no one in that position. Nor is Cilicia the only province with which the law is concerned. While the preserved text deals only with the assignation of Cilicia, it seems in its original, full version to have been a *lex de provinciis praetoriis* which assigned several of the overseas praetorian provinces for the year 100 BC. The intention of the legislators was not, however, to set a fixed pattern for the annual assignation of these provinces.[72]

It is convenient at this point to summarize the contents of the law, as it survives on the two versions from Delphi and Knidos, paying particular attention to matters relevant to piracy. The prescript to the law does not survive, although it may have been inscribed at the start of the Knidos copy. The first few lines of the Delphi copy (block A) may be part of a

---

[66] Crawford (1996): 262.

[67] Polyb. 2.12.4–6.

[68] See above Chs. 2 and 3.

[69] T. Didius was praetor in 101 BC and must have defeated the Scordisci in Thrace in this year (Cic. *Pis.* 61; Flor. 1.39; Jer. *Chron.* ad ann. 100). At the time of the law's promulgation, he may not yet have celebrated his triumph. *MRR* I 571, 573 and 575.

[70] Knidos copy, column IV, lines 5–30.

[71] Delphi copy, block C, lines 8ff.

[72] This is the view of Ferrary (1977), adopted in Crawford (1996): 236–7.

letter of introduction, but they are fragmentary. The rest can be divided into several sections:[73]

(i) Provisions for the safety of navigation for Romans, Latins and Rome's friends and allies.[74]

(ii) Limitations are imposed upon the consuls in office concerning troops stationed in Macedonia.

(iii) A list of matters which are not affected by the law. Reference is made to a statute concerning troops in provinces passed on 19 February by Marcus Porcius Cato.[75] At the end of this section mention is made of the province (ἐπαρχεία) of Lykaonia, which is part of the province (ἐπαρχεία) of Asia.[76]

(iv) Next come the instructions to the senior consul to write to various persons informing them of the designation of Cilicia as a praetorian province.[77]

(v) Further instructions follow, telling the senior consul to write to: '... the king ruling in the island of Cyprus,[78] and to the king [ruling at] Alexandria and in Egypt [and to the king] ruling in Cyrene and to the kings ruling in Syria [who have] friendship and alliance [with the Roman people, he is to send letters] to the effect that it is also right for them to see that [no] pirate (πειρατῆς) [use as a base of operations] their kingdom [or] land or territories [and that no officials or garrison commanders whom] they shall appoint harbour the pirates (πειρατάς) and to see that, insofar as [it shall be possible,] the Roman people [have (them as) contributors to the safety of all ...]'.[79] The senior consul is instructed to give the letters to the Rhodian ambassadors. The section ends with a general proviso that all magistrates see to it that the law is obeyed.

---

[73] The division into sections is my own. See Hassall et al. (1974) for the different proportions of the text which have been preserved at Delphi and Knidos. The lines on the Delphi copy are more than twice as long as those on the Knidos copy.

[74] Knidos copy, column II, lines 1–11.

[75] Ferrary (1977) is encouraged by this date to place the law in February 100. The identity of Cato is unclear; see Crawford (1996): 260.

[76] It is clear from this section that ἐπαρχεία is being used to translate *provincia*, and that it has both meanings of the Latin word, i.e. the sphere of activity of a magistrate *and* a territorial area. This dual meaning is important for understanding the provincial designations of the next three decades.

[77] Quoted above p. 109.

[78] The Knidos copy has 'the king holding power in the island of Cyprus' at this point, which indicates knowledge of very recent developments on that island; see Crawford (1996): 262.

[79] Delphi copy, block B, lines 8–12. The restorations are fairly clear, and enough of the text survives to leave no doubt as to the basic intent. The Latin translation in Crawford (1996) uses *pirata* to translate *peiratēs* here, but I think it is highly unlikely that this Latin word was in general usage at the time (it first occurs in Cicero). The original version of the law would probably have used *praedo*.

(vi) The consuls are also very clearly instructed to give a special senate audience to the Rhodian ambassadors.

(vii) There then follows a series of orders to the governor of Asia (who has apparently already received this province for 100 BC). The governor is instructed to see to the publication of the law and to the delivery of the consular letters.

(viii) The governor of Macedonia (whose identity is not yet known) is given more specific instructions, relating particularly to the territory 'which Titus Didius took by force in war'.[80] The instructions which survive in the Knidos text relate to the arrangement and collection of tribute from these areas. The law begins to deal with the possible resignation of the praetor or quaestor in Macedonia, but the text is incomplete.

(ix) The law next orders the governors of Asia and Macedonia to 'swear ⟨to do⟩ whatever (the people) order (him) to do in this statute and not [to do anything] otherwise [knowingly] with wrongful deceit'.[81]

(x) The final section of the law is a complex *iusiurandum in legem* intended to see that the law is obeyed, with a detailed set of provisions for the enforcement of fines for non-compliance.

The surviving contents of the law are consistent with the interpretation of Ferrary that it is intended to assign at least one of the overseas provinces for praetors in the year 100 BC.[82] As a result of the law a praetor must have been sent out in that year to 'Cilicia'. He was presumably intended to build upon the achievements of Marcus Antonius in 102 BC, which is possibly a further indication that his success was very limited. But who was this praetor, and did he achieve anything of note? The possible praetors of 100 whose names we know are:[83]

(1) Lucius Cornelius Dolabella.
(2) Gnaeus Cornelius Lentulus.
(3) Publius Licinius Crassus.
(4) Gaius Servilius Glaucia.
(5) ? Tremellius.

Of these men numbers (1) and (4) can be discounted. Dolabella seems to have celebrated a triumph from Further Spain and Glaucia could not have been out of Rome for the year. Numbers (2) and (3) were consuls in

---

[80] Knidos copy, column IV, lines 8–10. These clauses are a strong indication of the *popularis* nature of the law; see Ferrary (1977).
[81] Delphi copy, block C, lines 8–10.
[82] Ferrary (1977): 643–5.
[83] *MRR* I 574–5.

97 BC, and their praetorships are assumed for this year since it is the latest possible date under the *lex Villia*. Number (5) is a shadowy figure, the son of a quaestor of 142 BC and the father of a quaestor of 71 BC.[84] There seems no obvious way to decide if any of these men did receive Cilicia as his province, but it would perhaps be most likely that it was either an unrecorded sixth individual, or the almost unknown Tremellius, since we do have some further information about Crassus and Lentulus.[85] It does not appear that this praetor, or any of his immediate successors, achieved anything remarkable during their praetorships, since none of our sources have anything further to say about Cilicia until the praetorship of Sulla. In spite of the promises enshrined in the law and the energetic letter-writing of the senior consul, piracy must have remained as serious and unresolved a problem as it was before the law was promulgated.

It is important to emphasize that this law is the earliest clear statement of the position of Rome concerning pirates. They are effectively being declared enemies of the Roman people, and their friends and allies. The prohibitions on assisting pirates in sections (i) and (v) are similar to the prohibitions placed upon Roman allies with regard to the enemies of Rome.[86] The Romans are spelling out their opposition to piracy in terms which also reinforce their political dominance in the Eastern Mediterranean. The law articulates the Romans' assumption of the right to take aggressive, imperialistic measures in order to counter the threat of those whom they designate as pirates, in the same fashion as that which they have previously employed in the Western Mediterranean against the Balearic islanders.[87]

The clauses of the *lex de provinciis praetoriis* relating to the Rhodians indicate that they were most concerned of all the allies and friends of Rome about the problem of piracy in the Eastern Mediterranean. The fact that they are to be granted a special audience with the senate, and are to be given copies of the letters instructing or urging the kings to keep their kingdoms free of pirates, leads to the suggestion that they were, in some sense, behind the creation of Cilicia as a praetorian province. It seems safe to assume that many Rhodians participated in Marcus Antonius' campaign,[88] and they would have had plenty of opportunities to discover how serious the problem was. It has been suggested that the

---

[84] As mentioned in Varr. *Rust.* 2.4.2.
[85] *MRR* II 6, 8, 10, 12, 13 and 15.
[86] See, for example, the treaties between Rome and Methymna (*IG* XII.2.510) and Astypalaia (*IG* XII.3.173), which are both from the second century BC.
[87] See above pp. 92–6. For discussion of the connections between piracy and Roman imperialism see below pp. 134–6. This subject is developed further in de Souza (1996).
[88] See above pp. 103–8.

Rhodians had been 'fulfilling the maritime role of the praetor of Cilicia at this time'.[89] This is, however, an exaggeration of the island's importance. The *lex de provinciis praetoriis* makes it very clear that the Romans, through their consuls and other senior magistrates, are responsible for initiating and organizing any action to deal with pirates in this region. The Rhodians, like the kings and cities to whom the consul is to write, are merely agents of the Roman people in this matter. It was only the Romans who had the authority and influence to organize the necessary manpower to launch any effective attacks on Cilicia, or anywhere else. The impression which the law's provisions give concerning the Rhodians is that they are being reassured that Rome will continue to take her responsibilities in this matter seriously, and that everything possible is being done. It is open to doubt whether they would have believed this to be true.

Also worthy of emphasis is the method by which piracy is to be combated, according to this law. The most important thing is to deny bases to the pirates, wherever they may be. Some scholars have suggested that vast maritime commands were envisaged at this time as the most effective way to suppress piracy.[90] It is clear from this law, from the activities of Quintus Caecilius Metellus Balearicus, and from the campaign of Marcus Antonius the orator, that the Romans were well aware at this time that the most effective way to deal with pirates was to tackle them *on land*. This might involve some naval activity, in order to approach certain bases or strongholds, but the real test of the Romans' determination to ensure the safety of the seas for their friends and allies was their willingness and ability to overcome in their lairs those whom they declared to be pirates.

The law found at Delphi and Knidos is, therefore, a *lex de provinciis praetoriis* dating from the early part of the year 100 BC. It contains several provisions which announce the Romans' concern for the safety of seafarers and the suppression of piracy. In particular, a repeat of Marcus Antonius' campaign of 102 BC is envisaged with the designation of Cilicia as a praetorian province. Little or nothing seems to have resulted from this promise of action, however, and, as will be shown below, the problem of piracy in Cilicia (and elsewhere) seems, as far as we are able to tell from the surviving sources, not to have had a high place again on the list of political priorities at Rome for a considerable time.

After 100 BC we are very much in the dark about the course of Roman magisterial activity in Anatolia for nearly ten years.[91] Marius was touring

---

[89]   Sherwin-White (1977b): 65.

[90]   Ferrary (1977); Pohl (1993). On the latter see de Souza (1995b).

[91]   The 90s BC are a lean decade in terms of available source material. Since piracy was a marginal topic for the ancient authors anyway, it is hardly surprising that so little is known about Roman policy in this period.

the East in 99/8 BC, for the expressed purpose of fulfilling a public vow,[92] and he may have made some observations on the problem when he returned to Rome on the completion of his mission. There is, however, nothing in the sources to indicate this, nor would pirates have been as enticing as Mithridates for Marius' military ambitions.[93] Indeed, for the next twenty years, it was the King of Pontos whose depredations were to be the Romans' main cause for concern in the Eastern Mediterranean. In most cases pirates make appearances in our literary sources only in conjunction with Mithridates.[94] It has been suggested that further campaigning against pirates was carried out or was, perhaps, intended to be carried out by Lucius Cornelius Sulla as praetor of Cilicia in the 90s BC.[95] Sulla was praetor in 97 BC and for his proconsulship in 96 was assigned the province of Asia.[96] His immediate task, given to him by the senate, was to restore Ariobarzanes, the senatorial nominee, to the throne of Cappadocia.[97] Some of the sources make Cilicia his province.[98] It is clear, however, that he campaigned in Cappadocia and there was no reason for him to stay long in Cilicia itself.[99] His army was mostly supplied by Rome's allies.[100] There is no indication that he had any naval forces under his command.[101] To see pirates lurking behind every mention of Cilicia or adjacent regions is, in any case, to misunderstand the Romans' priorities in Anatolia during this period. On both the national and the personal level, there was far more prestige and profit to be gained against the likes of Mithridates, and other dynasts, than any campaign against pirates could hope to yield.[102]

---

[92] Plut. *Mar.* 31 says that he had an ulterior motive, which was to try and stir up trouble with Mithridates.

[93] See Luce (1970) on the Eastern designs of Marius.

[94] See below pp. 116–36.

[95] Reddé (1986): 461; Ormerod (1924): 210–12. See *MRR* III 73–6 for recent work on Sulla's praetorship and proconsular command.

[96] Badian (1964): 214 and *OCD*[3] 400.

[97] Ariobarzanes' epithet Φιλορώμαιος (Friend of Rome) neatly sums up his dependency on the Romans for the Cappadocian throne; Braund (1982): 106–7. See Sherwin-White (1984): 109–13 and 226 for the full story of his interrupted reign.

[98] App. *Mith.* 57: Κιλικίας ἄρχων; *De vir. ill.* 75: *praetor Ciliciam provinciam habuit.*

[99] Plut. *Sulla* 5 and Livy, *Ep.* 70 name only Cappadocia. The formal designation of the province need not have corresponded too closely with the geographical area of his activities.

[100] 'The force he brought with him was not large, being eagerly reinforced by the allies' (Plut. *Sulla* 5). See also Brunt (1971): 434.

[101] Contra Reddé (1986): 459–63, who cites no evidence for this opinion. Similarly Quintus Oppius, whom Reddé also associates with campaigns against Cilician pirates, seems not to have had any naval forces, nor to have been active against pirates, Cilician or otherwise. He was probably proconsul of Asia *c.* 89 BC, along with Gaius Cassius; see *MRR* II 32, 33 and 42; Crawford (1974): I 545–6; Reynolds (1982): 11–20.

[102] See Sherwin-White (1977b) and (1984) on the beginnings of what he calls 'the aggressive imperialism of individual army commanders of the late Republic'(1977b): 75.

### Mithridates

Mithridates VI Eupator, king of Pontos (120–63 BC), was one of Rome's most implacable and successful enemies. In a series of wars between 88 BC and his death in 63 BC he challenged Roman domination over the Eastern Mediterranean region and, briefly, threatened to wrest control of the Romans' Greek-speaking provinces from them. Three of Rome's greatest leaders, Sulla, Lucullus and Pompey, fought long campaigns against Mithridates and his allies, involving armies of thousands of Roman and allied soldiers. The impact of his exploits is illustrated by the fact that Appian devoted a whole book of his *Roman History* to the Mithridatic wars. The idea that the Mithridatic wars represent a significant phase in the development of Cilician piracy was current in ancient times. Appian, in the course of his account of these wars, attributes a speech to Sulla in which he lists the various ways in which the Asian communities have been punished for their submission to Mithridates' rule. They have had to suffer the pillage and slaughter of their inhabitants, redistribution of land, cancellation of debts, freeing of slaves, the establishment of tyrannical governments and: 'piracy all over the land and the sea' (App. *Mith.* 62).[103] This seems to me to represent a generalized catalogue of the worst crimes that a despot like Mithridates could commit in Appian's view. In his next chapter Appian describes the sorry state of the province of Asia after the end of the first war and the political and economic settlement imposed by Sulla: 'There sailed against her hordes of pirates, more like navies than pirate bands. They were initially established on the seas by Mithridates when he was despoiling all those regions, which he did not hold for long ...' (App. *Mith.* 63). Appian returns to this theme later in the same book, discussing the growth of piracy in Southern Anatolia in an extended passage which introduces his account of the campaign of Pompey in 67 BC:

When Mithridates first went to war with the Romans and conquered Asia (Sulla being busy with Greece), believing that he could not hold on to Asia for long, he despoiled it one way and another, as I have mentioned, and sent out pirates on the sea. At first they harassed people by sailing around in a few small boats, as pirates do, but, as the war dragged on, they became more numerous and sailed in larger ships. Having acquired a taste for rich plunder, they still did not cease their activities when Mithridates was defeated, made peace and retreated. For, having been robbed of their living and their homeland on account of the war, and having fallen into hardship and poverty, they harvested the sea instead of the land, first

---

[103] The words quoted are a translation of the Greek: καὶ ληστήρια πολλὰ ἀνά τε γῆν καὶ θάλασσαν.

in *myoparones* and *hemioliai*, then in biremes and triremes, cruising around in squadrons, under the command of archpirates just like generals in a war. (App. *Mith.* 92)

The suggestion that it was Mithridates who gave the pirates an initial boost is also found in Plutarch (*Pomp.* 24) and is probably also referred to by Cassius Dio (36.20–1). Appian himself repeats the point in his final comments on Mithridates (App. *Mith.* 119).

These general statements in the literary sources are the basis for modern scholars' views on the role of pirates in the Mithridatic wars. The most detailed discussion of this subject is to be found in a paper by the Hungarian academic Egon Maróti.[104] He sees the relationship between the king and the pirates as one of mutual assistance. Mithridates could not manage to control the whole of the Eastern Mediterranean unaided, and the pirates needed 'freedom' for their own activities. Therefore, Maróti argues, the king gave the pirates a 'free hand' in return for various military services, especially attacks on Roman naval forces and supply ships.[105] This seems at first sight to be a reasonable interpretation, but when the specific evidence cited by Maróti to back it up is examined closely, it seems to me that the generalizations lose much of their credibility and a different analysis is required. The suggestion that Mithridates gave the pirates a 'free hand' should not be taken seriously. How was he supposed to prevent them from going where they pleased and doing as they wished? Appian and Plutarch may, in fact be repeating the hostile propaganda of earlier Roman writers, aimed at discrediting Mithridates and putting a better interpretation on the Romans' wars against him. It would have been relatively easy to blame Mithridates for the problem of piracy, and Sulla may even have done so after the Peace of Dardanus, but the theme of promoting piracy was nothing new in political invective.[106] If Mithridates could be placed on the same level as pirates, it would be ample justification for Rome's ultimate destruction of the Pontic king.[107] This does not, however, mean that Mithridates had a pro-pirate policy. Given the confused political situation in large areas of the Eastern Medi-

---

[104] Maróti (1970). See also Ormerod (1924): 210–12; Jackson (1973): 243; Mattingly (1980); Sherwin-White (1984): 160; McGing (1986): 139; Garlan (1989): 192–3; Pohl (1993): 140–6.

[105] Maróti (1970): 485.

[106] See, for example, Ch. 2 above on the political invective of the second half of the fourth century BC.

[107] For further examination of the discourse of justifiable imperialism in the Late Republic and some illuminating comparisons from modern history see de Souza (1996). Jackson (1973) and Mattingly (1980) are both conscious of the dangers of believing everything that Appian and Plutarch say.

terranean at this time it was surely easy for pirates to flourish, without their needing to ask anyone's permission to profit from the chaos of war. What, then, of the services that the pirates performed for Mithridates in return for his generosity in allowing them the freedom of the seas? Maróti cites the adventures of Sulla's quaestor, Lucius Licinius Lucullus, as evidence of the close co-operation between the king and the pirates during the first Mithridatic war.

## Lucullus

Sulla arrived in Greece with five legions in 87 BC and soon had Mithridates' generals penned up in Athens and the Piraeus. But he was hampered in his attempts to take the Piraeus because he lacked any significant naval forces. Mithridates enjoyed a considerable degree of naval supremacy resulting from Sulla's lack of warships and transport vessels. The only Roman naval contingents in the East mentioned by our sources before the arrival of Sulla were under the command of Minucius Rufus and Gaius Popilius, and were stationed at Byzantion 'watching over the mouth of the Pontos' (App. *Mith.* 17). In spite of his initial successes in Greece and on the mainland of Asia Minor, Sulla was later unable to corner Mithridates because of the latter's ability to escape by sea. Nor, in the early stages of the conflict, could he prevent Mithridates from reinforcing his generals on the Greek mainland at will. An important aspect of Mithridates' naval strategy was the isolation of Rhodes, Rome's most important maritime ally in the Eastern Mediterranean. Mithridates possessed a substantial fleet, which he brought to Rhodes in 88 BC in an attempt to capture the city. Appian says that Mithridates' fleet greatly outnumbered the Rhodian forces, but they were able to defeat his ships several times before he retired and turned his attention to the Greek mainland (App. *Mith.* 24–7).[108] Part of his fleet remained behind to keep the Rhodians occupied.

Sulla tried to obtain naval support from the Rhodians in 87 BC, but the presence of Mithridates' fleet prevented them from reaching him. Desperate to find ships Sulla ordered Lucullus to put together a fleet from the resources of the kings who were still loyal allies of Rome (App. *Mith.* 37). Sulla cannot have expected Lucullus to take as long as he did over this task. He set out late in 87 BC and did not rejoin his commander until early in 85 BC, having had several adventures along the way. His problems were partly caused by Mithridates' own navy, but he also suffered at

---

[108] It is difficult to determine the size of Mithridates' fleet, but Appian refers to a squadron of 25 ships and mentions both triremes and quinqueremes.

the hands of opponents who are labelled pirates by the ancient sources. Both Appian and Plutarch describe him encountering pirates as well as the Mithridatic naval forces. Appian says that he was threatened with capture by pirates on several occasions (App. *Mith.* 56), and Plutarch specifies that on his journey from Cyrene to Alexandria he lost most of his ships in a pirate attack (Plut. *Luc.* 2.5), but neither author suggests that any pirates attacked him on Mithridates' instructions, or even on their own initiative with the intention of helping the Pontic king's cause. It is assumed by Maróti that these pirates were close allies of Mithridates on whom he relied to a considerable extent.[109] The activities of pirates in the Eastern Mediterranean at this time do, indeed, come to the attention of the literary sources, such as Appian, because of the Mithridatic wars, but it does not necessarily follow that they were closely involved in those wars. It would appear instead that Lucullus was simply the victim of some pirates who were based on the coast of Libya, somewhere between Cyrene and Alexandria. Pirates seem to have operated in this area with some success in the 90s BC, after the death of Ptolemy Apion in 96 BC, as is indicated by an inscription in honour of a certain Apollodoros, who helped to restore some degree of order to the city of Berenike at this time.[110] Lucullus may have tried to establish some kind of political order in Crete, where he went before coming to Cyrene, and he stayed in Cyrene long enough to be honoured by the Cyrenaicans as their lawgiver.[111] He does not, however, seem to have made any attempt to deal with local pirates in either of these places. Indeed, according to Plutarch, after leaving Egypt he went out of his way to avoid pirates: 'Then he proceeded to sail around collecting a large number of ships from the coastal cities, except for those which practised piratical misdeeds . . .' (Plut. *Luc.* 3.2). Lucullus' reluctance to become embroiled with pirates is understandable, especially after his mishap on the way to Alexandria. His job was to create an effective counter to Mithridates' naval power, not to waste his resources by relieving places like Berenike of the threat of further attacks by pirates. Sulla's embarassing lack of ships for the struggle with Mithridates was only partly rectified by Lucullus' efforts. In his quaestor's absence Sulla had been forced to begin his own shipbuilding programme (App. *Mith.* 51). He also demanded the surrender of a substantial part of the

---

[109] Maróti (1970); see also Ormerod (1924): 209–12 and Pohl (1993): 140–4.

[110] '. . . Later, when the city was lying unwalled and had already twice been sacked by pirates sailing against it in a fleet, he was placed in authority over the city and its territory . . .', Reynolds (1977): 234–46, no. 3 lines 13–15. The inscription explicitly describes events, 'after the death of the king' (lines 5–7), and so must be dated to later than 96 BC, but before the annexation of Cyrene in 75 BC.

[111] See Braund (1987).

Pontic king's navy as part of his peace terms. He did not, however, leave these ships in the Eastern Mediteranean: they were needed for his next great task, the return to Italy and the continuation of the Civil Wars.[112] The absence of Roman naval forces after Sulla's departure can largely explain the maritime activities of subsequent Roman commanders, activities which some scholars have interpreted as directed towards the suppression of piracy.[113]

As has already been indicated at several points in this book, the most effective method of suppressing piracy in antiquity was to neutralize the pirates in their bases on land, as it still is today. This would often entail some maritime action on the part of the attacking forces, in order to secure the approaches to the base, and to prevent their opponents from escaping by sea. Similarly, military action against Mithridates, or any other foe who was occupying territory which included a substantial coastline, could only be effective with a fleet to support and transport the land forces. This was demonstrated vividly in 85 BC when the Roman commander Flavius Fimbria, whose authority was not recognized by Sulla, was forced to allow Mithridates to escape his clutches at Pergamon because Lucullus would not allow his newly assembled fleet to act in conjunction with a rival, 'renegade' army (Plut. *Luc.* 3.4–7). It is, therefore, important to try to determine the real object of any campaign conducted by land or sea in Anatolia (or elsewhere) in this period, since it does not follow that all maritime or coastal activity involves the suppression of piracy, nor can it be assumed that largely land-based operations could not be directed against pirates.

The importance of Rhodes in Roman naval organization is again very noticeable at this time. Lucullus appears to have relied heavily on Rhodian ships and officers in his victories over Mithridates' fleet.[114] An inscription from Rhodes records honours voted to Sulla, Murena, Lucullus and the legate Aulus Terentius Varro.[115] In the years following Murena's departure, it is possible to detect a greater degree of difficulty in obtaining ships for Roman magistrates in the Eastern Mediterranean. This may be due to the considerable demands placed on the available resources, above all Rhodes, by Sulla, Lucullus and Murena, not to mention the activities

---

[112] App. *Mith.* 55; Granius Licinianus 26F. Some of the 70 ships, fitted out for action, which were handed over to Sulla, may have come from the Roman squadron stationed at Byzantion which had surrendered to Mithridates (App. *Mith.* 19).

[113] Reddé (1986): 461–3; Sherwin-White (1984): ch. 5.

[114] Plut. *Luc.* 3–4; App. *Mith.* 56.

[115] *IGRRP* 1.843. The names mentioned in the text are followed by a long list of naval officers. See also *CIL* I².2.738 from Delos, honouring the same Aulus Terentius Varro.

of Mithridates himself.[116] The sort of demands which Rome's military activities might make upon their 'maritime allies' are illustrated by a passage from Memnon, describing how the city of Herakleia sent ships to assist in the Jugurthine war. The ships and their crews did not return for eleven years![117] On the other hand, naval service with the Romans could be rewarding, as is seen in a bilingual inscription from the city of Rome which records the honours granted by the senate to three Greek naval officers in 78 BC.[118]

## Murena and his successors

Sulla's successor in the province of Asia, Lucius Licinius Murena, decided on his own initiative to continue the war with Mithridates.[119] In 83 BC, claiming that Mithridates was preparing for war, he invaded Pontus from Cappadocia with his two Roman legions, ostensibly in support of king Ariobarzanes of Cappadocia. After being ordered to desist by a senatorial envoy, he did the same again in 82 BC. Eventually Mithridates repulsed him and a settlement was arranged between Ariobarzanes and Mithridates in 81 BC, bringing this second Mithridatic war to an end.[120] The preparations which Murena construed as directed against Rome and her allies in 83 BC included the assembly of a fleet, which Appian says Mithridates intended to use against the Bosporan tribes (App. *Mith.* 64). These peoples were indeed subdued by the Pontic king after the Murena episode (App. *Mith.* 67). Murena also organized naval forces, requiring the cities of Asia to furnish ships as part of their tribute to Rome (Cic. *II Verr.* 1.89).[121] Cicero suggests that these ships were intended for use against pirates (Cic. *II Verr.* 1.86–9), but it is more likely that Murena wanted to avoid a repeat of Sulla's experiences by assembling his fleet in

---

[116] Reddé (1986): 463–6 is right to see the Late Republic as a time of improvisation and temporary arrangements, but he probably goes too far in his attempts to show that the East was better provided than the West. It was never easy for the Romans to obtain the ships they needed in the wars of the 80s, 70s and 60s BC.

[117] *FGrHist* no. 434 fr. 20.351.

[118] *IGRRP* 1.118; Sherk (1969) no. 22; *CIL* I². 518. The men were from Klazomenai, Karystos and Miletos. They had apparently been involved in the Social War, or the Civil Wars of the 80s, so they too may have seen a long period of service before being allowed to return home.

[119] Murena held the province of Asia in 84 BC, but initially he deferred to Sulla, who left for Italy in 83 BC. He celebrated a triumph in 81 BC. *MRR* II 61, 62, 64, 70 and 77.

[120] See Sherwin-White (1984): 148–52.

[121] This tribute should be seen as separate from the payments of indemnities and taxes which were imposed by Sulla, the collection of which was Lucullus' responsibility (Plut. *Sull.* 25.2; *Luc.* 4.1; App. *Mith.* 62–3).

advance of any clash with Mithridates.[122] Since Sulla had taken all his available ships with him when he returned to Italy (Plut. *Sull*. 25.3), it may well be that he specifically instructed Murena to gather a new fleet. Several inscriptions from Samothrake, Rhodes and Delos honour Aulus Terentius Varro, a *presbeutes*, along with Sulla, Murena and Lucullus.[123] He was apparently a legate in charge of a fleet, probably that which Murena had asssembled. In the text from Rhodes Varro's name is followed by a long list of Rhodian officers. Both Lucullus and Murena apparently relied very heavily upon the Rhodians, and other maritime allies, for naval resources at this time. Such demands could be both burdensome and rewarding for the communities and individuals involved.[124]

Appian credits Murena with some activity against pirates in Southern Anatolia. In the section of his *Mithridatika* which introduces Pompey's campaign of 67 BC, he describes how the problem of piracy had worsened during the Mithridatic wars, and the difficulty which the Romans had in dealing with it: 'Murena took them on, but he had no great success, nor did Servilius Isauricus who came after Murena ...' (App. *Mith*. 93). This brief notice should be interpreted cautiously, since it is clearly intended to make the campaign of Pompey, which Appian describes in the following chapters, seem all the more remarkable by comparison, and it is both selective and misleading.[125] Servilius was not Murena's successor, as Appian implies, nor is it fair to say that he was unsuccessful. Appian probably chose to mention (and dismiss as insignificant) the actions of Murena and Servilius at this point in his narrative because, in addition to Lucullus, whom he had already dealt with, they were the two best-known Roman commanders who were active in Southern Anatolia after Sulla and before Pompey. The only detailed evidence we have for the nature of Murena's exploits comes from the *Geography* of Strabo, who says that he captured Kibyra and overthrew Moagetes, the tyrant who ruled this South Anatolian tetrapolis, and handed two of the cities over to the

---

[122] The mention of pirates in this context fulfils an important function in Cicero's concerted attack on his subject, Gaius Verres. It may reflect the subsequent use made of these ships by Murena's successors, but I do not think that it is sufficient on its own to show that Murena's fleet was not organized initially for use against Mithridates. See below pp. 150–7 on Cicero, Verres and piracy.

[123] *IGRRP* 1.843 (Rhodes); *ILS* 8772 (Samothrake); *CIL*² 2.738 (Delos).

[124] See Memnon, *FGrHist* 434 fr. 20.351; *IGRRP* 1.118; Reddé (1986): 463–6.

[125] Appian chose to narrate the campaign of 67 BC as a prelude to Pompey's war with Mithridates because he could find no obvious place for it in the scheme of his work (App. *Mith*. 91). It seems likely to me that this decision to place the narrative within the context of the Mithridatic wars may have been partly responsible for Appian's emphasis on the relationship between Mithridates and the growth of piracy in Anatolia. In contrast Strabo, whose work is arranged according to a geographical scheme, does not mention Mithridates in his explanation of the rise of the Cilician pirates (Str. 14.5.2).

Lycian League (Str. 13.4.17). There is nothing to link Kibyra with piracy, however, and it is more likely that Murena was trying to re-establish Roman control over this area in the wake of the first Mithridatic war. I would tentatively date Murena's Kibyran campaign to the summer of 84 BC, before Sulla left for Italy. Murena was using the title of *imperator* (victorious general) in 83 BC, according to Greek inscriptions, which could have been the result of his victory in Karia.[126] It has been suggested that this action was in some way a preparation for a campaign against the pirates,[127] but it is difficult to see how this could be so: Kibyra is an inland region, far from the coast, and does not block any obvious route to the more piratical regions of Pamphylia and Cilicia. It is quite possible that Murena was acting in accordance with instructions left him by Sulla, although he departed from any such orders and attacked Pontos directly as soon as Sulla was gone. It is difficult to see when he might have taken on the pirates in any case, since he was mostly concerned with Cappadocia and Pontos. He did not even deal with the Asian city of Mytilene, which was still in a state of revolt, leaving it instead to his successor Minucius Thermus, and Lucullus.[128]

Minucius Thermus was praetor in 81 BC and probably went to Asia as governor in that year. It was under his command that Mytilene was captured after a siege.[129] He was succeeded by the proconsul Gaius Claudius Nero, who was active in the south of the province,[130] but an inscription from Ilion in the north is thought to record measures he took against pirates:

Since the proconsul Gaius Claudius Nero, son of Publius, instructed the Poimanenians to send us, for the protection of our city, some soldiers with their own commander, the Poimanenians, being our friends and well disposed towards our people, sent the soldiers and Nikandros, son of Menophilos, to command them . . .[131]

While it is certainly possible that the soldiers were intended to guard against the incursions of pirates, we cannot be sure that there was not some other danger necessitating their presence, which we are not informed of by the inscription. Appian (*Mith.* 63) mentions attacks on

---

[126] *MRR* II 64.
[127] Reddé (1986): 463. Pohl (1993): 259 argues that inscriptions in honour of Murena as εὐεργέτης (benefactor), πρόξενος (patron) and σωτήρ (saviour) from Kaunos, Rhodes and Messene imply his success in suppressing piracy; but there is no reason to interpret these relatively commonplace titles in this particular way.
[128] Plut. *Luc.* 4; Livy, *Ep.* 89; Sherwin-White (1984): 149.
[129] *MRR* II 76 and 81; Suet. *Jul.* 2.1; *De vir. ill.* 78.1.
[130] *MRR* II 76, 80 and 84. Cic. *II Verr.* 1.71–6 and 84.
[131] *IGSK* Ilion no. 73, lines 1–6; *IGRRP* 4.196. The event can be dated to either 80 or 79 BC. The connection with piracy is made by Ormerod (1924): 206.

Aegean islands and coastal cities in 83 BC, while Sulla was still in Asia. If similar attacks were continuing, then garrisons at selected points might help to deter them, but there is no further evidence that Nero did anything about piracy during his proconsulship.

The picture of Roman activity in Anatolia after the first Mithridatic war is complicated by the establishment of a new province, which was called Cilicia, but did not actually include any Cilician territory at this time. The addition of territory in Pamphylia and Rough Cilicia eventually made the name of this province a partial reflection of its extent. The first person to hold this provincial command was Gnaeus Cornelius Dolabella.[132] It is clear from Murena's campaign in Kibyra that some parts of the new province were not properly under Roman control at this time. The war with Mithridates must have contributed to the problem, inter-rupting Roman domination in Western Anatolia, and making it necessary for magistrates to reconquer certain areas on the fringes of the Roman province, especially those which had never before been fully absorbed. Eventually this reconquest seems to have involved confronting the pirati-cally inclined communities which existed along the coastline of Pamphylia and Cilicia. Dolabella's main task was probably to pacify Pamphylia, continuing the process which had been started by Murena against Kibyra, but which he had abandoned in favour of renewing the war with Mi-thridates. According to Cicero, he was involved in this war when he was called away to Asia to sort out the problems caused by his legate Gaius Verres (Cic. *II Verr.* 1.73). It has been suggested that Dolabella cam-paigned against pirates at this time.[133] Cicero certainly mentions the plundering of two cities on the coastal plain of Pamphylia, Aspendos and Perge, but this, he says, was done by Verres, presumably while on active service with Dolabella (Cic. *II Verr.* 1.53–8). We have no direct evidence, therefore, that Dolabella's enemies were pirates.[134]

If the interpretation argued for above, that Lucullus was not the victim of an alliance between Mithridates and the pirates in 87–85 BC, is correct, then there is no specific evidence to back up the claim that Mithridates *employed* pirates against Roman forces at this time. Nor is there any good evidence to show that the Roman commanders in Anatolia after Sulla's departure campaigned against pirates, whether they were allies of Mi-thridates or not, in the 80s BC.

---

[132] *MRR* II 76, 80 and 84; III 65. See also Sherwin-White (1976): 10–11 and (1984): 152–5.
[133] Sherwin-White (1976): 11 and (1984): 153–4.
[134] We are also told by Cicero that Dolabella despatched Verres to Bithynia on an un-specified mission which *might* have been to obtain some ships or crews (Cic. *II Verr.* 63), as Casear had done for Minucius Thermus in 81 BC (Suet. *Jul.* 2), but this does not mean that the purpose of such aid was to suppress piracy.

## Mithridates and the pirates

The first episode involving pirates and Mithridates for which we have any details occurs in the third Mithridatic war (74–63 BC), long after the establishment of the pirates by Mithridates had supposedly occurred. In 73 BC, with Lucullus instead of Sulla as the main Roman commander, the king of Pontos was forced to abandon his siege of Kyzikos and flee by sea back to his own country. Appian describes the situation as follows:

> When Mithridates was sailing towards Pontos another storm blew up. About 10,000 men and 60 ships came to grief and the rest were dispersed according to where the wind blew them. Mithridates, his flagship having been holed, went aboard a pirate ship, although his friends tried to dissuade him, and the pirates brought him safely to Sinope. From there he was taken on to Amisos . . .[135] (App. *Mith.* 78)

The (apparently fortuitous) intervention of a pirate ship at this point was timely, as it appears to have saved Mithridates from a watery grave, but it hardly constitutes the sort of major collaboration between the king and the pirates which Maróti envisaged. Both Appian and Plutarch suggest that Mithridates was unwise to entrust his safety to the pirates. Why should this be so, if they were his long-time allies? It seems unlikely that his rescuers were allies at all, but that these pirates happened to be near by and offered their assistance in expectation of some reward. It is quite reasonable to assume that the pirates mentioned in this instance were operating in a similar fashion to those who accompanied Demetrios Poliorketes to the siege of Rhodes, and other 'camp followers' who gathered around the fringes of major conflicts in the Hellenistic period, hoping to gain some profit from the misfortunes of others.[136] On the unsuccessful termination of the siege of Kyzikos they probably departed along with Mithridates' forces and were caught up in the same storm.

A few years later, when he had finished settling affairs in Asia, Lucullus renewed the offensive against Pontos. He laid siege to the city of Sinope, which according to Plutarch was held by Cilicians on behalf of Mithridates. They slaughtered many of the inhabitants and, after setting fire to the city, tried to abandon it under cover of darkness; 8,000 of them were killed by Lucullus when he entered Sinope (Plut. *Luc.* 23.2). Memnon also describes the end of this siege, and names the commanders of the Cilician garrison as Kleochares and Seleukos, referring to the latter as:

---

[135] See also Plut. *Luc.* 13.3. Ormerod (1924): 211 cites Orosius' brief account (6.2.24), in which the pirate vessel's commander is identified as Seleucus, but ignores Appian and Plutarch. For other versions in the ancient sources see Maróti (1970): 487, n. 24.

[136] See above pp. 43–8.

'Mithridates' general' (*FGrHist* 434 fr. 1.37–38.1). Orosius calls him 'the archpirate' and adds that Kleochares was a eunuch (Oros. 6.3.2). Strabo, on the other hand, refers to the commander of the garrison appointed by Mithridates as Bakchides (Str. 12.3.11). Memnon also describes an incident during the siege of Sinope involving the capture of some supply ships. The Roman admiral, Censorinus, had 15 escort triremes, but these were defeated by the Sinopian triremes under Seleukos who took the supply ships for their booty (*FGrHist* 434 fr. 1.37.2–3). It is on the basis of these references that Maróti concludes that the Cilician pirates operated extensively for Mithridates by disrupting Roman communications and attacking their supply and transport vessels.[137] While it is true that the sources do mention both pirates and Cilicians, the nature of these references does not suggest that Cilician pirates formed a particularly important part of Mithridates' forces. The (large) garrison at Sinope is more likely to have been made up of *mercenaries*, many of them no doubt of Cilician origin.[138] The only ancient source who mentions any pirates in connection with the siege of Sinope is Orosius, who reserves the label 'archpirate' for Seleukos. This may be a term of abuse taken from his sources, but it is hardly good evidence for the conclusion that all the cities of the Pontic coast were held for Mithridates by pirates.[139] Indeed, Jacoby argues that it is Strabo, a native of Pontos and closer in time to the events than most other sources, who is most likely to have the correct information about the commander of the Sinopian garrison and whose sources for the Mithridatic wars were generally very good.[140]

References such as those discussed above, sometimes in agreement, sometimes conflicting, are typical of the sources for the history of this period, as far as piracy is concerned. It is possible to fashion from them a relatively detailed narrative which fleshes out the skeleton provided by Appian's broad generalizations. Thus Seleukos becomes a leading Cilician pirate whose alliance with Mithridates makes him an important figure in the third Mithridatic war, and he is but one example of many such pirate-captains.[141] It is not even clear, however, that the term pirate is appro-

---

[137] Maróti (1970).

[138] Compare Polybius' reference to Cilicians serving in the army of Antiochos IV (Polyb. 30.25.4). Mithridates also recruited mercenaries in Crete, another place notorious for its pirates (Flor. 3.6; Memnon, *FGrHist*. 434 fr. 1.33). Pohl (1993): 140 n. 234 uses a comment in Appian's account of Sicily and the Islands (App. *Sic*. 6.1) to argue that Mithridates was closely allied with many Cretan pirate communities; on this see below pp. 145–8.

[139] So Maróti (1970): 487.

[140] *FGrHist*. 434 Kommentar *ad loc.*

[141] Maróti (1970): 486–8. Ormerod (1924): 209–10 compares them to the Barbary corsairs, who operated as naval allies of the Turks in the sixteenth century AD.

priately applied to Seleukos. Only Orosius, a Christian writer of the early fifth century AD, uses it to describe him, and he is hardly a reliable or unbiased source, since his aim was essentially to narrate pagan history in an unfavourable light.[142] If Seleukos was not a pirate, but rather a mercenary leader, or even a general, then his activities are of no great significance for Cilician piracy. It is impossible to choose a 'true version' among the conflicting accounts of the Sinope episode, but it seems that the main source which indicates that it should be included among the activities of the Cilician pirates is also the one least to be relied upon. The only clear evidence of the involvement of pirates in a specific part of the Mithridatic wars is the rescue of Mithridates in 73 BC, in circumstances which suggest that the pirates were not important allies but 'hangers-on'. This does not mean that pirates (from Cilicia and elsewhere) did not profit from the political instability in the Eastern Mediterranean which resulted from the wars between Mithridates and the Romans,[143] but it would seem to me that their activities were very marginal to the conflicts themselves. Perhaps the most important contribution which Mithridates made to the piracy problem of the region was to create a situation similar to that which had allowed Rough Cilicia to become a base for pirates in the second century BC.[144]

The threat posed by the king of Pontos to Roman domination in the East had been clearly demonstrated in the 80s BC. The uneasy truce which prevailed after Murena's withdrawal in 81 BC was not controlled by a formal treaty, because the terms of the agreement between Mithridates and Sulla, the Peace of Dardanus, were never formally ratified by the senate. Murena had used this as his excuse for war in 83 BC and it appears that in 78 BC, with Sulla dead, Mithridates' ambassadors in Rome were still trying to obtain access to the senate so that the treaty could be confirmed.[145] Sherwin-White, in his analysis of the strategic considerations facing the Romans in Anatolia, stresses the need for their commanders to recover lost ground and establish a strong position to defend their territory against any further attacks from the kingdom of Pontos. Fundamental to this strategy was the need to dominate Mi-

---

[142] See Momigliano (1963). Orosius is also the only source for the detail that Kleochares was a eunuch (6.3.2). In his selection from a variety of earlier sources, which he completed very quickly, Orosius was more interested in excitement and colour than accuracy.

[143] Appian says pirates sacked Iassos, Samos, Klazomenai and Samothrake, robbing the latter's temple of 1,000 talents when Sulla was near by, but that he allowed them to go unhindered. If they were *allies* of Mithridates, why did Sulla not try to punish them, or hold them to the same peace agreement as the king?

[144] See above pp. 97–101.

[145] App. *Mith.* 64 and 67. See also Sherwin-White (1984): 149–51.

thridates' southern flank, that is, Cappadocia, which was the Romans' principal buffer against Mithridates, and the southern and western regions of Anatolia which provided access to it from Asia.[146] Murena made some efforts in this direction with his Kibyran campaign, and Dolabella seems to have continued the work, but the most extensive series of campaigns in this region in the 70s BC were those of a magistrate of consular rank, Publius Servilius, who has been credited with considerable success against (Cilician) pirates. It is his operations which must be considered next.

### Servilius Isauricus

Publius Servilius Vatia was consul in 79 BC and went to his province of Cilicia as Dolabella's successor in 78 BC.[147] At this time the *provincia* called 'Cilicia' did not include any territory which was geographically Cilician. The appointment of an ex-consul as governor is itself an indication that great importance was being attached to operations in Cilicia at this time. The forces which Servilius had under his command included a fleet, containing 'heavy' warships, among which may have been some of the vessels handed over by Mithridates as part of the Peace of Dardanus.[148] His army was, perhaps, five legions strong, some of whom had been in the provinces of Cilicia or Asia since the early to mid-80s.[149] The crews of the warships and some of the ships themselves were most likely drawn from Rome's allies. It is reasonable to assume that the Rhodians once again played a prominent part in the campaign.

There is general agreement among historians about the broad outline of events relating to the campaigns carried out in Southern Anatolia by Servilius in the years 78–74 BC. In an important article published just two years before his book on ancient piracy Ormerod concluded that, after a year spent in preparations, Servilius conducted a campaign in Pamphylia and Eastern Lycia in the years 77–76 BC, and then attacked and defeated the Isaurians and the Orondeis in the years 76–75 BC.[150] In 74 BC he returned to Rome and celebrated a triumph, taking the cognomen 'Isauricus'.

It is the early stages of Servilius' actions which are most relevant to the problem of piracy and its supression. The sources speak of at least one

---

[146]  Sherwin-White (1984): 155–8.

[147]  *MRR* II 82 and 87.

[148]  Flor. 1.41.4 (*gravi et Martia classe*).

[149]  See Sherwin-White (1984): 157 and Brunt (1971): 452. One of his junior officers was (briefly) Gaius Julius Caesar, who returned to Rome after Sulla's death in 78 BC to further his political career (Suet. *Jul.* 3).

[150]  Ormerod (1922). A summary version is given in Ormerod (1924): 214–19.

naval battle, followed by attacks against bases on land.[151] The general shape of his campaign – a gathering of forces, a sea battle and then a series of attacks on strongholds – conforms to a typical pattern of anti-piracy actions in this period.[152] This suggests that Servilius' early activities were intended as a serious attempt to deal with pirates in Southern Anatolia at this time. His later victories, against the Isauri and Orondeis seem, however, to have little connection with piracy. It is also important to clarify as far as possible the nature and location of Servilius' piratical opponents. Although most of the sources speak of Servilius defeating pirates in 'Cilicia', it is clear from the details we have concerning his activities that he began by tackling strongholds in eastern Lycia. The places which are most commonly mentioned in the sources are Phaselis, Olympos and Korykos.[153] Strabo goes into some detail about Olympos, describing it in the following terms:

Near to the mountain ridges of the Tauros is the pirate base of Zeniketos – Olympos, the mountain and the citadel having the same name – from where the whole of Lycia, Pamphylia, Pisidia and Milyas can be seen. The mountain having been taken by Isauricus, Zeniketos burnt himself along with his household. He also controlled Korykos and Phaselis and many parts of Pamphylia, but Isauricus took them all.[154] (Str. 14.5.7)

Zeniketos emerges from this passage as a powerful local ruler; he also controlled other territory in Pamphylia[155] and his domain may, perhaps, have been similar to that of Moagetes, the tyrant of Kibyra in western Lycia, who was overthrown by Murena in 84 BC.[156] An important difference between the two is that Zeniketos controlled a substantial part of the Lycian coastline and is specifically labelled a pirate by Strabo.

Further evidence of piratical activities carried out in this area is provided by Cicero, who says of the city of Phaselis:

That Phaselis, which Publius Servilius captured, had not always been a city of Cilician pirates. It was the Lycians, a Greek people, who inhabited it. But, because of its situation, and because it projected so far out to sea that the pirates often had

---

[151] Flor. 3.6; Str. 14.5.7; Eutr. 6.3; Sall. *Hist.* frr. I.1.127–33; Cic. *II Verr.* 1.21 and 4.22; Cic. *Leg. agr.* 2.50.

[152] Compare the campaigns of Quintus Caecilius Metellus Balearicus in 123 BC and Marcus Antonius the orator in 102 BC (above pp. 92–6 and 102–08), as well as Pompey's Cilician campaign of 67 BC (below pp. 161–72).

[153] E.g. Str. 14.5.7; Oros. 5.23.21–3; Eutr. 6.3.

[154] Strabo places this account of Olympos and Zeniketos in the *Cilician* section of his *Geography*, between Seleukeia and Soli. This would appear to be the result of his confusing Korykos with the Korykos in Cilicia (see map 3). For the correct identifications see Ormerod (1922).

[155] Indicated by Cic. *Leg. agr.* 1.5.

[156] Str. 13.4.17; see above pp. 121–3.

cause to call in on their expeditions from Cilicia, both on the outward and the return journey, they made the city their own, first through commercial ties, then also by an alliance (Cic. *II Verr.* 4.21)

This passage provides an important insight into the practical aspects of piracy, which are all too easily overlooked by modern scholars. The journey by sea from Cilicia towards the west is not an easy one and Phaselis is one of the last suitable landfalls before the difficult stretch around Cape Gelidonya. Pirates are bound by the laws of navigation as much as ordinary sailors, and they need suitable ports to sell or exchange their booty, hence Cicero's mention of frequent landfalls at Phaselis. It was also an important commercial harbour for merchants passing between the Aegean and the Levantine coast. Cicero implies that piracy was a relatively recent problem at Phaselis, when Servilius captured the city, and that it was not the practice of its native population. It could be that Phaselis was overrun by outsiders, the 'Cilicians', who forcibly introduced piracy,[157] or, perhaps it is more likely, since Cicero portrays the relationship as an alliance, that the inhabitants willingly co-operated with the pirates in return for a substantial share of their profits. Phaselis certainly had elaborate public buildings in Roman times and there were three large harbours.[158] Olympos was one of the six largest cities in the Lycian League according to Strabo (Str. 14.3.3), which is a further indication of the power and size of Zeniketos' domain. Cicero called for an official list of the impressive booty removed from Olympos in his speech against Verres in 70 BC, which implies that Zeniketos and his subjects had amassed great wealth.[159] In defeating him, after a hard-fought campaign, it may be that Servilius was removing a troublesome nest of pirates, but the longer-term consideration of his governorship was to reassert Roman control over a strategically important region which had been lost to Mithridates in the first Mithridatic war.[160] The next part of Servilius' military activity, in Isauria, demonstrates the overriding strategic concerns which guided his actions. He spent another year or more fighting in rugged, mountainous country far from pirates and the sea, securing control of the overland route to Cappadocia. Although Ormerod has suggested that his purpose here was to prepare for an attack on Cilicia proper, it is clear from the subsequent course of events that the kingdom of Cappadocia, which

[157] On the leaders among Cilician pirates as outsiders see Rauh (1998).

[158] Blackman (1973). Little remains, however, of the Hellenistic city and its harbours.

[159] Another pirate leader mentioned by Cicero in connection with Servilius is Nico, who escaped but was recaptured (Cic. *II Verr.* 5.79). He gives no further information, but it seems reasonable to suppose that he was an associate of Zeniketos, presumably a leading figure in one of the Lycian or Pamphylian cities which Zeniketos controlled.

[160] See Sherwin-White (1976): 1–8.

Sherwin-White calls 'the soft underbelly of the Pontic Empire', was the principal concern.[161] In 74 BC, when war with Mithridates was imminent, Lucullus was perfectly placed in the newly acquired part of the province of Cilicia to counterattack.

## Pirates and propaganda

If the involvement of pirates, Cilician or otherwise, in the Mithridatic wars was limited to occasional appearances such as the rescue of Mithridates in 72 BC, why do some of the ancient sources present a great deal of the Roman provincial commanders' activities at this time in terms of the suppression of piracy? The answer to this question would seem to lie in the need for both Mithridates and his Roman adversaries to win the support of the social and political élites in the communities of the Eastern Mediterranean. In order to cultivate their support, both sides projected images of themselves and their actions which they expected would meet with approval among the wealthy cities and monarchs whose money, men and other resources were the ultimate objective in their wars. Mithridates, for example, seems to have stressed the aggressive, greedy and rapacious aspects of Roman imperialism in the Eastern Mediterranean, arguing that submission to Roman rule meant virtual slavery. He also portrayed himself as the innocent victim of Roman provocation, aimed at destroying a king who was the potential saviour of the Hellenistic Greeks.[162]

The Romans sought to portray Mithridates as a destructive tyrant, intent on overthrowing the established order and devastating the comfortable lives of the wealthy Greek communities. Such is the image of Mithridates which Appian offers in his version of the first Mithridatic war. He makes Mithridates terrorize many of the Aegean communities with the threat of attacks on their cities, mass deportations, the cancellation of debts, citizenship for foreigners and freedom for slaves (e.g. App. *Mith.* 46–8). Sulla's speech to the representatives of the cities of Asia at the end of the first war repeats the same imagery (App. *Mith.* 62). An important part of this negative picture of Mithridates is the alliance of Mithridates and the pirates, which is stressed by Appian (App. *Mith.* 62, 63, 92, 119). It made good sense for the Romans, who had recently adopted a role as the suppressors of piracy, to exploit the obvious fears which pirates engendered among many of the citizens of the Greek cities by presenting Mithridates as an ally of pirates. Pirates were viewed as common enemies

---

[161] Ormerod (1922); Sherwin-White (1976): 11.
[162] E.g. App *Mith.* 70; Sall. *Hist.* fr. IV.69M. For a detailed treatment of Mithridates' 'propaganda' see McGing (1986): 89–108.

to whom a severe punishment should be meted out, as the late second-century BC decree of Ephesos in honour of the Astypalaians shows.[163] The clearest expression of the Graeco-Roman élite's attitude to pirates in the first century BC is found in Cicero's work *On Duties*. In a passage which discusses the sanctity of oaths, Cicero distinguishes between oaths which should be kept, and oaths which it is not dishonourable to break:

> If, for example, you do not hand over to pirates the amount agreed upon as the price of your life, that is not perjury, not even if you have sworn an oath and do not do so, for a pirate is not included in the category of lawful enemies ... (Cic. *Off.* 3.107)

The notion behind this passage is clear: pirates are the worst kind of enemies, and they are not deserving of the normal respect due to enemies according to the conventions of war.[164] This prevailing view of piracy made the label pirate an attractive one for application to one's political opponents, as had been the case in earlier periods.[165]

### Sertorius

The Sabine senator Quintus Sertorius, who went to Spain as praetor in 83 BC is one of the most famous rebels in Roman history. In his life of Sertorius, Plutarch describes his adventures after withdrawing from Spain in 81 BC in order to avoid the forces of the Sullan magistrates who were sent to replace him. Plutarch recounts how, after a brief excursion to Mauretania, he tried to return to Spain:

> He was once more driven away from the coast, but, after joining forces with a number of ships from Cilicia, he attacked the island of Pityussa [Ibiza], overpowered the garrison which Annius had placed there, and forced a landing. Soon afterwards Annius arrived with a large fleet and a force of 5,000 infantry, whereupon Sertorius ventured to engage him in a full-scale naval battle, even though his own ships were frailly built and were designed for speed rather than for fighting.[166]

A storm then blew up and scattered Sertorius' ships, which eventually headed out through the straits of Gibraltar and round the coast of Spain to the Guadalquivir delta. He was tempted by glowing reports of the 'Isles

---

[163] *IGSK* Ephesos 1a no. 5; see above pp. 100–1.

[164] A similar sentiment is expressed in Cic. *II Verr.* 5.76: 'Could any one individual keep within the walls of his own house the bitterest and most dangerous enemy of the Roman people, or, rather, the common enemy of all peoples?' Maróti (1962a) takes these comments and other references much further, arguing that there was a Roman-led 'common war' (κοινὸς πόλεμος) against piracy in the second and first centuries BC.

[165] See above Chs. 2 & 3.

[166] Plut. *Sert.* 8; I quote from the translation of Scott-Kilvert (1965). For an alternative interpretation of these events, which places greater emphasis on the 'alliance' of Sertorius and the Cilicians see the commentary of Konrad (1994).

of the Blest' to settle his men there, but, according to Plutarch, '... his allies, the Cilician pirates, had no desire for peace or leisure; their interest was all in spoils and riches' (Plut. *Sert.* 9). The Cilicians sailed off to Africa to aid the restoration of Askalis, the son of Iptha, to the Mauretanian throne, but Sertorius joined the opposing side in this civil war and was duly victorious. Nothing more is said about these pirates by Plutarch. They seem to have been a relatively small force, apparently trying their luck away from the Eastern Mediterranean. They were prepared to engage Roman forces with Sertorius, and to join in civil war, but their interest, according to Plutarch, was in the booty rather than the political outcome. They disappear from Plutarch's account just before the arrival of Paccianus, with strong Roman forces sent by Sulla to help Iptha against Sertorius (Plut. *Sert.* 9). They seem to be acting as mercenaries, although how effective they were is difficult to assess. Sertorius was a very marginal political figure at this time, and would have been desperate enough for help to ignore his allies' dubious origins. From a literary point of view, it seems to me that Plutarch is trying at this point in his biography to illustrate the decline in Sertorius' fortunes. He has sunk so low that he has to associate with pirates, who prove to be very unreliable allies. A comparison might be made with the story which connects Spartacus and the Cilician pirates in Plutarch's life of Crassus (Plut. *Crass.* 10).[167] The episode is included by Plutarch to show the change in Spartacus' fortunes, which continue to decline to the point where he is defeated at the hands of Crassus and his army. It also neatly signals that things have changed for the better as far as Crassus and the Romans are concerned. Sertorius was later linked with Mithridates in an anti-Roman alliance of Eastern and Western Mediterranean. Plutarch describes Mithridates' 'flatterers' persuading the king that he is a new Pyrrhus and Sertorius a new Hannibal, which encouraged the king to negotiate an alliance between them in 76/5 BC, although Sertorius refused to acknowledge Mithridates' claim to the province of Asia, granting only recognition of his rights to Bithynia and Cappadocia.[168] Here the literary effect is clearly to show that although Sertorius has departed some way from the role of a true repre-

---

[167] This episode, in which Cilician pirates offer to transport Spartacus' forces to Sicily, but then sail away and leave him stranded in South Italy, is not mentioned in any other source for the Slave War of 73–71 BC. I think it unlikely that Cilician pirates would have risked a confrontation with the Roman forces gathering in South Italy and Sicily at this time, although the story could well be a contemporary invention, aimed at blackening Spartacus' name even further by associating him with pirates.

[168] Plut. *Sert.* 23–4. Compare Sall. *Hist.* fr. II.90, as renumbered by McGushin (1992), and Oros. 6.2.12, who claims the 'flatterers' were Lucius Magius and Lucius Fannius, two deserters from Fimbria's army, whom Cicero in 70 BC describes as carrying messages between all the enemies of the Roman people from Spain to the Black Sea (Cic. *II Verr.* 1.87).

sentative of the senate and People, he still tries to act as an upholder of Roman authority by denying the claims of a foreign king to possession of a Roman province. Contemporary sources presumably made a great deal of this 'unholy alliance' between the rebel magistrate and the Eastern king.[169] In both cases it seems highly likely that the links between Rome's enemies were being stressed by contemporary or near-contemporary sources in order to generate a kind of negative propaganda.

### Romans and pirates

Mithridates also seems to have exploited the pirate label, although, as would be expected from the loser in a major conflict, the criticisms and name-calling he employed against the Romans were less effective in the long run than their negative presentation of him. There are, however, two passages in the ancient sources which may be indicative of an attempt by the king of Pontus to turn the piracy accusation against his enemies. Sallust, in a letter he attributes to Mithridates in his *Histories*, makes the king call the Romans 'the race of pirates who plundered the globe'.[170] In his account of the speech given by Mithridates to his men before the invasion of Bithynia in 74 BC, Appian has the king claim that the Romans have so neglected their duty to keep the sea safe, that it has been overrun by pirates (App. *Mith.* 70). It is very difficult to assess how closely such references reflect the utterances of the protagonists, and how far they must be attributed to the literary skills of the historians in whose works they occur. Yet it does not seem unreasonable to conclude that both sides deliberately sought to blacken their opponent's name by associating it with the long-standing problem of piracy. The Roman commanders in particular found it convenient to justify their aggressive military actions in Anatolia in terms of the suppression of piracy, especially in situations where they might otherwise have appeared to be provoking their recent opponent to further ruinous wars. It should not be forgotten that the burden of such conflicts, whatever the nature of their resolution, fell heavily on Rome's provincial subjects and allies. Many of these were apparently disillusioned enough with Rome in the 80s BC to side with Mithridates, at least in the early stages of the first Mithridatic war.[171] Thereafter the Romans must have been conscious of the need to improve

---

[169]  Konrad (1994): 191 even suggests that Magius and Fannius were 'pirates', apparently on the basis of Cicero describing their ship as a *myoparon*. See also Rauh (1999a).

[170]  Sall. *Hist.* fr. IV.69M. The date of the letter, to the Parthian king Arsaces, is 69 BC. It is unlikely to be genuine, but it may reflect contemporary views. See McGushin (1994): 173–99; he renumbers the fragments, making the letter fr. 4.67.

[171]  See McGing (1986): ch. 4. Pohl (1993): 139–68 argues that piracy itself was another form of resistance to Roman oppression and the economic dislocation of the Mithridatic wars.

their image in the Eastern Mediterranean by presenting themselves as powerful benefactors.

Publius Servilius Isauricus seems to have understood very well the need for positive promotion of Rome's image as the suppressor of piracy. In the *Verrine Orations* Cicero draws his audience's attention to the captured pirates whom Publius Servilius displayed in public:

> One man, Publius Servilius, captured alive more pirates than all the previous commanders put together. And when did he ever deny to anyone the pleasure of seeing a captured pirate? On the contrary he displayed the most enjoyable spectacle of captive enemies in chains to all and sundry. And so they came from all around, not just from the towns through which the pirates were being led, to behold the sight. (Cic. *II Verr.* 5.66)

Cicero then goes on to boast about the large numbers of executions of pirates which followed Servilius' triumph. He says earlier in the *Verrine Orations* (*II Verr.* 1.56) that he witnessed this triumph and it seems to have made a considerable impression upon him. Cicero is presumably describing how the captives were paraded through the towns of Italy on their way to Rome, but it is reasonable to assume that Servilius would have made a similar show of his booty and prisoners in the Eastern Mediterranean, among Rome's Greek-speaking subjects and allies. In this way they could be presented with the tangible results of the campaign and show their approval for the Roman commander's actions. It should be noted that the labelling of Servilius' enemies as 'pirates' would have been his decision. Zeniketos and his subjects may not have thought of themselves as pirates, any more than Murena's opponent Moagetes or his people considered him to be a tyrant, but the historical verdict on them has been determined by the labels chosen for them by their Roman conquerors. Indeed, such captives could have been literally 'labelled' as pirates in the context of a Roman triumph, in which it was common practice to have the prisoners of war accompanied by descriptive placards. The fact that Servilius' captives were, ultimately, being marched off for execution, which another passage from the *Verrine Orations* confirms as the appropriate punishment for pirates (Cic. *II Verr.* 5.76), would be seen as the final 'proof' that through Servilius Rome was fulfilling her pledge to suppress piracy which she first outlined in the *lex de provinciis praetoriis* of 100 BC. Those whom Rome declared to be pirates were suffering the fate of pirates.

It was also stated in the *lex de provinciis praetoriis* that the Romans expected those who were their allies and friends to co-operate with them in suppressing piracy, by denying bases to the pirates.[172] How willing

---

[172] *Lex de provinciis praetoriis* Knidos copy column II, lines 2–4 and column III, lines 28–37. See above pp. 108–14.

were they to respond to the Romans' call for a common stand against pirates? It would seem likely that the depredations of pirates based in Cilicia and adjacent regions would have been most keenly felt by the communities of Southern Anatolia. While this might seem likely to make them eager to take anti-piratical measures, it is important to bear in mind that they could be potential partners of their piratically inclined neighbours, as Cicero outlines in the case of Phaselis (Cic. *II Verr.* 4.21). Alternatively, if they opposed piracy, their proximity might make them easier targets for reprisals from powerful enemies like Zeniketos. It was one thing to join in a general Roman-led chorus of disapproval, but quite another to turn words into deeds, especially when the Romans themselves showed a greater interest in the war with Mithridates and other imperialist ambitions. In any case, the resources of the individual kings, cities or groups of cities were not up to major campaigns, but required the political and military leadership of Rome. Hence there is very little evidence for local resistance to piratical communities, or attempts at suppression of piracy independent of the Roman proconsuls' efforts which have been considered above. This may partly be a reflection of the Romano-centric nature of the main literary sources, whose narratives concentrate on the actions of great men in great wars, but it is probably also due to a general reluctance on the part of communities in Lycia, Pamphylia and Cilicia to risk retribution and even destruction by acting without the reassurance of Roman protection, especially in the period after 88 BC, when the Romans' reputation for invincibility was severely dented by Mithridates. It is worth noting that one of the most prominent opponents of piracy, Rhodes, was a large *island* community, better placed than most others to escape or resist retaliation. Such considerations as these might lead to the conclusion that all the peoples inhabiting the coastline of Southern Anatolia were pirates, friends of pirates or helpless victims, but some scraps of literary and epigraphic evidence do indicate that there were places where piracy was rejected and even opposed without direct Roman involvement.

### Lycians and Pamphylians

Strabo, in his description of the coastline and the harbours of Lycia, is at pains to distinguish between the civilized, decent behaviour of the Lycians, and the deplorable practices of their less civilized, piratical neighbours. He briefly characterizes the Pamphylians and Cilicians as either pirates or the accomplices of pirates, but says of their western neighbours: 'The Lycians continued to live decently, according to the way of a *polis*, so that, in spite of the good fortune which made their neighbours a sea power even as far as Italy, they did not lust after shameful booty, but

stayed in their fatherland under the Lycian League' (Str. 14.3.2).[173]
Strabo is generally of the opinion that rugged or inhospitable countries
are the abode of 'uncivilized' peoples, who are likely to be poor and
practise banditry or piracy (Str. 1.3.2; 2.5.26; 3.3.5). He ends his *Geography* by contrasting the 'civilized' world inside the Roman Empire with the
'uncivilized' world of nomads and pirates outside it (Str. 17.3.25). The
Lycians, therefore, constitute something of an exception to this rule,
which is explained by their Hellenized lifestyle. They live in cities[174]
which are organized together into a league. This decent behaviour was
rewarded by the Romans, who allowed them considerable autonomy on
account of the good government which they lived under (Str. 14.3.3). Yet
not all the Lycians were as well behaved as Strabo claims. Cicero describes the piratical city of Phaselis in the eastern part of Lycia as: 'a city
of Cilician pirates' (Cic. *II Verr.* 4.21), and the cities of Olympos and
Korykos, which were captured along with Phaselis by Servilius Isauricus
from the piratical leader Zeniketos, were also in eastern Lycia (Str.
14.5.7). Strabo's general comments should not be dismissed as mere phi-
losophizing, in spite of the apparent contradictions. It is likely that he
drew heavily upon Lycian sources, written by people who would have
been keen to portray their homeland's past history in the best possible
light.[175] Cicero, on the other hand, was commenting upon recent events,
which had not yet been subjected to the reassessment of historians. It is
also noteworthy that Strabo's list of cities captured by Servilius does not
inlcude any of the major Lycian cities on the western side of the mountains which effectively divide Lycia in two. The existence of such diver-
gent views on Lycian attitudes to and participation in piracy in the first
century BC may well reflect divisions among the Lycians themselves over
the practice and support of piracy, and possibly over its suppression.

Internal Lycian divisions appear to lie behind a group of late second- or
early first-century BC inscriptions from Xanthos, which celebrate the
deeds of a Xanthian admiral called Aichmon. Two of these inscriptions
seem to have formed part of a *tropaeum* which was built into the wall
above the city gate. The third was found close to this location. Aichmon,
son of Apollodoros, is described in the first inscription as the commander
of the fleet of all the Lycians. He fought a sea battle around Chelidonia
and then invaded enemy territory, laid it waste and was victorious in three

---

[173] See above p. 97 for the preceding section of this passage.
[174] The words which Strabo employs to describe how the Lycians conducted themselves are:
πολιτικῶς καὶ σωφρόνως. For an account of Lycian civilization, which was far less
Greek than Strabo or Cicero believed, see Bryce (1986).
[175] For ancient works on Lycia see Bryce (1986): ch. 1.

battles.[176] The inscription on the reverse of this block gives further details, including some clues about the nature of Aichmon's command and the enemy whom he overcame. Aichmon is described as '... having been elected by the Lycians to command over their assembled war fleet ...', and he is credited with 'having persevered against the ones having been in a state of opposition to the nation, for the entire duration of the campaign, industriously and boldly ...'[177] The editor of *OGIS*, W. Dittenberger, drew attention to the peculiar phrase used in the second inscription to denote the Lycians' opponents. Instead of being described as 'the enemy', they are designated by the tortuous formula 'the ones having been in a state of opposition to the nation'.[178] Dittenberger suggested that this might indicate that the enemy involved were Lycians themselves. This idea is supported by the location of the battle, off the Chelidonia Islands, which would indicate that the landfall was probably in the same eastern half of Lycia, on the coastal plain. It is in this part of Lycia that Phaselis, Korykos and Olympos are located, all cities which felt the wrath of Rome during Publius Servilius' proconsulship. It would also seem that this action was taken independently of the Romans, who are not referred to in any way by these inscriptions.[179] It seems to me, therefore, that Aichmon's campaign, for which he received the praise of the Lycians in Xanthos, may well have been an attempt by some of the western Lycians to reduce the influence and curtail the piratical activities of their eastern neighbours. The events described must, I believe, date to before 78 BC, but they need not be any earlier than the beginning of the century and *could* be dated to the 80s BC. The context of a Lycian decision to undertake military action against their neighbours could be provided by the *lex de provinciis praetoriis* which invited Rome's friends and allies to undertake such measures. If this hypothesis is correct, then Aichmon's campaign, which was probably not a complete success, in spite of the triumphal tone of the inscriptions, was a remarkable display of initiative and

---

[176] *OGIS* 552; *ILLRP* 3.607B. The date of the entire group is deduced from the letter forms and the absence of anything to indicate the period of direct Rhodian control. I date the events to the early first century BC, but there is no conclusive proof.

[177] *OGIS* 553 = *ILLRP* 3.607A. The text of the latter is defective in line 3, printing ἐπαναχθήτος instead of συναχθέντος. The third inscription (*OGIS* 554 = *ILLRP* 3.620), found near the other two and clearly relating to the same episode, is much shorter. It is a simple dedication to the two Lycian heroes Glaukos and Sarpedon by those serving in his fleet.

[178] The Greek text reads: τῶν τὰ ἐναντία πραξάντων τῷ ἔθνει, instead of the simpler τῶν πολεμιῶν.

[179] So Magie (1950): 1167 n. 18. Sherwin-White (1984): 115 n. 22 dismisses the episode as irrelevant to Roman policy in the region. Ziebarth (1929): 35 assumes that the Lycians were 'Bundesgenossen der Römer gegen Zeniketes'. The absence of Roman involvement would help to explain why none of the extant literary sources make any mention of this episode.

determination, indicating that some of the Lycians were indeed worthy of the fulsome praise heaped upon them by Strabo.

Epigraphic evidence also indicates that Strabo was less than entirely fair to the Pamphylians. He implies that all the Pamphylians practised piracy or behaved like the citizens of Side, entering into partnership with pirates (Str. 14.3.2). An inscription found on the site of the ancient city of Syedra shows that such generalizations cannot be accepted at face value. The inscription is an oracular response, probably from the oracle of Apollo at Klaros, advising the Syedrans on how to deal with the problem of piracy. The oracle tells the Syedrans to set up a statue of Ares and Hermes, to which the inscription was probably attached. The advice continues: '... in addition, you should take up the violent battle, either driving away, or binding in unbreakable chains, and do not, through fear, pay a terrible penalty because of the pirates; in this way you will certainly escape all punishment'.[180] The implication of this inscription is that the Syedrans must resist the pirates by force, or suffer the consequences. Two questions arise from this: what form should the resistance take, and whose retribution are the Syedrans trying to avoid? It is reasonable to suppose that the answer to the first question is provided by the *lex de provinciis praetoriis*, with its clear statement of the responsibility of Rome's allies and friends to assist the Romans in their efforts to suppress piracy. The Syedrans could have been prompted to consult Apollo for guidance by the promulgation of the law itself, and the campaign of Marcus Antonius the orator which preceded it, or the events of the 80s and 70s BC, especially Servilius' spectacular advances in this area. All of these developments might have given the Syedrans reason to decide whether they would support Rome or her piratical enemies. A less certain, but still likely, conclusion is that the retribution to be feared is that of Rome. In a period when Rome's supremacy was not guaranteed, however, it would have been prudent to make the public record of the Syedrans' decision as ambiguous as possible, leaving the city's resistance to piracy to be implied rather than boldly stated. It is also worth noting that the inscription starts with a reference to Syedran lands as 'the homes of mixed peoples', which is probably an allusion to the presence of both Pamphylians and Cilicians in the community. The oracular message could have been intended to help provide a focus for unity among the Syedrans. The neighbouring city of Korakesion was notorious as a centre of piracy which resisted the Romans, especially Pompey in 67 BC (Plut. *Pomp.* 28.1; Vell. Pat. 2.32.4), so Syedra's decision to align with Rome would have been a risky under-

---

[180] Bean & Mitford (1965): 21–3. For a fuller discussion, text and translation of this inscription see de Souza (1997).

taking, with plenty of reason to fear retribution from the pirates as well as the Romans. I think it unlikely that such a small and vulnerable place as Syedra engaged in any independent military actions. Instead the inhabitants probably refused to allow those they considered pirates to use their harbour and town. They probably contributed in some fashion to the Roman forces which did eventually come into this area, particularly those of Pompey, who has a tenuous connection with the city in the 40s BC, possibly indicating that he had received assistance from there at an earlier date, and may even have been a patron of the Syedrans.[181] Another exception to the general rule of Cilician and Pamphylian co-operation with pirates is provided by Strabo, in his description of the city of Seleukeia on the river Kalykadnos, which he says kept aloof from the practices of the Cilicians and Pamphylians (Str. 14.5.4). He calls it a populous city, which may mean that the community felt sufficiently large and strong to take an independent line and avoid the bad reputation which neighbouring cities soon acquired.

There is a little evidence, therefore, to indicate that there were some cities and communities in Southern Anatolia that responded positively to Rome's call to join in the suppression of piracy. While it is for attacks across the other side of the Mediterranean that Cilician pirates have become infamous, in all periods of history pirates have tended to conduct most of their operations fairly close to home. The depredations of the Cilician pirates were probably felt most keenly by their own neighbours, in and around the coastal regions of Anatolia. The position which the Romans held as the leaders in a common struggle against piracy left the onus on them to organize and conduct effectve campaigns. It was, however, a long time before the Romans themselves undertook a major campaign to suppress piracy in this region, and then only after Cilician pirates had claimed many more victims and made a great impact across the entire Mediterranean.

The story of one such victim is worth relating briefly at this point as it seems to illustrate a general lack of enthusiasm among Roman magistrates in the Mediterranean for tackling the problem of piracy. In late 75 or early 74 BC, Gaius Julius Caesar was sailing to Rhodes, where he was to study rhetoric, when he was captured, off the island of Pharmakussa, by pirates who held him for about 40 days until he was ransomed.[182] Having been released, he collected together a small fleet in Miletos and

---

[181] Lucan and Florus mention Syedra as the place where Pompey held his last council of war before his fatal journey to Egypt in 48 BC: Luc. 8.259–60; Flor. 2.13.51.

[182] Suet. *Iul.* 4.1; Val. Max. 6.9.15; Plut. *Caes.* 2. The incident is also mentioned by Velleius (2.41–2) with some variations, such as crediting the pirates with a fleet, instead of one ship. See Ward (1977) for a detailed chronology.

went after the pirates, whose base he was able to locate, and captured them. In accordance with a promise made to them during his captivity he had them crucified.[183] Plutarch says that he initially detained the pirates in Pergamon, and went to the Roman governor of Asia, Juncus, to demand that he deal with them, but getting no satisfaction Caesar ordered the executions himself. On what authority he acted is unclear. It would appear from the Ephesian inscription, mentioning the execution of some pirates on Astypalaia, that no 'conviction' was necessary in such cases.[184] Caesar may have had the status of a legate, although he was not travelling on any mission at this time, but the fact that he approached the governor of Asia suggests that he lacked any real authority.[185] The incident clearly shows that pirates might strike against anyone,[186] but it seems to me that it demonstrates once again the necessity of Roman 'leadership' of allies or subjects against pirates, since Caesar must have used local forces to attack the pirates' base. His determination seems to have been unexpected and unwelcome. The governor preferred to ignore such matters, unless he could profit from them himself. There is no clear indication of where the pirates came from, but it does not seem to have been Cilicia.

## Marcus Antonius Creticus

After Publius Servilius Isauricus, the next Roman magistrate who is said to have taken action against pirates is Marcus Antonius Creticus, the son of Marcus Antonius the orator, whose Cilician campaign of 102 BC has been discussed above.[187] Marcus Antonius Creticus was elected praetor in 74 BC and he was assigned a special command.[188] His official title may possibly have been *curator tuendae totius orae maritimae*, which reflects

---

[183] Suet. *Iul.* 4.2; Val. Max. 6.9.15; Vell. Pat. 2.42; Plut. *Caes.* 2. Plutarch adds the detail that the pirates were found at their base. Caesar did not have to hunt for them.

[184] See above pp. 100–01. The pirates lacked recognized status as citizens of a *polis*, or a Roman province; they were 'outlaws' rather than 'enemies'.

[185] See Ward (1977) for discussion. Velleius specifically says that Caesar had no authority, but he may be exaggerating for effect. Plutarch says that Juncus wanted to obtain the pirates' loot, so he delayed a decision on their case. He neglects to say what happened to the plunder after they were executed. Perhaps it paid for Caesar's rhetoric lessons?

[186] A similar incident, dated to 67 BC, is the capture by pirates of Publius Claudius Pulcher (later Clodius) who was ransomed with the reluctant help of king Ptolemy Auletes (App. *Bell. civ.* 2.23; Str. 14.6.6; Dio. 36.16.3).

[187] See above pp. 102–8.

[188] *MRR* II 101–2. Antonius' supposed *imperium infinitum* has been the subject of much scholarly literature, but detailed discussion of it is not needed here. It is clear that he operated in more than one *provincia*, but his authority did not automatically override that of other magistrates. For further discussion see Jameson (1970) and Maróti (1971). His command was prorogued in the usual manner in 73, 72 and 71 BC; *MRR* II 102, 108, 111, 117 and 123.

the general nature of his command and is not specifically directed against piracy.[189] His *imperium* may have been valid only up to 50 miles inland, as was Pompey's in 67 BC.[190] A justification for Antonius' early campaigning in the Western Mediterranean can be found in the fragments of Sallust's *Histories*. A fragment of Book II refers to a shortage of corn at Rome in 75 BC, which provoked riots and threatened the safety of the consuls (Sall. *Hist.* fr. II. 45M). Soon after, in a speech to the people, the consul of 75 BC, Gaius Aurelius Cotta, says:

You have elected us consuls, citizens of Rome, when the state faces the severest difficulties both here and at the front. Our commanders in Spain are asking for pay, soldiers, weapons and food, and circumstances compel them to do so, since, with the defection of the allies and the flight of Sertorius over the mountains, they can neither come to grips with the enemy nor lay their hands on necessities. We are keeping armies in the provinces of Asia and Cilicia because of the excessive strength of Mithridates, Macedonia is full of enemies, and so are the coastal regions of Italy and the provinces, while in the meantime our revenues, small and unreliable because of the wars, barely meet even a portion of our expenses: thus the fleet we have at sea, which used to protect our food supplies, is smaller than previously.[191] (Sall. *Hist.* fr. II. 47M, 6–7)

In the same book, also referring to 75 BC, there is a letter from Pompey to the senate in which he accuses the senators of rewarding his achievements by reducing him and his army to starvation (Sall. *Hist.* fr. II.98M).

It is argued by Garnsey that shortages of grain in Rome were exacerbated by the need to supply the Roman armies operating in the provinces, and he cites the shortages of 75–73 BC as examples of this problem.[192] Cicero claimed to have done his bit to relieve the problems by sending grain to Rome in 75 BC, when he was quaestor in Lilybaeum in Sicily,[193] and he says that Verres was ordered to make extra grain purchases during his propraetorship in Sicily, although he misused the funds provided by the senate.[194] These references to problems with supplies indicate that both the Romans' overland and their maritime supply

[189]  Ps.-Asc. 121; a fragment of Sallust appears to refer to Marcus Antonius as a worse guardian of the coasts than the pirates had been: *Qui orae maritimae, qua Romanum esset imperium, curator ⟨nocent⟩ior piratis* (Sall. *Hist.* fr. III.2M). Maróti (1971) suggests that Pseudo-Asconius got the title from Sallust.

[190]  Vell. 2.31.2–3. See Maróti (1971) and Jameson (1970) for different views. Jameson must be right when she suggests that the idea of *imperium infinitum* is absurd.

[191]  I quote the fragments of Sallust from the translation by Carter (1970). The references are to the edition of Maurenbrecher.

[192]  Garnsey (1988): 203–4.

[193]  Cic. *Planc.* 64. In 74 BC the proconsul Gaius Licinius Sacerdos, Verres' predecessor as governor of Sicily, was able to lower the price of Sicilian grain, suggesting that the crisis had eased a little (Cic. *II Verr.* 215).

[194]  Cic. *II Verr.* 3.

routes in the Western Mediterranean were under serious strain at this time, threatening the armies in Spain, where the commanders Quintus Caecilius Metellus Pius and Pompey were fighting Sertorius and his allies, and the sources of Rome's grain supply. As far as the maritime aspect of this problem is concerned, there are numerous references in the accounts of Sertorius' activities to his use of ships. At one point Plutarch mentions a naval battle in the Straits of Gibraltar (Plut. *Sert.* 12; 80 BC) and sea-borne operations against the supply-lines of Metellus and Pompey (Plut. *Sert.* 21; in 75 BC?). At an earlier stage in his 'career' as a rebel Sertorius tried to occupy one of the Balearic Islands, but was driven away by Gaius Annius (Flor. 2.10; Plut. *Sert.* 7; 81 BC). In his dealings with Mithridates it was in return for ships that he promised to hand Asia and Bithynia over to the king of Pontos (Plut. *Sert.* 23–4; Cic. *Leg. Man.* 46; App. *Mith.* 68; 75 BC). His intention was to prevent supplies reaching the two Roman generals in Spain by sea.[195] There can be little doubt that he was meeting with some success. I would also suggest that pirates who had no connection with Sertorius were adding to the problem, since there is plenty of evidence in Cicero's *Verrine Orations* to show that piracy was a serious problem in the Western Mediterranean in the late 70s BC.[196] The items mentioned by Cotta in the speech quoted above – food, weapons and money – would obviously have been attractive targets for pirates as well as Sertorius and his allies. Antonius' initial task must have been to secure the western supply routes by attacking the bases of those who were disrupting them, whether they were 'rebels' or pirates.

The evidence for Marcus Antonius Creticus' activities in the Western Mediterranean is fragmentary. Cicero has cause to mention him several times in the *Verrine Orations*. In the speech against Quintus Caecilius he says that one of Marcus Antonius' officers appropriated some slave musicians for his fleet from a Sicilian woman, who got no help from Caecilius, and only a little from Verres.[197] Why the prefect wanted the slave musicians is not clear. Antonius himself comes in for some criticism from Cicero in the course of his prosecution of Verres.[198] It seems that his high-handed behaviour was not to Cicero's liking. He includes him among those magistrates other than the notorius Verres who have oppressed the Sicilians,[199] and pours scorn upon Verres' defence counsel

---

[195] See above pp. 132–4.

[196] See below pp. 150–7.

[197] Cic. *Div. Caec.* 55: *praefectus Antonii quidam*. I would date this incident to early 73 BC, soon after Verres' arrival in the province of Sicily (Cic. *II Verr.* 1.149).

[198] See below pp. 150–7 on Cicero and the *Verrine Orations* in general.

[199] Cic. *II Verr.* 2.8: '… and afterwards they had felt the power of that unlimited authority of Marcus Antonius' (*et postea Marci Antonii infinitum illud imperium senserant*).

Hortensius for trying, by citing Antonius as a precedent, to defend Verres' actions in respect of grain requisitions and purchases:

And so, out of all the praetors, consuls and generals of the Roman people, you have chosen Marcus Antonius, and it is his most infamous deed which you would imitate .... . Antonius, while he was doing and plotting many things contrary to the well-being of our allies and of no benefit to the provinces, was cut short by death in the middle of his injustices and pilferings. (*II Verr*. 3.213)

The particular injustice which Verres is accused of imitating seems to have been to do with a requisition of grain. Instead of the grain, however, he demanded a high cash equivalent at a time of very low prices, presumably because he was interested in obtaining other things with the money. Cicero points out that Verres did a similar thing but for a far longer period of time. The action occurred in the year in which Sacerdos was governor of Sicily (74 BC): 'Say rather, since you have a suitable authority for it, that he did for three years what Antonius did once when he arrived, and scarcely for a month's supplies' (Cic. *II Verr*. 3.214–15). It would appear, then, that Antonius visited Sicily in 74 BC and took a sum of money from the inhabitants which was the equivalent of a month's supply of grain. Some time in the following year one of his prefects requisitioned some slaves for his fleet. Cicero implies that Antonius was making the most of his authority as proconsul at the expense of the Sicilians, which might indicate that he was short of adequate resources for the task in hand.

Sallust's *Histories* provide the only detailed information about the course of Antonius' western campaigns. Unfortunately their fragmentary nature does not offer more than a few glimpses. Two episodes of reasonable length survive from the third book. In the first, Sallust describes an abortive attempt against a Ligurian harbour, after which Antonius and forces proceed to Spain, to tackle Sertorius.[200] While it appears that he was unable to capture the place, he did succeed in preventing it from being used, for a while at least. Once again the practice of depriving pirates of their bases is seen to be the most effective way of suppressing piracy. The second fragment is worth quoting in full:

... divided from the enemy by the deep river Dilunus, which even a handful of men rendered impossible for him to cross, he pretended to make some crossings not far away and ferried his army over with the fleet, which he had recalled, and some flimsily put together boats. He then sent his officer Manius on ahead with the cavalry and some of the warships and reached the island of [......], thinking that unexpected panic might make it possible for the town, which was conveniently situated for the receipt of supplies from Italy, to be recaptured. But the

---

[200] Sall. *Hist*. fr. III.5M. The Ligurians seem to have had a sizeable fleet and were able to hold Antonius off before retiring into the mountains.

enemy, relying on the strength of their position, remained unshaken in their re-
solve; indeed they [fortified with a double wall] a small hill whose sides rose
steeply on the seaward side and rear and had in addition a narrow sandy approach
from the front. (Sall. fr. III.6M)

The location of the river Dilunus and the island mentioned is unclear.
Some historians have suggested one of the Balearic Islands might fit the
bill.[201] The mention of a fleet, warships and an army which includes
cavalry, suggests that Antonius had considerable forces with him, but it is
the description of the town (also unidentified) as suitable for receiving
supplies from Italy which is most significant. There seems to me to be little doubt that Antonius was at this point engaged in securing the supply
lines to the armies in Spain, in response to the requests of Metellus and
Pompey.

Foucart has suggested that the Spanish operations took up most the
campaign season of the year 73 BC.[202] In 74 BC Antonius was mainly
concerned with preparing his forces. His exactions in Sicily (and the seizure of slaves by his prefect) suggest that he lacked adequate resources for
the task in hand, having to demand things from the neighbouring provinces. Although the preserved fragments of Sallust and the general comments of later writers portray him as incompetent,[203] I think it likely that
he was reasonably successful in the first part of his commission, namely to
enable supplies to reach Spain from Italy. He discouraged the Ligurians
who must have been harrying the route along the coast, and he secured
landing points for the supplies in Spain. His command was prorogued
several times, which is unlikely to have been the case if he was making a
complete mess of things.[204] The war against Sertorius was brought to a
successful conclusion in 73 BC, but Antonius' command was prorogued
for another year. This time he was to campaign in Crete.[205]

Why did Marcus Antonius turn his attention to Crete in 72 BC? Piracy
on Crete had a long history by the time Antonius came on to the scene,[206]
but there had been no attempt made by Rome to suppress it previously. Indeed, during the first Mithridatic war, Lucullus had apparently
been able to 'win over' Crete while on his quest for ships (Plut. *Luc.* 2.3).

---

[201]  See Foucart (1906): 571.
[202]  Foucart (1906): 571–5.
[203]  See, for example, Plut. *Ant.* 1; Livy, *Ep.* 97; Flor. 3.7.
[204]  It is instructive to compare the fates of the commanders in the early stages of the war
against Spartacus, which was going on at about the same time. They were not given the
opportunity to repeat their mistakes!
[205]  Ps.-Asc. 259. It was Antonius' Cretan campaign which attracted the attention of later
writers like Livy, Florus and Appian, because it provided some interesting moral anec-
dotes and a contrast with the successes of Pompey (Livy, *Ep.* 97; Flor. 3.7; App. *Sic.* 6).
[206]  See above Ch. 3.

Appian indicates that there were two charges which were levelled against the Cretans by Antonius:

> For it seemed that Crete had from the start been well disposed towards Mithridates, the king of Pontos, and it was said that Crete provided him with mercenaries during his war with the Romans ... It also appeared that, as a favour to Mithridates, they provided assistance for the pirates and openly took their side when they were fleeing from Marcus Antonius. (App. *Sic*. 6.1)

The charge of co-operating with Mithridates is also found in Memnon and Florus.[207] Like the claim that they were supporting pirates it may well have had some foundation, though perhaps not for all the cities of Crete. The Mithridatic war was finally going Rome's way, and it may have been that the Romans wanted to reassert their control over the Aegean. Only two years earlier the Romans had finally decided to take over the administration of Cyrenaica, and it has been suggested that the need to suppress pirates operating from this area was part of the reason for doing so.[208] Florus suggests that it was purely out of a desire for conquest that the Romans attacked Crete. In the context, however, this ignoble motive seems to function as an explanation for the humiliating defeat which Antonius suffered at the hands of the Cretans: 'First Marcus Antonius invaded the island with such confidence, and so overwhelming an expectation of victory, that he carried more chains than arms in his ships. And so he paid the penalty for his folly' (Flor. 3.7.2). Appian, Dio, Florus and Diodorus together preserve only a few details of the campaign. Antonius sent legates to the Cretans, but they got no satisfaction (App. *Sic*. 6.1). He attacked Crete and was defeated, the leader of the Cretans being a certain Lasthenes (Flor. 7; App. *Sic*. 6.1; Dio fr. 108; Diod. 40.1). A peace treaty was concluded, although it was later repudiated by the Romans (Diod. 40.1).[209] Appian adds that he acquired the surname 'Creticus' for his pains.

Foucart, in his lengthy discussion of Antonius' campaigns, drew attention to two inscriptions from the Peloponnese which indicate that he was active on the Greek mainland.[210] One, from Epidauros, honours a certain Euanthes, the *agoranomos*, who obtained exemption for Epidauros from

---

[207] Memnon, *FGrHist* 434.48; Flor. 3.7.1.

[208] See Reynolds (1962) and Badian (1965) for differing views. Note also Harris (1979): 154–5 and 267.

[209] I have not included all the lurid details which are to be found in the scanty sources for this campaign. See Ormerod (1924): 225–7. A further fragment from Sallust may refer to the Cretan campaign (Sall. *Hist*. fr. III.8). It mentions the loss of a cohort to an attack at sea by pirates.

[210] Foucart (1906). I do not accept all his conclusions concerning the nature of Antonius' campaigns or his activities in the Peloponnese.

the requirement to furnish soldiers to Antonius in 72 BC.[211] Nevertheless a garrison was installed in the city, which made it particularly difficult for Euanthes to carry out his duties and satisfy the needs of the population. The other inscription is from the port of Gytheion. It honours two Romans, Numerius and Marcus Cloatius, who have helped the city to cope with various debts incurred over a period of several years:[212] '... and in the year of Timokrates' magistracy, when Antonius had come here and our city had need of cash and nobody else was willing to enter into a contract with us, they loaned us 4,200 drachmas under contract at interest of four drachmas per mina per month ...' There is a familiar ring to what this inscription has to say about Antonius. He turns up in a province and starts ordering the provincials about, the kind of behaviour which caused resentment in Sicily and for which Cicero saw fit to censure him. As in the case of Sicily, it seems to be cash which is his main concern. With money he could buy supplies, feed and perhaps even pay his men. The garrison at Epidauros could have been a precaution against pirates, or it could have been a way of billeting some of his forces before proceeding to Crete.[213] The exemption from providing troops indicates that Antonius, like many other Roman magistrates in this period was dependent upon locally recruited men for his military personnel. Indeed, it may be that all his men came from allies and subjects of Rome.[214] There are several legates mentioned in the Gytheion inscription, including Gaius Julius Caesar, which would suggest that Antonius had considerable 'staff' to cater for, all at the expense of the local population, for whom the campaign must have been a considerable burden.[215]

There are two ways of looking at Marcus Antonius Creticus' campaigns. His four years of activity could be seen as a major attempt to suppress piracy, a logical follow-up to Servilius' Anatolian campaigns and a rather sorry prelude to the more successful operations of Pompey.[216] On the other hand, it could be argued that he was given his extraordinary *imperium* as a result of certain problems facing Rome in the mid-70s BC,

---

[211] *IG* IV.932. See Foucart (1906) for discussion of the date, given according to the Achaian era.

[212] *IG* V.1.1146; *SIG* 748. I quote from the translation in Sherk (1984): no. 74, lines 32–6. Gytheion is the main port of Lakonia. Six eponymous magistrates are mentioned, so the dealings mentioned in the inscription spanned at least six years.

[213] Ormerod (1924): 226, n. 5 thinks it unlikely that the garrison was for the Epidaurians' protection.

[214] Brunt (1971): 455 says, 'I can discover no evidence that M. Antonius ... had any legionary force.'

[215] Given Caesar's recently acquired experience of dealing with pirates, it is just possible that he was included as an 'expert' to advise Antonius.

[216] This is how the events are interpreted by Ormerod (1924): 224–7.

namely the war with Sertorius, the grain-supply difficulties and Cretan 'resistance' to Roman domination in the Mediterranean. It seems to me that Marcus Antonius had no single plan of action because he was called upon to perform several operations in succession, for which he lacked adequate resources. Firstly, he had to secure the supply route from Italy to Spain, in order to help with the war against Sertorius. This involved driving the Ligurians away from the coast and capturing suitable landing places in Spain. It is obvious from the problems which Verres had in Sicily that he did not succeed in clearing the Western Mediterranean of pirates, even for a brief spell.[217] Secondly, after the death of Sertorius, he was despatched to sort out the recalcitrant Cretans. In spite of a year spent gathering forces in the Peloponnese he was defeated by the Cretans and forced to abandon his campaign. He died soon after. It is instructive at this point to consider the remarks that Cassius Dio makes about the Romans' attitude to the threat of piracy before the campaign of Pompey in 67 BC. According to Dio the Romans had not been greatly concerned by the problem: 'But they used to send out fleets and generals, as and when they were prompted by specific reports. Nothing was achieved, except that the allies had to suffer even greater hardship as a result of these attempts, until their situation became quite desperate' (Dio 36.23.2). The Cretan campaign of Marcus Antonius Creticus seems to be what Dio has in mind here. The almost desperate tone of the inscriptions from Epidauros and Gytheion, as well as Cicero's biting condemnation of his intervention in Sicily, are a further indication that most Roman attempts to suppress piracy in this period were carried out largely at the expense of the friends, allies and subjects of Rome.

[217] See below pp. 150–7 on Verres and the pirates and also pp. 157–61 on Metellus Creticus.

# 5    Pompey and the pirates

Most of the ancient sources which have been used so far in the account of Roman activities against pirates have been non-contemporary ones. While such writers as Livy, Appian and Plutarch did base their accounts on the works of Greek and Roman historians of the second and first centuries BC, they provide only very limited access to the thought-world of that period, which is filtered through the prejudices, biases and misunderstandings of a later age. It is only in the 70s BC that a substantial amount of contemporary evidence becomes directly available, principally in the form of the speeches, letters and other works of Marcus Tullius Cicero. In consequence it is possible to explore the Roman response to piracy in the mid first century BC in considerable detail.

### Cicero on piracy

Cicero was born in the Central Italian hill-town of Arpinum in 106 BC. His father was a wealthy local aristocrat who provided Marcus and his younger brother Quintus with the education and financial resources to embark upon careers in the competitive world of Roman politics. The elder of the two used his considerable talents as an orator to establish himself as an influential member of the senate in the 60s BC. He achieved the office of consul in 63 BC. In order to broadcast his own views and to further his career Cicero published versions of his most important political and forensic speeches, usually soon after their delivery. He also published a series of rhetorical, philosophical and moral treatises which were based on Greek models but were thoroughly imbued with the values of the Roman aristocracy. In addition, hundreds of letters from Cicero's private and public correspondence were collected and published through the efforts of his freedman Tiro and his close friend Titus Pomponius Atticus. These rich veins of source material provide unrivalled insights into the ideology and political realities of the Roman ruling class in the period in which Rome approached the climax of her domination of the Mediterranean world.

There is a fairly consistent image of piracy to be found in the philosophical works of Cicero. Casual references to pirates in such works are indicative of the fact that they were a common feature of the Mediterranean world at his time.[1] Cicero clearly thinks of pirates as evil, dishonourable people who are not worthy of respect. This attitude is exemplified in a frequently quoted passage from his work *On Duties*. In the course of a discussion about the importance of keeping oaths and promises he says:

> If, for example, you do not hand over to pirates the amount agreed upon as the price of your life, that is not perjury, not even if you have sworn an oath and do not do so, for a pirate is not included in the category of lawful enemies, but is the common enemy of everyone. In his case good faith and sworn oaths should not be recognized. (Cic. *Off.* 3.107)

Pirates figure at several points in this work as examples of immoral people. Sometimes, however, they get the best of the comparison, as when Cicero comments on some sharp practice by the Roman senate concerning the allies: 'The faith of pirates is better than the senate's!' (*Off.* 3.87). Piracy is an activity which Cicero associates with Rome's past enemies, contrasting the honourable and civilized nature of the Romans with the dishonourable and barbarous practices of other peoples. The point is well illustrated by his comments on the superior, inland location of the city of Rome: 'For indeed among the barbarians there were in former times none who were seafarers, except the Etruscans and the Phoenicians, the one on account of trade, the other for the sake of piracy' (Cic. *Rep.* 2.9). Given the position assumed by the Romans in regard to piracy at the start of the first century BC,[2] it is not surprising that it is a recurrent theme in Cicero's political speeches. Indeed, the problem of dealing with piracy often figured in the political debates of Cicero's time. Equally unsurprising is the fact that Cicero uses his considerable rhetorical talents to make political capital out of piracy. This can be seen most clearly in his prosecution of the notorious proconsul of Sicily, Gaius Verres.

### Cicero and Verres

The prosecution of Verres in 70 BC was Cicero's entry onto the grand stage of Roman politics. His lengthy speeches, collectively known as the

---

[1] E.g. *Tusc.* 2.67: 'As if, for example, a god were to say to a sailor who is being pursued by pirates: "Throw yourself overboard into the sea: there is something there to rescue you, whether a dolphin..."' The word translated as 'pirates' here is *praedones*. Cicero also uses *pirata*, although this word seems not to have been fully established in the everyday Latin vocabulary of his time. For more detailed discussion of this topic see de Souza (1992): 70–3.

[2] See above Ch. 4.

*Verrine Orations*, touch on many of the most important issues of the last half-century of the Roman Republic. One of these themes is piracy, as a danger to Rome, her subjects and her allies which it is the duty of a Roman magistrate to suppress. In the course of his published versions of the *Verrine Orations* Cicero employs numerous references to pirates and piracy in order to present the object of his attack in the worst possible light.

Gaius Verres was born in about 115 BC. His father was a senator, and the younger Verres entered the senate in the mid-80s. His career, according to Cicero, was as dishonest and self-serving as any in the history of Republican politics.[3] In 84 BC, he was quaestor to the consul Gnaeus Papirius Carbo, a colleague of Cinna. Verres deserted Carbo, taking much of the consul's financial resources with him, and joined the forces of Sulla. After the victory of Sulla, Verres went to Cilicia as legate to Gnaeus Cornelius Dolabella (*pr.* 81) and remained with him until 79 BC, eventually becoming *legatus pro quaestore*. Cicero makes a great deal of the way in which the propraetor and his legate plundered the Greek East together, only for Verres to prosecute Dolabella in the *quaestio repetundarum* on his return. His next office was that of urban praetor in 74 BC. His proconsulship in Sicily, in 73 BC, was extended to 71 BC because his successor, Quintus Arrius (*pr.* 73), was diverted to the war with Spartacus,[4] providing Verres with a greater opportunity to plunder and abuse his province than he might normally have expected. On his return to Rome he was prosecuted by Cicero on behalf of the enraged Sicilians. The overwhelming strength of Cicero's prosecution compelled Verres to retire into exile in Massilia before the trial was finished.

The structure of the *Verrine Orations* reflects the peculiar nature of the trial. Cicero delivered only two of the published speeches in a form similar to that which we have now. These were the *divinatio in Caecilium*, in which he established his right to prosecute Verres, and the *actio prima* in which he presented his witnesses, and their damning evidence against Verres, for consideration by the jurors and examination by the defence. Cicero was short of time, owing to the manœuvres of his opponents, who were trying to get a more sympathetic president of the court,[5] so he passed over the opportunity to display all his rhetorical abilities and concentrated on a swift result. He published his attack on Verres' career and character in a full form later. The *actio secunda* is not, therefore, a written-

---

[3] The details of Verres' career are well established. For full references see *MRR* II 61, 64, 81, 85, 102, 112, 119 and 124.
[4] *MRR* II 109 and 117.
[5] For a reconstruction of the chain of events see Stockton (1971): 43–8.

up version of the speeches he delivered in court, but a combination of the speech with which he might have opened the proceedings, under normal circumstances, before the witnesses had been heard, and the speech with which he would have taken up the attack on Verres after the witnesses had been heard. The first book of the *actio secunda* deals with the career of Verres up to the end of his praetorship, establishing the rapacious and deceitful nature of the accused governor. The second book deals with his administration of justice in Sicily. The third is concerned with his handling of the corn supply, a major aspect of the governor's work in this province. In the fourth book Cicero details Verres' plundering of statues and other works of art from Sicily.[6] Finally, in the fifth book Cicero describes how Verres conducted his military duties and the manner in which he mistreated Sicilians and Roman citizens, building up to a climax with his unlawful executions.

There are several ways in which Cicero exploits the theme of pirates and piracy in his condemnation of Verres. In very straightforward terms he calls the proconsul of Sicily a pirate, as well as a bandit and a thief. Verres' associates are referred to as pirates and bandits. Cicero also on several occasions compares what Verres has done with what pirates have done, or might do, in order to suggest that he is a worse evil than pirates. On a slightly different tack, Cicero makes much of the way Verres handled the problem of piracy in his capacity as a Roman magistrate, especially during his governorship of Sicily, with the clear implication that a proconsul is expected to do much better than Verres did.

One of the main points which Cicero makes about Verres in the course of the speeches is that he has 'plundered' the inhabitants of all the places he has been to in his political career. In the first speech of the *actio secunda*, Cicero says of Verres' career: 'Not one hour was free of theft, wickedness, cruelty and disgrace' (*II Verr.* 1.34). Yet it will not do for Cicero to describe Verres merely as a thief: 'For it is no ordinary thief, but a plunderer... whom we have brought before your court' (*II Verr.* 1.9). In order to obtain the strongest condemnation for his subject's actions, Cicero's favourite way of referring to Verres, when describing his plundering, is with the word *praedo*, which can mean bandit or pirate. As will become clear, it is probably correct to translate it as pirate on most occasions, in order to convey Cicero's precise intention.[7] The term is introduced very

---

[6] The speech begins thus: 'I come now to that subject which Verres himself calls an interest (*studium*)... but which the Sicilians call piracy (*latrocinium*)' (Cic. *II Verr.* 4.1).

[7] *II Verr.* 4.23 refers to Verres as both *praedo* and *pirata*, which is best read as 'a bandit and a pirate'.

early on, in only the second section of the *actio prima*: 'He has stolen from the treasury, harassed Asia and Pamphylia, presided over the city like a pirate (*praedonem*), and was like a plague of devastation in the province of Sicily' (*I Verr.* 1.2). The theme is returned to regularly, with Verres being referred to as *praedo* in every book of the *actio secunda*[8] except the final one, in which the activities of other pirates play a major part.[9] He is also called *pirata* and there are several references to his *latrocinium*.[10]

Verres is not alone in being depicted in this way. The Mamertines, who were the only people of Sicily to support Verres at his trial, are described by Cicero as his partners in crime,[11] in the same way as the people of Phaselis were to the Cilician pirates.[12] The Mamertines also provided the pirate-proconsul with a ship to convey his plunder. Cicero describes it as *navem onerariam maximam* (a huge cargo ship)[13] and he chastises Verres for his behaviour, which was wholly inappropriate for a Roman governor, whose duty it is to protect his province: 'What you ought to have done was exacted a ship which could be sailed against pirates, not one for use in piracy; a ship to defend the province against plundering, not one to carry off plunder from the province' (*II Verr.* 5.59). In some respects, Cicero tells the jury of senators, Verres' behaviour was even worse than that of pirates. The example of the island of Melita (Malta) is selected. Its temple of Juno was the repository of many valuable objects which, says Cicero, neither Rome's long-time enemies the Carthaginians, nor, in recent times, even the pirates dared to remove.[14] For Verres, however, nothing was sacred:

The envoys sent by the people of Melita say that the Temple of Juno was ravaged. Nothing was left in that most holy of shrines; they say that a place where enemy fleets have often put in, where pirates spend the winter year after year, but which

---

[8] *II Verr.* 1.46, 154; 2.141; 3.76; 4.23, 80.

[9] He is, however, called an 'ally of pirates' (*praedonem sociorum*) at one point (*II Verr.* 5.122).

[10] *II Verr.* 1.90, 154 (*pirata*); *II Verr.* 1.57, 89, 129, 130; 2.18; 4.24.

[11] Verres' retinue are called *latrones* (*II Verr.* 5.114) and share in the plundering (*praedor*) of Sicily (*II Verr.* 2.29).

[12] 'Indeed, this city was the Phaselis for that Sicilian bandit and pirate' (*II Verr.* 4.23). 'That town was the receptacle for your booty, those men were the witnesses and receivers of your stolen goods...' (*II Verr.* 5.59).

[13] *II Verr.* 2.13. See also *II Verr.* 5.44 for a more elaborate description. For the whole story of Verres and the Mamertine ship see *II Verr.* 5. 43–59. In *II Verr.* 1.46 Verres deposits ancient and sacred statuary stolen from Delos *in onerariam navem suam* ('in his cargo ship'). The implication would seem to be that in Sicily he requires a larger ship because he has become a bigger pirate. The first vessel is also described as *navis illa praedonis* ('that pirate's ship') when a storm wrecks it and the statues are recovered.

[14] *II Verr.* 4.103.

no pirate has ever before violated, no enemy ever touched, has been so plundered by this one man, that nothing at all is left.[15] (*II Verr.* 4.104)

As the previous chapter has shown, piracy was a serious problem for the Romans and their allies in the first century BC. The governor of Sicily could expect to have to deal with attacks at sea and on land. As Cicero indicates in the passage quoted above, it was the Romans' usual procedure to require their allies and provincial subjects to furnish ships which could be used, amongst other things, to combat pirates. Cicero interweaves the theme of combating pirates with the theme of Verres' own acts of piracy in a deliberate fashion, designed to bring out the contrast between what Verres ought to have done, as a Roman magistrate, and what he actually did with regard to pirates. Verres' mishandling of this aspect of his responsibilities in Sicily is announced early in the *actio prima*:

[During Verres' governorship] ... well fortified harbours and the securest of cities lay open to pirates and bandits; Sicilian sailors and troops, our allies and friends, were starved to death; the finest and most excellently turned out fleets were lost and destroyed, bringing great disgrace to the Roman people. (*I Verr.* 1.13)

Before detailing these crimes, Cicero takes the opportunity to show how irresponsible 'Verres the pirate' has been in the past when it comes to the business of combating piracy. In the first book of the *actio secunda*, he tells the jury a long tale about a warship which was supplied to Verres by the city of Miletos in Asia.[16] The ship was one of ten which the Milesians built on the orders of Lucius Murena, Sulla's legate, in 83 BC. The other cities of the region did likewise. After he had used it as an escort to Myndus in Karia, Verres dismissed the crew and sold the ship.[17] Cicero casually introduces pirates into the story when he describes how the Milesians accounted for the loss of the ship in their public records: 'Therefore, they have entered into their public records that one of the ten was lost, not through a sudden attack of pirates, but through the piracy of a legate...' (*II Verr.* 1.89). Piracy is brought up again when Cicero concludes this section, by presenting his Milesian witnesses: 'They will make it clear that Gaius Verres, with regard to the fleet that was built to fight the pirates, himself played the part of the wickedest of pirates' (*II Verr.* 1.90). This is very rousing stuff, although it might be somewhat ex-

---

[15] A comparison might be made with Cicero's characterization of L. Cornelius Chrysogonus, the dictator Sulla's freedman, in his defence of Sextus Roscius: 'Was there ever a bandit so wicked, a pirate so cruel as, when he could get his booty intact without bloodshed, to prefer to take spoils dripping with blood?' (*Rosc. Am.* 146).

[16] *II Verr.* 1.86–90.

[17] The buyers, two Romans living in Miletos, used it, so Cicero says, to communicate between Sertorius and Mithridates (*II Verr.* 1.87); see above p. 133.

aggerated. Murena's ships could have been used to combat pirates, but that was not the reason for their construction. Murena's prime concern in 83 BC was Mithridates, not pirates.[18] To mention pirates here enables Cicero to create a neat rhetorical effect, even if he is not being strictly accurate. Summing up at the end of this book Cicero repeats his word-play:

Do we also inquire what Verres has got up to in deepest Phrygia, or in the furthest parts of Pamphylia, how in the war against the pirates he has played the pirate himself, he who was found to be an abominable pirate here in the Roman Forum? (*II Verr.* 1.154)

Cicero deals with Verres' own contribution to the war against the pirates in Book 5 of the *actio secunda*.[19] In this speech he accuses Verres of mishandling affairs in several ways. Firstly, he neglected to keep a proper fleet of warships ready to deal with any attack, pocketing the money which the Sicilian cities set aside for this, and then accepting bribes from them to discharge most of the sailors.[20] Cicero is quick to point out how ill-advised such behaviour was: 'And this most insane of men, when there was so much piratical activity about, and so much danger to the province, did it so openly that the pirates themselves were aware and the whole province witnessed it' (*II Verr.* 5.62). Not all the ships are empty, since a squadron does capture one pirate vessel.[21] Verres cannot restrain himself:

The whole night is taken up with emptying out the ship. The pirate captain himself, who ought to be executed, is seen by no-one. To this day everyone believes – you may judge for yourselves what truth there is in this conjecture – that Verres secretly accepted money from the pirates in exchange for their captain.[22] (*II Verr.* 5.64)

[18] See App. *Mith.* 64. In ch. 93 Appian includes Murena among those who prepared to attack the Cilician pirates before 67 BC. All he achieved was the annexation of Kibyra (Str. 13.4.17; *De vir. ill.* 74.2). Memnon calls him 'the governor sent by the senate', but this is a mistake (*FGrHist.* 434, fr. 1.26). See above pp. 121–3 for further details.

[19] Verres' adventures with the pirates are first mentioned at *II Verr.* 5.42 (After the war with Spartacus) and concluded at 5.138. They comprise approximately half of the fifth book of the *actio secunda*.

[20] *II Verr.* 5.60–2.

[21] *II Verr.* 5.63. Cicero does his best to play even this success down with sarcastic humour, observing that 'While Publius Caesetius and Publius Tadius were cruising around in their ten half-empty ships, they led away, rather than captured, a ship laden with pirate's booty, clearly overcome and sinking under its own weight.'

[22] Maróti (1956) suggests that Verres used the pirate captain as a bargaining counter with the pirates to persuade them not to transport the slave army of Spartacus across to Sicily. He bases his conjecture on a passage of Plutarch (Plut. *Crass.* 10) which is discussed above, pp. 133–4. I find it incredible that such a deal could have gone unnoticed by all the other sources, especially Cicero.

The rest of the pirates are gradually spirited away to Verres' own house, and other prisoners, some of whom are Roman citizens, are executed in their place.[23] It should be noted that, in the course of his indignant recounting of these events, Cicero says of the pirate captain: 'What is the law in this case? What do custom and precedent say? Could any one, private individual keep within the walls of his own house the bitterest and most dangerous enemy of the Roman people, or, rather, the common enemy of all peoples?' (*II Verr.* 5.76).

Secondly, Verres handed the command of his fleet over to a Syracusan called Cleomenes, whose conduct was not much better than his superior's. The undermanned vessels were laid up in idleness at Pachynus, while their starving crews looked for food.[24] Thirdly, when an attack of pirates did occur, the fleet was humiliatingly defeated, many of the crews captured or killed, and most of the ships were burnt at Elorus.[25] The pirates, led by a captain called Heracleo, sailed on to Syracuse and entered the harbour itself.[26] Cicero sums up the whole sorry episode as follows:

While you were praetor, Sicilian soldiers were fed on the roots of palm trees, and pirates on Sicilian corn! What a sad and sordid spectacle! The prestige of the city, the name of the Roman people and the huge crowd of onlookers made a laughing-stock by a pirate galley! In the harbour of Syracuse a pirate celebrates a triumph over the fleet of the Roman people, while the cowardly and worthless praetor gets his eyes splashed with water from the pirates' oars! (*II Verr.* 5.100)

In a sad aftermath, Verres turned against his own naval captains and had several of them executed, though not the infamous Cleomenes. Those who survived were the ones who were captured by the pirates and afterwards ransomed.[27]

Piracy is, therefore, a major theme of the *Verrine Orations*. Cicero

---

[23] At this point Cicero contrasts Verres' treatment of pirates with that of other Roman magistrates, notably Publius Servilius Isauricus, whose campaign against the pirates in Cilicia had recently brought him a triumph. Cicero says of Servilius: 'He captured more pirate leaders alive than anyone before him.' The difference is, of course, that they did not get away from him later (*II Verr.* 5.66 and 79). See above pp. 128–31.

[24] *II Verr.* 5.78–87.

[25] *II Verr.* 5.87–95.

[26] *II Verr.* 5.95–100. As Cicero reminds his audience, not even the Carthaginians and the Athenians in their heyday were as successful in the Syracusan harbour as mere pirates in the praetorship of Verres (*II Verr.* 5.97–8). This episode is anticipated in the fourth book, where Cicero makes similar comments (*II Verr.* 4.116). Oros. 6.3 seems to identify a certain Pyrganio, who was defeated by Verres' successor, with this captain.

[27] *II Verr.* 5.101–38. Note especially 137: 'In your praetorship, for the first time since the founding of Syracuse, pirates sailed around in the harbour which no enemy has ever penetrated.' Cicero even adds a few more mentions of pirates before the end of this speech, to remind his audience of the earlier pirate themes (*II Verr.* 5.144, 146, 156, 157).

presents Verres as a despicable pirate who has robbed and plundered Asia, Achaea, Sicily and even the city of Rome. 'Verres the pirate' is the antithesis of a good, Roman magistrate. The piratical characteristics which are emphasized by Cicero – lust for plunder and disregard of proper behaviour – present an image of piracy which is familiar to readers in any age. In his military dealings with real pirates Verres is shown to be incompetent and contemptible, his disgrace being compounded by the fact that he is facing not proper enemies, but mere pirates. The implication is that Verres cannot even deal with people as worthless as himself. The main function of all the references to piracy in the *Verrine Orations* is, however, to belittle Verres, not to inform us about piracy in the first century BC. Even casual mentions are calculated to add to the overall impression of the worthlessness of Verres. It is important to consider this carefully when attempting to use the Verrines for historical analysis of piracy. Nevertheless, it is clear that Cicero chose to exploit the theme of piracy so thoroughly in the *Verrine Orations* precisely because it was currently a very topical one. As the previous chapter has demonstrated, piracy was a considerable problem throughout the Mediterranean in the early decades of the first century BC, and the Romans, who liked to portray themselves as the benefactors and protectors of weaker states, were expected to do something about it by their subjects, allies and friends. The pirates of the Verrines, especially as presented by Cicero in his attack on Verres, are good evidence of the commonly held view among the communities of the Roman world that piracy was a serious menace which required strong action to suppress or control it. When such action finally did come, in the early 60s BC, it was partly in response to the pressure which Rome's allies and friends had been putting on the senatorial aristocracy, forcing them to restore their image as protectors of the Mediterranean. A close examination of the campaigns of Quintus Metellus Creticus and Gnaeus Pompeius Magnus shows, however, that there were also political gains to be made by individuals from exploiting the problem of piracy.

## Metellus Creticus

The embarrassing defeat suffered by Marcus Antonius at the hands of the Cretans in 72 BC was bound to have serious repercussions at Rome, and it seems that many of the Cretan cities realized this at the time. They tried to forestall retaliatory action by giving their side of the story, and appealing to the senate to renew their status as allies of Rome (Diod. 40.1.1–2). Unfortunately, a more bellicose group led by the tribune Lentulus Spinther opposed the deal which was put forward, forcing the senate to take a hard line with the Cretans:

> The senate, looking favourably upon their explanation, attempted to pass a decree which cleared them of all charges and declared them friends and allies of the leading power (Rome). But the decree was vetoed by Lentulus, surnamed Spinther, and the Cretans departed.[28] (Diod. 40.1 .2)

The Cretan ambassadors seem to have been given some kind of ultimatum to surrender all their ships and provide 300 hostages, including the 'pirate' Lasthenes, who was responsible for the defeat of Marcus Antonius Creticus.[29] This proved unacceptable (as was probably the intention) and war followed.[30] In Diodorus' account the senate are informed many times of the Cretans' collusion in piracy (Diod. 40.1.3) and this prompts them to declare war. It seems, however, that the piracy element had been conveniently overlooked until Spinther intervened. Velleius does not mention pirates at all in his account (Vell. 2.34; 38–9). He does, however, say that Crete was punished (*multata est*) by the consul of 69 BC, Metellus (Vell. Pat. 2.38.6), which might refer to accusations of piracy, or of siding with Mithridates. Neither does the Epitomator of Livy refer to pirates (Livy, *Per.* 99). The conquest of Crete should not, therefore, be seen simply as a further measure to suppress piracy. Florus is, perhaps, to be taken seriously when he says that desire for conquest was what spurred the Romans on after the defeat of Antonius (Flor. 3.7). Nor should it be forgotten that an extended campaign of this kind offered numerous opportunities to obtain booty and, for a victorious general, prestige and influence in Rome. The attempted conquest of Marcus Antonius in 72 BC can be compared with the successful annexation of Cyrenaica in 75 BC, which seems to have netted a lot of money for the public coffers at Rome.[31] It is not unreasonable to think that some Romans saw Crete as another potential treasure-chest and a profitable addition to their growing empire. It may be easier to understand why Metellus' campaign was launched by first looking briefly at what he achieved. He conquered the whole of Crete and brought the island under Roman control. Its harbours were no longer open to pirates, its mercenaries less readily available to

---

[28]    The motion must have been put forward after the restoration of the tribunician veto in 70 BC.

[29]    Diod. 40.1.3 and Dio 30/5.111; App. *Sic.* 6.1–2. According to Appian the senate declared war first, then demanded the ships and hostages. Diodorus' account seems more likely (why demand hostages when you have already declared war?), and Appian's allows no role for Spinther. It is Dio who combines the embassy and the ultimatum.

[30]    Technically, of course, it was the Cretans who chose war with the Romans. They refused to accept the senate's terms and so they were in the wrong.

[31]    See Crawford (1974): 705.

Rome's enemies. The victorious proconsul was saluted as *imperator*, one of the most desirable achievements of a political career in the Republic.[32] Metellus and his army must also have gained some booty from the capture of so many cities, and a great deal more would have gone into the public coffers in Rome.[33] Metellus' triumph is mentioned by several sources, largely on account of his quarrels with Pompey over some captured generals, but it seems to have been an impressive show.[34] On a less tangible, but still very important level, the ignominy of Antonius' defeat was cleansed: 'He celebrated a triumph and took the name Creticus, more deservedly than Antonius, having conquered the whole island' (App. *Sic.* 6.2). What seems to emerge from the ancient sources' presentation of the conquest, however, is a reluctance on the part of the Romans to admit openly that their goals were imperialist. They preferred to justify their actions in terms of defence of their honour and security and the protection of their friends and allies.[35]

The importance which the Romans attached to the Cretan situation is reflected in the senate's decision to make Crete a consular province for 69 BC, as a fragment of Cassius Dio reveals (Dio 36.1). The lot fell to Quintus Hortensius Hortalus, Cicero's main adversary in the trial of Verres, but he declined in favour of his colleague Quintus Caecilius Metellus. Metellus' campaign in Crete lasted three years. It is worth looking at in some detail because of the strange contrast it affords with the more celebrated campaign against the pirates conducted by Pompey in 67 BC. It is apparently a continuation of Marcus Antonius' attempt to subdue the Cretans, although Metellus had better resources and was ultimately more successful.[36] According to Velleius the Cretan leaders Lasthenes and Panares had collected together '24,000 young men assembled into a swift, tough, well trained force, renowned for their skill as archers' (Vell. 2.34.1). This number seems rather high, but there should have been no shortage of fighting men on Crete, where rigorous military training was still sponsored by many cities. Mithridates probably recruited mercenaries on Crete, as did many others in the Hellenistic period.[37] It is diffi-

---

[32] *CIL* I².2.746; *ICret.* 2.252.14.

[33] See Harris (1979) and North (1981) on booty as a motive for Roman imperialism, though it should not be seen as the most important one in this case.

[34] Vell. Pat. 2.40.5; App. *Sic.* 6.2; Dio 36.19.3. Appian mentions the great wealth of Lasthenes kept in Knossos, and Dio accuses Metellus of extorting money from Eleuthera. For a more detailed analysis of the prosperity of Late Hellenistic Crete and the motives for Roman conquest see de Souza (1998a).

[35] See de Souza (1996) for further discussion of the justification of Roman imperialism in this period.

[36] He had at least three legions, according to Phlegon of Tralles 12.12 (*FGrHist.* no. 257).

[37] See above pp. 145–8. Willetts (1955): 241–8 remains the best treatment in English of Cretan mercenaries, supplemented for piracy by Brulé (1978).

cult to assess the situation in Crete at this time, but it seems that the two leaders mentioned were supported by a substantial part of the island's population, including most of the main cities, which were controlled by aristocracies.[38]

The sources all lay heavy emphasis on the arduous and protracted nature of the Cretan War, making it essentially a series of sieges.[39] The early stages of Metellus' campaign seem to have been centred on western Crete. Livy's account dealt first with his siege of Kydonia in Book 98 (Livy, *Per.* 98), and Kydonia is the site of his first victory in Appian's version of events (App. *Sic.* 6.2). Only one battle is mentioned, at Hierapytna, which seems to have taken place at sea and resulted in defeat for Lucius Bassus, a legate of Metellus, at the hands of Aristion and Octavius.[40] Aristion is an otherwise unknown Cretan leader, Octavius' part is discussed below.

Recent excavations in western Crete have uncovered what seems to be hard evidence of Metellus' efforts to overcome determined Cretan resistance. The ancient harbour and city of Phalasarna, on the north-western tip of Crete, has been uplifted along with the rest of the area so that it now lies well above sea level. Excavations were begun in 1986 and have revealed that the harbour, which was approached via a narrow rock-cut channel, was deliberately blocked by large pieces of masonry. The excavators have plausibly associated this with Metellus' campaign. The blocked harbour and nearby finds indicate that Phalasarna was besieged and blockaded by land and sea. The inhabitants probably surrendered, either to Metellus or to one of his lieutenants, although it is possible that the place had to be taken by storm, since its fortifications are impressive.[41] The exact number of Cretan cities which were taken by Metellus is not known, but a list of the places mentioned in our literary sources gives a good idea of the extent of his campaign:

| | |
|---|---|
| Eleuthernai | (Dio 36.18.2; Florus 3.7.5.) Dio says that it was taken through treachery (ἐκ προδοσίας); presumably someone opened the gates. |
| Hierapytna | (Dio 36.19.1.) The city was abandoned to Metellus by Aristion, after his defeat of Lucius Bassus. |

[38] On the nature of Cretan society and politics at this time see Willetts (1955), Sanders (1982) and Karafotias (1997). Although Crete was still politically volatile, the cities seem to have banded together to resist the Romans. This may have come as a surprise to M. Antonius in 72 BC, if he was counting on exploiting inter-city rivalries to his advantage.

[39] Vell. Pat. 2.34.1; App. *Sic.* 6.2; Dio 36.18–19; Florus 3.7.4–6; Plut. *Pomp.* 29.

[40] Dio 36.19.1; *MRR* II 147. Dio uses the verb ἀντανάγω when referring to Bassus. This often means 'to put out to sea against someone', but could simply mean 'attack'.

[41] See Hadjidaki (1988a and b), Frost (1989) and Frost & Hadjidaki (1990). The latest sherds of pottery found at the site date from the first century BC. Several catapult stones have been found in the midst of the harbour complex.

| | |
|---|---|
| Knossos | (Livy, *Per.* 99; App. *Sic.* 6.2; Florus 3.7.5.) According to Appian there was a siege and Livy says that the city was taken by storm. |
| Kydonia | (Livy, *Per.* 98–9; App. *Sic.* 6.2; Florus 3.7.5.) Livy says it was stormed but Appian claims that Panares surrendered the city to Metellus in return for good treatment. |
| Lappa | (Dio 36.18.2.) Stormed, while Octavius was there. |
| Lyktos | (Livy, *Per.* 99.) Stormed. |

Three of these cities are located in central Crete (Eleuthernai, Knossos and Lappa), two in eastern Crete (Hierapytna and Lyktos) and the remaining one, Kydonia, along with Phalasarna, is in western Crete. The fullest accounts of the campaign come from Appian and Dio. The former says that Kydonia was taken before Knossos and the latter gives a sequence of Eleuthernai, Lappa and then Hierapytna. It therefore seems reasonable to conclude that Metellus began by securing the western part of the island and then moved eastwards, pursuing his remaining enemies and laying siege to those places which sheltered them or offered resistance.[42] The Cretan leaders Aristion, Lasthenes and Panares were most probably aristocrats from the leading cities, all three being associated with Kydonia at some point in the various literary accounts. This city seems to have been the main focus of Cretan resistance to the Romans. It would appear that Metellus was disinclined to strike any deals with the Cretans. He prosecuted the war vigorously, making sure that all the cities surrendered to him. In 67 BC, however, he came up against an unexpected problem in the shape of the rival campaign of Pompey. Their encounters are discussed below in the context of Pompey's commission to clear the seas of pirates.

### The background to the campaign of Pompey

In 67 BC Gnaeus Pompeius Magnus (Pompey) was appointed under a law proposed by the tribune Aulus Gabinius to clear the seas of pirates. He was given wide-ranging powers and enormous resources. The suppression of piracy had become so urgent a matter that the Romans risked, in the eyes of some at least, creating another Marius or Sulla in order to deal with it.[43] Why did the Romans choose to act in this fashion at this

---

[42] Appian (*Sic.* 6.2) speaks of Lasthenes fleeing from Kydonia to Knossos. Dio (36.19.1–2) has Aristion abandoning Kydonia and Hierapytna in succession.

[43] See Dio 36.21–37; Plut. *Pomp.* 25–7; App. *Mith.* 92–6; Cic. *Leg. Man.* for the political uproar caused by the Gabinian law.

time? In the first place it seems that there was a growing recognition at Rome that piracy had become so widespread, and the pirates so great a menace, that the practice of requiring allies and subjects to be largely responsible for the suppression of piracy, backed up by occasional campaigns directed at specific targets (e.g. in Cilicia or Crete), was no longer adequate. There are several episodes and events recorded in our sources which can be used to illustrate this growth in the menace of piracy. The capture of Julius Caesar by pirates in 75/4 BC, described in the previous chapter, showed that even a high-ranking Roman could become the victim of pirates. The problem of piracy was also put forward as a justification for the activities of Marcus Antonius Creticus in 74–72 BC. The attacks of pirates on the island of Sicily during the governorship of Gaius Verres have already been discussed.[44] The measures undertaken by Verres to deal with these attacks were not very successful, but it appears that his successor, Lucius Metellus, was more effective in suppressing piracy in this area. Livy recorded his achievement in the 98th book of his history (Livy, *Per.* 98) and Orosius goes into some detail about the matter, claiming that one of the pirate leaders he captured, called Pyrganio, was the same man who had earlier embarrassed Verres by sailing in triumph into the harbour at Syracuse and mocking the efforts of the Roman governor to capture him (Oros. 6.3.5).[45] The name which Cicero gives to this leader, however, is Heracleo, so it may be that Orosius was guilty of a flight of fancy here. Metellus' victory must have been reasonably spectacular to merit a mention in Livy's account, although it could be argued that his success was made all the more impressive by the scale of Verres' failure.

In his speech to the assembly of the Roman people on the Manilian law in 66 BC, Cicero recalled for his audience how the friends, allies and subjects of Rome had been left at the mercy of pirates until Pompey drove them away.[46] One of the places he described was Delos, '... situated so far away from us in the Aegean sea, where people from all over gathered together, bringing their wares and cargoes to trade, crammed full with riches, small, unwalled, accustomed to fear nothing...' (Cic. *Leg. Man.* 55). Cicero goes on to contrast this happy position of Delos in former days with the vulnerability of Rome in more recent times. He must have had some particular reason to mention Delos at this point and the explanation of his reference is provided by a fragment from the Greek historian Phlegon of Tralles: 'And Athenodoros the pirate, having reduced the

---

[44] See above pp. 154–7.
[45] For the details of the incident see Cic. *II Verr.* 5.95–100.
[46] Cic. *Leg. Man.* 31–5 and 54–7.

Delians to slavery, shamefully desecrated the statues of their gods. But Gaius Triarius rectified the damage to the city and built a wall round Delos' (*FGrHist* 257, fr. 12.13). The event can be dated to 69 BC on the basis of the inscriptions mentioned below, and a reference to Metellus Creticus which precedes it. The remains of Triarius' wall have been excavated at Delos, along with inscriptions bearing dedications to him.[47] It was probably this event, occurring only a few years earlier, which prompted Cicero to mention Delos in his speech. Triarius was a legate of Lucullus involved in naval campaigns against Mithridates' fleet.[48] An inscription of 58 BC, recording a law of the consuls Aulus Gabinius and Lucius Calpurnius concerning the restoration of shrines and temples on Delos, also refers to the piracy which 'troubled the whole world for many years'.[49]

A comparable view of the vulnerability of Aegean communities to piracy is offered by an inscription from the island of Aigina in honour of one Diodoros, who was *agoranomos* in the year 69 BC, which mentions an attack by pirates: '... during the recent war, when the pirates overran and laid waste our territory, and at the same time we were greatly in need on account of the tax, he provided enough grain for the whole period to those who required it...'[50] This inscription indicates that there was a crisis on Aigina, partly as a result of an attack by pirates, in the same year that Athenodoros sacked Delos. It is tempting to see some close connection between the two. Perhaps the attack on Aigina was also carried out by Athenodoros? In any case, it is clear that piracy, from whatever sources, was a problem in the Aegean at this time, in spite of the presence of Triarius and a Roman fleet. His principal concern was obviously the war, mentioned in the Aigina inscription, and not the suppression of piracy.

A similar crisis on the island of Tenos is indicated by another inscription from this period, this time honouring a Roman banker, Lucius Aufidius Bassus, the son of Lucius, for remitting interest on loans owed by the people of Tenos. The inscription refers to events at the time of the first Mithridatic war, involving the elder Lucius. He reached an agreement concerning loans which were particularly onerous, 'when the war was going on and the island was continually under attack from pirates'. His

---

[47] See Rostovtzeff (1941); *ILS* 8774; Maier (1959): nos. 41 and 42. Coin hoards found on Delos which have been dated to 69 BC indicate that considerable loss of life and property may have resulted from Athenodoros' attack. See Hackens & Lévy (1965): 503–17.

[48] See *MRR* II 113, 120, 125, 130 and 134; *MRR* III 214–15.

[49] *SEG* 1 no. 355 (from Mykonnos).

[50] *IG* IV.2 lines 9–14. The date is given in lines 4–5 as the 64th year of the era. The editor, M.Fraenkel, believes that the first year of this era was 133 BC, so the 64th year is 69 BC.

son had to be generous in much the same way, apparently because the circumstances had not improved.[51]

In more general terms there are several references in the literary sources to the attacks of pirates on islands and cities of the Eastern Mediterranean in this period. Cicero, in his speech on the Manilian law, picks out Knidos, Kolophon and Samos, as well as mentioning Delos (Cic. *Leg. Man.* 31–3 and 55). Plutarch lists 13 plundered sanctuaries and claims that pirates captured 400 cities at the height of their power (Plut. *Pomp.* 24). Dio is less specific in his description of the pirates' depredations, saying that they began by attacking shipping and then became bold enough to raid harbours and cities (Dio 36.20–1). Appian paints a similar picture of the increasing boldness of the pirates who attacked ships, harbours and even fortified cities until they dominated the whole Mediterranean (App. *Mith.* 92–3). It is not clear from these literary sources exactly when particular places were plundered by pirates. Appian, Plutarch and Cicero mention several cities and islands which seem to have been notable victims of the pirates shortly before Pompey's campaign. Samos is mentioned by all three, Samothrake by Plutarch and Appian, and the list of sanctuaries given by Plutarch covers a considerable part of the Eastern Mediterranean. The context in which Appian mentions Samothrake and Samos, however, is the end of the first Mithridatic war, while Sulla is still in Asia (App. *Mith.* 63).[52] It may be that the lists of specific locations attacked by pirates, which are given by our literary sources in the early parts of their accounts of Pompey's campaign, cover many years of piracy, rather than just a few, as the authors seem to imply. Thus, it is reasonable to infer from Cicero's speech *On the Manilian Law* that the Romans had for some considerable time been aware of the vulnerability of their subjects and allies in the eastern and western provinces. The allies themselves were very concerned, and Cicero speaks of them as requesting Pompey's appointment in 67 BC.[53] I am, however, reluctant to see a sudden, dramatic wave of piratical attacks across the whole Mediterranean, encompassing hundreds of cities and islands as the primary motivation for the Gabinian law.

That is not to say that piracy was not a very serious menace in the years leading up to 67 BC. The kidnapping of Julius Caesar, the piratical activity around Sicily in the time of Verres, the inscriptions from Aigina and Tenos, and the sack of Delos, taken together with the statements of

---

[51] *IG* XII.5.860. See also *RE* II.2 col. 2291 and *SEG* 29 (1979) no. 757. Further discussion in Hatzfeld (1919); Ormerod (1924): 233; Ziebarth (1929): 41 and 116.

[52] Appian's account is not strictly chronological, however, so chapter 63 of his *Mithridatic Wars* may refer to events of the 60s and 70s BC.

[53] Cic. *Leg. Man.* 67 '[the people of] the coastal regions' (*ora maritima*).

all the main sources that piratical attacks were widespread and numerous at this time, are clearly enough a cause for concern. But they do not seem to me to represent a worsening of the situation since the early 70s BC. The attacks on Delos, Aigina and possibly even Tenos might be ascribed to pirates operating from Crete. In this case Metellus' appointment in 69 BC to the war with Crete[54] seems to be the same kind of response as were the commands of Marcus Antonius the orator in 102 BC, Publius Servilius Isauricus in 78 BC and even Marcus Antonius Creticus in 74 BC. In these instances, as with that of Metellus, the suppression of piracy seems to have been a less important reason for the campaign than Rome's 'imperialist' ambitions.[55] Something more dramatic is needed to explain the sudden change of approach which the appointment of Pompey represents, since the expressed purpose of the command was to suppress piracy. It is clear from the various sources which describe the immediate build-up to his appointment, and the discussion which Gabinius' law provoked, that it was the threat to Italy and Rome itself which finally stung the Romans into more drastic action.

Cicero, recalling the dire straits which the Romans found themselves in before Pompey's campaign against the pirates, contrasts earlier days of maritime tranquillity with the current period of insecurity:

We used to guarantee not just the safety of Italy, but were able, through the prestige of our imperial power, to preserve unharmed all our far-flung allies ... yet we are now not only kept out of our provinces, away from the coasts of Italy and its harbours, but we are even driven off the Appian Way! (Cic. *Leg. Man.* 55)

The places in Italy which Cicero says have been attacked are Caieta, Misenum and Ostia (Cic. *Leg. Man.* 33). Velleius speaks of pirates plundering 'certain cities of Italy' (Vell. Pat. 31.2), Florus mentions Sicily and Campania (Flor. 3.6). According to Appian the pirates attacked Brundisium[56] and Etruria (App. *Mith.* 92), and Dio says that they pillaged and burned Ostia and other cities in Italy (Dio 36.22). It has also been suggested that evidence of burning and destruction found in some of the houses excavated at Cosa should be attributed to pirate raids in this period.[57] While such an explanation is possible, I do not find it particularly plausible, especially in the case of the town of Cosa, which is a very defensible site and unlikely to have seemed to pirates to be worth attack-

---

[54] See above pp. 157–9.
[55] A different emphasis is offered by Pohl (1993), who sees the campaign of 67 BC as the culmination of a gradual increase in military and political commitment by Rome to the solution of the piracy problem; see further de Souza (1995b).
[56] See also Cic. *Leg. Man.* 32.
[57] Brown (1980): 74 n. 112. See also McCann (1987): 28.

ing. Low-lying, prosperous places like Ostia and Brundisium are a different matter.[58] Indeed, according to some of the literary accounts, the
pirates had singled out Italy and the Romans as targets for their attacks,
raiding cities, harbours, roads and villas. Plutarch, in an often quoted
passage, describes the humiliation and insults which pirates enjoyed inflicting upon their Roman victims (Plut. *Pomp.* 24). As well as general
comments he includes two specific examples:

On one occasion they seized two praetors in their purple trimmmings, Sextilius
and Bellinus, making off with them, servants, lictors and all. They also captured
the daughter of Antonius, a man who had celebrated a triumph, as she was on her
way to the country, and ransomed her for a great deal of money.[59] (Plut. *Pomp.*
24)

These examples are also mentioned by Cicero (*Leg. Man.* 32) and Appian
(*Mith.* 93). Another shocking event to which attention is drawn by Cicero
and Dio is the destruction of a Roman fleet at Ostia by pirates.[60]

Plutarch concludes his long description of the growing menace of
piracy in the following fashion:

Their power was felt in all parts of the Mediterranean, so that it was impossible to
sail anywhere and all trade was brought to a halt. It was this which really made
the Romans sit up and take notice. With their markets short of food and a great
famine looming, they commissioned Pompey to clear the pirates from the seas.
(Plut. *Pomp.* 25.1)

It would seem that the one thing which no one could ignore at Rome was
a threat to the grain supply. Dio mentions that there had been periodic
interruptions caused by pirates before 67 BC, and one such occasion has
been discussed above.[61] Appian stresses the threat to the grain supply as a
factor in provoking the Romans to respond to the pirate menace. He
blames the enormous population of the city for the distress which resulted
(App. *Mith.* 93). Livy also recorded that the supply was cut off by pirates
in 67 BC (Livy, *Per.* 99).

The political response to this crisis was a proposal by the tribune Aulus
Gabinius for an extraordinary provincial command aimed at 'clearing

---

[58] The full report of the Cosa excavations is still awaited. It may well be that the evidence
Brown refers to can be explained more appropriately by another hypothesis.

[59] Presumably this refers to the daughter of Marcus Antonius the orator.

[60] Cic. *Leg. Man.* 33; Dio 36.22.2. It is often asserted, on no particular evidence, that this
fleet had been prepared specifically to fight the pirates. It would be wrong to imagine a
huge fleet of pirate ships waiting off the mouth of the Tiber to pre-empt a Roman strike
against them. Only a few pirate vessels would have been needed. The mission of the
Roman fleet is unknown.

[61] Dio 36.23.2. See above pp. 142–3 on the shortage in 75 BC. See Garnsey (1988): 200–1
for other possible shortages.

the seas' of pirates. Someone would be appointed for three years with authority to raise troops in all provinces and to override other magistrates anywhere within fifty miles of the sea. Up to 25 legates were proposed[62] for the commander and a large budget to pay for the outfitting of a huge fleet and army.[63] In the end Pompey did not make use of all the resources that were offered to him, and once again allied forces were prominent.[64] The political uproar caused by Gabinius' proposal forms the longest part of two of our major accounts of Pompey's campaign, and is referred to by Cicero in his speech of the following year on the Manilian law.[65] Although Pompey was not named in the law, it was clearly intended for him, and the urgency of the matter was reflected in the way that the people shouted down the opponents of Gabinius.[66] All they wanted was someone to restore their food supplies. If Cicero can be believed, when the appointment of Pompey was confirmed the grain crisis virtually disappeared (Cic. *Leg. Man.* 44).

### Pompey: the secret of his success

Pompey's early military activity confirms that securing the grain supply was his first priority:

In spite of the unsuitability of the weather for sailing he crossed to Sicily, checked out the coast of Africa, took his fleet to Sardinia and established military and naval garrisons to guard these three granaries of the state ... The two seas around Italy were secured with huge fleets and strong armies. (Cic. *Leg. Man.* 34)

Plutarch's account of the campaign also demonstrates this point. According to him Pompey gathered his naval forces and concentrated them in the Western Mediterranean. Plutarch picks out exactly the same places as Cicero – Africa, Sardinia and Sicily – as well as Corsica and the Tyr-

---

[62] Only 15 seem to have been used, *MRR* II 148–9. Brunt (1971): 456 n. 10 thinks there were only 14.

[63] The actual figures given by Appian and Plutarch for the forces allotted to Pompey seem far too high (App. *Mith.* 94; Plut. *Pomp.* 26.2). 'Within so short a time he could not have raised the huge forces of which Appian and Plutarch tell' (Brunt (1971): 456). Also the suggestion of unlimited funds, men and ships (Dio 36.37.1) is incredible. Appian puts the number of ships at 270, which might be possible. The attempt by Gröbe (1910) to rationalize the figures is largely guesswork.

[64] E.g. Flor. 3.6.8 on Pompey's Rhodian allies; see also *SIG* 749.

[65] Dio 36.25–36; Plut. *Pomp.* 25.3–26.1. Cic. *Leg. Man.* 56.

[66] See Plut. *Pomp.* 25; Dio 36.30. The opposition to Gabinius' proposal concentrated on the wide scope of the *imperium* which the appointed commander would have, enabling him (theoretically) to override other holders of *imperium*. It is difficult to say whether these powers were vital to the job. Their most conspicuous use was in Crete, where Pompey's intervention was unnecessary; see below pp. 170–2. For further discussion of the 'constitutional' aspects see Pohl (1993): 186–99.

rhenian Sea (Plut. *Pomp.* 26.4).[67] Most of the sources agree that the first part of his campaign was completed in 40 days (Livy, *Per.* 99; App. *Mith.* 95). The remarkable speed with which Pompey cleared the seas before heading for Cilicia makes it unlikely that a thorough operation was carried out.[68] He divided up the seas among his legates, assigning each to a particular area. The forces which they had at their disposal are not known, and there are no details in the sources of their activities, only generalizations.[69] In short, it is unclear whether they did much at all. Plutarch's account of the procedure is one of the fullest:

> Notwithstanding this achievement, he divided up the coasts and seas into 13 regions, assigning a number of ships to each one, with a commander. His forces were spread out, threatening the pirate hordes from all sides so that they were swiftly caught and brought to land. The more elusive ones were driven together towards Cilicia, like bees swarming to their hive. Pompey made ready to move against them with 60 of his best ships. (Plut. *Pomp.* 26.3)

The sources are equally brief in what they say about the Cilician part of the campaign. Cicero sums it up in one sentence: 'He himself, however, set out from Brundisium and in 49 days he had brought Cilicia into the Roman Empire' (Cic. *Leg. Man.* 35). A few more details are given by some of the later sources, particularly those writing in Greek, but they do not suggest that there was a hard struggle, or even that there was much fighting.[70]

In spite of the numerous superlatives that have been used to describe Pompey's campaign of 67 BC, a close scrutiny of the sources leaves the distinct impression of a 'rush job'.[71] Even if it is allowed that the first stage, clearing the seas around Italy to secure the grain supply, could have been carried out so quickly with reasonable thoroughness, the conquest

---

[67] I think it quite likely that Plutarch had read Cicero's speech *On the Manilian Law*. He also read other sources which provided details of the political wrangling before the appointment and the course of the campaign.

[68] According to Florus (3.6.15) it took him only 40 days to complete the entire commission, including the conquest of Cilicia!

[69] Breglia (1970–1) discusses the legates and the sources at length, concluding only that Appian is more reliable than Florus.

[70] E.g. Dio's account in Book 36 of his *Roman History*. The military operations of Pompey and his legates occupy less than 30 lines of Greek text (in the Loeb volume), as compared with the 16 pages (incomplete) devoted to the story of the rise of the pirates and the debates at Rome over the Gabinian law.

[71] The sources are unanimous in their opinion that Pompey's campaign was as outstanding as it was swift. Modern authorities have tended to follow suit. E.g. Casson (1991): 182–3: 'It was a spectacular operation, brilliantly conceived and magnificently executed. In three months Pompey had accomplished what no power had been able to do for centuries.'

of Cilicia in 49 days seems incredible, especially in the light of previous actions by Roman magistrates in this area.[72] I think that a clue to understanding this 'miracle' is provided by the cursory way in which the Cilician part of the campaign is treated by everyone from Cicero to Orosius.[73] Once the grain supply had been secured, the people of Rome were far less interested in the progress of the 'pirate war'. What Pompey did after his initial forty days was a matter of little interest to them, and thus of less interest to the ancient sources, especially as his subsequent part in the Mithridatic wars was much more significant.

After 40 days spent sorting out the Western Mediterranean, Pompey went directly to Cilicia, pausing only to stop off at Athens and tell its population how wonderful he was (Plut. *Pomp.* 27.3). It would seem logical that the most difficult and demanding part of his job should now have been about to begin. All the remaining pirates were supposedly gathered in their Cilician 'lairs' waiting for him to arrive. There is an obvious tendency for the ancient sources, and some modern scholars, to assume that all those labelled pirates at this time were Cilicians, but even allowing for such an exaggeration it is clear that the ports and cities of this region were the source of many of the worst marauders. Having ruled the seas and successfully resisted the Romans for 35 years, since the brief campign of Marcus Antonius the orator, they could hardly be expected to give up without a fight. Yet, astonishingly, according to some ancient sources this is exactly what they did. Florus and Appian claim that there was no need even to spill blood! Pompey's reputation and his earlier successes were enough to make the Cilician pirates surrender to his army and fleet on sight:

His reputation and his preparedness reduced the pirates to panic, and in the hope that, through not fighting, they would make him benevolent towards them, first those who held Kragos and Antikragos, the largest strongholds, surrendered, and after them those who lived in the Cilician mountains, and, eventually, all the rest followed suit.[74] (App. *Mith.* 96)

Even those who admit there was some fighting can find very little of it. There was a naval battle off Korakesion, followed by a siege of the city

---

[72] See above Ch. 4 on Marcus Antonius the orator, Sulla, Murena, Servilius Isauricus.

[73] Appraisals of Pompey's campaign are to be found in the following writers: Cic. *Leg. Man.* 31–6; Livy, *Per.* 99; Str. 14.3.3; Vell. Pat. 2.32.4; Plut. *Pomp.* 26–8; App. *Mith.* 95–6; Flor. 3.6.15; Dio 36.37; Eutr. 6.12; Oros. 6.4.1. There are others, but they are much shorter and not worth considering here.

[74] Appian then proceeds to contradict himself (or, perhaps, to correct himself) by saying that 10,000 pirates were killed in fighting. See also Flor. 3.6.13–14. On the location of Kragos and Antikragos see Rauh (1999b).

(Plut. *Pomp.* 28.1; Vell. Pat. 2.32.4).[75] How many troops and ships Pompey had it is impossible to tell. He may have been entitled to recruit as many as 120,000 men and deploy around 200 ships (App. *Mith.* 95; Plut. *Pomp.* 25.3), but the best modern estimate of his actual army strength in 66 BC, just before the passing of the *lex Manilia* transferring the Mithridatic war to him, is 30,000, including the army of Quintus Marcius Rex, whom he had superseded in Cilicia.[76] I would estimate, without any strong evidence to refer to, that the fleet with which Pompey attacked Cilicia was about 100 strong, with perhaps about 50 good-sized warships. Part of his forces had been posted to guard various points on the grain supply route. While this force is not insignificant, it hardly seems enough to inspire terror. How, then, did Pompey conquer Cilicia so quickly?

The answer is the famous Roman virtue *clementia* (mercy), something more often associated with Pompey's political rival Julius Caesar:[77]

For he had at his disposal great forces, both in his fleet and his army, so that at sea and on land he was irresistible. Just as great was his clemency[78] towards those who made terms with him, so that he won over many of them by this policy. For those men who were beaten by his forces and experienced his great benevolence, put themselves at his disposal most readily. (Dio 36.37.4)

According to Plutarch, Pompey never thought of putting any of his prisoners to death, the punishment which others regularly meted out to pirates (Plut. *Pomp.* 28.2).[79] Appian claims that he was able to distinguish between pirates who were 'wicked' and others who had been driven to piracy by poverty (App. *Mith.* 96). In effect, Pompey offered the Cilicians another chance, giving them land in exchange for their ships. He settled them in various cities of Cilicia and also in Dyme, a city of Achaia.[80] This philanthropic attitude contrasted strongly with that of Metellus Creticus. Indeed, it was the cause of a violent disagreement between the two. Some of the Cretans, fearing the approaching army of Metellus, offered to sur-

---

[75] Other sources (Dio, Livy, Eutropius, Orosius) clearly assume some fighting took place, but give no details.

[76] Brunt (1971): 460. See Dio 36.17 and Sall. *Hist.* fr. V.14M for Quintus Marcius. Brunt describes his conclusions on this matter as 'precarious', but I can offer nothing better.

[77] See Caesar, *The Civil Wars*, passim.

[78] Dio here uses the Greek word φιλανθρωπία.

[79] See above pp. 128–31 on the treatment of pirates by Verres, Servilius, Caesar and the Astypalaians.

[80] Plut. *Pomp.* 28.4; App. *Mith.* 96 and 115; Dio 36.37.6; Str. 8.7.5 and 14.3.3; Livy *Per.* 99; Vell. Pat. 2.32.5–6. Velleius is the only ancient source to mention any contemporary criticism of this policy, which he immediately dismisses by saying that it was so good it would have made the reputation of anyone.

render to Pompey, on the basis that his *imperium* could override Metellus'. There had already been problems over jurisdiction in the early stages of the campaign, when the governor of Gallia Narbonensis refused to allow Pompey's legates to recruit in his province (Dio 36.37.2). In Metellus' case it came to blows.

The legate whom Pompey despatched to Crete to accept the surrender of various Cretan communities, Octavius, went so far as to use his troops, and those of the governor of Achaia, to fight for the Cretans at Lappa and Hierapytna against Metellus (Dio 36.19; App. *Sic.* 6.2). The capture of Lappa neatly demonstrated the opposing sides' different attitudes to their prisoners. Metellus, finding some Cilicians among Octavius' men, had them executed as pirates. Livy recorded an exchange of letters between Metellus and Pompeius (Livy, *Per.* 99) and Dio even suggests that Pompey was on the point of going to war with Metellus, when news of the Manilian law made him change his plans (Dio 36.45.1; App. *Sic.* 6.2). It appears that the two Cretan leaders, Lasthenes and Panares, both offered themselves to Pompey, but were eventually captured by Metellus. Pompey later insisted that they be withdrawn from Metellus' triumphal procession, as they were not his prisoners (Vell. Pat. 2.40.5; Dio 36.19.3). In his speech on the Manilian law Cicero mentions the Cretans' offer to surrender to Pompey, using it to emphasize his reputation among Rome's enemies:

All pirates, wherever they were, suffered capture and death, or handed themselves over to this singularly powerful commander. Even the Cretans, when they sent emissaries to him in Pamphylia to plead their case, learned that there was hope for their surrender, and were ordered to give hostages. (Cic. *Leg. Man.* 35)

Although Cicero is careful to say that Pompey did not spare all his prisoners, it is, nevertheless, clear that the only reason the Cretans had for turning to him was the chance of a better deal. They obviously thought that surrender to Pompey would be easier for them than giving in to Metellus. They must have reached this conclusion fairly soon after Pompey arrived in Cilicia, if not before, otherwise there would have been no time for negotiations before he turned to the war with Mithridates. Pompey's policy of clemency must, therefore, have been advertised from the beginning of his campaign. In other words, the secret of his remarkable success lay in his declared willingness to come to terms without a fight. He was able to conquer so quickly because he did not act in the same fashion as previous Roman commanders, who behaved as Florus depicts Metellus in Crete: 'He exercised the rights of the victor over the vanquished' (Flor. 3.6.6). Pompey, to put it simply, was 'soft' on his opponents. Thus he was able to complete a three-year mission in less than three months.[81] Yet this short, largely uneventful campaign greatly enhanced his reputation as a military genius, a liberator of the Mediterranean world from the evil of piracy and a hero of the Roman people. How was this possible? The answer would seem to lie in the way that both contemporary and later writers portrayed the campaign, with Cicero playing a leading role.

### Cicero and Pompey

Pompey's swift conclusion of his mission left him in the Eastern Mediterranean region in 66 BC, in a perfect position to take over the war with Mithridates VI. Once again a tribune, Gaius Manilius, proposed a motion in the tribal assembly appointing Pompey to this command in place of Manius Acilius Glabrio, who had just succeeded Lucullus.[82] Cicero, aligning himself with Pompey for the first time, spoke to the popular assembly in favour of this motion. The published version of his speech *On the Manilian Law*, also known as *On the Command of Gnaeus Pompeius*, goes into considerable detail about Pompey's military record, especially the campaign against the pirates. In sharp contrast to his treatment of Verres, in this speech Cicero uses the struggle against pirates to present his subject in the best possible light.

To begin with, Cicero deliberately avoids referring to Pompey's campaign as 'the war against the pirates'. Instead he calls it 'the naval war' (*bellum maritimum*).[83] This contrasts markedly with his references to 'the war against the pirates' in the *Verrine Orations*.[84] Similarly, in a speech delivered in the senate some ten years later, he refers to Gabinius' proposal as 'the measure concerning the war against the pirates' (*rogationem de piratico bello*).[85] It is not simply a different turn of phrase which can be observed here, but a calculated change in emphasis. In spite of the amazing things which Pompey had achieved in his early years, there was relatively little which could stand comparison with the great Republican leaders of the past. Put bluntly, all his successes had been against Romans and Italians, with the exception of the war with Spartacus, and that was

---

[81] A further indication that the pirate war was not properly finished comes from the comment Dio makes about Pompey, after he heard about the passing of the Manilian law: 'Crete, and the other maritime places where something still remained to be done, he considered as nothing' (Dio 36.45.2).

[82] See Sherwin-White (1984): 187–8.

[83] *Leg. Man.* 44, 58; also 28 (*navale bellum*). Appian uses the phrase 'the campaign at sea' (τὰ περὶ τὴν θάλασσαν) to describe the war against the pirates (App. *Mith.* 91).

[84] E.g. *II Verr.* 1.154; 5.42; see above pp. 150–7.

[85] *Red. sen.* 11.

against slaves. Aware of this shortcoming, Cicero invites the people to compare Pompey with Scipio Aemilianus and Gaius Marius, both granted special commands in contravention of customary Roman practice.[86] Scipio and Marius, however, were facing *foreign* enemies – Carthage, Numantia, Jugurtha, the Cimbri and Teutones. Pompey's opponents therefore have to be displayed with similar credentials:

> What form of warfare can there be, in which the fortunes of the Republic have not made use of his abilities? The Civil War, the African War, the Transalpine War, the Spanish War (against a mixture of citizens and men from the most warlike of nations),[87] the Slave War, the Naval War, represent a tremendous variety of conflicts and enemies. They were not only conducted, but concluded by this one man, whose experience can be said to embrace every possible form of military endeavour. (Cic. *Leg. Man.* 28)

It should be noted that Cicero here enumerates the exploits of Pompey as the senate's henchman in terms of their location – the African War was against Gnaeus Domitius, the Spanish War against Sertorius. In this form, however, they appear more like the Punic Wars, or the Gallic Wars of Scipio and Marius. Nor is Cicero being scrupulously honest when he gives Pompey sole credit for the completion of these wars. His contribution to the Civil War was marginal, and against Sertorius in Spain he was sent out to reinforce and assist Quintus Caecilius Metellus Pius, who celebrated a triumph in 71 BC, on his return from Spain.[88] To claim that Pompey finished the war with Spartacus is a considerable exaggeration,[89] but in keeping with Cicero's intention. Only the campaign against the pirates can truly be said to have been conducted and concluded by Pompey himself. Cicero carefully magnifies the importance of this campaign by calling it the Naval War,[90] and associating the pirates with the most powerful of Rome's former enemies.

In order to make Pompey into a great Republican hero, Cicero has to find him a 'dragon' of suitable stature to slay. The pirates whom Pompey

---

[86] *Leg. Man.* 47 and 60. Cicero is attempting to rebut the arguments of Quintus Catulus and Quintus Hortensius by finding precedents for the extraordinary nature of Manilius' proposal.

[87] Some editors and translators have found the words used here, *mixtum ex civitatibus atque ex bellicosissimis nationibus*, problematical. The phrase is clumsy, but this seems to me to be due to the awkwardness of what Cicero is trying to do, namely to demonstrate that Pompey's dubious military credentials are sound.

[88] Vell. Pat. 2.30; *ILLRP* 1.266; *CIL* I².733.

[89] See *II Verr.* 5.5 where Cicero shares the credit between Pompey and Crassus.

[90] Cicero uses the same term (*navalis*) to refer to operations in the Punic wars around Sicily (Cic. *II Verr.* 4.103). Pompey and his supporters also seem to have preferred this designation for the campaign of 67 BC, judging by the coin celebrating his exploits issued by Faustus Cornelius Sulla in 56 BC. It depicts the stern ornament of a ship (*aplustre*) as a symbol of the 'naval war'; Crawford (1974): 449/4b. See Pl. 3.

Pl. 3. A silver Roman *denarius* minted by Faustus Cornelius Sulla in 56 BC, in praise of his former commander Pompey the Great. The obverse shows a head of Hercules, while the reverse has symbols of Pompey's achievements, including an *aplustre* (ship's stern ornament) signifying his victory in the 'naval war' against the pirates.

defeated in 67 BC are, therefore, shown to have wielded enormous power: 'For, in the past few years, what part of the coast has been so well defended that it was safe, or so well concealed that it escaped disaster? Who could set sail without running the risk of death, or capture and slavery? Except for the winter season, the sea was full of pirates' (Cic. *Leg. Man.* 31).[91] Cicero then chooses some recent events to remind the people of the extent of the pirates' influence, mentioning attacks on two Roman praetors, the capture of the cities of Knidos, Kolophon and Samos, and raids on the Italian ports of Caieta and Misenum (Cic. *Leg. Man.* 32–3). His account of the pirates' atrocities culminates in the embarrassing capture of the children of Marcus Antonius the orator. The purpose of this catalogue of disasters is to make the power of the pirates appear to be overwhelming and inescapable, so that the act of defeating them, and rendering the seas safe for the Romans and their allies, assumes almost mythical proportions: 'Immortal gods! Was it not the incredible, divinely inspired ability of this one man, that was able, in so short a time, to give such help to the state that instead of seeing the Tiber's mouth full of enemy ships, you hear that the seas are empty of pirates as far as the Ocean?' (Cic. *Leg. Man.* 33).[92] Cicero goes on to explain how even the mention of Pompey's name was enough to bring down the price of corn in

[91] Similarly *Leg. Man.* 32: 'What province did you keep free of pirates in those years? What revenue of yours was safe? Which allies did you defend? Whom did you protect with your fleets? How many islands do you think were deserted, and how many allied cities were abandoned in fear or captured by the pirates?'

[92] Cic. *Leg. Man.* 54–6 is very similar in tone and content.

anticipation of his victory.[93] The 'naval war' has formed the climax to Cicero's exposition of Pompey's military credentials, and he proceeds to advocate that he be given the command against Mithridates, so that he can continue in the same vein. Cicero uses the campaign against the pirates to establish Pompey as the saviour of the Roman Republic, in the tradition of Scipio and Marius. It is portrayed as the crowning achievement of an illustrious military career. Everything which he says about it is intended to glorify Pompey. In order to impress upon his audience the magnitude of the victory, therefore, the pirates are portrayed as powerful enemies,[94] whose defeat could only be accomplished by an exceptional commander after a brilliant campaign. The Roman people were apparently happy to give Pompey great credit for his victory, and subsequent accounts of the period, by Appian, Dio, Plutarch, Velleius and other writers of the Imperial period followed suit, creating the myth of Pompey's spectacular victory over the pirates.

## Pompey's treatment of the vanquished pirates

The extravagant praise which is heaped upon Pompey for his suppression of piracy is made even more fulsome by the ancient sources, who see further evidence of his genius in the policy of 'resettlement' which he devised for those who surrendered to him. Essentially it is seen as an attempt to convert pirates into farmers by removing then from the coast and giving them land to farm. Plutarch describes the idea thus:

Therefore wisely weighing with himself that man by nature is not a wild or unsocial creature, neither was he born so, but makes himself what he naturally is not by vicious habit; and that again, on the other side, he is civilized and grows gentle by a change of place, occupation, and manner of life, as beasts themselves that are wild by nature become tame and tractable by housing and gentler usage, upon this consideration he determined to translate these pirates from sea to land, and give them a taste of an honest and innocent course of life by living in towns and tilling the ground.[95] (Plut. *Pomp.* 28.3)

Florus also praises Pompey for the remarkable intelligence which he showed in adopting this policy of removing the pirates far from sight of

---

[93] Cic. *Leg. Man.* 44.

[94] Cicero also refers to the pirates as 'enemies' (*hostes*), *Leg. Man.* 33 and 46. In an earlier work, however, he notes that Lucius Licinius Crassus (*cos.* 95) was denied a triumph for his victory against bandits (*latrociniis*) because they were not worthy of the title *hostes* (*Inv. rhet.* 2.111).

[95] I have quoted this passage in the elegant translation of Dryden, revised by Clough (1910): 410. The last phrase reads, in Greek: ἐν πόλεσιν οἰκεῖν καὶ γεωργεῖν. Compare Strabo 14.3.2 on the Lycians, above pp. 136–7.

the sea (Flor. 3.6.14).[96] The places he is said to have chosen for the new settlements were thinly populated or deserted sites, some as a result of the Mithridatic wars (App. *Mith.* 96; Dio 36.37.6). On the face of it this seems be a brilliant way of solving the problem of piracy, worthy indeed of a statesman like Pompey. Even dispassionate modern scholars have been generous in their praise of this innovative approach to the suppression of piracy.[97]

Where were the places which Pompey gave to the pirates turned farmers? Most were in the region of Cilicia itself. All those ancient writers who mention particular sites include Soli, which was renamed Pompeiopolis, as one of the two main locations.[98] The only others specifically referred to are Adana, Mallos and Epiphaneia.[99] In addition, a large number were transferred to Dyme, in Achaia.[100] Even the most cursory glance at a map reveals, however, that the idea of taming the pirates by moving them away from the sea is nonsense. Dyme is on the northern *coast* of the Peloponnese, close to the mouth of the gulf of Corinth. Soli is on the *coast* of Cilicia, north-east of Seleukeia. Adana and Mallos are not coastal, but both lie close to the sea on navigable rivers, and Epiphaneia, the most distant of these places from the sea, is less than 15 km inland. It is abundantly clear that Soli and Dyme, the main cities turned over to the pirates, were ideally situated not for farming, but for piracy. No wonder the Cretans were so anxious to surrender to Pompey!

The principal objective of Pompey in his campaign against the pirates in 67 BC was to reach a conclusion as swiftly as possible. It was vital for his prestige at Rome that he secure the corn supply, and this he did by committing substantial forces to the Western Mediterranean to guard the approaches to Italy. With regard to the notorious pirate stronghold of Cilicia he was trying, to a certain extent, to follow up the successes of Murena, Dolabella and, especially, Publius Servilius Isauricus. It was only necessary for him to subdue the pirates of Rough Cilicia, but his victory had to be swift in order to obtain his coveted posting to the war with Mithridates.[101] To this end Pompey avoided long, hard fighting and drawn-out sieges in Cilicia and instead agreed generous terms with the pirates, treating them more like political enemies than pirates.[102]

---

[96]  *a conspectu longe removit maris.*
[97]  E.g. Seager (1979): 37–8; Leach (1978): 66–74; Greenhalgh (1980): 91–100; Pohl (1993): 278–80.
[98]  Plut. *Pomp.* 28.4; App. *Mith.* 115; Dio 36.37.6; Str. 8.7.5, 14.3.1,3 and 5.8. See Map 3.
[99]  App. *Mith.* 96. See Map 3.
[100] Plut. *Pomp.* 28.4; App. *Mith.* 96; Str. 8.7.5, 14.3.3.
[101] Although some may have thought in 67 BC that the Mithridatic war was nearly over, Cicero, in the speech on the Manilian law, and Dio (36.45.1–2), describing Pompey's joy at the passing of the law, suggest otherwise. See also Sherwin-White (1984): 188.
[102] For a similar reappraisal of another aspect of Pompey's achievements in the Eastern Mediterranean see Freeman (1994).

Metellus Creticus, embarking upon his campaign in the wake of an humiliating defeat inflicted on the Romans by the Cretans, and operating with limited resources,[103] did not have such short-term political objectives in mind. As a result he scorned the idea of negotiated settlements, in favour of beating his opponents into submission. His Cretan war was a thorough, hard-fought affair, which followed in the tradition of previous campaigns, in being not just an attempt to suppress piracy, but an aggressive war intended to achieve political and economic gains for the general, his army and the people of Rome. The contrast between the two in style and approach is remarkable and instructive. Even Cicero, in his famous work *On Duties*, written in the 40s BC, while discussing the question of the conflict between moral duty and expediency, criticizes Pompey's generous treatment of the Cilician pirates of Soli, comparing Rome with Athens: 'They were far better than us, for we give immunity to pirates and make our allies pay tribute' (Cic. *Off.* 3.49).

The long-term effectiveness of Pompey's and Metellus' campaigns will be assessed in the next chapter, which also considers the problem of piracy during the Imperial period. Before proceeding to this, however, it is appropriate to draw some conclusions about the nature of attempts to suppress piracy during the Late Roman Republic. Firstly, although there were some attempts by local communities, particularly Rome's allies in the Greek East, to deal with piracy, the initiative rested with the Romans. They made extensive use of their allies in all operations connected with the suppression of piracy, but the leadership and organization was their responsibility. Rome inherited the position of the Classical Athenians, the Ptolemies and the Rhodians in this respect. Whether or not they were capable of being effective, they were regarded as being responsible for the suppression of piracy.[104] This was a responsibility that the Roman people took seriously only when their own interest (or honour) seemed to be directly threatened. It is surely no coincidence that the political circumstances of Pompey's appointment bear some resemblance to those of Metellus Creticus' three years earlier. In both cases popular pressure, led by a tribune, overcame senatorial opposition and resulted in action against those designated as pirates, in the interests of the Roman people. While it is possible to explain away the two cases to a certain extent by pleading the special circumstances, there remains the persistent impression that, in spite of the good intentions voiced in the *lex de provinciis praetoriis*,[105] and echoed eagerly by Cicero, the senate was reluctant to

---

[103] See Brunt (1971): 455.
[104] I find the theory of a 'common war' against piracy in this period, advocated by Maróti (1962b), unconvincing. Although Cicero refers to pirates as the common enemies of all he is not describing them in terms of political enemies; see above pp. 149–50.
[105] Itself most likely a piece of tribunician legislation; see Ferrary (1977).

take specific measures to suppress piracy in this period. Why was this so? It seems to me that the explanation must be connected with the method of suppression. It became clear in the first century BC that only through controlling the regions where the pirates had their bases could piracy itself be controlled. *The suppression of piracy required the conquest of territory.* Indeed, it required more than that, because the territory had to be firmly controlled in order to prevent a recrudesence of piracy. The senate's reluctance to 'annex' territory in this period has been the subject of much debate in recent years, and there is no space to review all the arguments here.[106] The Roman aristocracy of the Late Republic were constantly competing among themselves for military glory, and the economic and political rewards which accompanied it. As the stakes got higher, so the competition became more intense and more destructive to the political order. Pompey's career was extraordinary only in the sense that it represented, in an exaggerated form, the inherent contradictions of city-state politics played out on a Mediterranean-wide stage. There was a great fear among Roman senators, vindicated by the likes of Marius and Sulla, that individuals might become too powerful to be controlled by their peers, if they were given extensive authority and large armies for long periods. Yet this was precisely what was needed in order to campaign effectively against piracy, allowing the co-ordination of resources across the whole Mediterranean where necessary. All that the authorities at Rome were prepared to permit, however, was the occasional, brief operation in a particular area, with definite strategic objectives and limited 'annexation' of territory. While an operation like that of Metellus Balearicus could be effective on a small scale, the campaigns of Marcus Antonius the orator and Publius Servilius Isauricus serve to indicate how ineffective localized actions were against piracy on a large scale. At the same time, it was the turbulent political atmosphere of the period, with Rome's attention far more firmly focussed on Mithridates than on the pirates, which was partly to blame for the prevalence of piracy. The ultimate solution, both to the problem of piracy and the political troubles of the Late Republic, had to be Empire-wide.[107]

---

[106] See Harris (1979); North (1981).

[107] Pohl (1993) also argues that the suppression of piracy was hindered by political concerns. For discussion of his analysis see de Souza (1995b).

# 6    Pax Romana

It is very difficult to determine the importance of piracy in the Mediterranean after 67 BC. There are only a few references in the literary and epigraphic sources, but I think that it would be wrong to ascribe the lack of information to a lack of pirates. The literary sources are much less concerned with piracy after Pompey's campaign, and they therefore devote little space to it. That is not to say that it has ceased to be an issue in Roman politics, but the civil wars of the 40s and 30s BC and the build-up to them overshadow everything else. Nevertheless, from the occasional references which can be discovered, it seems clear that piracy was still a major concern in the Mediterranean during the last few decades of the Republic and at the beginning of the Principate.

### After Pompey

According to Cicero the effect of Pompey's campaign in 67 BC was dramatic. The pirates were completely removed from the seas and Rome's food supply was restored. He was, as has been shown above, exaggerating when he claimed this. His portrayal of Pompey the 'pirate-slayer' in the speech on the Manilian law was intended to convince people that Pompey was the right man to finish off Mithridates.[1] A few years later, however, when he was defending Gaius Valerius Flaccus on a *repetundae* charge, although he was forced to admit that Pompey's success had not meant an absolute end to piracy, the political situation still did not permit him to be entirely candid in admitting the inadequacy of Pompey's campaign of 67 BC. The great man and his supporters had to be mollified with due praise for his success against the pirates.

Flaccus had been urban praetor in 63 BC and had aided Cicero in suppressing the 'conspiracy' of Lucius Sergius Catilina.[2] In 62 BC he went out as governor to Asia. His period as proconsul lasted only one year,

[1] See above pp. 172–5.    [2] *MRR* II 167.

after which he was succeeded by Cicero's brother Quintus.[3] Flaccus' association with Cicero made him a suitable target for a politically motivated prosecution, though this did not actually take place until 59 BC. Among the accusations made by the prosecutor, Decimus Laelius, was the suggestion that Flaccus had extorted money from the cities of his province for a fleet, a measure which was either unnecessary, or else it was merely an excuse for obtaining money, because the sum raised was not used for this purpose.[4] Cicero makes the most of Pompey's prestige to support Flaccus in this speech. Having reminded the jury that Pompey's influence is particularly strong in Asia at this time, as a result of his liberating the province from the menace of pirates and kings (i.e. Mithridates and Tigranes), Cicero explains that a fleet is needed in Asia both to maintain Roman prestige, and to protect the province against pirates. He rebuts objections to the latter idea as follows:

'There were no pirates.' Indeed? Who could be sure that there might not be some in the future? 'You are diminishing Pompey's glory,' he says. On the contrary, you are adding to his troubles. For he destroyed the pirates' fleets, their cities, their harbours and refuges. He bestowed peace upon the maritime world through his great courage and incredible speed. But he never undertook, nor should he have undertaken, to be held responsible if a single pirate ship should happen to appear somewhere. Therefore he himself, when he had already brought an end to all the wars on land and sea, nevertheless ordered those same cities to provide a fleet.[5] (Cic. *Flacc.* 29)

Cicero goes on to explain that Pompey also proposed a fleet for the protection of Italy in 62 BC, and that the following year 4,300,000 sesterces were spent on protecting the Adriatic and Tyrrhenian seas, presumably with a fleet stationed on each.[6] According to Cicero, Pompey's undiminished 'glory' comprises the prestige gained from two things. Firstly the fact that the pirates are no longer free to wander at will over the seas, and secondly, that Syria, Cilicia, Cyprus and Crete are controlled by Rome, ensuring that they cannot be used as pirate bases (Cic. *Flacc.* 30).[7] Cicero argues that even if there were no pirates at all, a cautious approach on Flaccus' part would not merit criticism. In fact, he claims that several witnesses of impeccable equestrian rank could testify that piracy was rife

---

[3] *MRR* II 177, 178 (Flaccus), 181, 185 and 191 (Quintus Cicero).

[4] See Cic. *Flacc.* 27–33. The precise nature of the accusations is hard to discover. Cicero seems to be deliberately avoiding or skipping over potentially embarrassing details.

[5] The implication is that Flaccus was simply following Pompey's wishes.

[6] Cic. *Flacc.* 30. Cicero also mentions cavalry stationed on the coasts. This arrangement seems to correspond to Cicero's description of the forces protecting Italy during the campaign of 67 BC (Cic. *Leg. Man.* 35).

[7] The last two, of course, were not controlled by Rome thanks to Pompey's efforts, but to those of king Ptolemy Alexander and Quintus Caecilius Metellus Creticus.

around Asia in 62 BC: '... should Flaccus still be censured for his con-
scription of rowers? Even if a member of the aristocracy of Adramyttium
was killed by pirates, someone whose name is familiar to almost all of us,
Atyanas the Olympic boxing champion?' (Cic. *Flacc.* 31). In reply to the
point that no prisoners were taken by Flaccus' fleet, Cicero reminds the
judges that such things are a matter of luck, for it is a difficult job to find
and pursue pirates across the sea. In this way he neatly restores the 'glory'
of Pompey, whose luck in 67 BC must have been outstandingly good.

It remains for Cicero to counter three further points made against his
client. Firstly, that the fleet never actually put to sea, which he flatly de-
nies, claiming that all of Asia knew there was one flotilla operating above
Ephesos and one below, following the pattern established by Sulla and
continued by Pompey. He also claims that Flaccus spent far less money
on a fleet than either of these two (Cic. *Flacc.* 32). Secondly, that there
was no entry in the governor's accounts, a point which Cicero brushes
aside as a mere technicality. Finally, he has to face the fact that his own
brother Quintus, who succeeded Flaccus as governor of Asia, did not find
it necessary to obtain any contributions at all from the cities of Asia. This
Cicero explains as a difference of approach. His brother preferred to wait
until the pirates made their presence known before he raised a fleet (Cic.
*Flacc.* 33).

Several important points emerge from this section of the speech *On
behalf of Flaccus*. Even in 59 BC Cicero is still very careful to maintain
the impression that Pompey completely defeated the pirates in 67 BC and
that his mission was a great success. He also provides a few scraps of information about further measures to protect the coasts of Italy and other
important areas.[8] He is unable to deny that piracy has continued to be a
serious problem in recent years, in spite of Pompey's efforts.[9] The measures being employed to suppress it are similar to those adopted before and
during 67 BC. We can be fairly sure that Cicero is not exaggerating the
continued extent of piracy in this speech, as it would not help his case to
do so. There is also no reason to doubt what Cicero says about Pompey's
arrangements for fleets in Asia and Italy. Rome had no obvious maritime
enemies other than pirates in the 60s BC, so it is reasonable to conclude

---

[8] For the importance attached to the security of Asia at this time see Cic. *Leg. Man.* 14–16.
[9] It has been argued that the appearance of large amounts of Roman coinage in hoards
buried in the Lower Danube basin from the 60s BC onwards, should be attributed to a rise
in Roman demand for slaves from this area, brought about by the curtailing of piratical
slave-trade in the Eastern Mediterranean by Pompey; Crawford (1977) and (1985): 224–
36. This interpretation of the Dacian coin hoards presupposes a higher reliance on piracy
as a source of slaves than I think is appropriate (see above pp. 60–5) and has been challenged by other scholars; see Fulford (1985); Howgego (1995): 102–5.

that these fleets were intended for use against them. The Adriatic fleet may have been on guard against pirates operating from Illyria and Dalmatia, areas which Rome did not properly control until the first century AD.[10] The Asian fleet might have been needed to respond to pirates operating out of Cyprus, Anatolia or the Aegean islands, wherever local authorities were not strong enough to prevent them. The expenditure of 4,300,000 sesterces on a fleet in one year indicates a considerable naval commitment by the Romans, perhaps enough to equip and maintain more than 100 ships.[11] Do these commitments amount to the establishment of a 'standing fleet' in Italian waters? Starr points to the gradual increase in the number of ships available since 88 BC and suggests that, by confiscating ships and constructing some new vessels, the Romans had amassed a considerable reserve in Italian docks by 67 BC.[12] Ships are much less costly in dry docks than when they are in the water, especially if they are manned and operational,[13] and what Cicero says only accounts for two years of expenditure. It may be that their period of active service was brief, although there seems to be no particular reason why the years 62–61 BC should require such activity.[14] The problem for any modern historian is that the kind of details which Cicero provides in his speech for Flaccus only cover a small period. Thus it is impossible to reconstruct Roman naval policy in the last few decades of the Republic with any degree of certainty. I think it is unlikely that there was any time in the Late Republic when the Romans did not have some warships operating in Italian waters, based at Ostia and other commercial ports. I do not, however, think that it is appropriate to see these as representing a standing fleet.[15]

Incidental references in the literary sources for the 50s BC suggest that there continued to be substantial numbers of pirates active in the Eastern

[10] See below pp. 195–6.

[11] There are no figures which can be used to estimate the cost of building, equipping and crewing ships during this period, and I have simply taken a guess at the size of fleet which could be maintained from the money mentioned by Cicero.

[12] Starr (1941): 1–4, following Kromayer (1897) and citing Cic. *Leg. Man.* 33 and 67 and Dio 36.23.2 on new constructions; the latter is irrelevant since it refers in only the most general terms to 'fleets being sent out from time to time'.

[13] Caesar describes how in 49 BC some ships which had been used during Pompey's campaign of 67 BC and beached at Utica were recommissioned by Publius Attius, after they had been repaired (Caes. *Bell. civ.* 2.23.2). This was probably common practice at the time.

[14] Starr (1941): 4. Comparison might be made with the naval 'reserves' of Athens in the fourth century BC and the difficulties of commissioning an operational fleet. The years after 61 BC are not directly relevant to Cicero's point here, which may explain his 'silence'. Reddé (1986): 463–70 is of the opinion that Roman naval efforts at this time were sporadic and concentrated on the Eastern Mediterranean.

[15] See Reddé (1986): 457–72. On Ostia see Meiggs (1960) and Reddé (1986): 201.

Mediterranean, reinforcing the impression that Pompey's solution was far from effective. Aulus Gabinius, the proposer of the law creating Pompey's extraordinary command in 67 BC, was governor of Syria from 58 to 55 BC. He carried out a reorganization of Judaea, but his proconsulship is chiefly remembered for checking the activities of the *publicani* and for the restoration of King Ptolemy XII Auletes to the throne of Egypt, apparently in return for an enormous bribe. The account of his actions in Dio contains repeated accusations that he left his province at the mercy of pirates while he was away in Egypt (Dio 39.56.1, 6; 59.2).[16] If there is any truth in this claim, then it is likely that the pirates were operating out of Cilicia or, possibly, Cyprus. The latter had been added to the province of Cilicia by the Romans in 58 BC (Dio 38.30.5; 39.22–3), supposedly because the king, Ptolemy, had been aiding pirates, but it seems that financial reasons were uppermost in the mind of Clodius when he proposed the 'annexation'.[17] Piracy seems more like a convenient excuse than a serious reason for Roman intervention, but that does not mean that pirates were not operating from bases in Cyprus. The Syrians may have been exaggerating the seriousness of the piracy, but Dio also says that they were unable to pay the *publicani* what they owed as a result (Dio 39.59.2). If this were so, then the pirates' raids must have been on a considerable scale.

A further indication that piracy was still a serious problem in the 50s BC comes from the other side in the Gabinius story. In his speech in defence of Gaius Rabirius Postumus Cicero deals briefly with the legitimacy of Gabinius' actions in Egypt: 'Gabinius said that he had done it for the sake of the Republic, since he was worried about the fleet of Archelaus, because he thought that he would fill the seas with pirates. In addition, he said that it was permissible for him under the law' (Cic. *Rab. Post.* 20). Archelaus was a son of Mithridates' general of the same name. He had been made High Priest of Comana. In 56 BC he married Auletes' daughter Berenike and ruled as her consort. It was on Pompey's instruction that Gabinius drove him out of Egypt and restored the king.[18] That Gabinius should accuse him of piracy, or, at least, the threat of piracy, and that Gabinius himself should be accused of abandoning his province to

---

[16] 'Gabinius did much to ruin Syria, so much that he caused more harm than did the pirates who were flourishing still' (Dio 39.56.1).

[17] See Oost (1955) and Badian (1965). Garnsey (1988): 215–16 stresses the connection between grain supply costs and the revenues raised from Cyprus. Note that Cicero *may* be referring to pirates in Cyprus in the speech *On behalf of Flaccus* quoted above.

[18] See Sherwin-White (1984): 271–5. The law referred to by Cicero is presumably the *Lex Clodia* which gave Gabinius Syria as his province, instead of Cilicia which was originally assigned to him.

pirates, are indications that piracy was acknowleged to be still a great menace in this region, in spite of Pompey's campaign ten years before. If it were not, then none of the accusations made would have had any force.[19] It is also worth noting that the historical literature of this period indicates considerable interest in the suppression of piracy among the élite. Two writers of the last decades of the Roman Republic who present the ideal of the great leader suppressing piracy are Nepos, who (implausibly) credits Themistokles with the suppression of piracy (Nep. *Them.* 2.3), and Diodorus, also a product of the political and moral values of the Late Republic,[20] who praises Dionysios II, Timoleon, Eumelos and the Rhodians for suppressing piracy at various times (Diod. 16.4.3; 16.82.3; 20.25.2; 20.81.3).

Accusations of piracy, or acting like a pirate, continued to have force, and to be made, in the 40s and 30s BC. On several occasions in his *Civil Wars* Caesar accuses his opponents of acting like pirates, or of having pirates, bandits and slaves in their armies.[21] Pompey's son, Sextus Pompeius, was accused by Augustus of employing pirates in the 30s BC (App. *Bell. civ.* 5.77).[22] Such accusations have to be treated with caution; they are, as has been shown above, commonplace in the political invective of the period.[23] This does not mean, however, that these references are worthless as evidence. What they do indicate is that piracy can still be assumed to be prominent in the Eastern Mediterranean at this time, especially as some, more reliable, evidence is available to substantiate this point.

Cicero mentions in a letter of 44 BC to his friend Atticus one group who appear to be practising piracy: 'It is not surprising that the Dymaeans, having been driven out of their land, are making the sea unsafe.

---

[19] Cicero defended Gabinius in 54 BC, but in 56 BC he was arguing that he needed to be replaced (Cic. *Prov. cons.* 1–17). It is likely that a lot of false accusations were being flung around at this time. What is remarkable is the extent to which the problem of piracy is still a useful weapon in political invective. Cicero had earlier accused Gabinius and Lucius Calpurnius Piso, his fellow consul of 58 BC, of being 'not consuls but pirates', and suggested that Gabinius would have had to turn to piracy to make money, had it not been for his law of 67 BC, and the favour which it earned him from the grateful Pompey (Cic. *Red. sen.* 11).

[20] See Sacks (1990).

[21] E.g. Caes. *Bell. civ.* 3.110 (pirates), 1.24 and 34 (slaves and shepherds). He also accuses the inhabitants of the island of Pharos of behaving like pirates (*Bell. civ.* 3.112). See also *Bell. Hisp.* 40.2.

[22] See below pp. 185–95.

[23] Compare Cicero calling Mark Anthony a 'bandit' and saying in his correspondence of 44 BC that he is hated by everyone except bandits (Cic. *Fam.* 10.5; 10.6; 12.12 = SB nos. 359, 370, 387). Strabo preserves another example of someone being called a 'bandit chief' (τῶν λῃστηρίων ἡγεμών) as a term of abuse in his account of the Lycian petty dynast Kleon, who served both Anthony and Octavian (Str. 12.8.8–9).

There should be some protection in a joint voyage with Brutus, but I imagine it will only be a matter of very small craft.'[24] Cicero is referring here to the inhabitants of Dyme, which is one of the places settled by Cilician 'ex-pirates' after Pompey's campaign of 67 BC. Their expulsion from the land seems to have resulted from the establishment of a Caesarian colony there, as at Buthrotum.[25] The resettled Cilicians would appear to have reverted to their old practices, if, indeed, they had ever abandoned them. It is tempting to believe that the numerous 'pirates' who were resettled by Pompey in cities in Cilicia itself also resumed their former practices. As I showed in the previous chapter, the claim that they were prevented from practising piracy by their removal from the coasts is patently absurd. They might account for some of the pirates who are referred to in the sources for the 60s and 50s BC, especially by Cicero, who would be at pains to conceal or ignore their origins, if they were known.

Another instance of piracy in this period may be recorded in an inscription from Syros in the Cyclades. It is an honorific decree for a Siphnian called Onesandros. He had assisted a slave from Syros who was the victim of a pirate raid.[26] Scholars who have commented on this text have been inclined to assign it to the period before 67 BC, in spite of the indications of a later date which the letter forms provide.[27] They apparently did this on the assumption that pirates could not have been active in the Aegean after 67 BC because Pompey had eradicated piracy. Since this was not so, there is no reason to date the inscription earlier than the second half of the first century BC, in which case it may well be from the 40s or 30s BC.[28]

## Sextus Pompeius

It is often said that the history of any war is written by the victors, and historians of the ancient world need to take particular account of this truism in their own treatment of events. The following extract from the *Achievements of the Divine Augustus*, a monumental inscription recording the services which Rome's first emperor had rendered for her citizens, shows that the practice of labelling political opponents as pirates was ex-

---

[24] Cic. *Att.* 16.1 = SB no. 409. I quote from Shackleton Bailey's translation. The Latin reads: *Dymaeos agro pulsos mare infestum habere nil mirum.*

[25] See Salmon (1969): 136.

[26] *IG* XII.5.653.

[27] E.g. Ziebarth (1929): 40 and Appendix I no. 111; Ormerod (1924): 206 n. 5. See the editor's comments in *IG* ad loc. where it is included among inscriptions of imperial date.

[28] Compare also *IG* IX.1.873, an epitaph from Corcyra of similar date, which appears to mention pirates. It was dated to before 227 BC by the editor of *IG* IX because the Romans had suppressed Illyrian piracy by this date!

ploited by the adopted son of Julius Caesar to enhance his own position at
the end of the first century BC:

I made the sea peaceful and freed it of pirates. In that war I captured about 30,000
slaves who had escaped from their masters and taken up arms against the republic,
and I handed them over to their masters for punishment.[29]

In these few words Augustus deals with the Sicilian War of 42–36 BC
against the last of the republican or 'Pompeian' leaders – Sextus Pompeius. The son of Pompey the Great is not mentioned by name, nor does
Augustus include the war in his account of the 'many civil and foreign
wars by land and sea throughout the world' at the start of the *Res gestae*.[30] There is no doubt that he is referring to the Sicilian War, but he has
made it an affair of pirates and runaway slaves. While modern writers are
prepared to acknowledge that the importance of the Sicilian War in the
establishment of the Principate is greater than Augustus makes it appear,
they nevertheless accept his characterization of the war, assigning a leading role to the slaves and the pirates.[31] In the light of what has been suggested above, concerning the participation of pirates in ancient warfare,
and the use of piracy in ancient 'propaganda', the idea of a war against
pirates and slaves is worthy of some suspicion. One should ask, how realistic is this version of the Sicilian War? How important were the pirates
(and the runaway slaves) in this episode of Roman history?

There are several ancient accounts of the exploits of Sextus Pompeius
and the Sicilian War, but none of them is written from a standpoint which
is entirely independent of Augustus. They all date from the first or second
centuries AD and are influenced to some extent by the 'propaganda' of
the Augustan regime. Nevertheless, it is possible to assess the evidence for
the involvement of pirates (and slaves) in the Sicilian War, and to show
how Augustus came to write his victor's version. The most comprehensive
single account of the civil wars of the Late Republic is contained in the
five books of the *Civil Wars* which comprised part of Appian's *Roman
History*. Having dealt with the history of the Republic in a series of books
which showed how the Romans fought and conquered various peoples to
gain control over the Mediterranean region, Appian proceeds to tell the
story of how they then fought among themselves. The *Civil Wars* begins
with Tiberius Gracchus' tribunate (133 BC) and ends with the defeat and

[29] Augustus, *Res gestae*, ed. Brunt & Moore (1967): 31. I follow what has become the conventional practice by referring to Augustus as Octavian when dealing with matters before
27 BC and as Augustus thereafter. The *Res gestae* was largely composed in the period up
to 2 BC; see Brunt & Moore (1967): 6.

[30] Brunt & Moore (1967): 19.

[31] Ormerod (1924): 250–2; Hadas (1930); Maróti (1961).

death of Sextus Pompeius (36 BC). Thus, for Appian, the Sicilian War was not only an integral part of the Civil Wars, it was, in fact, their climax. He preferred to place the struggle with Mark Antony in an account of the Egyptian Wars of Augustus, which does not survive.[32] Similarly, Cassius Dio makes the war with Sextus Pompeius an integral part of his account of the rise of Octavian in his *Roman History* (Books 46–9). And Suetonius, who calls it the Sicilian War, says: 'It would be safe to say that the Sicilian was by far his most dangerous campaign' (Suet. *Aug.* 16). There is also a strong historical tradition which follows Augustus' version (in the *Res gestae* as we have it and probably also in his official biography), playing down the status of the war, though not its seriousness, and making it a conflict against pirates and runaway slaves. The Livian sources (based upon the now lost later books of Livy's *History of Rome*), including the *Periochae*, Orosius' *History Against the Pagans* and Florus' *Breviary*, along with Velleius Paterculus' *Roman History*, all demonstrate this tendency in the highly moralizing style of their accounts. Plutarch and Suetonius are similar in their tone and emphasis.

It is Appian and Cassius Dio, however, who provide most of the detailed information on which my own interpretation is based. Both agree that Sextus Pompeius was not in conflict with Caesar and took no part in his assassination, but he was drawn into the war with Octavian as a result of his proscription in 43 BC. Dio says: 'When, however, he discovered his name was on the tablet and he knew that he was being proscribed, he prepared for war. He began building triremes and received deserters, he took the pirates on to his side and brought the exiles under his protection' (Dio 48.17). Leaving aside the mention of pirates for the moment, the course of events is typical of many of the political struggles of the Late Republic. One side seizes control in Rome and proscribes leading opponents, who then gather together in order to continue the struggle. Sextus Pompeius had already been recognized as a legitimate commander of Roman forces, with the title of 'Commander of the fleet and the coasts (around Italy)', which he received from the Senate early in 43 BC.[33] He was outlawed under the *Lex Pedia* of August of the same year and then proscribed, as were many others, including Cassius and Brutus.

Appian describes how Sextus, based in Sicily and Sardinia, collected many republican exiles around him: 'The wealthy citizens fled from a country that they could no longer consider their own and took refuge with Pompeius, who was near by and greatly loved at that time' (App. *Bell. civ.*

---

[32] See Goldmann (1988) for a more favourable assessment of Appian than has been the norm in modern historiography. I have not always highlighted differences in the versions of Dio and Appian.

[33] See Crawford (1974), no. 511 for coins proclaiming this appointment.

4.5). These men were to play a major part in determining the course of his actions. He waged war on Octavian and the other triumvirs by raiding the coasts of Italy and blockading the city of Rome, cutting off its vital grain supply. The sources tend to condemn him for his timidity and failure to press the attack more vigorously. His aim was to put pressure on Octavian through famine and popular unrest, so that he could extort concessions for himself and his fellow republican exiles. Hindsight may enable us to doubt the wisdom of his long-term strategy, but there can be no doubting the effectiveness of his immediate tactics. His naval victories and his raids on the Italian coast produced a feeling of unease and dramatically reduced the prestige of Octavian in Italy. They encouraged Mark Antony to consider the idea of an alliance with Sextus against Octavian. It was, however his disruption of the grain supply which had the most spectacular effect:

And famine laid hold of Rome, for the merchants of the East were afraid to sail out because of Pompeius, and his forces in Sicily, while those in the West were baulked by Sardinia and Corsica, which were held by Pompeius' men, and those in Libya were kept in check by the fleets which controlled both sides. (App. *Bell. civ.* 5.67)

The gravity of the situation was brought home to Octavian by the populace at Rome, who rioted and even attacked him personally: 'As soon as he appeared they stoned him furiously, and they did not relent even when they saw how he stood up to them, and endured the wounds' (App. *Bell. civ.* 5.67–8). According to Appian Octavian was eventually rescued by Mark Antony and his soldiers, who were obliged to cut their way through the massed citizens in order to reach Octavian.[34]

There had been crises over the grain supply before, but, as a recent study notes: 'These riots were more serious and prolonged, and the situation more desperate, than in any earlier food crisis.'[35] The tactics employed by Sextus Pompeius worked. Octavian and Antony were forced to make peace and negotiate a treaty – the 'Misenum Accord' of 39 BC. The terms of this treaty reveal the significance of the 'Sicilian War' and demonstrate very clearly that it was an integral and important phase of the Civil Wars. The terms were as follows:[36]

(1) All slaves who had deserted to the republican side were to be free.
(2) All exiles were to be restored with $\frac{1}{4}$ of their property. (Julius Caesar's assassins were excepted.)

---

[34] The version in Dio (48.31–2) is only slightly less dramatic.
[35] Garnsey (1988): 207.
[36] Dio 48.36; App. *Bell. civ.* 5.72.

(3) The exiles were to get political offices immediately – praetorships, tribunates and priesthoods.
(4) Sextus Pompeius was to become consul and augur.
(5) He was to receive 70 million sesterces from his father's estate.
(6) He was to be governor of Sicily, Sardinia and Achaia for five years.
(7) He was to receive no more deserters, obtain no more ships and keep no garrisons in Italy.
(8) He was to devote his efforts to securing peace for the western coast of Italy.
(9) He was to send a stated amount of grain to the city of Rome.

Point (1) indicates that slaves did form part of the forces under Sextus' command, though they had been given their freedom when they joined him, a grant they were anxious to have confirmed. Thus, they were not considered slaves by their commanders. Point (7) is clearly intended to reduce the power of Sextus by removing him from the Italian mainland and curbing his ability to recruit. He already had a considerable advantage in ships. Octavian had his own uses for the manpower of Italy.[37] Points (2) and (3) were the main aims of Sextus Pompeius' republican followers. With the deaths of Brutus and Cassius in 42 BC Sextus Pompeius became the last resort of the republicans. We have no impressive list of names, consulars, ex-praetors and leading senators, such as might be compiled from the adherents of his father on the eve of the battle of Pharsalus in 48 BC. This is because many of the exiles with Sextus Pompeius were senators who had not had the chance to pursue normal careers and obtain the higher offices. They wanted to get back into the political arena which the Civil Wars had driven them out of, and they needed wealth to do so. For the reconciliation of the two sides to be effective and lasting their demands had to be met. Points (4), (5) and (6) created a fourth partner in the triumvirate. In return for his cessation of hostilities, Sextus Pompeius obtained the rich prize of Achaia, in addition to his western holdings. This was a major concession by the triumvirs. The role envisaged for him in points (8) and (9) did not require him to hold Achaia, and the province was to be a stumbling-block for the process of peace. It is doubtful whether Octavian and Antony really intended to be bound by the agreement in any case, the negotiations being to some extent forced upon them by their own followers and popular pressure.

A brief review of the Sicilian War up to 39 BC brings us to the following conclusions. Sextus Pompeius was forced into a position as leader of

---

[37] See Brunt (1971): 498–500 and 507–8 for calculations of the relative strengths of the two sides in terms of legions and ships. Kromayer (1897) suggests that he had 350 ships in 36 BC, but many would not have been warships.

the surviving republicans, firstly through his proscription by the triumvirs, and secondly as a result of the battle of Philippi. From his Sicilian base he put military and economic pressure on Octavian at Rome to wrest concessions from the triumvirs. His successes brought about a treaty which met the main demands of his republican followers, in return for an end to the pressure he was exerting.

The Misenum Accord was a recognition of the strength of Sextus Pompeius' position. Dio says that he called the shots at the meeting because his forces were far larger, and records the suggestion of one of his admirals that he assassinate Octavian and Antony (Dio 48.38). He had no reason to do this, however, since his demands were apparently being met. Why, then, did the war continue after Misenum? According to Dio and Appian, it was because his demands were not met. The exiles were not restored, as had been agreed, and Achaia was not handed over by Antony (Dio 48.46; App. *Bell. civ.* 5.77). In reply, Sextus Pompeius renewed his attacks on the Italian coasts through his admiral Menekrates. Octavian also complained that Sextus had broken the treaty by accepting more 'deserters' and building triremes (App. *Bell. civ.* 5.77). Whatever the truth of these accusations, it seems clear that neither side trusted the other. The struggle for supremacy had to continue. Antony returned to the East and left the heirs of Caesar and Pompey to slug it out. Octavian needed a lot of manpower and expertise (and luck) to defeat Sextus, but his eventual victory signalled the final demise of the republican or 'Pompeian' side and, according to Appian, the end of the Civil Wars. If the Sicilian War was, as I have shown, another chapter of the Civil Wars, why did Augustus and many other sources call it a 'pirate war'? What part did pirates play in the conflict? In order to answer this question it is first necessary to show that the label 'pirate war' is an inappropriate one.

The case for pirates playing a major role in the Sicilian War is argued most fully by Egon Maróti. He begins by pointing out that piracy was still a problem after 67 BC, in spite of the extravagant claims made concerning Pompey's successes. Pirates, he claims, played a significant part in Roman history only once more, as the adherents of Sextus Pompeius. He makes various points to justify this view. All the sources agree in calling it a 'pirate war', they confirm that pirates (and slaves) were very important in deciding the outcome. The methods employed by Sextus Pompeius were very similar to those of pirates. This, according to Maróti, was because his admirals were all ex-pirates. Their influence waxed as that of his republican followers waned, partly because of conflicts over what to do. Maróti traces Sextus Pompeius' connections with the pirates back to his change of location in 43 BC, and his reaction to being proscribed. It was the pirate admirals who forced him to take a stand against a peaceful settlement of grievances in order to plunder Italy.[38]

The unanimity of the sources will be dealt with shortly. To argue that Sextus Pompeius' use of piratical methods justifies the label 'pirate war' is too simplistic. I have already considered other cases of piratical methods (and pirates themselves) being used in ancient warfare, but there is no question, for example, of calling the siege of Rhodes a 'pirate war'. Sextus Pompeius' blockade of Italy was on a far larger scale than the blockade of Rhodes.[39] It was also largely effected by the possession of vital territory – namely Sicily, Sardinia and places in Italy.[40] Such raiding as was carried out (e.g. App. *Bell. civ.* 5.77; Dio 48.46) was intended to put pressure upon Octavian by stretching his military resources, damaging his prestige and undermining his support in Italy.[41] It is also the aims rather than the methods which count in deciding such cases, as I have shown above. To ascribe eight years of sustained conflict to a lust for plunder is going too far.

The recruitment of exiles, deserters and runaway slaves on Sextus Pompeius' part is not evidence of the influence of pirates. It seems likely that many of his 'recruits' came to him in Sicily from local towns and cities, or from Italians who preferred his side in the Civil Wars. There is also the likelihood that many of the 'exiles' would have brought clients and dispossessed tenants with them.[42] On the subject of slaves it is worth noting that Octavian himself was not above recruiting servile oarsmen into his fleet. He 'requested' a large number from his friends, and took them when he was not offered enough (Dio 48.49; Suet. *Aug.* 16). His levies of money and men were also on a large scale. It is noteworthy that the number given for these slaves in Suetonius' *Life of Augustus* is 30,000. This is the same as the number 'returned' to their masters from the runaways recruited by Sextus Pompeius (*Res gestae* 25). It is tempting to see the runaways as convenient replacements for those conscripted in 37 BC. Brunt reckons the number would have manned less than half of Octavian's ships.[43] Whereas Maróti wants to connect slaves and pirates in a

---

[38] Maróti (1961). He is followed by Garlan (1989) and Jackson (1973). See Hadas (1930) for similar views.

[39] See above pp. 43–6.

[40] See Garnsey (1988) and Rowland (1990) on the significance of Sicily and Sardinia for the food supply of Rome.

[41] The scale of Octavian's response is indicated by Brunt (1971): 499, who calculates that Lepidus sent him about 35,000 men in 36 BC for the war, and Octavian invaded Sicily with 12 legions. See Paget (1968) for the impressive harbour works undertaken at Cumae to accommodate Agrippa's fleet which were then abandoned as soon as the war was over.

[42] See Brunt (1971): 500.

[43] Brunt (1971): 507–8.

way which I feel is due to the Augustan bias of our sources and the reputation of pirates as slave dealers, I would see in the association of Sextus Pompeius with slaves and pirates a deliberate attempt to illegitimize him and to justify Octavian's war against him.

Another point which is relevant in this context is the activity of Gnaeus Domitius Ahenobarbus, who acted in a very similar fashion to Sextus Pompeius in the Adriatic: 'For Domitius was one of Caesar's murderers, he escaped after the battle of Philippi, gathered together a small fleet, and made himself master of the Gulf for a while, and did a lot of damage to the cause of his opponents' (Dio 48.7.5). Domitius, whom none of the ancient sources ever accused of piracy, or even of associating with pirates, eventually defected to Antony, through the agency of Asinius Pollio (Dio 48.16; App. *Bell. civ.* 5.55). He was consul in 32 BC, but he managed to switch sides at the crucial moment in 31 BC. His better reputation must be partly due to his ending up on the side of the victor.[44]

It is also suggested by Maróti that two of Sextus Pompeius' most important admirals were ex-pirates. Menekrates and Menodoros (called Menas by Dio) are names which could have a Cilician origin. Both are credited with considerable naval expertise and both are described as freedmen of Sextus Pompeius.[45] In the account of Appian, in particular, Menodoros is portrayed as his main confidant, until he defects to Octavian in 38 BC. The two freedmen encountered each other in a naval battle soon after and Menekrates was killed. It is possible that they could both have been enslaved as pirates by Pompey in 67 BC and subsequently freed, but their previous histories are not commented on in our sources, a strange omission if they had indeed been pirates.[46] What is more significant about the pair is their skill in naval warfare (e.g. Dio 48.46), which they are unlikely to have acquired as pirates. They were both admirals and it was as admirals that they were important to Sextus Pompeius and the republicans. Until Menodoros defected Octavian was at a serious disadvantage due to a lack of experience among his own commanders. He was lucky to have the services of the remarkable Marcus Agrippa, whose

---

[44] His forces were quite considerable; see Brunt (1971): 486–9, 504, 507.

[45] Menodoros/Menas is also said to be a former slave of Pompey the Great. Mark Antony is said to have claimed him as a fugitive slave because Pompey's property had passed to Antony (App. *Bell. civ.* 5.79). Velleius (2.73) says that both were Pompey's freedmen.

[46] Plutarch does call Menas a pirate on one occasion, and describes them both as being in charge of a 'pirate fleet' (Plut. *Vit. Ant.* 32) but this is the only explicit statement and is probably there for literary effect. Menas is acting dishonourably at this point in the narrative (unlike Sextus Pompeius) and Sextus has just undertaken to clear the sea of pirates in Plutarch's version of events. I find the silence of Appian and Dio on this point more compelling than the sole explicit testimony of Plutarch.

skills helped to turn the tide of the war in his favour after the disastrous experiences under Salvidienus and Calvisius Sabinus (Dio 48.47–9).

Menodoros had ambitions far above the possibilities of an ex-pirate (Dio 48.45). He changed sides twice more, ending up with Octavian. He died in Octavian's service in Pannonia in 35 BC. There was obviously considerable rivalry in the camp of Sextus Pompeius between his various commanders. One casualty of this was Lucius Staius Murcus, a former legate of Julius Caesar. He joined Sextus after Philippi, but was murdered in 40 BC (Dio 48.19; App. *Bell. civ.* 5.70).[47]

If, as I have suggested, the connections made between Sextus and pirates are the result of propaganda on the part of his opponents, it remains to be explained why they would choose to do this, and to show how he was discredited and illegitimized. There was nothing remarkable in the Late Republic about an attempt to make a political enemy out to be a pirate, or the associate of pirates. In 70 BC Cicero used every opportunity he could to discredit Gaius Verres, the former governor of Sicily, when he prosecuted him in Rome.[48] There was also a strong image of pirates as 'the enemies of all mankind' in the first century BC, which was not diminished by the campaign of Pompey in 67 BC.[49] In the 40s BC there are also examples of political opponents being labelled as pirates or bandits. Julius Caesar, in his description of the forces arrayed against him at Alexandria in 48 BC, says they were 'collected from the pirates and bandits of the provinces of Cilicia and Syria' (Caes. *Bell. civ.* 3.110). Cicero and his correspondents in 44/3 BC constantly refer to Mark Anthony as 'the Bandit'.[50] In the case of Sextus Pompeius there was, of course, the added irony that his father had been the most successful of a series of Roman generals who campaigned against pirates in the first century BC. His piratical tactics lent themselves to the accusation that he was employing pirates himself. The point is brought out by several of the ancient sources, including Florus, who exclaims: 'O how unlike his father! He exterminated the Cilicians, his son supported the pirates ...' (Florus 2.18.1). Velleius' description is similar in tone: 'Through his father's freedmen,

---

[47] The 'admirals' in the service of Sextus Pompeius exhibit characteristics which are similar to those found among the *condottieri* of the 15th and 16th centuries AD; see Mallett (1974).

[48] E.g. 'Do we also inquire what Verres has got up to in deepest Phrygia, or in the furthest parts of Pamphylia ... he who was found to be an abominable pirate here in the Roman forum?' (Cic. *II Verr.* 1.154). For further examples see *II Verr.* 1.90, 4.29 and 5.5 and above pp. 150–7.

[49] See Maróti (1962b), although I am not convinced by his arguments for a 'common war' against pirates. See also Ormerod (1924): ch. 2 and de Souza (1996).

[50] Cic. *Fam.* 10.5; 10.6; 12.12; 12.14 = SB nos. 259, 370, 387 and 405.

Menas and Menekrates, the commanders of his fleet, he infested the seas
with raiding and piracy, using plunder to support himself and his army.
Nor was he ashamed to plague with the wickedness of piracy the very sea
which had been cleared of it by his father's arms and leadership' (Vell.
Pat. 2.73.3).

Sextus Pompeius and the triumvirs were involved in a competition for
the support of the Roman world. In order to maintain their challenge for
the supreme position in the Roman Republic they needed men and ma-
terials. Dio says of Sextus in 43 BC:

> He anchored off Italy, and sent agents to Rome and to the other cities, offering,
> among other things, a reward to those who saved any one which was double that
> announced for murdering them, and he promised the men themselves a place of
> safety, help, money and honours. As a result many came to him. (Dio 47.13)

He recruited in Sicily and Italy, making his own position stronger by
demonstrating that Octavian was vulnerable and offering a choice between himself and the triumvirs (App. *Bell. civ.* 4.85). His 'plundering
raids' should be seen as an attempt to undermine the position of Octavian
in Italy. It was hardly a gentle form of persuasion, but they were not
gentle times. He portrayed himself as the son of Neptune, the lord of the
seas, both on coins and in public spectacles (Dio 48.19; App. *Bell. civ.*
5.100).[51]

Sextus was undoubtedly popular, for his own sake as well as for his
father's. The popular approval which was demonstrated for him in Rome
in 40 BC must have seriously worried both Octavian and Anthony (Dio
48.31; App. *Bell. civ.* 5.67). It is at this point, in my estimation, that the
'propaganda war' can be most clearly seen in operation. Dio preserves
one side: 'Sextus, on his part, noised it abroad that Anthony did not think
he was being treated justly, and pursued his own projects more eagerly.
Finally he sailed to Italy, and made many landings, inflicting and suffering a great deal of damage' (Dio. 48.46). Such accusations and recrimi-
nations had been flying back and forth on both sides over the Misenum
Accord. Octavian was very unpopular in Rome, where the effects of Sextus' tactics were most keenly felt. In order to revive his fortunes and gain
the support he needed he tried a 'smear campaign', which Appian's account relates: 'Octavian captured and subjected to torture some bands of
pirates, who said that Pompeius had sent them out, and Octavian announced this to the people and wrote about it to Pompeius himself, who

---

[51] See Crawford (1974): no. 511. Lucius Staius Murcus also issued coins of a similar kind,
possibly an indication of their rivalry. See Zanker (1988): 39–42 on the similar images
used by Octavian and Sextus on coins proclaiming naval victories over each other.

rejected the claim and made his own protest about the Peloponnesos' (App. *Bell. civ.* 5.77).[52]

Sextus had been accepted into a kind of partnership with the triumvirs. In order to justify turning against him, it was necessary to illegitimize him in Roman eyes. By accusing him of harbouring slaves and making him into a pirate, Octavian could justify breaking faith with him, and ignoring a treaty which had been deposited with the Vestal Virgins in Rome (Dio 48.37). Escaped slaves had long been a nightmare image for the Romans, especially in Sicily. The pirate was not a proper enemy, and so no promise to him was binding (Cic. *Off.* 3.107).[53] Maróti is right to say that all the sources agree about the importance of pirates in the Sicilian War, but that is because they have all been influenced, directly or indirectly, by the 'propaganda' of Augustus and his victor's version. It should be noted that the references to pirates in the sources tend to be very vague. No details are suggested about who they were, or where they came from. Appian even refers to 'mysterious bands of pirates' (App. *Bell. civ.* 5.77).[54]

## Piracy and the Principate[55]

Octavian's defeat of Sextus Pompey did not mean the end of the Mediterranean piracy any more than Pompey's campaign of 67 BC had done. As the first and greatest of the Roman emperors he was, however, credited with having suppressed piracy, in keeping with the traditional image of successful rulers in the Graeco-Roman world. Immediately after his victory in the Sicilian War he subdued the barbarous tribes of Illyria, thereby, it was claimed, freeing Italy from their raids (App. *Ill.* 16). Appian continues his list of defeated pirates with the Liburnians and the islanders of Malta and Corcyra. Several other writers of the Imperial age offer similar praise of Augustus as the deliverer of safe seas for the people of the Roman world. As he nears the end of his Life of Augustus, and recounts the last days of his subject's life, Suetonius includes the following anecdote:

After coasting past Campania, with its islands, he spent the next four days in his villa on Capreae, where he rested and amused himself. As he had sailed through the gulf of Puteoli, the passengers and crew of a recently arrived Alexandrian ship had put on white robes and garlands, burned incense, and wished him the greatest of good fortune – because, they said, they owed their lives to him and their liberty to sail the seas: in a word, their entire freedom and prosperity. This incident gra-

---

[52] Starr (1941): 6–7 also sees Sextus Pompey as the victim of propaganda.
[53] See above pp. 149–50.
[54] ληστήριά τε ... ἀφανῆ.
[55] This topic is discussed along similar lines in the excellent article by Braund (1993).

tified Augustus so deeply that he gave each member of his staff forty gold pieces, making them promise under oath to spend them only on Alexandrian trade goods.[56] (Suet. *Aug.* 98)

This charming story illustrates what both contemporaries and later writers have perceived as one of the major benefits which the Augustan Principate brought to the Mediterranean world. An increasing volume of trade was conducted in the relative security of the Roman Empire. Similar sentiments can be found in other works from the Augustan period and later. Strabo, in his description of Iberia, remarks on the advantageous conditions for trade between Spain and Italy, including the absence of piracy, which has been suppressed by the Romans (Str. 3.2.5). Praise of the Augustan maritime peace can be seen in Horace (Hor. *Carm.* 4.5.17–20) and Propertius (Prop. 3.4.1 and 11.59). Inscriptions proclaim Augustus as supreme ruler over both land and sea,[57] a theme also found in Suetonius' biography (Suet. *Aug.* 22). After the death of Augustus the ideology of the Roman imperial peace continued to be applied to maritime conditions. Philo, in his invective against the Emperor Gaius Caligula, praised Augustus and his successors for opening up the seas to commercial navigation by removing the threats of war, banditry and piracy: 'He it was who abolished wars, both open and of the hidden kind, which result from the attacks of pirates. He it was who managed to empty the sea of pirate vessels and fill it with cargo ships' (Philo, *Leg.* 146).[58] The same idea is contained in the second book of Pliny's *Natural History* (Pliny, *NH* 2.118). Even Epictetus was prepared to grant that the emperors might be able to make life better in these respects: 'For see how Caesar seems to provide us with a great peace, so that there are no longer any wars, or battles, nor is there much banditry or piracy, but it is possible to travel at all times, to sail from sunrise to sunset' (*Discourses* 3.13.9).[59] The philosopher goes on to enumerate those things which the emperor cannot prevent, like shipwreck, fire and earthquake, but the common theme is clear. It is the imperial peace which enables men to travel and trade, without much fear of piracy and war. The repeated praise of this peace in various forms of ancient literature served two purposes: it both thanked the providers and exhorted them to continue their efforts. Suetonius' Alexandrians and others were certainly reflecting a widespread perception among Rome's subjects when they said that they owed their liberty to sail to the emperor, but they were also communicating their desire that this liberty be maintained. The period *c.* 31 BC – AD 300, commonly referred to by

---

[56]  This quotation is from the translation by Robert Graves (1957).
[57]  E.g. *IGRRP* 3.718, 719 and 721.
[58]  See paragraph 141 for similar praise of Tiberius.
[59]  See also Antipater of Tarsus in Plut. *De tranq. anim.* 466e.

modern historians as the Principate, would, therefore, seem to be one during which piracy was kept at much lower levels in this region than at any time previously. It is impossible to quantify this statement, but the sources for the Principate make fewer references to piracy, especially in the Mediterranean itself, than those for the preceding periods. Claims are made that piracy has disappeared, in both literary and epigraphic sources, but this is hardly a new development.[60] Why then, should piracy have been a less serious problem during the Principate than in previous periods?

In the first place there is what has been called the *Pax Romana* or 'Roman Peace'. For over two centuries the Mediterranean region was part of a single political unit, with a reasonably stable government. The ultimate providers of this stability were the armed forces. The territory of the Roman Empire was conquered and pacified by the armies of the Republican generals and later by those of the Emperors. Peace was maintained by the use or potential use of force. By the end of the reign of Augustus virtually the whole of the Mediterranean coastline was under direct Roman control. Those areas which were not directly ruled by Rome were 'satellites' of the Empire, the so-called 'client kingdoms', whose rulers were politically subordinated to the Emperors. I have stressed on several occasions the importance of attacking the pirates' bases in order to suppress piracy.[61] The Emperors could call on huge forces for the suppression of piracy in almost any part of the Roman world. There is evidence that they did, on several occasions, to good effect. I suggest, though this cannot easily be demonstrated, that there were many more occasions when they did so, for which no evidence has survived, probably because such activities were not particularly remarkable or significant in the eyes of contemporaries.

Secondly, and this point is closely linked to the first, the inhabitants of the Empire were less likely to choose piracy as a means of obtaining what they wanted. There were, it can be argued, greater opportunities for prosperity through peaceful activities, as well as less incentive to attempt violent seizure of people and property, as a result of the establishment of Roman rule. The impulse to turn pirate was less likely to be found among the relatively prosperous, contented inhabitants of the Roman provinces, than it had been amongst their predecessors, especially those who had been outside the Empire. This economic argument for a decrease in piracy requires some elaboration.

The celebrated historian Michael Rostovtzeff considered the Classical period to have been one of economic growth and progress, but he also thought that in the Mediterranean world a peak was reached in the fourth

---

[60] See above pp. 179–83.     [61] E.g. pp. 110–4 above.

century BC.[62] This argument was essentially followed by F. M. Heichelheim, who suggested that there was a decline in economic activity in the eastern half of the Mediterranean at the end of the Hellenistic period, which was never fully compensated for by growth in the economy of the western half.[63] Keith Hopkins, however, has argued that from *c.* 1000 BC there was a period of gradual and uneven economic growth, during which the volume of surplus production in the Mediterranean region gradually increased, reaching a peak in the first and second centuries AD. He suggests several reasons for this development: political change, especially the growth of empires, culminating in the Roman Empire, diffusion of technical innovations, and the spread of social institutions, particularly absentee landlords and chattel slavery.[64] Another view of the economic and political history of the Roman Empire which is, in my opinion, complementary to Hopkins' is that put forward by Greg Woolf. He argues that the Roman Empire can be viewed as an early form of World Empire, with a core and periphery, defined in both economic and political terms along the lines proposed by Immanuel Wallerstein.[65] Both these analyses of the Roman Empire necessitate a period of economic and political development during which the principal features may not have evolved fully. That transitional stage ought to extend well back into the Hellenistic and Classical periods, and it follows that any long-term developments should have their origins in these periods, or be present in an early form.

Among the components of the strong upward trend in economic activity in the first two centuries AD Hopkins identifies the 'Roman Peace' as an important factor:

For more than two centuries, the Roman peace more or less freed the inhabitants of the Roman world from major military disturbances; the Mediterranean was free of pirates, major roads were usually clear of brigands; tax burdens were by and large predictable. I do not wish to eulogize the grandeur of the Roman Empire. But it seems likely that these conditions allowed the accumulation of capital.[66]

Hopkins also argues that long-distance trade, particularly, but not exclusively maritime, was stimulated by the Roman peace and the taxation system of the Roman Empire. The probable increase in the quantity and frequency of maritime trade in the Principate cannot be properly mea-

[62]  Rostovtzeff (1941).
[63]  Heichelheim (1965–70).
[64]  Hopkins (1983). See also Hopkins (1980) on the stimulation of trade in the Roman Empire through the exaction and expenditure of taxes.
[65]  Woolf (1990).
[66]  Hopkins (1983): xix.

sured,[67] but it is a logical companion to the other components outlined by Hopkins. This long-term trend should have been already well under way in the Classical and Hellenistic periods. The statement that the Mediterranean was 'free of pirates' is clearly an exaggeration. Piracy may still have been very common in the Principate. The ancient novels suggest this is so, as do several references in historical literature and some inscriptions. For example, a second-century AD inscription from Olympia, concerning regulations for the Sebasta festival at Neapolis includes the following clauses: 'If someone arrives after the deadline given in the announcement, he must report the reason for the delay to the contest officials; valid excuses shall be, illness, *piracy* or shipwreck ...'[68] The literary sources do, however, provide numerous indications that the period from the reign of Augustus onwards was *perceived* as one of peace, stability and prosperity. Relative to the preceding centuries, it is reasonable to characterize the Principate as a period in which piracy was a lesser problem, in the Mediterranean at least. The same is obviously not true for the Classical and Hellenistic periods, although the Late Republic was a time when piracy was gradually beginning to be suppressed, becoming a less serious menace to trade and to economic production in general.

Who did practise piracy during the Principate, and why? Some must have found piracy attractive because of the excitement and risk. This is a phenomenon which can be seen in many periods of history. Others may have turned to piracy through desperate need, or as a way to supplement meagre resources. Fishermen and merchants, already equipped with boats, would be obvious candidates for 'occasional' bouts of piracy. Finally, it is likely that those who did not have easy access to the 'benefits' of Roman rule, either because they were outside the Empire, or because they were 'outsiders' within its territory, would have found piracy an attractive option, as a way of plundering the riches of the Empire. The armed might of Rome, which was greater in this period than ever before, was, however, a powerful deterrent to would-be pirates. For the people who lived under these political and economic conditions, piracy would have had a quite different meaning from that which it had for those who lived during earlier periods. Many of the written sources for these periods

---

[67] I am sceptical about the attempt made by Hopkins (1980) to quantify the increase in maritime trade through a 'head count' of shipwrecks in the Mediterranean. Underwater surveys currently being carried out in the Eastern Mediterranean may go some way towards correcting and altering the apparent patterns of distribution which emerged in the 1970s. See Parker (1992) and *The International Journal of Nautical Archaeology* for more recent work.

[68] *IvO* 56, lines 24–6 as restored by Merkelbach (1974); see *SEG* XXII no. 334. I think 'piracy' is a more likely translation than 'banditry' because of the mention of shipwreck. ληστεία, the word used, could indicate both or either.

were written by people who flourished during the Principate. Such people's understanding of piracy and its history must have been profoundly influenced by their historical perspective, which would have led them to make unfavourable comparisons between the pirate-ridden past and the more tranquil, secure present. This perspective can best be illustrated through an examination of the work of the Greek historian and geographer Strabo.

### Strabo on piracy

Strabo is a very important source for the study of ancient piracy, as the numerous references which have already been made in this book to the text of his *Geography* indicate. He was born *c.* 63 BC in the city of Amaseia in Pontos, and he died at some time after AD 21. He was thus a contemporary of the first Roman emperor, Augustus, and his life spanned the period which saw the collapse of the Roman Republic and the establishment of the Principate by Augustus and his successor, Tiberius. Strabo seems to have lived in Rome in the 40s and 30s BC, to have been in Egypt in the late 20s BC and probably returned to Amaseia *c.* 7 BC. He wrote 47 books of *Historical Notes*, which are lost, and a *Geography* in 17 books which has survived.[69] A certain amount of Strabo's work is based on autopsy, some of which is particularly good, such as his description of Rome in Book 5 (Str. 5.7–8), which is a valuable eyewitness description of the city in the first century. The bulk of his *Geography* is, however, clearly based on a wide variety of written sources, including Homer, Eratosthenes, Polybius and Poseidonios. He lists those places which he has visited himself, and those which he has not, acknowledging that his dependency upon written sources means that he is at the mercy of much oral information and hearsay in them (Str. 2.5.11).

The general plan of the work is a tour of the known world, stretching from Britain to India. He begins with Iberia and ends with Egypt. It is essentially the Roman world which he describes, although he does venture beyond the boundaries of the Roman Empire in some places, and his comments reflect a view of the world as the dominion of the Romans:

This, then, is the lay of the different parts of the inhabited world; but since the Romans occupy the best and best-known portions of it, having surpassed all former rulers of whom we have record, it is worthwhile, even though briefly, to add the following account of them.[70] (Str. 17.3.24)

[69] See Jones (1917–32): I; *RE* s.v. Strabo (3), by W. Aly.
[70] He then proceeds to give a general account of the Roman Empire and the lands around it. I quote from the translation of Jones (1917–32). See Nicolet (1988) on the Roman 'world view' of Strabo.

Strabo is an unashamed admirer of the Romans and what he says about piracy largely reflects that admiration. His purpose in writing the *Geography* is to provide a useful work for the philosopher and the statesman, particularly commanders and men of high rank, who will benefit from studying that which is grand, honourable, practical, worth remembering and entertaining (Str. 1.1.23). It seems likely that his intended audience was both Greek and Roman men involved in public affairs. He devotes a lot of space to maritime affairs. He describes coastlines and harbours in detail, but is rather brief and vague about the inland regions. In his account of Attica, for example, he goes into considerable detail about the coastal demes and the harbours at Mounychia and Peiraeus, but he does not bother with any of the inland ones (Str. 9.1.15–22). Sea power, or thalassocracy, is an historical element which he makes a lot of, recording the succession of maritime domination among the Greeks, from the Athenians to the Spartans and on to the Thebans (Str. 8.5.5). He is also much interested in harbours as the destinations of merchants. Trade is a major theme of his work. For example, he points out that the advantages that Turdetania in Iberia enjoys stem partly from its trading links with Rome (Str. 3.2.1). It is important to note that maritime trade between Spain and Italy is, in Strabo's view, particularly facilitated by the current peaceful conditions under Roman rule, with the seas clear of pirates (Str. 3.2.5).

Among the major sources of Strabo's *Geography* were the authors of accounts of harbours and coastal itineraries, whom he criticizes in Book 1 for their lack of theoretical content (Str. 1.1.21), but who have obviously left their mark on large parts of his work. It appears that Books 8 and 9 are particularly indebted to the admiral of Ptolemy II, Timosthenes, who compiled ten books on harbours in the Eastern Mediterranean (Str. 9.3.10). In Strabo's view the availability of good harbours can also promote piracy, however, as he remarks concerning the Illyrians, whose coastline has many natural harbours (Str. 7.5.10), and the harbour at Jaffa is described as a pirates' lair (16.2.28). In the Western Mediterranean the barbarians, according to Strabo, were overwhelmed by the Greeks and the Carthaginians because of the lack of co-operation and trade among them (Str. 3.4.5).

Piracy and banditry are another constantly recurring theme in Strabo's work. In one of his earliest comments about the work of the Hellenistic geographer Eratosthenes, whom he constantly refers to and corrects, he approves of Eratosthenes' comment that the early seafaring of the Greeks was done for either piracy or trade (Str. 1.3.2).[71] Piracy and trade are

---

[71] Πλεῖν μὲν κατὰ λῃστείαν ἢ ἐμπορίαν.

closely linked, of course, by the activities of pirates who prey on maritime trade (e.g. Str. 13.1.32). One explanation which Strabo offers for the practice of piracy (and banditry) is poverty. Thus the victors of the Trojan war, and the descendants of the ancient ruler of the sea, king Minos, turned to piracy because of their poverty, having been deprived of their gains from the war as well as their possessions at home (Str. 1.3.2). The link between the two is made again in Book 2, where he comments that the Romans have brought even the regions where deprivation and piracy are found under good administration (Str. 2.5.26). Rough and mountainous country leads to banditry also. The mountain-dwelling Artabrians, for example, were constantly practising banditry until the Romans stopped them (Str. 3.3.5).[72]

The absence of strong, unified rule among a particular people is seen by Strabo as likely to result in piracy, as was the case with the Etruscans, whose *hybris* was especially annoying to the Greeks (Str. 5.1–2; 6.2.2). The Cilicians are another example of how the absence of strong rule, in this case due to the internal struggles of the Seleukids, can result in piracy becoming dominant (Str. 14.5.2). Piracy can also be the result of corruption and the bad influence of others. Even the Greeks are not exempt from Strabo's criticisms. It is their bad influence on the Scythians, the result of trading contacts, which he blames for the piracy of these people, who have also 'taken to the sea' (Str. 7.3.7; 7.4.2). Pirates are cunning and impious as well as corrupt, a good example being the Cilicians, who not only broke into the temple of Samothrake and robbed it, but did so secretly (Str. 7. fr. 50a)![73] Just as the rule of the sea can pass from one people to another, so pre-eminence in piracy is seen by Strabo to have changed hands, passing from the Tyrrhenians to the Cretans and thence to the Cilicians. But, significantly, he says that the progress has been halted by the Romans, whose destruction of the Cilicians has ended the 'history' of piracy (Str. 10.4.9).[74]

Those who prevent or suppress piracy and keep the seas clear for navigation and trade earn fulsome praise from Strabo, like the Greeks of Massilia, who established strongholds along the coast to keep the sea free (Str. 4.1.9), or the Rhodians who preferred trade to piracy (Str. 13.2.5). Similarly those who refrain from piracy, while their neighbours practise it, are worthy of special mention: 'The Caeretani were highly praised among

---

[72] This is probably an idea taken from Poseidonios. See also the Cilicians in Book 14.2, the Corsicans in Book 5.7, the Frentani, who live on cliff-tops in Book 5.4.2. Note also the differentiation between piracy and banditry, and warfare (e.g. 17.3.15).

[73] Compare the impious bandit Kleon in Str. 12.8.9.

[74] But note the revival of banditry in Cilicia when it passes out of direct Roman rule (Str. 12.1.4). See Hopwood (1983) on Cilician banditry.

the Greeks both on account of their bravery and their righteousness. For they did not practise piracy, although they were well equipped to . . .' (Str. 5.2.3).[75] The pirates of Italy whom Strabo mentions are all non-Roman peoples, including the Etruscans or Tyrrhenians, and the Volscian inhabitants of Antium (5.3.5). When these people, who were under Roman domination, did practise piracy and were 'caught in the act', the Romans quickly responded by suppressing their activities.

But in earlier times the people of Antium used to possess ships and to take part with the Tyrrheni in their acts of piracy, although at that time they were already subjects of the Romans. It was for this reason that Alexander, in earlier times, sent in complaints, and that Demetrios, later on, when he sent back to the Romans what pirates he had captured, said that, although he was doing the Romans the favour of sending back the captives because of the kinship between the Romans and the Greeks, he did not deem it right for men to be sending out bands of pirates at the same time as they were in command of Italy, or to build in their Forum a temple in honour of the Dioscuri, and to worship them, whom all call saviours,[76] and yet at the same time to send to Greece people who would plunder the native land of the Dioscuri. And the Romans put a stop to such practices.[77] (Str. 5.3.5)

For Strabo the march of Roman imperialism has been a civilizing and ordering process for the whole world. His summary of Roman history at the end of Book 6 includes praise of the physical advantages of Italy, which have enabled the Romans to rise to such great heights, and a eulogy of the achievements of the Romans up to and including Augustus and Tiberius (Str. 6.4.2). Those parts of the world which the Romans do not control are dismissed as the homes of nomads and pirates, unworthy of Roman rule: 'Similarly also, the entire Mediterranean coastline of Asia is under their control, unless you include the lands of the Achaians and the Zygoi and the Heniochoi, who live as nomads and pirates in narrow and barren territories' (Str. 17.3.25).[78] Strabo ends his *Geography* with an account of the Roman provincial system, which taxes the legitimate activities of its subjects. In very simple terms, for Strabo the Romans have installed order and prosperity throughout the world, and one of the important ways in which they have done this is by suppressing piracy and encouraging peaceful use of the sea for trade. As for those barbarian and 'uncivilized' peoples who do not recognize the 'correct' way of life and the

---

[75] Compare his comments on the Phoenicians of Arados, who refrained from piracy in favour of trade (Str. 16.2.14), and the Lycians (Str. 13.3.2).

[76] The Dioscuri themselves later get credited with being suppressors of piracy in Lucius Ampelius' third-century AD *Handbook of Knowledge* (2.3).

[77] Translation from Jones (1917–32).

[78] See 11.2.12 and above pp. 54–6. Note, however, the rather apologetic tone with which Strabo recounts the long failure of the Romans to deal with Cilician piracy (Str. 14.5.2). This seems to represent a stain on their clean record, which he feels compelled to excuse.

'civilized' practices which he singles out for praise, in his view they do not deserve to be part of the Roman world.

Strabo was not alone in seeing piracy as something which the Romans had suppressed within the Mediterranean region for benefit of all. As the passage from Suetonius' *Life of the Divine Augustus* quoted above and other references show, the prevailing wisdom among the writers of the Principate was that piracy had long been a terrible curse, but that it no longer represented a significant problem. How was this happy state of affairs maintained?

### Suppression of piracy

The suppression of those pirates who were active during the Principate was carried out mainly by the considerable armed forces which the Roman Emperors maintained, for their own security as well as that of their subjects. The standing army was a creation of Augustus, but there had already been many legions in existence at the same time in different parts of the Roman Empire before the Principate, so that the step to a professional, standing army was not so great as might at first be thought.[79] The Roman imperial navy is, however, a new thing in this period and its role requires some discussion.

Octavian recovered from the naval disasters of the early 30s BC with the able assistance of Marcus Vipsanius Agrippa. The same naval forces which were used to defeat Sextus Pompeius at Mylasa and Naulochus were victorious at Actium in 31 BC, and eventually formed the basis of the Augustan navy. Its principal units were the praetorian fleets based at Misenum and Ravenna, with further squadrons stationed in other parts of the Mediterranean, especially in the Eastern half. Our literary sources pay very little attention to the development of the navy of the Principate, giving the impression that it was not thought to be at all important and that the establishment of standing fleets in numerous bases was not considered a remarkable act.[80] By the middle of the second century AD, the imperial navy was a large, widespread force, with extra squadrons having been added under several emperors. There were fleets in Syria, Egypt, the Black Sea, Africa, Britain and on some major rivers, like the Rhine and the Danube.[81] The size of the navy is difficult to establish, but the Byzantine scholar John the Lydian reckoned that the navy of the reign of

---

[79] See Keppie (1984).
[80] Tac. *Ann.* 5 and Suet. Aug. 49 refer briefly to the fleets at Ravenna and Misenum, but disregard any others. Surprisingly, there is no mention of any fleets in the *Res gestae*.
[81] See Reddé (1986) for the most comprehensive and up-to-date account, especially parts 2 and 4.

Diocletian comprised 45,000 men, compared with 800,000 for the army (*Mens.* 1.27). Such figures are a poor guide for the first and second centuries AD, but, if they reflect the relative sizes of fleets and army at all well, then it is easy to see why ancient writers found little to say about the navy.

The main function of the navy was to carry out maritime tasks in times of war. It is at such times that we most often hear of it in our literary sources. Although direct combat was rare, logistical support and the conveyance of troops and their equipment formed the main part of naval activity. In addition, naval forces might take action to ensure freedom of movement for civilians and military personnel, protect coastal settlements and prevent navigation by hostile forces within the area of Roman influence. Such activity would include the suppression of piracy.[82] Roman forces can be observed responding to disruptions to the maritime security of the Empire on several occasions during the first, second and third centuries AD. It is appropriate at this point to consider whether there were regular restrictions on the liberty of mariners in the Principate. Starr maintains that the Roman attitude to commercial activity was one of *laissez-faire*.[83] Reddé, however, cites a small amount of evidence which suggests some control of navigation, at Alexandria, at Ostia and along the rivers and coastlines away from the Mediterranean itself.[84] It is, however, unlikely that the ideology of rule over land and sea extended to any practical attempts to regulate the use of the Mediterranean. There was little that could be done away from ports and river stations to prevent anyone who wished from building boats or ships and using them. Only when violence threatened the security of Rome or her subjects did the imperial authorities take steps to suppress certain forms of maritime activity.

Those who dwelt on the coasts of the Roman Empire had, to some extent, to be ready to protect themselves and their property from unexpected seaborne visitors. They may also have been tempted into more predatory actions, from time to time. At one point in Petronius' *Satyricon* the three adventurers, Giton, Encolpius and Eumolpius, are on the ship of Lichas when it is caught in a storm and badly damaged. Their plight is

---

[82] See Reddé (1986): part 3 for a thorough survey of the duties of the imperial fleets. He is more positive than Starr (1941): ch. VIII about the 'security' role of the navy, although both seem to be looking for 'excuses' to explain the rather uneven distribution of the fleets.

[83] Starr (1941): ch. VIII.

[84] Reddé (1986): 399–412. He cites Strabo 2.3.5 on control of entry/exit at Alexandria and various instances of military personnel connected with trade, especially the corn supply of Rome.

observed from the nearby shore: 'Some fishermen in small boats rushed out to seize the plunder. Then as they saw people prepared to defend their belongings, they turned from cruel thoughts to come to our aid ...' (Petron. *Sat.* 114). This was probably a regular occurrence on the shores of the Roman Empire. The fishermen can hardly be classed as pirates, since they do not intend to fight for their plunder, but rather to take it from those who are unable to retain it as a result of storm or shipwreck, in which case 'wreckers' seems a more appropriate term for them. Plundering wrecks is quite a common theme in the literature of the Principate,[85] and it was also the subject of imperial legislation. Ownership of goods from a shipwreck is discussed by the second-century AD Roman legal writer Callistratus in the *Digest*, and seizure of such goods was prohibited by an edict of the Emperor Hadrian (*Dig.* 47.9.5–7). Hadrian also authorized those whose goods had been seized to take their case to a prefect. The penalties for unlawful seizure were the same as those for piracy or banditry.[86]

Wreckers of this kind were probably a great menace to merchants and seafarers, as the section of the *Digest* cited above implies, because of the extremely hazardous nature of ancient seafaring. Evidence of deliberate wrecking, using false lights or other signals to lead ships onto rocks or sandbanks, cannot be found in the literary sources, although it is referred to in the *Digest* (47.9.10). I suspect that it happened only rarely, as ancient ships were much less reliant on coastal signals than their more modern counterparts. On the other hand, shipwreck was a commonplace occurrence, as evidenced by the numerous ancient wrecks which have been located around the coasts of the Mediterranean and other seas. During the Principate, and at other times, it might be a major cause of losses in terms of both goods and people. Emperors, as Epictetus observed (3.13.9), could do nothing to prevent shipwrecks, but they could afford some protection and redress for merchants and travellers against the 'wreckers' who preyed on the unfortunate victims.

There is an early example of the suppression of piracy by official Roman forces during the Principate in an inscription from the reign of Tiberius, found at Ilion: 'The council and the people [of Ilion] honoured Titus Valerius Proclus, the procurator of Drusus Caesar [for] destroying the pirate groups[87] in the Hellespont and guarding the city in all ways without

---

[85] See, for example, Sen. *Controv.* 1.6 & 7; 7.1; Dio Chrys. *Or.* 7.31. For a Roman definition of wrecking see *Dig.* 47.9.10.

[86] The prefect concerned may be the rather shadowy *praefectus orae maritimae*. See Reddé (1986): 417–22 for speculation about his duties. Note also Rougé (1966): 339–43 and 465 on wreckers.

[87] The word used is ληστήρια which may refer to bandits, but seems in context to refer to pirates. See also the Aelius Alexander inscription from Rhodes discussed below, pp. 218–19.

burdening it.'[88] This inscription seems to refer to a special operation (or series of operations) undertaken in the reign of Tiberius to root out several groups of pirates operating in the Hellespont. It is unclear whether the procurator himself directed the military action, which would be unusual in this period, or was simply responsible for financial arrangements and organization.[89] The Hellespontine region was a potential weak link in the chain of the Roman frontiers. The point at which the Black Sea communicates with the Mediterranean had to be guarded, and some protection afforded to the cities on the long coastline of Northern Anatolia against the marauding tribes from across the Black Sea.[90] In the early part of the first century AD Strabo described the piratical ways of the people of the eastern seaboard of the Black Sea, especially the Heniochoi: 'They live by piracy, using small boats which are lightly built, narrow and agile, holding twenty-five men, though occasionally they can manage up to thirty. The Greeks call them *kamarai* ... And so by fitting out fleets of these *kamarai* and sailing against merchant ships, coastlines and even cities they dominate the sea' (Str. 11.2.12).[91] The raids of the Heniochoi were resisted and even punished by the local dynasts, but, according to Strabo, the Roman governors of his time were ineffective against them (Str. 11.2.12).[92]

The military action undertaken by Antiochos IV Epiphanes of Commagene, in the reign of Claudius, against a group of Cilician pirates is a good example of a local ruler suppressing piracy. It is the kind of activity which may have been commonplace in the Principate, but would go unnoticed because it would not reach the main literary sources. In this case, however, Tacitus chose to include the episode in his account of the notable events of the year AD 52:

Soon after this, under the leadership of Troxoboros, the Cietae, one of the wild Cilician tribes, a constant source of trouble, set up camp in the rough mountains and made descents from here to the coast, or to the cities. They dared to use violence against farmers and townspeople and even to attack merchants and shipowners. They laid siege to the city of Anemurion and defeated a cavalry force under the prefect Curtius Severus sent to relieve it. (Tac. *Ann.* 12.55)

The peace and prosperity of the Cilician coastal plain, and the safety of passing ships, were once again threatened. Damage was done to the local

---

[88] *IGSK* Ilion no. 102; *IGRRP* 4.219. See also Reddé (1986): 329.
[89] The editor of *IGSK* Ilion, P. Frisch, sugggests (pp. 208–9) that he put his slaves at the disposal of the cities, but he cites no evidence to prove this.
[90] See above pp. 54–6 for similar efforts by the Greek states and the Hellenizing monarchs of the region in the Hellenistic period.
[91] Compare Arr. *Peripl. M. Eux.* 11.1–2.
[92] Arrian seems to suggest that he personally would be more effective in this role than his predecessors (Arr. *Peripl. M. Eux.* 11.2).

rural population, but the impression which Tacitus gives is that it was the threat to traders and seafarers which provoked Roman intervention. Anemurion was a coastal city, a convenient staging-post on the voyage to or from Syria. The problem was eventually dealt with by the local dynast Antiochos IV Epiphanes, who used treachery and bribery to split up the Cietae and capture their leader.

After the Roman take-over of the Polemonid kingdom of Pontos in AD 63, the royal fleet of the Polemonid rulers was to have been maintained as the basis of the *Classis Pontica*. This fleet, based at Trapezos, seems to have been partly intended for use against such raiders.[93] The potential vulnerability of this region was illustrated soon after the establishment of Roman rule when the former commander of the Royal fleet, Annicetus, a freedman of king Polemo, raised a force in the name of the emperor Vitellius and attacked the city of Trapezos. He defeated the forces there and captured and burned what remained of the Pontic fleet (Tac. *Hist*. 3.47). The main fighting ships, the 'liburnians', had already been removed to Byzantium under the command of one of Vespasian's supporters, Mucianus (Tac. *Hist*. 2.83). Having eliminated the immediate naval presence, Annicetus and his men turned to piracy, using *kamarai*. Vespasian eventually got to hear about them and sent Virdius Geminus to deal with them. Having no ships he was compelled to build a fleet of 'liburnians' and use them to hunt down Annicetus. He attacked and defeated some of the opposing forces and tracked Annicetus to the territory of the Sedochezi, whose king had been bribed by Annicetus to protect him. This worthy monarch was persuaded that peace with Rome was better than pirate gold and so he betrayed his allies (Tac. *Hist*. 3.48). Tacitus closes his account with the words: 'And so an end was brought to this slave war.'[94] It is significant that Annicetus had military experience, of a naval character. He turned from war to piracy after a change in the political situation which was obviously not to his liking. It was not a difficult step to take, since he was able to recruit a sizeable following and take advantage of the crisis of AD 69 and the removal of Roman forces to profit from piracy. Presumably the advent of direct Roman rule had created a certain amount of discontent among the former subjects of Polemo.[95] In effect, Annicetus and his comrades had become, or had made themselves, outsiders by refusing to accept the terms on which they were being

---

[93] On the Pontic fleet see Reddé (1986): 258 and 507–8.

[94] *belloque servili finis impositus*. Although Tacitus never uses the words *praedo*, or *latro*, or *pirata* in recounting this incident, it can, nevertheless, be classed as piracy.

[95] Tacitus says the soldiers defeated at Trapezus were from the royal army and had recently received Roman citizenship. There seems to be some rivalry between those who benefited from the annexation of Pontos and those who suffered as a result.

brought inside the Roman Empire.[96] The use of *kamarai* for piracy seems to be common in this area, as can be seen from Strabo's comments (Str. 11.2.12). Geminus seems to have attacked the pirates on land, driving them away from the vulnerable cities, and then to have constructed ships to pursue them. If ships of the *Classis Pontica* had been available he would not have needed to do so. In the second and third centuries AD the importance of a strong naval and military presence in this area became apparent. The *Classis Pontica* not only provided facilities for transport and communication in this region, it also played an important role in protecting those parts of the provinces which were open to the sea. Reddé sees this as part of the development of what he calls the Pontic *limes*.[97] At the point where the European provinces met the Anatolian ones the approach to the Mediterranean from the Black Sea was well guarded, but once it could be breached, or circumvented, large areas were exposed for plunder. The raid of the Kostoboki, who came from the north-western shores of the Black Sea, in AD 170 was the result of a failure of the landward defences, from the Danube to the Aegean, which allowed them to penetrate as far as southern Greece, before they were defeated by local forces under the command of the Olympic victor Mnesiboulos.[98]

In the latter part of the Jewish rebellion of AD 66–74, after the fall of Jerusalem in AD 70, some of the survivors gathered together in the coastal city of Joppa and decided to turn to piracy: 'And so they built themselves a fleet of piratical ships and engaged in raids on the coastline of Syria and Phoenicia and the sea route to Egypt, making those seas unnavigable for all' (Joseph. *BJ* 3.9.2). Vespasian sent a force of cavalry and infantry to attack the city. The inhabitants took to their ships rather than resist the Romans, but the rough coastline and the bad weather wrecked many of them. Some died in the sea and many others were killed by the Roman legionaries on the shore. The city itself was occupied to prevent its further use. The pirates of Joppa are another example of a group turning to piracy after being defeated in war. Their initial success, possibly exaggerated by Josephus, stemmed from the potential of Joppa as a place from which to attack the prosperous coastline and shipping of the Levant and Egypt. The Roman response seems to have been swift, however, and was relatively easy to effect because there were large forces

---

[96] Compare Arrian's threat to 'drive out' the piratical barbarians of the Southern coast of the Black Sea if they will not submit to Roman rule and pay tribute (Arr. *Peripl. M. Eux.* 11.2).

[97] Reddé (1986): 442–3. A comparison might be made with the 'Saxon Shore' system in the English Channel during the Late Empire; see below, pp. 225–8.

[98] Paus. 10.34.2 on Mnesiboulos; see also *CIL* VIII.14667; *CIL* VI.31856 on part of Pontic fleet sent to help deal with them under Lucius Julius Vehilius Gratus; *PIR* 4. no. 615.

already in the area. The circumstances of this particular episode meant that it was unneccesary to employ any naval units in its suppression. The pirates' base was not difficult to locate and there were plenty of Roman forces in the area which could approach directly by land. Vespasian sent cavalry and infantry to attack the city. The inhabitants put up no resistance, but tried instead to escape in their ships. The weather and the inhospitable coastline were their undoing. The operation was completed by the occupation of the former pirate base by the Roman army (Joseph. *BJ* 3.9.1–4).

Starr has argued that a naval squadron to watch the Levantine coast would have been essential after Augustus' pacification of Cilicia.[99] If such a squadron was in existence, then there is no clear record of it. Some ships are to be found operating here in the first century AD, but the earliest attestation of the *Classis Syriaca*, based at Seleukeia in Syria, comes from the reign of Hadrian. It may be that the fleet which was formed by Augustus out of the remainder of the Ptolemaic navy after Actium, the *Classis Alexandrina*, was felt sufficient to fulfil any naval duties in the area, with the occasional help of praetorian detachments from Italy.[100] The suppression of piracy might involve some naval operations, but, as several of the examples in this section demonstrate, this was by no means always the case. The one unchangeable facet of anti-piracy operations in this period was the paramount importance of depriving the pirates of a base, which usually involved extensive use of land forces.

### Outsiders

Piratical raids on the provinces of Gaul by barbarians from outside the empire are mentioned occasionally in our literary sources. In AD 41 the Chauci, who lived in the area around the mouth of the River Weser, attacked the coast of Gallia Belgica and were driven off by the governor, Gabinius (Dio 60.8.7). According to Suetonius Gabinius assumed the surname Chaucius as a result of his victory over the Chauci (Suet. *Claud.* 24.3). In AD 47 the Chauci were on the rampage again, this time attacking Lower Germany:

At the same time the Chauci, free from internal quarrels, and taking swift advantage of the death of Sanquinius, attacked Lower Germany while Corbulo was still on his way. Their leader, Gannascus of the Canninefates tribe, an auxiliary of long service, had now deserted and was using light ships to plunder and lay waste to the coasts, especially of Gaul, which he knew to be wealthy and pacified. (Tac. *Ann.* 11.18)

---

[99] Starr (1941): 114–15.
[100] See Reddé (1986): 493–5 for the creation of the Syrian and Alexandrian fleets.

Gannascus was defeated by a detachment of the *Classis Germanica* which came down the Rhine from its base at Köln. He escaped and fled back to the territory of the Chauci, but Domitius Corbulo persuaded the Chauci to betray him into a trap, which Tacitus remarks was not a dishonourable thing as he was a deserter. He was killed by the Chauci (Tac. *Ann.* 11.19). It is probable that such raids continued to be a problem in this area, although there is very little evidence and nothing to suggest that the Roman provinces were being constantly attacked in the first century AD. The main attraction for the barbarians would have been the prosperity of the Gallic, and later the British provinces. A group of auxiliaries from the Usipi, who came from the east bank of the Rhine, deserted in AD 83 while on service with Julius Agricola in Scotland. They captured three liburnians and used them to sail round the northern coast of Britain and across the North Sea to the German coast, plundering for supplies as they went south. They were eventually shipwrecked on the Frisian coast and captured by the local people, who assumed they were pirates. Some of those who survived were sold as slaves to Romans and so their story became known (Tac. *Agr.* 28; Dio 56.20). The attitude of the Frisians to the shipwrecks suggests that they were used to pirates appearing on their shore at this time.[101]

It is noteworthy that the Chauci seem to have been raiding the Empire because of the comparative wealth and vulnerability of the provinces. Their resources were limited, hence the 'light ships' mentioned by Tacitus, and they probably found their neighbours the Frisians easier victims than the Romans. Internal quarrels may also have hindered the organization of attacks. The special knowledge and military skills of barbarians who had served as auxiliaries seems to have encouraged such raids. The function of the Roman army and navy as protectors of the provincials is clear from the way that they are defeated and driven off by Roman forces. Once outside the empire, however, they are dealt with by local tribes rather than by punitive expeditions. Claudius is said by Tacitus to have rebuked Corbulo for provoking an uprising among the Chauci as a result of his trapping of Gannascus, and ordered him to desist from his operations immediately (Tac. *Ann.* 11.19–20). The Chauci mentioned in Tacitus' *Germania* are described as a peaceful people, although this does not necessarily mean that they had by Tacitus' time entirely ceased to raid the rich provinces of the Roman Empire, or their neighbours (Tac. *Germ.* 35). In the reign of Marcus Aurelius, some time around AD 170, the governor of Gallia Belgica, the future emperor Didius Julianus, had to raise local

[101] Haywood (1991): 5–7 and 25 credits the Usipi with considerable experience of rowed ships and navigation on the high seas, on the strength of this episode. It is not clear, however, whether the auxiliaries had learnt their maritime skills in service with the Romans, or even if they had captured the crews of the liburnians along with the vessels.

auxiliary troops in order to defeat a raiding party of the Chauci, but there is no other record of their activity before or after this incident (SHA *Did. Jul.* 1.7).

In a recent work, John Haywood has argued that the Chauci continued to attack both Gaul and Britain from this period until the middle of the third century AD, when their position as the main pirate menace in the North Sea was usurped by the Franks and the Saxons.[102] He bases his conclusions on the evidence of coin hoards in northern Gaul and destruction by fire or other means of buildings and settlements here and in southern Britain. Haywood's book is a bold new approach to the maritime history of the northern barbarians, and this is not the place for a detailed criticism of it, but it should be pointed out that the pattern which he claims to have detected in the archaeological evidence has no basis in the literary sources. He is attempting to write a 'comprehensive history of barbarian Germanic seafaring', laying particular stress on the (previously unnoticed) 'continuity of barbarian seafaring activity'[103] (i.e. piracy), from the end of the first century BC to the Carolingian period. Faced with a lacuna in the literary sources he attempts to manipulate the archaeological evidence, in order to continue the historical narrative of Germanic piracy at this crucial point. He also tries to argue that exposed coastal areas of Britain and Gallia Belgica were provided with forts and other defences in order to create a 'Chaucian Shore', specifically intended to repel Chaucian pirates, who were raiding the prosperous provinces of Britain and Gaul with increasing intensity.[104] It does not seem to me likely that the evidence does, or even might, fit this hypothesis, especially when it is borne in mind that the raid of *c.* AD 170 is the only indication that the Chauci were active as 'pirates' in this period at all.[105] Haywood has gone far beyond what is reasonable in his interpretation of the archaeological evidence.[106] The raid defeated by Didius Julianus is best treated as an isolated incident, included in the *Historia Augusta* not for its intrinsic importance, but because of the identity of the Roman governor. There may have been others, but the evidence for them is lacking, and cannot be compensated for by imaginative interpretations of the archaeological data. There is clearly a similarity between Haywood's argument

---

[102] Haywood (1991): ch. 1.

[103] Haywood (1991): 1.

[104] Haywood (1991): 21–2. The only evidence for their tactics is the raid defeated by Didius Julianus.

[105] It is conceivable that the raid was not even carried out in ships, although this is not the most obvious interpretation of the notice in the *Historia Augusta*.

[106] See Drinkwater (1983): 76 and 90–1 nn. 24 and 25 for alternative interpretations and further bibliography. The discussion of the Saxon Shore and other 'maritime defences' in Salway (1981) indicates some of the weaknesses of Haywood's approach.

and that which I have advanced above with regard to the Eastern Mediterranean after Pompey's campaign of 67 BC. The crucial difference, however, is the almost total absence of literary evidence for Germanic piracy in the period for which Haywood is postulating continuous raids, whereas there is a substantial amount of such evidence for piracy in the Mediterranean during the (shorter) period after 67 BC.

Another group of barbarians who appear to be carrying out acts of piracy in the literary sources during the reign of Marcus Aurelius are the Mauri from North Africa. Two mentions are made in the *Historia Augusta* of their attack on the province of Baetica, both probably referring to the same incident, which may have taken place about AD 171. The first is in the *Life of Marcus*: 'When the Mauri were laying waste to most of Spain, good deeds were done by the legates' (SHA *Marc.* 21). The second occurs in the *Life of Severus*: 'After his quaestorship he was allotted to the province of Baetica, and he went next to Africa in order to settle things after his father's death. But while he was in Africa he was reassigned to Sardinia because the Mauri were devastating Baetica' (SHA *Sev.* 2).[107] It has been suggested that piracy was a common problem in this area, but there is little evidence to back this up beyond the references quoted above. Starr says that there was a permanent fleet stationed at Caesarea in Mauretania to cope with the local tribes, whom he describes as 'addicted to piracy'.[108] This fleet is assumed by Starr to have been established in the reign of Claudius, after the annexation of Mauretania in AD 40. Reddé argues, more persuasively, that there was only an occasional naval presence, with detachments of the *Classis Augusta Alexandrina* stationed there from time to time. In about AD 170 a vexillation from the *Classis Syriaca* seems to have reinforced them, perhaps to assist in the suppression of the piratical Mauri.[109] If so, this would suggest that the attack on Baetica was a unique, or very rare, occurrence. A *Classis nova Libyca*, apparently founded in the reign of Commodus, might be interpreted as a response to the recently perceived threat of piracy in this area, but this can only be speculation.[110]

Outside the boundaries of the Empire, where the Romans did not even nominally control the coastline, and the local population were hostile, navigation could be extremely hazardous at all times. The Red Sea was

---

[107] Some scholars see these as two separate raids, dating them as far apart as AD 168 and AD 198, using also the evidence of two inscriptions *ILS* 1354 and *CIL* VI.31856 (Julius Vehilius Gratus). See Reddé (1986): 328 for bibliography.

[108] Starr (1941): 119, also citing Calp. *Ecl.* 4.40: *trucibus Mauris*.

[109] Reddé (1986): 224–8 and 561–7 with full references. There is no clear evidence that Caesarea was a naval port.

[110] This fleet is mentioned in an inscription (*CIL* VIII.7030) of the period AD 180–8 and perhaps also in the *Historia Augusta* (*Comm.* 17). See Reddé (1986): 566–7.

one such place. The author of the *Circumnavigation of the Erythraean Sea*, describing the voyage from Egypt to India, is careful to inform his readers of points on the journey where piratical attacks from the natives are likely, such as the Ichthyophagoi, who prey on passing vessels and the victims of shipwreck (*Peripl. M. Eryth.* 20). The islands off the coast are also perilous: 'Then come the Sesekreinai Islands, as they are called, the Islands of the Aigidioi, the Island of the Kaineitoi, near to the so-called peninsula, which places abound with pirates, and after them is the White Island' (*Peripl. M. Eryth.* 53).[111] Strabo also mentions the piratical methods of the Nabataeans, who used rafts to attack ships, and who were the object of a punitive expedition launched by one of the Ptolemies (Str. 16.4.18). In order to protect themselves and their cargoes merchants carried armed men in their ships: 'Indeed, all year round the Red Sea was navigated with cohorts of archers placed in the ships, for it was greatly infested with pirates' (Pliny, *NH* 6.101). The coast of Africa was liable to be equally dangerous, for anyone who was bold enough to venture so far: 'The rest of the ancient writers do not consider it possible to sail here on account of the heat of the sun; but, indeed, the trade here is attacked by Arabs from the islands, called Ascitae, who, riding rafts made of inflated ox-hides, practise piracy using poisoned arrows' (Pliny, *NH* 6.167).

### Pirates in fiction

While piracy was seen to be a substantially reduced problem for most inhabitants of the Roman Empire, pirates flourished in the fictional works of the first four centuries AD. It may at first seem rather odd that the literary pirate is most prominent when his factual counterparts are declining in significance. Yet the development of the dangerous and romantic pirate, a figure familiar to modern readers from countless books and films, could probably have occurred only in the context of the Roman Peace. The suppression and marginalization of piracy under the Romans allowed a greater separation between the everyday world of the Graeco-Romans and the strange, unpredictable but exciting world of the fictional pirate.

It cannot be denied that pirates add spice to a story. They can be romantic, exciting, repulsive and generally more interesting than other figures because of the nature of their activities. They also represent a very convenient plot device, enabling people to be suddenly transported to faraway places, or turned from respectable citizens into slaves. The

---

[111] Casson (1989) plausibly suggests that the author of this work was a Greek merchant from Egypt, writing for other merchants at some point in the middle of the first century AD.

earliest fictional pirates to consider here are those who appear in the rhetorical works of the Elder Seneca. These exercises, especially the *Controversies*, written in the early first century AD, include several scenarios involving pirates on which the invention and ingenuity of famous orators is tried out. Pirates figure in *Controversies* 1.2; 1.6; 1.7; 3.3; 7.1 and 7.4. They create both legal and moral problems which the speakers try to solve using their rhetorical powers. Pirates are useful for this kind of exercise because they are outside the conventions of civilized law and their actions, usually capturing people for ransom or sale, create unusually awkward situations.

The comic novel *The Satyricon* by Petronius Arbiter, who wrote around the middle of the first century AD, contains several adventures involving bandits and pirates. Similar experiences are found in Greek novels of the first four centuries AD, including Xenophon of Ephesus' *Ephesian Tale*, Longus' *Daphnis and Chloe*, Chariton's *Chaireas and Kallirhoe*, Achilles Tatius' *Klitophon and Leukippe*, and the greatest of all the Greek novels, Heliodoros' *Ethiopian Tale*, dating probably to the mid-fourth century AD.[112] The pirates in these stories separate the hero and the heroine and put their lives in danger. They also condemn them to slavery and despair, testing the limits of their love and devotion. The story of *Klitophon and Leukippe* is a good example of this genre and the role of pirates within it. One of the earliest perils which the heroine faces is an attempted kidnap by a gang of pirates, who take the wrong woman (Ach. Tat. 17–18) Later on, both hero and heroine are captured by various bandits and pirates (Ach. Tat. 3.10; 3.20; 5.7). One of these incidents includes a night attack by pirates to seize the heroine on land, followed by an exciting chase and grisly death at sea:

> When the pirates saw our vessel closing in and us prepared to fight, they stood Leukippe on the top deck with her hands tied behind her, and one of them cried out in a loud voice, 'Here's your prize!' and so saying, he cut off her head and toppled the rest of the body into the sea.[113] (Ach. Tat. 5.7)

There is no doubt that pirates will stop at nothing in the novels. In Chariton's novel Kallirhoe is removed from Syracuse by pirates who have come to rob a tomb (Charit. 7–10). They escape with the maiden and her funeral gifts.[114] As well as violence and greed, pirates represent lust.

---

[112] Note also the similar functions of the bandits who appear in Apuleius' *Metamorphoses* and in the *Golden Ass*.

[113] Needless to say it is not the heroine who has been killed. Quotation from Reardon (1989).

[114] Compare the image of greedy and bloodthirsty pirates presented by Alkiphron, writing in the second or third century AD (e.g. 1.6.8).

Seneca's *Controversies* 1.2 is the case of a virgin who was captured by pirates and sold into slavery as a prostitute. She kills a soldier to defend her virginity, is acquitted and seeks to be a priestess. The function of the pirates in this scenario is to place the virgin in situations where her virginity is likely to be lost. Several of the speakers claim that it is unbelievable that she could have remained pure while among pirates, who are notorious for their cruelty and lust. The unlikely idea that a virgin can preserve her virtue among pirates is, however, found in the novels (e.g. Ach. Tat. 6.21). Achilles Tatius also uses the image of a pirate plunging a sword into the heroine, Leukippe, to represent Klitophon's first attempt to have sex with her (Ach. Tat. 2.23).

The pirates of the novels and the *Controversies* live outside civilization and cities. Theron, who steals Kallirhoe from her tomb, does so at night, and then takes her away from the city. When he does approach a city to sell his prize he is cautious and secretive (Charit. 1.12–14). Pirate crews are recruited away from cities, among fishermen and ferrymen (e.g. Charit. 1.7; Ach. Tat. 2.17). Their lairs are in deserted and lonely places, also away from cities (e.g. Charit. 1.12; Xen. Eph. 1.14). Another point to note about these fictional pirates is that as barbaric outlaws they are likely to suffer severe punishment. In the opening section of the *Satyricon* the writer claims, ironically, that, 'pirates in chains standing on a beach' are among the ordinary things that young men who have had too much schooling miss out on (Petron. *Sat.* 1). Chariton's principal pirate, Theron, is saved by the gods for a public execution in Syracuse (Charit. 3.3–4).[115]

Another remarkable aspect of these fictional works is the extent to which they cover the pirate's typical range of experiences. Everything from recruitment (e.g. Ach. Tat. 2.17) to execution (Charit. 3.4) can be found. Ransoming (Sen. *Controv.* 1.6; 7.4) and sale of captives as slaves (Charit. 2.12) are very common, but pirates also take a great deal of booty which is divided, hoarded and quarrelled over (Heliod. *Aeth.* 5.30; Charit. 1.10). They pursue and attack ships at sea (Heliod. *Aeth.* 5.22; Ach. Tat. 5.8), and also raid coastal sites (Charit. 1.7–10). These activities are generally presented in a realistic and believable fashion, although the tendency of the chief pirates to fall in love with the heroines clearly owes a lot more to romance than to realism.[116]

Scholarly debate about the ancient novels has raised the question of

[115] See Ach. Tat. 3.13, Xen. Eph. 2.13 and Heliod. *Aeth.* 3.32 for bandits and pirates getting their just deserts in a massacre. Pl. 4 has a similar theme.

[116] Their behaviour seems generally to resemble that of the famous Anglo-American pirates of the seventeenth and eighteenth centuries. See Defoe (1724); Botting (1978); Thrower (1980); Rediker (1987).

Pl. 4. Mosaic of the third century AD from Dougga in North Africa, showing the god Dionysos/Bacchus turning the Tyrrhenian pirates who tried to kidnap him into dolphins. This mythical story of pirates being punished for their impiety was a very popular theme in Graeco-Roman art.

whether the social and political conditions which are portrayed can be taken as representative of any historical period. It is clear that the periods in which the authors set their works are not serious candidates.[117] Some scholars have argued that the Greek novels are essentially products of the Hellenistic period, and reflect the conditions of the third and second centuries BC.[118] There are clearly some contemporary references, which suggest that a better general context is the first four centuries AD.[119] But, like the other forms of fiction discussed in this section, they also have a 'timeless' quality, since they are stories for entertainment, and not historical narratives. As far as the treatment of piracy is concerned however, it seems to me that they are most likely to reflect the attitudes of con-

---

[117] E.g. Chariton's and Heliodoros' Classical settings. Petronius is an obvious exception.
[118] Hägg (1983); Reardon (1971).
[119] E.g. the *eirenarch* in Xen. Eph. 2.13. See Millar (1981a) for a detailed argument in favour of 'contemporary' conditions for *The Golden Ass*.

temporaries and the nature of piracy after the establishment of the Principate. The strong tone of disapproval for their actions and the nature of pirates as 'outsiders', beyond the bounds of normal civilization, seem in particular to be good arguments for an imperial context.[120] The pirates of Roman imperial fiction are evidence of both the extent of the Roman Peace and the new way in which piracy and pirates were viewed by those who benefited from it.

### The third-century crisis

It has been suggested that piracy became a more serious problem in the early third century AD than it had been at any time since the establishment of the Principate. Several scholars have found evidence of a rise in the level of piratical activity in the Mediterranean, indicated by extraordinary measures undertaken by the Roman authorities to suppress it.[121] An inscription from Rhodes, dated to the Severan period, perhaps around AD 220, honours Aelius Alexander, who was charged with suppressing piracy at this time:[122]

> The people of the Rhodians and the council ... Aelius Alexander ... *prytanis*, having been *strategos* in the city justly and with integrity, having been *limenarch* honourably, carrying out the duties of treasurer ... frequently having been an overseer of public works faithfully, and in all things being praised by the council ... and in his period as *strategos* acting with justice and integrity also in the Chersonese, during which period he provided safety and security for sailors, seizing and handing over for punishment[123] the piratical band active at sea, in return for which the people and the council, by reason of their good will towards this man [dedicated this] to the gods.[124]

The scope of Alexander's activity is hard to estimate. He was clearly a local magistrate, in charge of the security of a small area, presumably for only a brief period. His achievement was, perhaps, comparable to that of Valerius Proclus in the reign of Tiberius, although Alexander is likely to have been directly responsible for the capture of the pirates mentioned.[125]

In AD 232 an extraordinary command was given to Publius Sallustius Sempronius Victor, an equestrian of the rank of *ducenarius*, as is recorded

---

[120] But see Winkler (1980) on the purely fictional elements in ancient novels, and the dangers of using them as historical sources.

[121] Starr (1941): 191–7; von Domaszewski (1903); Courtois (1939): 43–4.

[122] *BE* 1946–7: 337–8 no. 156.III; *AE* 1948: 78 no. 201. This inscription was unknown to the three scholars mentioned in the previous footnote.

[123] Lines 16–17 as restored by Robert in *BE* 1946–7: ποτὶ κ[ὸ]/λασιν.

[124] The lacunae indicated are between four and seven spaces only.

[125] See above pp. 206–7 on Valerius Proclus. For *strategoi* of the Chersonese and Syme in the same period as Alexander see *IGSK* Rhodischen Peraia nos. 161 and 163.

on an honorific inscription from Cos, describing him as: '... the most excellent *praefectus vehiculorum, praeses* and *ducenarius* of Sardinia, charged with establishing peace over all the sea with the power of life and death, *procurator Augusti* for Pontus and Bithynia'.[126] What was the nature of ·Victor's command? Starr concludes from his rank, and the location of the stone, that it was a local commission to suppress piracy in the Aegean.[127] M. Christol, in a more recent study of the period, has suggested that he was in charge only of securing maritime routes in connection with Severus Alexander's Parthian campaign of AD 232.[128] The inscription is inconclusive and there is very little other evidence to compare it with. A few years later Gaius Julius Priscus, brother of the future emperor Philip, and also a *ducenarius*, was put in charge of vexillations of the praetorian fleets from Ravenna and Misenum in the Mediterranean, possibly also to deal with piracy.[129] An inscription from the city of Oinoanda of the Termessians in Pisidia honours Valerius Statilius Castus, a *praepositus vexillationum*, '... who provided peace by sea and by land ...' during the reign of Gordian III.[130]

All these people may have been involved in the suppression of piracy in the Mediterranean, but in only one of these cases – Aelius Alexander – is it absolutely clear that pirates were the main concern of the person mentioned. Indeed, it could be argued that none of the others had anything to do with the suppression of piracy, because it is not mentioned explicitly in any of their inscriptions. If mention of providing peace by sea and land does refer to measures taken to suppress piracy, the level of activity need not be taken as unusual. These inscriptions do not have to be interpreted as evidence of a 'crisis', they may simply be a group of references to run-of-the-mill activities, which simply happen to come from the beginnings of a period of political instability and a decade or so before the Gothic raids of the middle of the third century AD.

At least one of the 'pretenders' who challenged the established emperors in this period was called a pirate. The *Augustan History*, when referring to Trebellian, one of the rivals for imperial power in the reign of Gallienus (AD 253–68), says: 'He gave himself the title of emperor, although others called him an archpirate'[131] (SHA *Tyr. trig.* 26.2). It is

---

[126] *IGRRP* 4.1057, lines 11–20. I have given the Latin terms for his offices, which appear in Greek form in the inscriptions. See also *PIR* 160 no. 69. For the date see von Domaszewski (1903) and Pflaum (1960–1): II 840–2.

[127] Starr (1941): 206.

[128] Christol (1978) n. 28, followed by Reddé (1986): 606.

[129] According to *CIL* VI.1638 as interpreted by Starr (1941): 193. A date of around AD 240 seems most likely. See also Reddé (1986): 678; *PIR* 4 no. 488.

[130] *IGRRP* 3.481 lines 8–10; *ILS* 8870. Dated to AD 256–8 by Christol (1978).

[131] *quem cum alii archipiratam vocassent.*

probably no coincidence that Trebellian's power base was in Isauria, a region which was famous for its bandits and pirates. The label pirate could still be used in the third century as a term of political abuse which implied that an opponent was not politically legitimate, in much the same way as it could in the Late Republic.[132] Another example of the same phenomenon is the rival to the tetrarchs in the late third century AD Carausius, who, although he was originally commissioned to deal with piracy on the coasts of Gaul and Britain, ends up being called a pirate himself (*Pan. Lat.* VIII.12.1).

The height of the third-century crisis, in terms of piracy, is usually placed in the period AD 250–70, when several large groups of 'Gothic' barbarians penetrated deep into the Mediterranean region, plundering and destroying as they went. The extent to which this resulted from a collapse of Roman naval defences has been the subject of some debate.[133] If the Roman navy was principally responsible for the suppression and control of piracy during the first and second centuries AD, it may well be that the successes of the Goths should be blamed upon Roman naval weaknesses. According to Courtois' interpretation,[134] the Mediterranean navy in the third century decayed, through neglect, until there was virtually nothing left. The proof of this decay is to be found in the resurgence of piracy in the third century. Starr puts it this way: '... the Augustan navy collapsed, but only on the Northern frontiers did a solid substitute take the place of its fragments. Hampered by universal war, the emperors of this period tended to abandon the Mediterranean to pirates and barbarians.'[135]

Kienast, however, has used much of the evidence cited by Courtois and Starr to demonstrate almost exactly the opposite.[136] He finds abundant evidence for the continued activity of the imperial navy during the third century and into the fourth. I find it unlikely that naval weakness or decline was a major factor in the growth of barbarian raids, especially as there is evidence of Roman naval forces involved in serious attempts to hinder the barbarians. A prime example of the difficulty of interpreting evidence for this period is an episode which is mentioned by the sixth-

---

[132] See above Ch. 5. See Amm. Marc. 14.2; 19.13; 27.9 for references to banditry in Isauria in the fourth century AD. Ammianus also accuses the Persians of banditry (*furta et latrocinia*) in describing their border raids in AD 356 (Amm. Marc. 16.9). See also Hopwood (1983).

[133] See Courtois (1939); Starr (1941): 194–8; Kienast (1966): 124–57; Demougeot (1969): 391–428; Reddé (1986): 572–623.

[134] Courtois (1939): 42–7 and 225–38.

[135] Starr (1941): 194.

[136] Kienast (1966): 124–57. Reddé accepts Kienast's arguments and adds some comments of his own.

century historian Zosimus and one of the fourth-century Latin Panegy-
rics. During the reign of the emperor Probus (AD 276–82) some Franks
who had been settled in Pontus by the Emperor decided to return to their
homeland. They obtained some ships, quite possibly from a Roman naval
base on the Black Sea, and set out across the Mediterranean, attacking
and plundering several places on their way (Zos. 1.71; *Pan. Lat.* VIII.18).
According to Haywood:

> The failure of the Romans to intercept the Frankish fleet at any point on its voy-
> age is a measure of the extent to which Roman sea power had been allowed to
> decay in the Mediterranean after more than two centuries of unchallenged domi-
> nance following the suppression of the Liburnian and Cilician pirates at the end of
> the first century BC.[137]

This may seem at first to be a reasonable assumption, but the Franks had
several advantages over their would-be interceptors. They had a clear idea
of their destination and seem to have made steady progress towards it. As
a result, although they seem to have stopped several times on the way,
they did not establish themselves in a base and launch attacks from there.
Had they done so the Roman authorities could easily have located and
dealt with them. They sacked Syracuse, but were defeated by a Roman
force from Carthage when they tried to land in Africa. Their earlier pillaging of Greece and some parts of Asia Minor was probably helped by a
lack of military forces in the area and, of course, the element of surprise.
The Roman navy could not have expected to intercept the Franks, because no one but they knew where they were going. To see this strange
episode, all the more unusual for being reported in our sources at all, as a
sign of naval decline is to misunderstand the nature of the Roman navy. It
was never meant to be patrolling the Mediterranean 'looking for trouble'
all the time.[138]

The Gothic raids of the third century AD varied considerably in both
their nature and their scale. They are occasions when warfare and piracy
seem to have come closer together than at any time since the Hellenistic
period, making it difficult to classify such incidents as either one or the
other. To call the barbarians 'pirates' is too simplistic, and does not ade-
quately reflect the nature of the threat which they posed to the inhabitants
of the Roman Empire. They often employed the methods of pirates –
moving from place to place by sea, attacking and plundering relatively
unprotected targets, aided by the unexpectedness of their action. The
Goths, like the Chauci, came from outside the Empire. Some of their

---

[137] Haywood (1991): 156 n. 46.
[138] On the inappropriateness of patrolling as a means of suppressing piracy see above pp.
29–40. See also Reddé (1986): part 3 on the operating methods of the navy.

raids were carried out entirely by land, and so cannot be considered as piracy at all. While they attacked only the fringes of the Empire they were not considered a great problem, and were not easy to suppress, since they did not operate from easily accessible bases. The attacks of the Boranes, from the coast of the Sea of Azov, upon the trading port of Pityous, and other cities along the Black Sea coast, are a good example of this. In about AD 254 they were defeated and driven away from Pityous by Successianus (Zos. 1.32).[139] They returned in about AD 258 and this time were more successful. After capturing Pityous they sailed along the coast as far as Trapezos, capturing the city with a large amount of booty and many slaves (Zos. 1.32–3). Their mobility was a big problem for the Romans, since they had initially obtained ships from the inhabitants of the Bosporan region, but later, probably after the capture of Trapezos, they seem to have been using Roman naval vessels.[140] An earlier raid in AD 253, perhaps also carried out by the Boranes, had got as far as Ephesos, moving mainly by land (Zos. 1.27–8). According to Zosimus, the example of the Boranes encouraged other barbarians to try their luck at building boats and raiding the Roman Empire:

When the neighbouring Scythians saw the Boranes' spoils, they were anxious to follow this example, and so they built a fleet with the assistance of their prisoners of war and the merchants who lived among them. They determined, however, that they would not sail the same way as the Boranes, which was long and difficult, and past places already plundered.[141] (Zos. 1.34)

The scale of some of these raids was clearly much greater than the relatively petty piracy which was a common problem in the Principate, but in some cases it seems little different. In AD 266 Herakleia Pontike was attacked by 'Scythian' ships:

At a time when Odaenathus was engaged in war with the Persians, and Gallienus was indulging in his usual trivial pursuits, the inhabitants of Scythia built some ships and attacked Herakleia. They returned from there to their own country with their booty, although many of them were lost in shipwrecks and defeated in naval engagements. (SHA Gall. 12.6)

This notice suggests that the attack was only a small raid, and that some, at least, of the Roman naval units in the area were active in defence of the city and territory of Herakleia. In AD 267 the maritime defences of the

---

[139] See Demougeot (1969): vol. I for a detailed account. The chronology of these invasions is uncertain. I have followed what seems to be the most widely accepted version of events in the period AD 250–70; e.g. Millar (1981b): 216–17. See Salamon (1971) for discussion and a proposed chronology, which I have not followed in all respects.

[140] See Reddé (1986): 610–11.

[141] Quotation from Ridley (1982): 11.

Mediterranean were put to the test by the Herulians and their allies, who came in much greater numbers than ever before.[142] In a naval battle in the Dardanelles a Roman fleet, commanded by Venerianus and Cleodamus, was victorious (SHA *Gall.* 13). A return engagement resulted, however, in defeat and the death of Venerianus. The Goths broke through into the Aegean, with devastating results. The city of Athens was sacked and the barbarians were pursued around the coast of Greece by Roman naval forces. Other battles were fought on land and at sea, with the large numbers of the Goths being gradually depleted. The Herulians came through from the Black Sea again in AD 268, this time reaching as far as Crete, Cilicia and Cyprus (Zos. 1.46; SHA *Claud.* 6–12).[143]

There is obviously a considerable difference between barbarians as 'invaders' and barbarians as 'pirates'. A large raid causes similar problems to a small one, but on a much greater scale. The ability of the Roman authorities to deal with these raids is, however, bound to be dependent on their size. The attack on Herakleia Pontike in AD 266 was, it could be said, repulsed and partly defeated by the naval forces in the area. On several occasions the Herulians or Scythians were unable to plunder cities because they were met with sturdy walls and determined defenders (e.g. Tomi and Markianopolis: Zos. 1.42; Byzantion: SHA *Gall.* 13.6 and *Claud.* 9.7). The great invasion of AD 267 was able to penetrate into the Aegean only after a fierce naval battle in the Dardanelles. In addition, all of this occurred at a time when other external pressures and internal struggles had significantly weakened the defenders of the Empire. Even Zosimus, who looks for disasters and débâcles throughout his history, does not hide the fact that the invading barbarians could not plunder as freely as they wished.[144] These raids were serious and damaging for the eastern provinces of the Empire, but they do not indicate a complete breakdown of the military framework which had kept piracy to reasonable levels for over two centuries. The Roman Peace was cracked, but not wholly shattered. When political stability was restored, the military and naval authorities were able to return to the suppression of piracy in the same fashion as before, until more damaging invasions destroyed the framework of Roman control entirely.

---

[142] Zos. 1.42–5; SHA *Claud.* 2 and 9; *Gall.* 13; Amm. Marc. 31.5.16–17; Syn. p. 717. See Millar (1969) on Dexippus' 'eyewitness' account of the invasions. On the scale of the invasions see Demougeot (1969): 422–8.

[143] See also *AE* (1934) no. 257, which may be a reference to piracy on the coast of Mamarica. The author of the *Historia Augusta* includes a letter, supposedly written by Claudius himself, in which he claims 'We have destroyed 320,000 Goths and sunk 2,000 ships' (SHA *Claud.* 8.4). Similar numbers in Zos. 1.42.

[144] See Goffart (1971) on the character of Zosimus' *New History*.

It should be clear from the events discussed in this chapter that, in spite of the relative peace and prosperity of the Principate, piracy did not disappear wholly from the Mediterranean and its surrounding seas in the Principate. The Roman military authorities expended a lot of energy in keeping piracy to a minimum, which was a great benefit to the inhabitants of the Empire, especially traders. In times of civil strife, and under the pressure of barbarian invaders, the maritime peace of the Roman Empire could appear very fragile, even to the point of disappearing at certain times and in certain places, but it was maintained with a considerable degree of success from the reign of Augustus to the late third century AD at least. The relative success of the Romans in this period must be largely attributed to their superior resources. At no time previously did any state maintain such huge forces, military and naval, to be used not exclusively, but in large numbers, to suppress piracy in the Mediterranean and adjacent regions. The political unity of the Empire, preserved in spite of power struggles among the élite, enabled the Emperors to harness its economic resources effectively, financing army and navy through the taxes extracted from the provinces. As has already been suggested, there was an element of co-operation between Emperor and subjects, who both benefited from the tranquillity which the suppression of piracy produced. When the Empire began to disintegrate, however, the circumstances which had enabled piracy to be kept to a minimum were altered, and piracy became, once more, a great menace in the Mediterranean region.

# 7    Piracy in Late Antiquity

It is common practice among English-speaking ancient historians to refer to the period after AD 284 as 'Late Antiquity'. A terminal date for this period is less easy to establish than its inception. I have continued my research into the early seventh century AD, but I shall include only a brief survey of the period after the reign of the emperor Justinian (AD 527–65). With the end of the Roman Empire in the West the Mediterranean world was transformed. The conflict between Christians and Muslims produced its own pirates, but they are not part of the history of the Graeco-Roman world. The transition from the Roman Empire to medieval Christendom was a long one, however, and its progress was uneven. The threat of piracy had never been completely removed by the Roman Peace, and, as has been shown in the previous chapter, for some parts of the Roman world the problem of piratical raids by barbarian peoples seems to have worsened in the third century AD. It has been argued that in the north-western corner of the Empire this problem was dealt with by the development of a defensive system known as the 'Saxon Shore'.

## The Saxon Shore

Was the system of fortifications and harbours which existed along the English Channel and around the coast of East Anglia in the third and fourth centuries AD created as a direct response to the threat of barbarian piracy? The case for a positive answer is quite strong. Several scholars have argued that the forts of the so-called 'Saxon Shore' can only be explained in this fashion. Among the latest is John Haywood, who argues: 'The most certain indicator of the seriousness of the pirate threat faced by the Romans is the great extension of the system of coastal fortifications between c. 250 and c. 280 AD on both sides of the Channel.'[1] It seems most likely that the forts of the channel coast were established as naval

---

[1] Haywood (1991): 34. I am indebted to Haywood's work for several of the more obscure references discussed in this chapter.

bases, with harbours or beaches from which the ships of the *Classis Britannica*, or a new naval command of the late third century, and the units of the army stationed with them could be despatched, either to attack hostile ships at sea, or, possibly, to cut off raiders on land before they could return to their ships.[2] The concept of an integrated system of fortified bases, containing naval and military units (on both sides of the Channel) to protect the provinces against pirates is not explicitly attested in any surviving literary or documentary sources. Nevertheless, the modern arguments for the existence of the Saxon Shore system are persuasive ones, and I am satisfied that the bases were intended to be used for the suppression of piracy.

How did the system work? I have already had occasion to remark on the impracticability of seaborne patrols to 'detect' pirates in the Mediterranean region.[3] It may be, however, that the Saxon Shore is an exception to this point. Squadrons of ships operating out of the bases at Richborough, Dover, Lympne and Pevensey, as well as Boulogne and Etaples on the French coast could, possibly, have patrolled the Channel at its narrowest point, on the look-out for pirates.[4] It is, however, more likely that the main intention behind the establishment of the Saxon Shore was to provide bases from which units could be despatched quickly to attack or intercept raiders whose location had already been discovered, or whose route was predictable. The label Saxon Shore clearly refers to the coastline which was liable to be attacked by the Saxons, and also by the Franks, who crossed the North Sea to attack the coast of East Anglia, or sailed down the channel to plunder the shores of Britain and Gaul, possibly even reaching as far as Spain.[5] Their routes were, more or less, predictable, either they had to cross the North Sea to East Anglia, or they had to sail along the English Channel, and it was in precisely these areas that the forts were constructed.

That there were such raiders in the mid third century AD is well established. Several of the narrative sources for this period mention raids by

---

[2] See Johnson (1976) and Maxfield (1989) for details of the individual forts and the military units. The term 'Saxon Shore' (*litus saxonicum*) comes from the *Notitia dignitatum* of AD 408, but the forts and, presumably, the defensive system are third-century. On the possible continuity of the *Classis Britannica* from third to fourth century see Reddé (1986): 622–8; contra Maxfield (1989): 18–22.

[3] See above pp. 29–40, 221.

[4] Vegetius says that small scouting vessels, painted sea-blue in order to camouflage them, operated in this area, along with land-based scout-troops (*exploratores*), under the command of the Count of the Saxon Shore (Veg. *Mil.* 4.37). Although he is writing at the end of the fourth century his information may derive from earlier accounts. On *exploratores* see Austin and Rankov (1995).

[5] See Haywood (1991): ch. 2 for detailed discussion of these raids.

the Franks and Saxons in the 260s, 270s and 280s AD (Aur. Vict. *Caes.* 33.3; Eutr. 9.8 and 21; Oros.7.22.7–9 and 25.3).[6] The impact of the raids is difficult to assess. There is some evidence of depopulation in Belgica and Armorica, mainly the disappearance of villages and villa sites being abandoned.[7] Some scholars have argued that the location of Romano-British coin hoards can be interpreted as evidence of the widespread problem of Frankish and Saxon piracy, especially when taken in conjunction with evidence of destruction by burning on certain villa sites, e.g. Fishbourne and Lullingstone.[8] Attempts have also been made to interpret the distribution of coin hoards in Spain along similar lines.[9] These forms of evidence are extremely difficult to interpret, however, and they do not amount to a clear indication that Frankish and Saxon piracy was causing havoc in the region, necessitating the building of the Saxon Shore forts.[10] Nevertheless there is some evidence from the 280s AD for the importance which the tetrarchs attached to this problem, and the way in which it was to be dealt with.

In AD 285 the Caesar Maximian appointed Carausius to a maritime command in Gaul and Britain, based in Boulogne.[11] His duties are described by Eutropius: 'At this time Carausius, who, although of very low birth, had achieved a high reputation through his military career, was put in command at Boulogne to clear the seas along the coasts of Belgica and Armorica, which were plagued by Franks and Saxons' (Eutr. 9.21). Such a command presupposes that there was a serious piratical threat which had to be countered. The authority given to Carausius was considerable, extending to both sides of the English Channel. This was something of a risk for the tetrarchy, especially in the light of the recent career of Postumus.[12] Carausius was quickly successful,[13] and the report of his activities in Eutropius seems to give some indication of how the anti-piracy defences were supposed to work:

Often he captured many barbarians and did not return their plunder in its entirety to the provincials, nor did he send it to the Emperor, which made people start to

---

[6] Haywood (1991): ch. 2 identifies three contributory factors: changes in the tribal structure of the barbarians, the political problems of the empire, and the start of a marine transgression in Belgium and Northern France.

[7] See Percival (1976): 42–5 and 204.

[8] Frere (1987): 216; Haywood (1991): 32–3.

[9] See Balil (1959) on the difficulty of using Spanish coin hoards as evidence of piracy.

[10] See Robertson (1974) on the wide dispersal of third-century AD coin hoards, especially those from the reign of Tetricus (AD 271–4) or later, which does not fit well with the idea that many of them can be accounted for by the activities of pirates.

[11] For an account and discussion of Carausius see Salway (1981): 285–313.

[12] On the rise and demise of the Gallic Empire see Drinkwater (1987).

[13] Diocletian assumed the title *Britannicus Maximus* as early as AD 286, presumably as a result of Carausius' operations; Barnes (1982): 9.

suspect that he was deliberately allowing the barbarians through, so that he could catch them as they came back with their plunder, and make himself rich in the process. Maximian ordered his execution, so he assumed the purple of an emperor and took control of Britain. (Eutr. 9.21)

This passage suggests two ways in which the Saxon Shore system might have operated. Either the pirates could have been intercepted before they had passed through the Channel, or they could have been caught on their return journey, laden with plunder. Either method would depend upon the use of signalling stations and scouting ships to give the naval and land-based units sufficient time to mobilize. If this is indeed how the system was intended to work, then it indicates a strategic approach similar to the 'Pontic *limes*' discussed above.[14] Carausius' rebellion was eventually put down by Constantius Chlorus, but only after the pretender himself had been assassinated by one of his own officers. It is ironic that the panegyric addressed to Constantius in AD 297 refers to Carausius in the following fashion: 'Indeed, by this wicked act of piracy the fleeing pirate first of all commandeered the fleet which had up to that time been protecting Gaul...' (*Pan. Lat.* VIII.12.1). In the Later Roman Empire as in earlier periods the pejorative force of the term pirate was a useful tool, to be employed in 'propaganda', both legitimizing the victor and illegitimizing the vanquished in an internal struggle.

There is very little evidence of piracy in the northern provinces or in the Mediterranean region during the first half of the fourth century AD. A panegyric of AD 310 addressed to Constantine refers to Frankish raids on the coast of Spain, some time in the first quarter of the century (*Pan. Lat.* VI.10.1–2). Constantine's campaign of AD 314 against the Franks may in part have been a punitive expedition in response to these. Although our sources are not very good for this period, it is reasonable to suppose that the measures taken by the imperial authorities were meeting with some success. The Saxon Shore may have proved its worth in this period, without the narrative sources leaving any record of its success. In the second half of the century, however, the raids of the Franks and Saxons, and possibly the Scots and Picts, seem to have become a greater problem, beginning in the 360s AD (Amm. Marc. 26.4.5). During the so-called 'Barbarian Conspiracy' of AD 367 mention is made of a *comes maritimi tractus*, who may have been carrying out the same duties as the *comes litoris Saxonici* of the Notitia Dignitatum (Not. Dign. (*occ.*) 28):[15] 'Valentinian had left Amiens and was hurrying to Trier when he heard the news that Britain was in dire straits as a result of the plundering attacks of the united barbarians; also that Nectaridus, the count of the coastal area,

---

[14] See above pp. 208–9 and Reddé (1986): 608–9.     [15] See *PLRE* I Nectaridus vi.

had been killed and that Duke Fullofaudes had been captured by the enemy in an ambush' (Amm. Marc. 27.8.1). Valentinian eventually sent Count Theodosius to deal with the problems in Britain, especially the Picts and Scots. He also made a punitive attack on the Saxons, though nothing is said about the Franks (*Pan. Lat.* II.5.2–4; Claud. *Carm.* 8.30–2). After his successful campaigns nothing more is heard of imperial action to suppress piracy in the north-western provinces. The decline of Roman authority in Britain and the settlement of the Saxons created severe problems for the inhabitants of the western provinces, but it became the responsibility of the Visigoths and the Merovingians to respond to the problem of piratical raids in the fifth and sixth centuries.[16]

There is a brief mention of pirates ravaging the Eastern Mediterranean and the Black Sea in the *Ecclesiastical History* of Philostorgius, a continuator of Eusebius (Philostorg. *Hist. eccl.* 11.8), probably in the late 370s AD. He does not say anything about attempts to suppress them. Ammianus and Zosimus make a great deal of the banditry which afflicted both eastern and western provinces in the same period (Amm. Marc. 14.2; 19.13; Zos. 4.20; 5.15–20), and it is possible that a reference in Symmachus concerns the use of an imperial fleet (from Ravenna) to protect grain convoys to Rome in AD 384 (Symmachus *Relat.* 9.7), but no general conclusions can be drawn about the ability of the imperial authorities to suppress piracy on the basis of these references. In the West it seems that the imperial fleets were no longer active by the end of the fifth century AD.[17] Most of the military forces had also disappeared, or been superseded by barbarian 'allies'.

### The Visigoths and fifth-century piracy

The inhabitants of Spain and Gaul were troubled by piratical raids from the north and east during the fifth century AD. The *Chronicle* of Hydatius mentions a sudden attack by 'Vandals' on the coast of Galicia in AD 445 (Hydat. *Chron.* 131). They carried off numerous families as prisoners.[18] In AD 455–7 Hydatius' *Chronicle* records that the north coast of Spain was attacked by Herulians: 'A considerable force of Herulians had been conveyed to the shore at Lugo in seven ships, and almost 400 men were got ready to meet them. On the arrival of the assembled crowd they fled, with only two of their number killed. Returning to their own land they

---

[16] See below on the Visigoths. On the Saxon settlements and the Frankish response to piracy see Haywood (1991): chs. 3, 4 and 5.
[17] See Reddé (1986): 647–52.
[18] See below for discussion of the identity of these barbarians.

plundered several coastal places around Cantabria and Vardullia with great cruelty' (Hydat. *Chron.* 171). At about the same time Saxons raided Armorica, then under the control of the Visigoths (Sid. Apoll. *Carm.* 7. 369–71). It is possible that by this time both groups of barbarians were operating from bases in Britain.[19] The Herulians were clearly anxious to avoid a fight, and it would appear that nothing could be done to prevent them raiding settlements further along the coast once they had been driven away from Lugo. In AD 459 they were back again: 'The Herulians attacked several coastal places in the territory of Lugo with great cruelty and then proceeded on to Baetica' (Hydat. *Chron.* 194). Once again the entry in the *Chronicle* is brief but clear. The Herulians use the main advantage of the pirate, mobility, to plunder their way around the coast of Spain. It seems unlikely that they met with much resistance.

Another source records a raid carried out by Saxons in the region of Bordeaux, some time in the fifth century: 'It happened that on a particular occasion a multitude of hostile Saxon barbarians, with many ships, attacked a place called Marsas, driven on by the lust for plunder' (*Vita Viviani* ch. 7).[20] Marsas is a place near the River Garonne, in the territory which the Visigoths settled during the fifth century AD. The only evidence of counter-measures taken by the Visigothic kings to deal with piracy in this period concerns a naval establishment on the Garonne. It comes from a letter of Sidonius Apollinaris to Namatius, a Gallo-Roman who is a naval commander, some time in the reign of Euric (AD 466–84):

Joking aside, let me know at last what you and your family are doing. But look! Just as I want to finish this letter, which has rambled on too long, suddenly a messenger comes from Saintes. During a lengthy conversation with him about you, I obtained his repeated affirmation that you had sounded the war trumpet for the fleet, and that, taking the part of both soldier and sailor, you were cruising the sinuous shores of the Ocean against the curving galleys of the Saxons, who make one think that for every oarsman you see you can count an archpirate: thus do they all issue orders at once, giving and receiving instructions in piracy.

Indeed, right now there is very good reason for a strong warning to you to take the greatest care. Those enemies are the worst. They attack without warning and disappear as soon as they are seen. They avoid those who oppose them directly and strike down those they catch unawares.[21] If they chase they catch, if they flee they escape. They are not afraid of being shipwrecked, it is something they exploit, being not merely acquainted with the dangers of the sea, but even accustomed to them. Since a storm, whenever it comes along, makes their victims incautious of

---

[19] Thompson (1982): 180–1; see also Myres (1986) on barbarian settlements in Britain.

[20] This incident can be dated to the reign of either Theodoric I (AD 419–51) or Theodoric II (AD 453–66). See *MGH SRM* III (ed. B. Krusch) 92.

[21] This is what I take to be the meaning of the Latin, which reads: *spernit obiectos, sternit incautos.*

them, and hides their approach, they revel in the perils of the waves and the jagged rocks, risking all in the hope of a surprise attack.[22] (Sid. Apoll. *Ep.* 8.6.13–15)

From what Sidonius says about Namatius' duties it would appear that he was supposed to use his fleet to find and defeat Saxon pirates. It would seem that their raids on the coasts of France and Spain were sufficiently regular and troublesome to make a naval detachment based in the Garonne Estuary a worthwhile counter-measure. The size of Namatius' fleet and its effectiveness in the suppression of piracy can only be guessed at, but it does seem to indicate that the Visigothic kings were prepared to try to fulfil the role of protecting the Atlantic and Channel coastline from pirates, one which they had inherited from the Roman imperial authorities.[23] The manner in which Sidonius describes the Saxons in his letter suggests that he was well acquainted with their reputation, which he doubtless exaggerates, through the rumours of their raids. The letter would also indicate that they had been attacking that part of Gaul for a long time on a regular basis. There is some further evidence for the activities of Visigothic naval units during the sixth and seventh centuries, although none of it refers specifically to the suppression of piracy.[24] An obvious but important difference between the fifth and fourth centuries is that there were no longer any attempts to make punitive expeditions against the pirates in their own bases. The Herulians and the Saxons in Britain or Germany and Denmark were far beyond the reach of Namatius and his small fleet.

### The Vandals

The occupation of Africa by the Vandals began in AD 429, when they crossed from Spain, probably using a variety of fishing and merchant ships taken from the local ports of Spain and Mauretania. In AD 439 they captured Carthage and used the *annona* fleet to carry out maritime raids. They may have built some vessels while they occupied Carthage, but essentially their fleet was a merchant one used for military transport and

---

[22] In order to obtain a smoother flow to the English version I have translated singular as plural in the second paragraph.

[23] See Wallace-Hadrill (1962): 28–9 for the suggestion that the Visigoths were settled in this area precisely in order to defend it against the Saxons. Namatius' fleet was presumably in existence before the arrival of the Visigoths in Aquitaine.

[24] See Haywood (1991): 58–61 and 171–2. Isidore, in his *History of the Goths* ch. 70, seems to suggest that it was in the reign of Sisebut in the seventh century that the Visigoths first 'took to the sea'. There is some reason to doubt the reliability of Isidore on this point, however, as he was inclined to overdo praise of Sisebut; see Wallace-Hadrill (1967): 123–5.

piracy.[25] It should not be thought, however, that the Vandals were only interested in piracy and plunder. In the first place, the period during which Vandal pirate raids were a serious menace in the Mediterranean seems to have been only about 35–40 years from the capture of Carthage. Secondly, the label pirates is not sufficient to describe a people who ruled a considerable empire during the fifth century AD. In his monograph on the Vandals, C. Courtois makes an important distinction between raiding carried out by Gaiseric and his followers for plunder and operations conducted for conquest and the establishment of control over certain places.[26] In some areas it is clear that strategic considerations lay behind the Vandals' attacks; to others they came only as pirates, in search of plunder and slaves.

Sicily, for example, was one of the first places that they raided, and was fought over by the Vandals and the Ostrogoths for a long period. It seems that Sicily was first attacked in AD 440, when Gaiseric launched a major expedition against the island (Prosper, *Chron.* 1342; Hydat. *Chron.* 120). The Vandals continued to campaign in Sicily throughout the 440s, 450s and 460s. By AD 468 it seems that they had established control of the entire island, which they used as a base for attacks on Italy and other places in the Western Mediterranean. Italy was, like Sicily, an early target for Gaiseric and his followers. A novel of the emperor Valentinian III indicates that Italy was put on the defensive in anticipation of their attacks after the fall of Carthage: 'Gaiseric, the enemy of our Empire, was reported to have led a large fleet from the port of Carthage ... and although the care of our mercy arranged defences throughout many places ... however, because there is in the summer good weather for sailing, the ships of our enemy were able to reach that shore.'[27] The emperor was virtually powerless against the highly mobile Vandals. Raids on Italy are recorded in AD 445, 458, 461 and 463,[28] but they seem to have ceased after AD 468.

Following the decline in their raids in the Western Mediterranean the Vandals turned to the potentially more lucrative eastern provinces (Pro-

---

[25] See below on the extent of the Vandal raids. The nature of their 'navy' is discussed by Courtois (1955): 205–9 and Diesner (1966): 123–8; see also Reddé (1986): 647–50. The suggestion of Morales Belda (1969) that they had a regular navy before AD 439 is without serious foundation.

[26] See Courtois (1955): 197 and 212–14; the latter section is mainly concerned with the economic basis of the Vandal empire.

[27] *Nov. Val.* III.9 (June 440).

[28] John of Antioch fr. 201 *FHG* IV 615; Sid. Apoll. *Carm.* 5.388–440 (highly exaggerated in its description of Majorian's 'resistance'); Priskos frr. 29 and 30 *FHG* IV 104. See also Courtois (1955): 194–6. Victor of Vita specifies Campania, Lucania, Bruttium, Calabria and Apulia as places which suffered from attacks by the Vandals.

cop. *Vand.* 1.5.22–5; Victor of Vita 1.51). In AD 474 there is evidence of raids on Zakynthos (Procop. *Vand.* 1.22.16–18) and Nikopolis in Epiros (Malchos fr. 3 *FHG* IV.115). It also seems likely that Rhodes was raided by Vandal pirates at about this time.[29] In AD 474 the emperor Zeno brought about an end to the Vandal raids by agreeing to recognize Gaiseric's possession of Africa. It is clear that Vandal piracy was a far less serious problem in the Mediterranean thereafter.[30] In AD 474 Gaiseric concluded a treaty with the emperor Zeno by the terms of which his authority in Africa was recognized, in return for a cessation of Vandal attacks on the eastern provinces (Procop. *Vand.* 1.7.26). There were no attempts to conquer or control territory in the eastern provinces, and the Vandal raids on Greece and in the Aegean can be described as piracy. Spain was another place which seems largely to have escaped the wrath of the Vandals. If the raid on Galicia recorded by Hydatius in 445 (Hydat. *Chron.* 131)[31] was not carried out by the Vandals, then their only activity on the Spanish mainland would seem to have been the defeat of Majorian's expedition at Alicante in AD 460, which is discussed below. Similarly, the Vandals' occupation of the Balearic Islands can be accounted for by their concern over Majorian's fleet. Sardinia and Corsica were conquered under Gaiseric and used as bases for raids on the Italian mainland, but they were also convenient for the exiling of recalcitrant clergy and political opponents from Africa.[32]

The economic effects of the Vandal raids will be considered below, after I have outlined the measures taken to deal with Vandal piracy in the Mediterranean.[33] Although the rulers of Italy were faced with a series of Vandal raids in the 450s and 460s AD they seem to have taken relatively few measures to defend against them, and did not attempt, at first, to suppress them by attacking the Vandals at their base in North Africa. Ricimer, the Germanic patrician and 'kingmaker', seems to have organized some resistance to the Vandals in Italy, although this was only in the form of land-based forces (Sid. Apoll. *Carm.* 2.348–56; Procop. *Vand.* 1.5.22).[34] In AD 460, however, Majorian organized an expedition against Carthage. The account of this in Procopius (*Vand.* 1.7.5–14) is an obviously invented tale of daring espionage and deserves no credence what-

---

[29] Nest. *Herac.* II.2.
[30] See Courtois (1955): part 2, ch. II.
[31] See Tranoy (1974) ad loc. for the alternative suggestion that it was Herulians who carried out the raid.
[32] See Courtois (1955): 185–90 for the details. Victor of Vita records numerous banishments to these islands.
[33] For what follows I am heavily indebted to Courtois (1955), especially part 2.
[34] Courtois characterizes the imperial reaction up to the reign of Majorian (AD 457–61) as 'une politique de capitulation tacite'; Courtois (1955): 199.

soever. It is, however, possible to establish what happened from the annalistic sources. Majorian assembled about 300 ships at Cartagena in Spain with the intention of crossing over to Mauretania, and presumably of marching overland to Carthage. Unfortunately, Gaiseric seems to have been warned and was able to capture the assembled fleet at Cartagena, before it had a chance to set out.[35] It is possible that the 'traitors' who warned Gaiseric were ship owners or merchants operating between Africa and Spain or Italy.[36] Majorian was forced to recognize the Vandal kingdom and was himself assassinated the following year.

In AD 468 the Eastern Emperor, Leo I (AD 457–74), launched a maritime expedition against Carthage. After reaching the Gulf of Tunis unopposed the Byzantine forces headed for the eastern headland (Ras Addar). Here the Vandals approached them from the rear with fire-ships and were able, with the help of a following wind, to destroy or disperse most of them.[37] Leo made another attempt in AD 470. This time his troops managed to land in Africa and attacked the city of Carthage, forcing Gaiseric to negotiate. After this promising start, however, he was compelled by political problems back in Constantinople to recall his men.[38] From c. AD 476 the Vandals were at peace with most of their neighbours and devoted their energies to consolidating their position in Africa. Their political achievements were considerable. Gaiseric had forced the Byzantine emperor to recognize his control of Africa, and the rulers of Italy were, at least for a time, his vassals. The territories which the Vandals controlled by the end of the third quarter of the fifth century AD constituted a substantial part of the main grain-producing areas of the Western Empire. It can be reasonably assumed that part of Gaiseric's political 'muscle' resulted from this advantageous position.[39] Piracy had been a profitable activity for Gaiseric, but it was only one aspect of the 'foreign policy' of the Vandal kingdom in the fifth century. No further imperial expeditions were launched against the Vandals until the reign of Justinian I (AD 527–65).

The Ostrogothic king Odovacer (AD 476–93) was able to negotiate with Gaiseric for control of Sicily, which had been 'conquered' by the

---

[35] Hydat. *Chron.* 200; see also Priskos fr. 27 *FHG* IV 103. Further references in Courtois (1955): 199.

[36] The possible effect of the Vandal conquest of North Africa on Mediterranean trade will be discussed below.

[37] Priskos fr. 42 *FHG* IV 110; Hydat. *Chron.* 247; Procop. *Vand.* 1.6.11; Lydus, *Mag.* 3.43. See Courtois (1955): 201–3 for a detailed discussion and reconstruction of this expedition. The numbers of ships given in the sources are clearly an exaggeration, e.g. 1,100 in Priskos fr. 42.

[38] Theophanes, *Chronographical History* a.5963; Procop. *Vand.* 1.6.9 and 11.

[39] See Courtois (1955): 213–14 on the pursuit of power through control of 'l'empire du blé'.

Vandals by AD 468. In AD 476/7, according to a passage in Victor of Vita's account of the Vandal persecutions, most of it was ceded to Odovacer as Gaiseric's tribute-paying vassal:

After Valentinian died he [Gaiseric] gained control of the coastline of all Africa, and with his customary arrogance he also took the large islands of Sardinia, Sicily, Corsica, Ibiza, Mallorca and Menorca, as well as many others. (14) One of these, namely Sicily, he later conceded to Odovacer, the King of Italy, by tributary right. At fixed times Odovacer paid tribute to the Vandals, as to his lords; nevertheless they kept back some part of the island for themselves.[40] (Victor of Vita 1.13–14)

Courtois explains this development partly by the growth of Ostrogothic power, and partly by a lack of money and manpower available to Gaiseric.[41] In AD 491, however, Gunthamund was forced to abandon the tribute claims on the Ostrogoths and recognize their possession of almost all of Sicily (Cassiod. *Chron.* 1327). Vandal interest in Sicily remained strong for strategic reasons, but their presence was reduced to a small area around Marsala. The island is the closest to Carthage and has obvious strategic importance. Vandal raids seem to have decreased greatly in the last quarter of the fifth century AD. Courtois has drawn attention to the difference between raids carried out for the acquisition of booty and slaves (i.e. piracy), and the larger expeditions against islands in the Mediterranean near Carthage, mainly intended to secure control of these places for strategic reasons (i.e. warfare). Gaiseric's kingdom was founded on a combination of these two forms of raiding, both using the same personnel and the same fleet of transport ships, but launched at different targets and with different results. The imperial response to piratical attacks on Italy and the Aegean was a series of unsuccessful expeditions against Carthage. The usual approach of destroying the pirates at their home base having failed, both Eastern and Western leaders were compelled to negotiate settlements with the Vandal king which provided recognition of his authority and a cessation of hostilities in return, it would appear, for a reduction or possibly even a complete abandonment of piracy. While it would be unwise to assume too much on the basis of a lack of evidence, I do think that the general absence of mention of Vandal raids (or piracy of any kind) in sixth-century sources seems to indicate that the Vandals had been 'bought off'. The suppression of piracy by force had become something which Roman authorities could no longer manage, owing to the shrinking resources and fragmented organization of

---

[40] I quote from the translation by Moorhead (1992). His interpretation of the crucial part of (14) is in accordance with the suggestion of Courtois (1955): 190–3; the edited Latin text is given there on p. 192.

[41] Courtois (1955): 196.

the Empire in the fifth century AD. Belisarius' successful campaign to reconquer North Africa in AD 533 was undertaken after careful preparations, and the emperor was in great fear for its outcome. Although the imperial forces were able to land unopposed in Africa, owing to a pre-arranged rebellion by the Vandal governor of Sardinia, which required king Gelimer to send most of his army there to recover control, two battles had to be fought. The first of these was against the Vandal forces which remained in Carthage. The second was against the main army which was recalled from Sardinia. Belisarius' complete victory was a tremendous boost to Justinian in his mission to reunite the Roman empire under one ruler and one faith.[42]

In a celebrated discussion of the work of Henri Pirenne, Norman Baynes laid the blame for the disruption of the Roman peace not on the Muslims of the seventh and eighth centuries, but on the Vandals: 'My own belief is that the unity of the Mediterranean world was broken by the pirate fleet of Vandal Carthage and that the shattered unity was never restored.'[43] Neither the original 'Pirenne thesis' nor Baynes' counterproposal are much favoured by modern historians,[44] but it cannot be denied that the Vandals did have a profound influence on the Mediterranean world in the fifth century AD. The piracy practised by Gaiseric and his followers was widespread and highly disruptive. It is worthwhile, therefore, to consider its possible effect upon maritime trade in this period. Did the Vandal occupation of North Africa seriously disrupt trade in the Western Mediterranean? To some extent it may have done. The grain fleet no longer made regular journeys between Carthage and Rome, and any merchant vessels which were accustomed to accompany it would have had to make other arrangements, but that would not have been too difficult. The Vandals do not, however, seem to have attacked or hindered shipping; their raids were made against places on land. The impact on the North African provinces of no longer having to supply the *annona* must have been considerable and it must have had some consequences for overseas trade. Courtois detected evidence of an agricultural decline in the region following on from the Vandal conquest,[45] although some African (and Sicilian) grain was being sent to Constantinople in the sixth and

---

[42] The main narrative of the reconquest of North Africa is in Procopius' *Vandal Wars* chs. 10–25.

[43] Baynes (1955): 315. The original review was published in the *Journal of Roman Studies* in 1929.

[44] For a recent discussion of the breaking of the unity of the ancient Mediterranean see Collins (1991): chs. 8, 9 and 13.

[45] Courtois (1955): 316–23. See pages 209–11 on the importance of Africa as a supplier of food, especially grain, to other parts of the Mediterranean.

seventh centuries AD.[46] Nor did the African provinces have to produce the surpluses needed to pay taxes to Rome, and rents to absentee landlords in Italy. On the other hand, the majority of the 80,000 or so Vandals seem to have lived apart from the local population, as a kind of occupying élite, and would have needed to be fed and supplied by local producers and traders.[47] It could be argued that the Vandals created an independent and relatively wealthy state out of what had previously been a dependency of imperial Italy. Gaiseric's raids brought slaves and booty to Carthage and its hinterland in large quantities.

The concentration of wealth and power ought to have encouraged both production and trade. Evidence is difficult to find, but it seems from the wide dispersal of North African pottery, especially 'red slip ware', in Italy, Southern Gaul, Spain and even parts of Greece, that the activities of North African traders were not curtailed in the fifth and sixth centuries AD.[48] The picture seems to be one of continuity in this area of trade at least. It is also worth considering that the Vandal fleet need not have been used solely for piracy and conquest. This fleet of mainly merchant ships was surely used in overseas trade, from time to time in the 450s, 460s and 470s AD, and to a greater extent thereafter, when piracy ceased to be a major Vandal activity.

There is some evidence to suggest that Vandal Carthage was a major destination for the products of other regions. Excavations carried out in the 1970s seem to indicate that the city was a prosperous trading centre which only ran into trouble after the Byzantine conquest of AD 533.[49] The Vandals did not, as far as can be seen from our meagre sources, direct their piratical activities against merchant ships. The threat of raids on coastal areas of the Mediterranean might have acted as something of a deterrent to free movement of shipping. The possibility of arriving at a harbour in the middle of a raid would not have been relished by many, but such considerations are unlikely to have prevented the movement of goods for long periods of time. The knowledge that there were markets in Carthage and other Vandal-controlled places, with potentially rich customers, should have compensated for the occasional fear of piracy. The period of 'growth' in imports would appear to coincide with a period of

---

[46] Teall (1959), esp. Appendix C. He makes no use of archaeological evidence, relying on literary sources and numismatics only.

[47] See Courtois (1955): part 2, ch. II; Courtois et al. (1952).

[48] Hayes (1972): 128–50, 162–3.

[49] 'Imports of all main classes of pottery increased during the later Vandal period, reaching a peak about AD 525–50, followed by a gradual decline from c. AD 550–75 until the mid 7th century when they registered only as a slight trickle' (Fulford (1983): 7). See also Fulford (1980) and Tortorella (1983).

relative security and peace, after the initial 30 or so years of warfare and piracy.

Indeed, the period of about a hundred years after the reconquest was one during which the importance of maritime links, if not actual trade, increased. Carthage was one of several Byzantine enclaves in the West which were maintained and supplied by sea in the sixth and seventh centuries. But, as the pottery finds indicate, time began to run out for Carthage in the middle of the seventh century. The final conquest was certainly delayed, but by the end of the century the Arabs were in control of the whole of the North African coastline. The political changes which were wrought from c. AD 634 to 698 were what caused the 'rupturing' of the unity of the Mediterranean. Conquest of territory on a scale unheard of since the Late Roman Republic brought with it a change in emphasis for trade in the Mediterranean.[50] Piracy certainly flourished again, beginning with the raids of the Arabs on the coast of Anatolia and the Aegean islands, but it was never on a scale to stifle trade entirely, as was also true of the piracy of Antiquity.

### The Arabs

After the Byzantine reconquest of Carthage there was a resurgence of 'Roman' seapower which lasted for nearly a century. In many cases it was only the ability of the Emperors in Constantinople to dispatch large forces overseas that kept their Empire together. The distant enclaves of Carthage, Dalmatia and Campania were maintained against their foes by the dromons of the imperial fleet, which had no major rivals in the Mediterranean.[51] This situation changed completely with the arrival of the forces of Islam in the seventh century. Within a few years of the death of Muhammad they had reached Syria. Acre, Tyre, Sidon, Beyrouth and Laodikeia all fell in AD 637, Jerusalem and Antioch a year later, and in AD 640 Caesarea was captured. The remorseless advance continued westwards until Cyrenaica was taken from the Emperor's hands in AD 642, the same year in which the long siege of Alexandria was brought to an end by the Arab commander Amr. Northwards the penetration of Syria was slowed and although Cyprus was lost in AD 649, Anatolia was largely preserved, but by AD 674 an Arab army was encamped opposite Constantinople, across the Sea of Marmora at Chalkedon.[52]

---

[50]  See Collins (1991): ch. 9; Crone (1987).
[51]  Ahrweiler (1966): introduction; Eickhoff (1966): 9–13; Hocker (1995).
[52]  For more detailed narrative and discussions see Butler (1978); Kennedy (1986).

Warfare at sea was also a chapter of disasters, ending in the defeat of the fleet of the emperor Constans II (AD 641–68) in the Aegean in AD 655. Contact with Carthage was maintained almost until the end of the century, but the main preoccupations of the rulers were with the land battle in the East, and a determined effort from the base of Kairouan in the Sahel resulted in the conquest of Carthage in AD 698. By AD 711 the armies of the Prophet were poised to cross the Straits of Gibraltar and enter mainland Europe through Spain.[53] Some of the early attacks on Anatolia and the Aegean were made by small flotillas and in a manner which could be described as piratical. Within a few years of the conquest of Egypt it is also clear that regular raids were being made from there against the Christians. These expeditions, known as the *koursa*, are mentioned in numerous papyri from the seventh century and were organized by the authorities of the Caliphate.[54] This form of institutionalized piracy lasted long into the medieval period.

The revival of 'Roman' seapower which enabled the Byzantine Emperors to maintain something of a maritime Empire in the sixth and early seventh centuries AD did not encompass any significant efforts to suppress piracy. The Adriatic was made dangerous by Slav pirates who operated from the mountain-shielded coastline and numerous islands of Dalmatia. Imperial dromons were hard pressed to maintain their own safety and could do nothing to prevent this menace, which was to continue long into the modern period.[55] The conquest of the North African coastline and part of Anatolia by the Arabs in the seventh century brought a far greater menace. Piracy afflicted the coastline of Greece, Anatolia and the Aegean islands. It was effectively beyond the power of the rulers of Constantinople to prevent, since they were engaged in a desperate struggle to keep the Muslims out of Constantinople itself, and could not contemplate attempts to deal with the pirates in the only way that worked – attacking their home bases. There was some sporadic and often unsuccessful naval activity. A reorganization of the military might of the Roman Empire in the late seventh century created a force capable of intervening across almost the whole of the Mediterranean, but the availability of so many potential bases made suppression of piracy impossible.[56] The political

---

[53] See Collins (1989): ch. 1.
[54] See Brooks (1898), a summary of excerpts from the major chroniclers, including al-Yaqubi and al-Tabari, on the raids against Syria and Anatolia. See Bell (1910) on the *koursa*, as revealed by the Aphrodito papyri.
[55] See Eickhoff (1966): 11–13; Tenenti (1967).
[56] See Ahrweiler (1966): 19–35 on Byzantine naval resistance to the Arabs, and the organization of the *karabisianoi*.

structure of the medieval Mediterranean, with Christians to the north and Muslims to the south and east, provided ideal conditions for the 'endemic' piracy which Braudel described in his work on the sixteenth century.[57]

[57] Braudel (1972).

# 8    Conclusions

The Homeric poems, which are the earliest evidence for piracy in the Graeco-Roman world, reveal an ambivalent attitude towards pirates, but piracy does not seem to have been a disreputable activity at the time of their composition. Analysis of these and other sources for the Archaic period does not indicate any great distinction between piracy and warfare in the Mediterranean. It was only in the fifth and fourth centuries BC that the scale of inter-state warfare in the Greek world increased to a point where piracy could be clearly separated from warfare, although they continued to be closely related during the Classical and Hellenistic periods, and into the Late Republic. Indeed, the constant warfare of these periods tended to encourage piracy at its margins.

The close relationship between war and piracy is reflected in the literature of the Classical and Hellenistic periods. In many cases, however, the reputation which certain groups or individuals acquired as pirates is due wholly or in part to the application of a useful pejorative label to political opponents. The pejorative implications of the terms pirate and piracy were widely exploited, especially in rhetorical invective, with enemies being labelled pirates in order to illegitimize them. The enemies of Athens, Rhodes and Rome are regularly described as pirates in these periods. This development continued in the Late Republic and reached a climax with the image of pirates as violent, rapacious evildoers, the enemies of all mankind, which is found in the historical and fictional literature of the late first century BC and the first four centuries AD. This image has had a significant effect on the way that piracy in earlier periods is portrayed by the later sources. In the Graeco-Roman world pirates often appears to be the victors' term for the vanquished.

The threat which piracy posed to coastal areas and to maritime trade encouraged some localized efforts at suppression in the Classical and Hellenistic periods, but the claims made by or on behalf of various states and rulers appear to have more to do with a desire to be seen as powerful protectors than any effective control of piracy. The reputation which the Athenians enjoyed as the suppressors of piracy in the Aegean region in the fifth century BC was not deserved. In the fourth century BC Athens and Philip of Macedon quarrelled over who had the right to suppress piracy, whilst simultaneously promoting it in the Eastern Mediterranean. The Rhodians and others were commended for their efforts to suppress piracy, but their actions fell far short of the level of achievement which some sources suggest. Various strategies were developed by communities of the Mediterranean to cope with the problem of piracy. Defensive treaties, agreements of *proxenia*, *asylia* and *isopoliteia* between states helped to alleviate some of the effects of widespread piracy. The relative importance of combating piracy varied considerably according to the perspectives of different communities. In the latter part of the Hellenistic period the Rhodians and their allies perceived the Cilicians as a major problem, but the Romans were slow to respond until their own interests were threatened.

In the Late Republic the Romans began to assume a role as the suppressors of piracy, as the *lex de provinciis praetoriis* of 100 BC and the works of Cicero demonstrate. This role had been well rehearsed for them in the Greek literature of the Classical and Hellenistic periods. Links between piracy and the slave trade did not hinder this development, but the higher political priorities and the practicalities of effective suppression, which required the conquest and control of territory, made progress uneven, in spite of the extravagant claims made for Roman aristocrats like Marcus Antonius the orator, Publius Servilius Isauricus and Pompey the Great. Pompey's famous campaign of 67 BC against the pirates was nothing like the great success which his supporters and later writers presented it as. It was only as a result of the political transformation of the Roman state and the establishment of a monarchy under Augustus that Rome's claim to be the protector of the Mediterranean became reality.

The peaceful conditions established in the Principate did produce a considerable reduction in the amount of piracy in the Mediterranean, a situation which was loudly praised by Strabo and many other writers. Roman control of territory and military dominance continued to promote maritime trade and discourage piracy, until the gradual collapse of the Roman Empire and the political instability of the fifth and sixth centuries AD saw a return of circumstances in which piracy could flourish. The image of legitimate authorities taking strong action to clear the seas of pirates continued to be exploited for political ends, because it was such an appealing one to the inhabitants of the Graeco-Roman world.

# Bibliography

Ahrweiler, H. (1966) *Byzance et la mer*, Paris.

Almagro, J. M. & Vilar Sancho, B. (1973) 'Sello inédito de madera en el pecio del "Cap Negret" (Ibiza)', *Rivista di Studi Liguri* 33: 323–6.

Andrews, K. R. (1964) *Elizabethan Privateering*, Cambridge.

(1985) 'Elizabethan privateering', in Youings, J., ed., *Raleigh in Exeter 1985: Privateering and Colonization in the Reign of Elizabeth I*, Exeter.

Austin, M. M. (1981) *The Hellenistic World from Alexander to the Roman Conquest*, Cambridge.

(1986) 'Hellenistic kings, war and the economy', *Classical Quarterly* 36: 450–66.

Austin, N. J. E. & Rankov, N. B. (1995) *Exploratio. Military and Political Intelligence in the Roman World from the Second Punic War to the Battle of Adrianople*, London.

Avidov, A. (1997) 'Were the Cilicians a nation of pirates?', *Mediterrranean Historical Review* 10: 5–55.

Badian, E. (1952) 'Notes on Roman policy in Illyria (230–201 BC)', *Papers of the British School at Rome* 20: 72–93.

(1964) *Studies in Greek and Roman History*, Oxford.

(1965) 'Marcus Porcius Cato and the annexation and early administration of Cyprus', *Journal of Roman Studies* 55: 110–21.

Bagnall, R. S. (1976) *The Administration of the Ptolemaic Possessions outside Egypt*, Leiden.

Balil, A. (1959) 'Hispania en los años 260 a 300 D.J.C.', *Emerita* 27: 269–95.

Barnes, T. D. (1982) *The New Empire of Diocletian and Constantine*, Harvard.

Barnett, R. D. (1975) 'The Sea Peoples', in *The Cambridge Ancient History*, vol. II.2³, London: 359–78.

Bass, G. F. (1967) 'Cape Gelidonya: a Bronze Age shipwreck', *Transactions of the American Philosophical Association*, New Series no. 57 (8).

ed. (1972) *A History of Seafaring Based on Underwater Archaeology*, London.

(1987) 'Oldest known shipwreck reveals splendours of the Bronze Age', *National Geographic* 172: 692–733.

Baynes, N. H. (1955) *Byzantine Studies and Other Essays*, London.

Bean, G. & Mitford, T. B. (1965) *Journeys in Rough Cilicia in 1962 and 1963*, Vienna.

Bell, H. I. (1910) 'The naval organisation of the Khalifate', in *Greek Papyri in the British Museum*, vol. IV, London.

Benabou, M. (1985) 'Rome et la police des mers au 1er siècle avant J.C.: la répression de la piraterie Cilicienne', in Galley, M. & Sebai, L., eds., *L'homme méditerranéen et la mer* (Actes du troisième congrès de la Méditerranée Occidentale, Jerba, 1981), Paris.

Benecke, H. (1934) *Die Seepolitik der Aitoler*, Hamburg.

Berthold, R. M. (1984) *Rhodes in the Hellenistic Age*, Ithaca.

Billows, R. A. (1990) *Antigonos the One-Eyed and the Creation of the Hellenistic State*, Berkeley.

Blackman, D. J. (1973) 'The harbours of Phaselis', *International Journal of Nautical Archaeology* 2.2: 355–64.

Blinkenberg, C. (1938) 'Triemiolia', in *Lindiaka* VII, Copenhagen.

Boardman, J. (1980) *The Greeks Overseas*[3], London.

Bosworth, A. B. (1975) 'The mission of Amphoterus and the outbreak of Agis' War', *Phoenix* 29: 33–43.

Botting, D. (1978) *The Pirates*, Amsterdam.

Braudel. F. (1972) *The Mediterranean and the Mediterranean World in the Age of Philip II*, London.

Braund, D. C. (1982) *Rome and the Friendly King*, London.

(1987) 'The social and economic context of the Roman annexation of Cyrenaica', in Barker, G., Lloyd, J. & Reynolds, J., eds., *Cyrenaica in Antiquity*, Oxford: 319–25.

(1993) 'Piracy under the principate and the ideology of imperial eradication', in Rich, J. & Shipley, G., eds., *War and Society in the Roman World*, London: 195–212.

Braund, D. C. & Tsetskhladze, G. R. (1989) 'The export of slaves from Colchis', *Classical Quarterly* 39: 114–25.

Bravo, B. (1980) 'Sûlan: Représailles et justice privée contre des étrangers dans les cités grecques', *Annali della Scuola Normale Superiore di Pisa, Classe di Lettere e Filosofia* ser. III, X.3: 675–987.

Breglia, L. (1970–71) 'I legati di Pompeo durante la guerra piratica', *Annali della Facoltà di Lettere e Filosofia Università di Napoli* 13: 47–66.

Briscoe, J. (1973–81) *A Commentary on Livy Books xxxi–xxxvii*, 2 vols., Oxford.

Bromley, J. S. (1987) *Corsairs and Navies*, Cambridge.

Brooks, E. W. (1898) 'The Arabs in Asia Minor (641–750), from Arabic sources', *Journal of Hellenic Studies* 18: 182–208.

Brown, F. E. (1980) *Cosa: the Making of a Roman Town*, Ann Arbor.

Brulé, P. (1978) *La piraterie crétoise hellénistique*, Paris.

Brunt, P. A. (1971) *Italian Manpower 225 BC – AD 14*, Oxford.

Brunt, P. A. & Moore, J. M. (1967) *Res Gestae Divi Augusti*, Oxford.

Bryce, T. R. (1986) *The Lycians*, vol. I, London.

(1989) 'The nature of Mycenaean involvement in western Anatolia', *Historia* 38: 1–21.

Buck, R. J. (1962) 'The Minoan thalassocracy re-examined', *Historia* 11: 129–37.

Butler, A. J. (1978) *The Arab Conquest of Egypt and the Last Thirty Years of Roman Dominion*[2], Oxford.

Carter, J. M. (1970) *Sallust: Fragments of the Histories and Letters to Caesar* (LACTOR 6), London.

(1996) *Appian: The Civil Wars*, London.

Cartledge, P. & Spawforth, A. (1989) *Hellenistic and Roman Sparta*, London.

Casson, L. (1954) 'The grain trade of the Hellenistic world', *Transactions of the American Philological Association* 85: 168–87.

(1971) *Ships and Seamanship in the Ancient World*, Princeton (revised edition 1986).

(1989) *Periplus Maris Erythraei: text, translation and commentary*, Princeton.

(1991) *The Ancient Mariners*², Princeton.

Catling, H. W. (1975) 'Cyprus in the Late Bronze Age', in *The Cambridge Ancient History*, vol. II.2³, London: 188–216.

Charlin, G., Gassend, J.-M. & Lequément, R. (1978) 'L'épave antique de la Baie de Cavalière (Le Lavandou, Var)', *Archaeonautica* 2: 9–93.

Christol, M. (1978) 'Un duc dans une inscription de Termessos (Pisidie)', *Chiron* 8: 529–40.

Clough, A. (1910) *Plutarch's Lives* (Dryden's translation revised for the Everyman Library), London.

Coarelli, F. (1982) 'L'agora des Italiens a Delo: il mercato degli schiavi?' in Coarelli, F., Musti, D. & Solin, H., eds., *Delo e l'Italia. Opuscula Instituti Romani Finlandiae* 2: 119–39.

Collins, R. (1989) *The Arab Conquest of Spain 710–797*, Oxford.

(1991) *Early Medieval Europe 300–1000*, London.

Company, F. (1971) 'Nuevo yacimiento submarino en aguas de Ibiza', in *Atti del III Congreso Internazionale di Archaeologia Sottomarina, Barcelona (1961)*: 87–90.

Cornell, T. J. (1995) *The Beginnings of Rome. Italy and Rome from the Bronze Age to the Punic Wars (c. 1000–264 BC)*, London.

Courtois, C. (1939) 'Les politiques navales de l'Empire romain', *Revue historique* 186: 17–47 and 225–59.

(1955) *Les Vandales et l'Afrique*, Paris.

Courtois, C., Leschi, L., Perrat, C. & Summagne, C., eds. (1952) *Les Tablettes Albertini*, Paris.

Crawford, M. H. (1974) *Roman Republican Coinage*, 2 vols., Cambridge.

(1977) 'Republican denarii in Romania: the suppression of piracy and the slave-trade', *Journal of Roman Studies* 67: 117–24.

(1978) 'Trade and the movement of coinage across the Adriatic in the Hellenistic period', in Carson, R. & Kraay, C., eds., *Scripta Nummaria Romana. Essays Presented to Humphrey Sutherland*, London.

(1985) *Coinage and Money under the Roman Republic: Italy and the Mediterranean Economy*, London.

(ed.) (1996) *Roman Statutes*, 2 vols., London.

Crone, P. (1987) *Meccan Trade and the Rise of Islam*, Oxford.

Cunliffe, B. (1985) *Greeks, Romans and Barbarians: Spheres of Interaction*, London.

Defoe, D. (1724) *A General History of the Pyrates*, London (ed. M. Schonhorn, Charleston, 1972).

Dell, H. J. (1967) 'The origin and nature of Illyrian piracy', *Historia* 16: 344–58.

(1970) 'Demetrios of Pharos and the Istrian War', *Historia* 19: 30–8.

Demougeot, E. (1969) *La formation de l'Europe et les invasions barbares*, vol. I, Paris.

Derow, P. S. (1973) 'Kleemporos', *Phoenix* 27: 118–34.

de Sélincourt, A. (1972) *Herodotus: the Histories*, translation revised by A. R. Burn, London.

de Souza, P. (1992) 'Piracy in the ancient world: from Minos to Mohammed', PhD thesis, University of London.

(1995a) 'Greek piracy', in Powell, A., ed., *The Greek World*, London: 179–98.

(1995b) 'Piracy and republican politics', review of Pohl (1993), *Classical Review* 45: 99–101.

(1996) ' "They are the enemies of all mankind": justifying Roman imperialism in the Late Republic', in Webster, J. & Cooper, N., eds., *Roman Imperialism: Post-Colonial Perspectives*, Leicester: 125–33.

(1997) 'Romans and pirates in a Late Hellenistic oracle from Pamphylia', *Classical Quarterly* 47: 477–81.

(1998a) 'Late Hellenistic Crete and the Roman Conquest', in Cavanagh, W. & Curtis, M., eds., *Post-Minoan Crete: Proceedings of the Colloquium held by the British School at Athens in November 1995*, British School at Athens Studies, vol. 2, London: 112–16.

(1998b) 'Towards thalassocracy? Archaic Greek naval developments', in Fisher, N. & van Wees, H., eds., *Archaic Greece: New Approaches and New Evidence*, London: 271–93.

Diesner, H. J. (1966) *Das Vandalenreich. Aufstieg und Untergang*, Stuttgart.

Drinkwater, J. F. (1983) *Roman Gaul: the Three Provinces*, London.

(1987) *The Gallic Empire*, Historia Einzelschriften 52, Stuttgart.

Ducrey, P. (1968) *Le traitement des prisonniers de guerre dans la Grèce antique. Des origines à la conquête romaine*, Paris.

Durrbach, F. (1921) *Choix d'inscriptions de Délos*, Paris.

Ebeling, H. (1885) *Lexicon Homericum*, Leipzig.

Eickhoff, E. (1966) *Seekrieg und Seepolitik zwischen Islam und Abendland*, Berlin.

Ferrary, J. L. (1977) 'Recherches sur la législation de Saturninus et de Glaucia', *Mélanges d'archéologie et d'histoire de l'Ecole française de Rome* 89.1: 619–60.

Fine, J. V. A. (1940) 'The background to the Social War of 220–217 B.C.', *American Journal of Philology* 61: 129–65.

Finley, M. I. (1962) 'The Black Sea and the Danubian regions and the slave trade in Antiquity', *Klio* 40: 51–59.

Fitzgerald, R. (1961) *Homer: the Odyssey*, London.

Flacelière, R. (1937) *Les Aitoliens à Delphes*, Paris.

Fornara, C. W. (1983) *Archaic Times to the End of the Peloponnesian War. Translated Documents of Greece and Rome*, vol. I, Cambridge.

Forrest, W. G. (1980) *A History of Sparta 900–192 B.C.* (2nd edn), London.

Foucart, P. (1906) 'Les campagnes de M. Antonius Creticus contre les pirates', *Journal des Savants* 4: 569–81.

Fraser, P. M. & Bean, G. (1954) *The Rhodian Peraea and Islands*, Oxford.

Freeman, P. W. M. (1994) 'Pompey's eastern settlement: a matter of presentation?', in C. Deroux, ed., *Studies in Latin Literature and Roman History*, vol. VII, Brussels: 143–79.

Frere, S. S. (1987) *Britannia*[3], London.

Frost, F. J. (1989) 'The last days of Phalasarna', *Ancient History Bulletin* 3: 15–17.

Frost, F. J. & Hadjidaki, E. (1990) 'Excavations at the harbor of Phalasarna in Crete: the 1988 season', *Hesperia* 59: 513–27.

Fulford, M. G. (1980) 'Carthage: overseas trade and the political economy', in *Reading Medieval Studies* 6: 68–80.

(1983) 'Pottery and the economy of Carthage and its hinterland', in *Opus* 2.1: 5–14.

(1985) 'Roman material in barbarian society', in Champion, T. C. & Megaw, J. V. S., eds., *Settlement and Society: Aspects of Western European Prehistory in the First Millennium BC*, Leicester: 91–108.

Gabbert, J. J. (1986) 'Piracy in the Early Hellenistic period: a career open to talents', *Greece & Rome* 33: 156–63.

Gabrielsen, V. (1997) *The Naval Aristocracy of Hellenistic Rhodes*, Aarhus.

Garlan, Y. (1969) 'Etudes d'histoire militaire et diplomatique', *Dialogues d'histoire ancienne* 4: 1–16.

(1972) *La guerre dans l'antiquité*, Paris.

(1978) 'Signification historique de la piraterie grecque', *Dialogues d'histoire ancienne* 4: 1–16.

(1987) 'War, piracy and slavery in the Greek world', in Finley, M. I., ed., *Classical Slavery*, London: 7–21.

(1989) *Guerre et économie en Grèce ancienne*, Paris.

Garnsey, P. D. (1988) *Famine and Food Supply in the Graeco-Roman World*, Cambridge.

Gianfrotta, P. (1981) 'Commercio e pirateria: prime testimonianze archeologiche sottomarine', *Mélanges de l'Ecole Française de Rome: Antiquité* 93: 227–42.

Giovannini, A. (1978) *Rome et la circulation monétaire en Grèce*, Basel.

Giovannini, A. & Grzybek, E. (1978) 'La lex de piratis persequendis', *Museum Helveticum* 35: 33–47.

Gofas, D. C. (1989) 'Epiplous: une institution du droit maritime grec, antique, hellénistique, byzantin et postbyzantin', in Thür, G., ed., *Symposion 1985. Vorträge zur griechischen und hellenistichen Rechtsgeschichte (Ringberg 24–26 Juli 1985)*, Cologne–Vienna: 425–44.

Goffart, W. (1971) 'Zosimus: the first historian of Rome's fall', *American Historical Review* 76: 421–41.

Goldmann, B. (1988) *Einheitlichkeit und Eigenständigkeit der Historia Romana des Appian*, Hildesheim.

Grant, M. (1969) *Cicero: Selected Political Speeches*, London.

Greenhalgh, P. (1980) *Pompey: the Roman Alexander*, London.

Greenidge, A. & Clay, A. (1960) *Sources for Roman History 133–70 B.C.* (2nd edn revised by E. W. Gray), Oxford.

Griffith, G. T. (1968) *The Mercenaries of the Hellenistic World* (2nd edn), Cambridge.

Gröbe, P. (1910) 'Zum Seeräuberkriege des Pompeius Magnus (67 v. Ch.)', *Klio* 10: 374–89.

Grote, G. (1888) *History of Greece* (revised edition in 10 vols.), London.

Hackens, T. & Lévy, E. (1965) 'Trésor hellénistique trouvé à Délos en 1964', *Bulletin de correspondance hellénique* 89: 503–66.

Hadas, M. (1930) *Sextus Pompey*, New York.

Hadjidaki, E. (1988a) *The Classical and Hellenistic Harbor at Phalasarna: a Pirates' Port?* (PhD dissertation), Santa Barbara.

(1988b) 'Preliminary report of the excavations at the Harbor of Phalasarna in Western Crete', *American Journal of Archaeology* 92: 463–79.

Hägg, R. & Marinatos, S., eds. (1984) *The Minoan Thalassocracy: Myth and Reality*, Stockholm.

Hägg. T. (1983) *The Novel in Antiquity*, Oxford.

Hammond, N. G. L. & Walbank, F. W. (1988) *A History of Macedonia*, vol. III, Oxford.

Harris, W. V. (1979) *War and Imperialism in Republican Rome 327–70 BC*, Oxford.

(1989) 'Roman expansion in the West', in *The Cambridge Ancient History*, vol. VIII²: 107–62.

Hassall, M., Crawford, M. & Reynolds, J. M. (1974) 'Rome and the eastern provinces at the end of the second century BC', *Journal of Roman Studies* 64: 195–220.

Hatzfeld, J. (1919) *Les trafiquants italiens dans l'Orient Hellénique*, Paris.

Hauben, H. (1977) 'Rhodes, Alexander and the Diadochi from 333/332 to 304 BC', *Historia* 26: 307–39.

Hayes, J. W. (1972) *Late Roman Pottery*, London.

Haywood, J. (1991) *Dark Age Naval Power: a Reassessment of Frankish and Anglo-Saxon Seafaring Activity*, London.

Heichelheim, F. M. (1965–70) *An Ancient Economic History*, 3 vols. Leiden.

Herrman, P. (1965) 'Antiochos der Grosse und Teos', *Anadolu* 9: 29–159.

Hiller, F. (1895) 'Inschriften aus Rhodos', *Mitteilungen des Deutschen Archäologischen Instituts. Athenische Abteilung* XX: 222–9.

Hocker, F. M. (1995) 'Late Roman, Byzantine, and Islamic galleys and fleets', in Morrison, J., ed. (1995) *The Age of the Galley. Mediterranean Oared Vessels since Preclassical Times*, London: 86–100.

Hopkins, K. (1978) *Conquerors and Slaves*, Cambridge.

(1980) 'Taxes and trade in the Roman Empire (200 BC – AD 400)', *Journal of Roman Studies* 70: 101–25.

(1983) 'Introduction', in Garnsey, P., Hopkins, K. & Whittaker, C. R., eds., *Trade in the Ancient Economy*, Cambridge: ix–xxv.

Hopwood, K. (1983) 'Policing the hinterland: Rough Cilicia and Isauria', in Mitchell, S., ed., *Armies and Frontiers in Roman and Byzantine Anatolia*, London: 173–87.

(1990) 'Bandit elites and rural order', in Wallace-Hadrill, A., ed., *Patronage in Ancient Society*, London: 171–87.

(1991) 'The links between the coastal cities of western Rough Cilicia and the interior during the Roman period', *De Anatolia Antiqua* 1: 305–9.

Hornblower, J. (1981) *Hieronymus of Cardia*, Oxford.

Hornblower, S. (1983) *The Greek World 479–323 BC* (revised edition 1991), London.

(1991) *A Commentary on Thucydides*, vol. I, Oxford.

Howgego, C. (1995) *Ancient History from Coins*, London.

Jackson, A. H. (1973) 'Privateers in the ancient Greek world', in Foot, M. R. D., ed., *War and Society: Historical Studies in Honour and Memory of J. R. Western 1928–1971*, London: 241–53.

(1969) 'The original purpose of the Delian League', *Historia* 18: 12–16.

(1985) Review of Nowag (1983), *Gnomon* 57: 655–7.

(1993) 'War and raids for booty in the world of Odysseus', in Rich, J. & Shipley, G., eds., *War and Society in the Greek World*, London: 64–76.

(1995) 'An oracle for raiders?', *Zeitschrift für Papyrologie und Epigraphik* 108: 95–9.

Jameson, S. (1970) 'Pompey's imperium in 67: some constitutional fictions', *Historia* 19: 539–60.

Johnson, S. (1976) *The Roman Forts of the Saxon Shore*, London.

Jones, H. L. (1917–32) *The Geography of Strabo*, 8 vols., London.

Karafotias, A. (1997) 'Crete and international relations in the Hellenistic period' (PhD thesis), Liverpool.

Kennedy, H. (1986) *The Prophet and the Age of the Caliphates*, London.

Keppie, L. J. (1984) *The Making of the Roman Army: from Republic to Principate*, London.

Kienast, D. (1966) *Untersuchungen zu den Kriegsflotten der römischen Kaiserzeit*, Bonn.

Konrad, C. F. (1994) *Plutarch's Sertorius: a Historical Commentary*, Chapel Hill.

Kromayer, J. (1897) 'Die Entwicklung der römischen Flotte vom Seeräuberkriege des Pompeius bis zur Schlacht von Actium', *Philologus* 56: 426–91.

Kuhrt, A. (1995) *The Ancient Near East c. 3000–330 BC*, 2 vols., London.

Larsen, J. A. O. (1968) *Greek Federal States*, Oxford.

Leach, J. (1978) *Pompey the Great*, London.

Lintott, A. W. (1976) 'Notes on the Roman law inscribed at Delphi and Cnidos', *Zeitschrift für Papyrologie und Epigraphik* 20: 65–82.

Lloyd, A. B. (1975–88) *Herodotus Book II: Introduction and Commentary*, 3 vols., Leiden.

Long, L. (1988) 'L'épave antique des basses de Can (Var)', *Cahiers d'Archéologie Subaquatique* 7: 5–19.

Luce, T. J. (1970) 'Marius and the Mithridatic command', *Historia* 19: 161–94.

McCann, A. M. (1987) *The Roman Port and Fishery of Cosa*, Princeton.

Macdonald, B. R. (1982) 'The authenticity of the Congress Decree', *Historia* 31: 120–3.

McDonald, A. H. (1967) 'The Treaty of Apamea (188 BC)', *Journal of Roman Studies* 57: 1–8.

McDonald, A. H. & Walbank, F. W. (1969) 'The Treaty of Apamea (188 BC): the naval clauses', *Journal of Roman Studies* 59: 30–9.

McGing, B. C. (1986) *The Foreign Policy of Mithridates VI Eupator King of Pontus*, Leiden.

McGushin, P. (1992) *Sallust: The Histories*, vol. I, Oxford.

(1994) *Sallust: The Histories*, vol. II, Oxford.

McKechnie, P. (1989) *Outsiders and Outcasts in the Greek Cities in the Fourth Century B.C.*, London.

Magie, D. (1950) *Roman Rule in Asia Minor*, 2 vols., Princeton.

Maier, F. G. (1959) *Griechische Mauerbauinschriften*, vol. I, Heidelberg.

Mallett, M. (1974) *Mercenaries and their Masters*, London.

Marasco, G. (1987a) 'Aspetti della pirateria cilicia nel I secolo A.C.', in *Giornale Filologico Ferrarese* 10: 129–45.

(1987b) 'Roma e la pirateria cilicia', in *Rivista Storica Italiana* 99: 122–46.

Maróti, E. (1956) 'ПИРАТСТБО ОКОЛО СИЦИЛИИ БО БРЕМЯ ПРО-ПРЕТОРСТБА БЕРРЕСА' (Piracy around Sicily at the time of C. Verres' propraetorship), *Acta Antiqua Academiae Scientiarum Hungaricae* 4: 197–210.

(1961) 'Die Rolle der Seeräuber unter den Anhängern des Sextus Pompeius', in H. Diesner et al., eds., *Sozialökonomische Verhältnisse im Alten Orient und Klassischen Altertum*, Berlin.

(1962a) 'Ο ΚΟΙΝΟΣ ΠΟΛΕΜΟΣ', *Klio* 40: 124–7.

(1962b) 'Diodotus Tryphon et la piraterie', *Helikon* 9–10: 24–42.

(1970) 'Die Rolle der Seeräuber in der Zeit des Mithridatischen Krieges', in *Ricerche storiche ed economiche in memoria di Corrado Barbagallo, a cura di Luigi de Rosa*, vol. I, Naples: 479–93.

(1971) 'On the problem of M. Antonius' *imperium infinitum*', *Acta Antiqua Academiae Scientiarum Hungaricae* 19: 259–72.

Mattingly, H. (1980) 'M. Antonius, C. Verres and the sack of Delos by the pirates', in *Miscellanea di Studi Classici in Onore di Eugenio Manni*, vol. IV, Rome: 1491–1515.

Maxfield, V., ed. (1989) *The Saxon Shore: a Handbook*, Exeter.

Meiggs, R. (1960) *Roman Ostia*, Oxford.

Meritt, B. D. (1935) 'The treaty between Athens and Halieis', *American Journal of Philology* 56: 65–71.

(1977) 'Athenian Archons 347/6–48/7 B.C.', *Historia* 26: 161–91.

Merkelbach, R. (1974) 'Über ein ephesisches Dekret für einen Athleten aus Aphrodisias und über den Athletentitel ΠΑΡΑΔΟΞΟΣ', *Zeitschrift für Papyrologie und Epigraphik* 14: 91–6.

Millar, F. G. B. (1969) 'P. Herennius Dexippus: Athens, the Greek world and the third-century invasions', *Journal of Roman Studies* 59: 12–29.

(1981a) 'The world of the Golden Ass', *Journal of Roman Studies* 71: 63–75.

(1981b) *The Roman Empire and its Neighbours*[2], London.

Miller, H. F. (1984) 'The practical and economic background to the Greek mercenary explosion', *Greece and Rome* 31: 153–60.

Miller, N. P. (1987) *Menander: Plays and Fragments*, London.

Momigliano, A. (1963) 'Pagan and Christian historiography in the fourth century AD', in *The Conflict between Paganism and Christianity in the Fourth Century*, Oxford: 79–99.

Moorhead, J. (1992) *Victor of Vita: History of the Vandal Persecution*, translation, introduction and notes, Liverpool.

Morales Belda, F. (1969) *La marina Vandala. Los Asdingos en España*, Barcelona.

Morgan, M. G. (1969) 'The Roman conquest of the Balearic Isles', *California Studies in Classical Antiquity* 2: 217–31.

Morrison, J. S. (1980) 'Hemiolia trihemiolia', *International Journal of Nautical Archaeology* 9: 121–6.

Myres, J. N. L. (1986) *The English Settlements*, Oxford.

Nicolet, C. (1988) *L'inventaire du monde. Géographie et politique aux origines de l'empire romain*, Paris.

North, J. A. (1981) 'The development of Roman imperialism', *Journal of Roman Studies* 71: 1–9.

Nougayrol, J., ed. (1968) *Ugaritica*, vol. V, Paris.

Nowag, W. (1983) *Raub und Beute in der archaischen Zeit der Griechen*, Frankfurt-on-Main.

Oost, S. I. (1955) 'Cato Uticensis and the annexation of Cyprus', *Classical Philology* 1: 98–112.

Ormerod, H. A. (1922) 'The campaigns of Servilius Isauricus against the pirates', *Journal of Roman Studies* 12: 35–56.

(1924) *Piracy in the Ancient World*, Liverpool.

Osborne, R. (1996) *Greece in the Making 1200–479 BC*, London.

Paget, R. F. (1968) 'The ports of ancient Cumae', *Journal of Roman Studies* 58: 148–69.

Parker, A. J. (1992) *Ancient Shipwrecks of the Mediterranean and the Roman Provinces*, Oxford.

Percival, J. (1976) *The Roman Villa*, London.

Pflaum, H. G. (1960–61) *Les carrières procuratoriennes équestres sous le haut-empire romain*, Paris.

Podlecki, A. J. (1971) 'Cimon, Skyros and Theseus' bones', *Journal of Hellenic Studies* 91: 141–3.

Pohl, H. (1993) *Die römische Politik und die Piraterie im östlichen Mittelmeer vom 3. bis zum 1. Jh. v. Chr.*, Berlin.

Potter, D. S. (1984) 'I.G. I (2nd edn) 399; Athenian involvement in the war of Agis III', *Annual of the British School at Athens* 79: 229–35.

Pritchett, W. K. (1971) *The Greek State at War*, vol. I, Berkeley.

(1974) *The Greek State at War*, vol. II, Berkeley.

(1991) *The Greek State at War*, vol. V, Berkeley.

Raaflaub, K. A. (1998) 'A historian's headache: how to read "Homeric society"', in Fisher, N. & van Wees, H., eds., *Archaic Greece: New Approaches and New Evidence*, London.

Rauh, N. K. (1993) *The Sacred Bonds of Commerce: Religion, Economy, Trade and Society at Hellenistic and Roman Delos*, Amsterdam.

(1998) 'Who were the Cilician pirates?', in *Res Maritimae: the Cities on the Sea* (CAARI/ASOR), Chicago.

(1999a) 'Pirates, prostitutes and the maritime mob: sexual democracy and labour discontent at the end of the Hellenistic world', in Hopwood, K., ed., *Organized Crime in the Ancient World: Banditry, Piracy, Corruption*, London, forthcoming.

(1999b) 'The Rough Cilicia Survey Project', forthcoming.

Reardon, B. P. (1971) 'Le Roman', in *Courants littéraires grecs des IIe et IIIe siècles après J.-C.*, Paris: 309–403.

ed. (1989) *Collected Ancient Greek Novels*, Los Angeles.

Reddé, M. (1986) *Mare Nostrum*, Rome.

Rediker, M. (1987) *Between the Devil and the Deep Blue Sea. Merchant Seamen, Pirates and the Anglo-American Maritime World 1700–1750*, Cambridge.

Reed, C. M. (1984) 'Maritime traders in the archaic Greek world. A typology of those engaged in the long-distance transfer of goods by sea', *Ancient World* 10: 31–44.

Reynolds, J. M. (1962) 'Cyrenaica, Pompey and Cn. Lentulus Marcellinus', *Journal of Roman Studies* 52: 97–102.

(1977) 'Inscriptions from Berenike', in Lloyd, J. A. et al., eds., *Berenike I*, Tripoli.

(1982) *Aphrodisias and Rome*, London.

Rice, E. E. (1991) 'The Rhodian navy in the Hellenistic age', in Roberts, W. R. & Sweetman, J., eds., *New Interpretations in Naval History*, Annapolis: 29–50.

Richardson, J. S. (1986) *Hispaniae*, Cambridge.

Ridley, R. T. (1982) *Zosimus: New History. Translation and Commentary*, Canberra.

Ritchie, R. C. (1986) *Captain Kidd and the War against the Pirates*, Cambridge, MA.

Robertson, A. (1974) 'Romano-British coin hoards: their numismatic, archaeological and historical significance', in Casey, J. & Reece, R. eds., *Coins and the Archaeologist*, London: 12–35.

Rostovtzeff, M. I. (1941) *Social and Economic History of the Hellenistic World*, 3 vols., Oxford.

Rougé, J. (1966) *Recherches sur l'organisation du commerce maritime en Méditerranée sous l'empire romain*, Paris.

Rowland, R. J. (1990) 'The production of Sicilian grain in the Roman period', *Mediterranean Historical Review* 3: 14–20.

Sacks, K. R. (1975) 'Polybius' other view of Aetolia', *Journal of Hellenic Studies* 95: 92–106.

(1990) *Diodorus Siculus and the First Century*, Princeton.

Şahin, S. (1994) 'Piratenüberfall auf Teos: Volksbeschluss über die Finanzierung der Erpressungsgelder', *Epigraphica Anatolica* 23: 1–36.

Salamon, M. (1971) 'The chronology of the Gothic incursions into Asia Minor', *Eos* 59: 109–39.

Salmon, E. T. (1969) *Roman Colonization under the Republic*, London.

Salway, P. (1981) *Roman Britain*, Oxford.

Sandars, N. K. (1985) *The Sea Peoples*[2], London.

Sanders, I. F. (1982) *Roman Crete*, Warminster.

Schmitt, H. H. (1957) *Rom und Rhodos*, Munich.

Scott-Kilvert, I. (1979) *Polybius: the Rise of the Roman Empire*, London.

Scullard, H. H. (1982) *From the Gracchi to Nero* (5th edn), London.

Seager, R. (1969) 'The Congress Decree: some doubts and a hypothesis', *Historia* 18: 129–40.

(1979) *Pompey: a Political Biography*, Oxford.

Sealey, R. (1966) 'The origin of the Delian League', in *Ancient Society and Institutions: Studies Presented to Victor Ehrenberg*, Oxford: 233–55.

Sestier, J. M. (1880) *La Piraterie dans l'antiquité*, Paris.

Sherk, R. K. (1969) *Roman Documents from the Greek East*, Baltimore.

Sherwin-White, A. N. (1976) 'Rome, Pamphylia and Cilicia 133–70 BC', *Journal of Roman Studies* 66: 1–14.

(1977a) 'Ariobarzanes, Mithridates and Sulla', *Classical Quarterly* 21: 173–83.

(1977b) 'Roman involvement in Anatolia 167–88 BC', *Journal of Roman Studies* 67: 62–75.

(1984) *Roman Foreign Policy in the East*, London.

Sherwin-White, S. M. (1978) *Ancient Cos: an Historical Study from the Dorian Settlement to the Imperial Period*, Göttingen.

Shipley, G. (1987) *A History of Samos 800–188 BC*, Oxford.

Starr, C. G. (1941) *The Roman Imperial Navy 31 BC – AD 324*, Ithaca.

(1955) 'The myth of the Minoan thalassocracy', *Historia* 3: 282–91.

Stockton, D. (1971) *Cicero: a Political Biography*, Oxford.

(1979) *The Gracchi*, Oxford.

(1981) *From the Gracchi to Sulla* (LACTOR 13), London.

Sumner, G. V. (1978) 'The "Piracy Law" from Delphi and the law of the Cnidos inscription', *Greek, Roman and Byzantine Studies* 19: 211–25.

Tarn, W. W. (1913) *Antigonos Gonatas*, Oxford.

Taylor, L. R. & West, A. B. (1928) 'Latin elegiacs from Corinth', *American Journal of Archaeology* 32: 9–22.

Teall, J. L. (1959) 'The grain supply of the Byzantine Empire', *Dumbarton Oaks Papers* 13: 87–139.

Tenenti, A. (1967) *Piracy and the Decline of Venice 1580–1615*, London.

Thiel, J. H. (1946) *Studies in the History of Roman Sea Power in Republican Times*, Amsterdam.

Thompson E. A. (1982) *Romans and Barbarians*, Madison.

Thrower, R. (1980) *The Pirate Picture*, London & Chichester.

Tod, M. N. (1946) *A Selection of Greek Historical Inscriptions to the End of the Fifth Century BC*, 2nd edn, Oxford.

Torelli, M. (1975) 'TYPPANOI', *Parola del Passato* 165: 417–33.

Tortorella, S. (1983) 'Produzione e circolazione della ceramica africana di Cartagene (V–VII sec.)', *Opus* 2.1: 15–30.

Tranoy, A. (1974) *Hydace. Sources Chrétiennes no. 218*, Paris.

van Effenterre, H. (1948) *La Crète et le monde grec de Platon à Polybe*, Paris.

van Gelder, H. (1900) *Geschichte der alten Rhodier*, Den Haag.

van Wees, H. (1992) *Status Warriors. War, Violence and Society in Homer and History*, Amsterdam.

von Domaszewski, V. (1903) 'Die Piraterie im Mittelmeere unter Severus Alexander', *Rheinisches Museum* 58: 382–90.

Walbank, F. W. (1957–79) *Historical Commentary on Polybius*, 3 vols., Oxford.

(1980) 'Cretan piracy', review of Brulé (1978), in *Classical Review* 30: 82–3.

Wallace-Hadrill, J. M. (1962) *The Long-Haired Kings*, London.

(1967) *The Barbarian West*, London.

Ward, A. M. (1977) 'Caesar and the pirates', *American Journal of Ancient History* 2: 27–36.

Welles, C. B. (1934) *Royal Correspondence in the Hellenistic Period*, New Haven.

Wells, P. S. (1980) *Culture Contact and Culture Change: Early Iron Age Central Europe and the Mediterranean World*, Cambridge.

Wilhelm, A. (1914) 'Urkunden aus Messene', *Jahreshefte des österreichischen archäologischen Instituts in Wien* 17: 1–120.

Will, E. (1979–82) *Histoire politique du monde hellénistique*², 2 vols., Nancy.

Willetts, R. F. (1955) *Aristocratic Society in Ancient Crete*, London.

Winkler, J. J. (1980) 'Lollianos and the Desperadoes', *Journal of Hellenic Studies* 100: 155–81.

Woolf, G. D. (1990) 'World systems analysis and the Roman Empire', *Journal of Roman Archaeology* 3: 44–58.

Zanker, P. (1988) *The Power of Images in the Age of Augustus*, Ann Arbor.

Ziebarth, E. (1929) *Beiträge zur Geschichte des Seeraubs und Seehandels im alten Griechenland*, Hamburg.

# General index

# Index of sources

Abbreviations follow the scheme used in *The Oxford Classical Dictionary*[3]